Visual QuickStart Guide

WordPerfect 6.0
for Windows

Glen Waller

Webster & Associates

Peachpit Press

WordPerfect 6.0 for Windows: Visual Quickstart Guide
Webster & Associates

Peachpit Press, Inc.
2414 Sixth Street
Berkeley, CA 94710
(510) 548-4393
(510) 548-5991 (fax)

© 1994 by Webster & Associates Pty Ltd

All rights reserved. No part of this book may be reproduced or transmitted in any form or by any means, electronic or mechanical, including photocopying, recording, or by any information storage and retrieval system, without prior written permission from the Publisher. For information, contact Peachpit Press.

Notice of Liability

The information in this book is distributed on an "As is" basis, without warranty. While every precaution has been taken in the preparation of this book, neither the author nor Peachpit Press shall have any liability to any person or entity with respect to any liability, loss, or damage caused or alleged to be caused directly or indirectly by the instructions contained in this book or by the computer software and hardware products described therein.

Trademarks

Throughout this book, trademarked names are used. Rather than put a trademark symbol in every occurrence of a trademarked name, we are using the names only in an editorial fashion and to the benefit of the trademark owner, with no intention of infringement of the trademark. Where those designations appear in this book, the designations have been printed in initial caps.

0 9 8 7 6 5 4 3 2

ISBN: 1-56609-109-8
Printed and bound in the United States of America

 Printed on recycled paper

Why a Visual QuickStart?

Virtually no one actually reads computer books; rather, people typically refer to them. This series of **Visual QuickStart Guides** has made that reference easier thanks to a new approach to learning computer applications.

Although conventional computer books lean towards providing extensive textual explanations, a **Visual QuickStart Guide** takes a far more visual approach—pictures literally show you what to do, and text is limited to clear, concise commentary. Learning becomes easier, because a **Visual QuickStart Guide** familiarizes you with the look and feel of your software. Learning also becomes faster, since there are no long-winded passages through which to comb.

It's a new approach to computer learning, but it's also solidly based on experience: Webster & Associates have logged thousands of hours of classroom computer training, and have authored several books on computer applications.

Chapter 1 introduces you to the basic screen elements of WordPerfect.

Chapter 2 introduces you to basic editing and formatting techniques and concepts.

Chapters 3 through 17 outline graphically the major features of WordPerfect 6 for Windows. These chapters are easy to reference and use screen shots to ensure that you grasp concepts quickly.

Acknowledgments

The author wishes to acknowledge the effort and dedication of the following people:

- Catherine Howes
- Jenny Hamilton
- Sean Kelly
- Carrie Webster
- Stephanie Berglin
- Tony Webster

The author and Webster & Associates would also like to thank the following people from WordPerfect Australia for their contributions to the technical accuracy of the manual:

- Doug Ruttan
- Bran M'cithech
- Sonelina Pal
- Sanjay Israni

Contents

Chapter 1. WordPerfect for Windows

The Screen 1
The Screen Components 2
    The mouse pointer 2
    The title bar 2
    The menu bar 3
    The scroll bars 4
    The status bar 5
    The button bar 5
    The power bar 6
    The ruler bar 6
    QuickMenus 9
    Feature bars 10

Chapter 2. Editing Text

Introduction 11
Simple Editing Methods 11
    Moving the insertion point 11
    Insert and Typeover modes 12
    Editing keys 13
    Undo and Undelete 13
    Selecting text 14
    Cut, Copy, Paste, and Append 15
    Drag and Drop 16
    Convert Case 17
    Codes 17
    Find and Replace 21
    Abbreviations 25
Formatting 27
    Font 27
    QuickFormat 30
    WordPerfect Characters 31

Chapter 3. Page Formatting

- Page Views 33
- The Layout Menu 35
  - Line 35
  - Paragraph 40
  - Columns 43
  - Page 44
  - Document formatting 53
  - Typesetting 59
  - Placement of text 61

Chapter 4. Creating and Managing Files

- WordPerfect Files 63
- Accessing Files 63
  - New 63
  - Template 64
  - Open 64
  - Insert File 66
  - Switching between documents 67
- Finalizing 68
  - Save and Save As 68
  - Close 69
  - Exit 70
- File Management 70
  - File Options 71
  - QuickList 71
  - Setup 73
  - QuickFinder 74

Chapter 5. Setting Preferences

- The Preferences Dialog Box 75
- Selecting Printers 80
- Customizing the Screen 81
  - The button bar 81
  - The power bar 85
  - The status bar 88

Chapter 6. Speller, Thesaurus, and Grammatik
The Speller 91
    Using the Speller 91
Thesaurus 97
    Using the Thesaurus 98
Grammar Checker 102

Chapter 7. Printing
Previewing Documents 107
Printing Documents 108
    Selecting printers 109

Chapter 8. Tables
WordPerfect Tables 113
Creating Tables 113
    Selecting cells 115
    Selecting text in cells 116
The Table Menu 116
    Formatting text in tables 117
    Editing the table structure 123
    Working with tables 126
    Inserting formulas 129
    Naming tables 130

Chapter 9. Charts
WordPerfect Chart 135
    Charting your tables 135
    The Chart Editor 136

Chapter 10. Styles and Outlines
Styles 143
    Creating styles 143
    Applying styles 147
    Editing styles 148
    Saving styles 149

Retrieving styles 150
Deleting styles 151
Graphics, tables, and text in styles 152
Using Outlines 152
Moving families 154
Outline displays 155
Outline options 156

Chapter 11. Graphics
Graphics 159
Retrieving graphics 159
Moving graphics 161
Resizing graphics 163
Editing graphics 164
Creating a caption 169
Text wrap 170
Borders and fills 171
Graphics box contents 172
Putting text in boxes 173
Equations 174
Creating lines 175
Object Linking and Embedding (OLE) support 177
Deleting graphics 179

Chapter 12. WP Draw
Opening WP Draw 181
The Tool Bar 182
Function Tools 182
The Select tool 182
The Zoom tool 186
The Chart tool 187
The Figure tool 188
The Object Outline/Fill tools 189
The Set Line Style/Fill Pattern tools 189
The Set Line/Fill Color tools 190
Drawing Tools 190

    The Text tool 191
    The Freehand tool 191
    The Curve tool 192
    The Closed Curve tool 193
    The Line tool 193
    The Polygon tool 194
    The Elliptical Arc tool 194
    The Ellipse tool 195
    The Rectangle and the Rounded Rectangle tool 195
Updating Your Document 196
The WP Draw Menus 196

Chapter 13. TextArt

TextArt 197
Starting TextArt 197
    Creating text 198
    Text attributes 200

Chapter 14. Merging

The Merge Command 205
    The data file 205
    The form file 210
Merging Files 211

Chapter 15. Creating Macros

Using Macros 213
    Recording a macro 213
    Playing macros 215
    Putting macros in the menu 216

Chapter 16. Document Tools

Introduction 219
    Bookmark 219
    Document information 222
    Date 223
    Document comments 224

Footnotes and endnotes 227
Document summary 230
Document compare 231
Master document 232
Sort 235

Chapter 17. Referencing Tools
Mark Text, Define, and Generate 239
    Creating an index 239
    Creating a concordance file 240
    Defining an index 240
    Generating an index 242
    Creating lists 243
    Table of contents 245
    Cross-reference 248
    Table of Authorities 250
Hypertext 250
    Creating Hypertext links 250
    Using Hypertext links 251
    Editing Hypertext links 252

Index 255

WordPerfect for Windows

The Screen

WordPerfect offers a range of powerful editing and text manipulation features that help you simplify and speed up the way you prepare documents.

Figure 1. The WordPerfect screen is shown below. On start-up, your screen includes the menu bar, status bar, button bar, power bar, and scroll bars. However, the ruler bar is only displayed if you select it from the **View** menu. Also, you can now customize almost all of the screen elements in WordPerfect 6.0 to suit your needs.

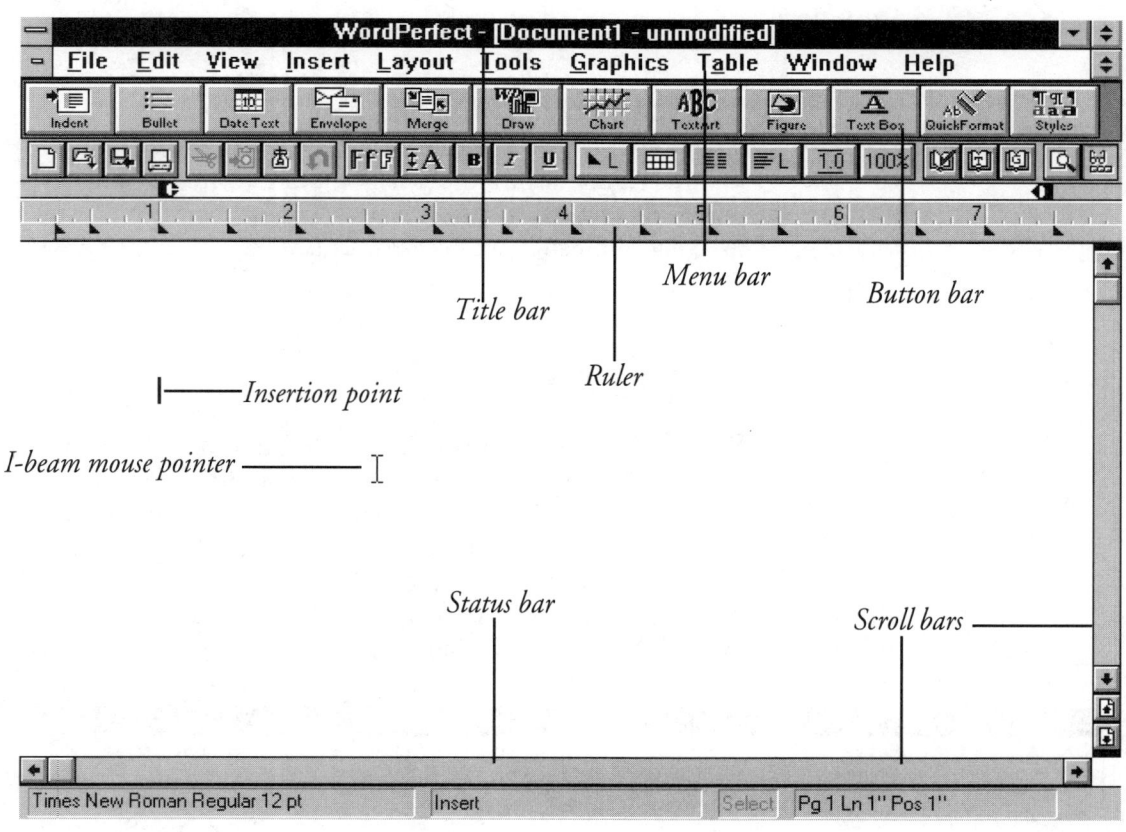

Chapter 1: WordPerfect for Windows

This chapter deals with the main features of the WordPerfect screen. For information on customizing the WordPerfect screen elements, see **Chapter 5**.

THE SCREEN COMPONENTS

THE MOUSE POINTER

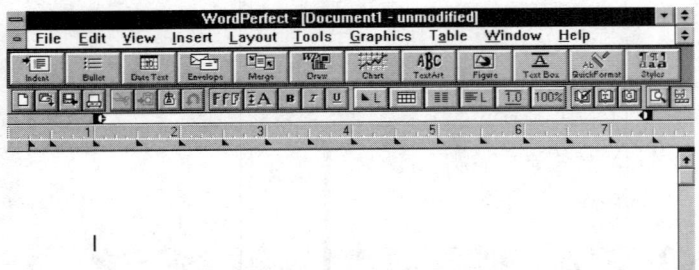

Figure 2. The insertion point is the flashing bar in the top left-hand corner of the screen. You can reposition this cursor in text by using the mouse or the arrow keys on the keyboard. The insertion point is where new text appears whenever you start typing.

The mouse pointer, on the other hand, represents the position of the mouse on the screen. When the mouse pointer is in the editing window it usually appears as an "I-beam," however, the mouse pointer changes to an arrow when you are selecting commands or screen elements.

THE TITLE BAR

Figure 3. The title bar is common to all Windows applications. It shows the program name and the title of the current document. If you haven't made any changes to the current document, the title bar reads *Document 1 - unmodified* (when you create your document the word *unmodified* disappears). The title bar also contains the Control menu box and the maximize and minimize buttons.

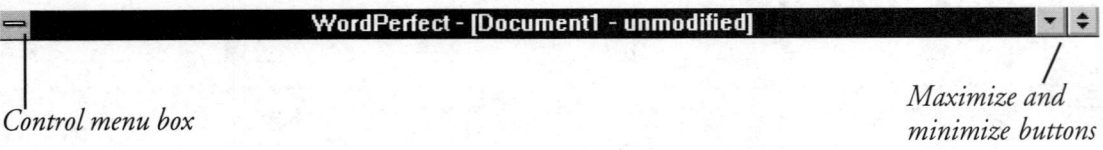

Control menu box

Maximize and minimize buttons

2

Occasionally the title bar displays help prompts to give you information about menu items or buttons you select.

Figure 4. Clicking once on the Control menu box activates the Windows **Control** menu. From this menu you can exit from the program, minimize, or maximize the current window, or activate the Windows *Task List* dialog box.

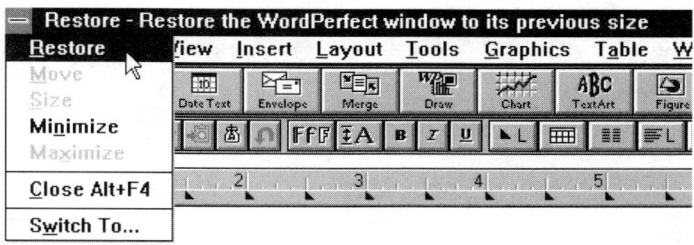

Figure 5. The minimize and maximize buttons are on the title bar at the right. The minimize button minimizes the program window to an icon at the bottom-left of the screen. You can double-click on this icon to reactivate the window. Clicking on the maximize button causes WordPerfect to fill the entire screen or application window with the document; and the maximize button becomes the restore button. Clicking on the restore button returns the screen to its previous size.

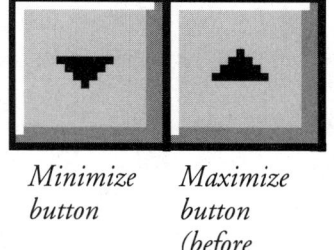

Minimize button   *Maximize button (before maximizing)*

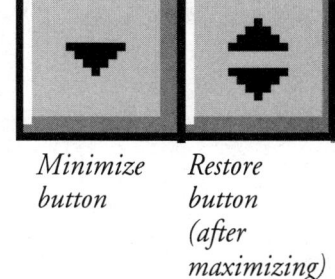

Minimize button   *Restore button (after maximizing)*

THE MENU BAR

Figure 6. The menu bar runs along the top of the screen below the title bar. If you click the mouse and hold it down on a menu option name, WordPerfect displays a list of further options or commands under this menu. Menus are common to all Windows applications. The WordPerfect menu bar also contains minimize and maximize buttons and a Control menu box that apply to the current WordPerfect document.

THE SCROLL BARS

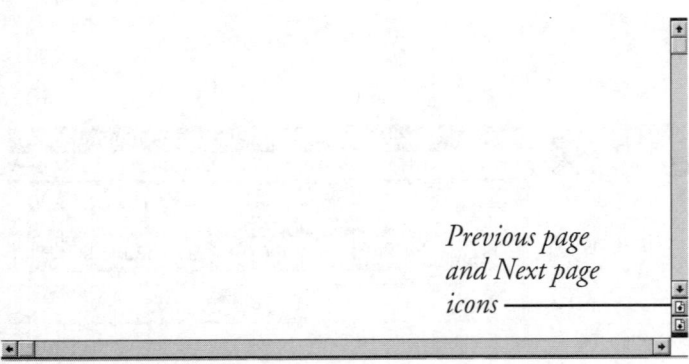

Previous page and Next page icons

Figure 7. You can use the scroll bars in conjunction with the mouse to move quickly around your page. Click on the gray area of the scroll bars to move up, down or across the page in large steps. To move one page at a time through your document you can click on the Previous page and Next page icons at the bottom of the vertical scroll bar.

You can also move in smaller steps by clicking on the arrows at either end of the scroll bars. To move around in arbitrary steps, hold the mouse button down on the scroll button, move it to the position you want, then let go of the button. When the scroll button is at the very top of the vertical scroll bar, you are at the top of your document; similarly, when you are at the end of your document, the scroll box is at the bottom of the vertical scroll bar.

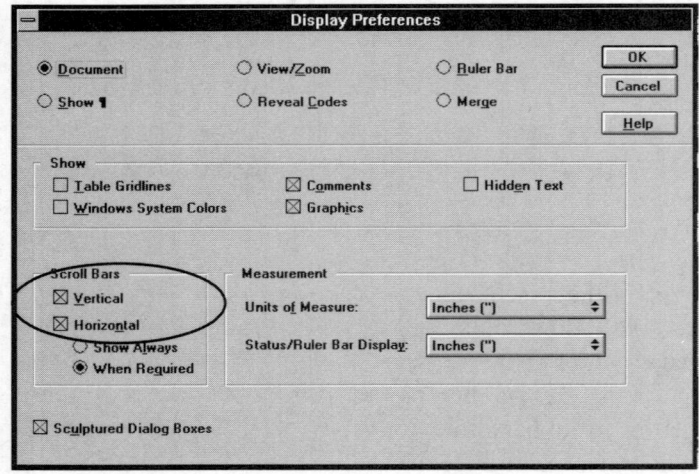

Figure 8. WordPerfect displays the scroll bars by default. However, you can change when WordPerfect displays the scroll bars through the *Display Preferences* dialog box from the **File** menu. See **Chapter 5** for more information on setting preferences.

THE STATUS BAR

Figure 9. Whenever you open WordPerfect, the status bar is at the bottom of the screen. This bar changes to reflect what you are doing in your document. Before you make any changes, the left of the status bar tells you the default font and size. The right of the status bar shows which page the cursor is on and exactly where it is. *Pg* tells you the page number, *Ln* signifies the line, and *Pos* stands for the horizontal position of the cursor on that line. The word "Insert" on the status bar indicates the current text entry mode, and the grayed out word "Select" becomes active whenever you select text in your document (see **Chapter 2**). In a new WordPerfect document, the default settings for line and position are one inch. This indicates that the top and left margins are at one inch.

THE BUTTON BAR

Figure 10. The button bar is now a default screen element and appears directly below the menu bar. The button bar lets you select commands and functions as an alternative to using menus, dialog boxes, or shortcut keys.

Each button on the button bar contains a picture and a command name, representing a function or command from the WordPerfect menus. To activate a command, click on one of the available buttons. For example, the first button on the button bar represents the *Indent* command from the *Paragraph* submenu in the **Layout** menu. Clicking on this button is the equivalent of directly selecting the *Indent* command from the menus.

You can also create, edit and customize the button bar or choose from a variety of default button bars (see **Chapter 5** for more information). You can turn the button bar on or off at any time by selecting *Button Bar* from the **View** menu. A check mark beside the command shows that it is active.

Chapter 1: WordPerfect for Windows

THE POWER BAR

Figure 11. The power bar, which appears directly below the button bar, is a new feature in WordPerfect for Windows 6.0 that you use in the same way as you do the button bar.

However, unlike the button bar, the buttons on the power bar do not contain text. If you want to see which command each button represents, simply put the mouse pointer over the button and WordPerfect shows what that button does on the title bar.

For instance, putting the mouse pointer over the first button on the power bar brings up the explanation "New Document - Create a new document in a new window - CTRL+N" in the title bar. Selecting this button is the same as selecting *New* from the **File** menu.

You can edit the buttons on the power bar (see **Chapter 5**) and you can turn it off by selecting *Power Bar* from the **View** menu.

THE RULER BAR

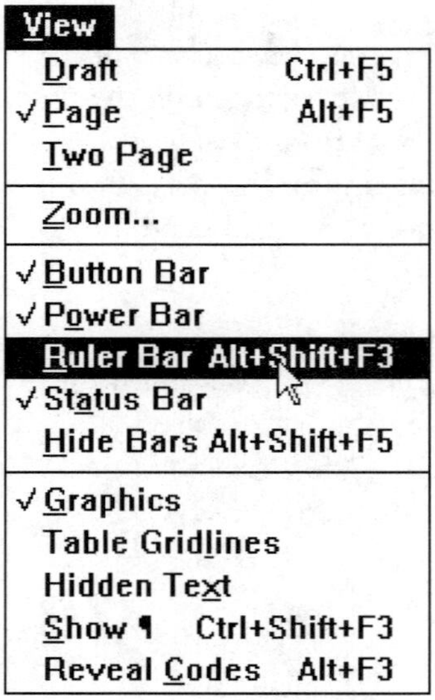

Figure 12. You can turn the ruler bar on and off in WordPerfect by selecting *Ruler Bar* from the **View** menu. Although the ruler bar is not a default screen element, it is a very useful feature that gives you quick and easy access to a variety of options and commands when you are formatting your document.

6

Chapter 1: WordPerfect for Windows

Figure 13. After you select the *Ruler Bar* command, the ruler bar appears below the power bar.

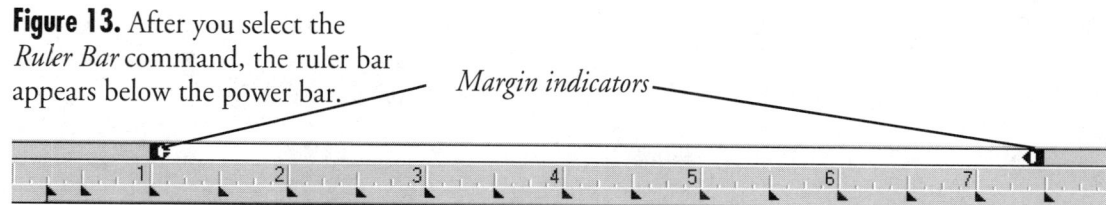

Margin indicators

Along the top of the ruler bar is the margin guide containing the margin markers. These markers display the current left and right page margins. The white area between them shows you where you can put your text on the page.

MARGINS

Figure 14. By double-clicking anywhere in the margin guide in the ruler bar, you activate the *Margins* dialog box. Here you can change the current margin settings by typing in a new measurement for each option or by using the arrows to increase or decrease the current settings. This dialog box also has a representation of a page containing text. This page shows you the effect of changes you make on the overall layout of your page.

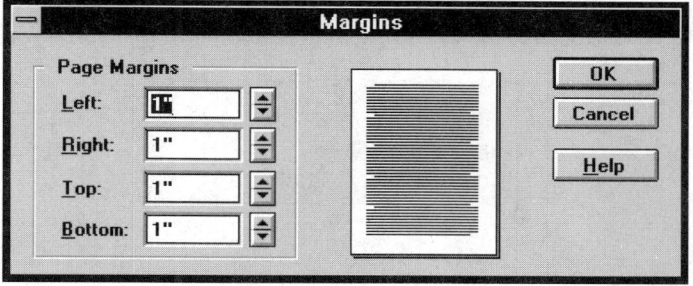

Figure 15. You can also alter horizontal margins by holding the mouse button down on the margin markers in the margin guide (left or right) and dragging it to a new position.

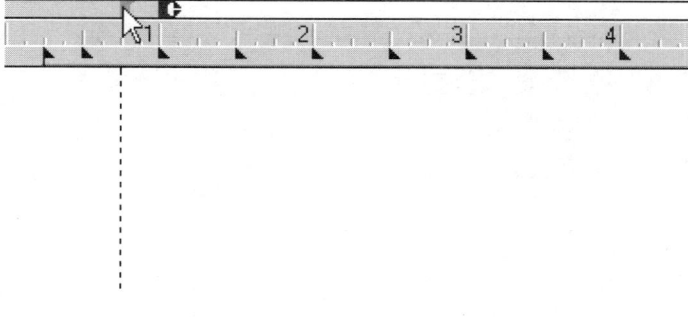

7

Chapter 1: WordPerfect for Windows

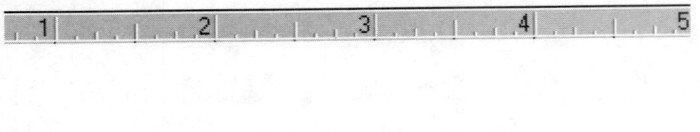

Figure 16. Below the margin guide is the ruler itself. You set the unit of measurement for the ruler in the *Display Preferences* dialog box (see **Chapter 5**). You use the ruler to set up the current margin and tab settings.

TABS

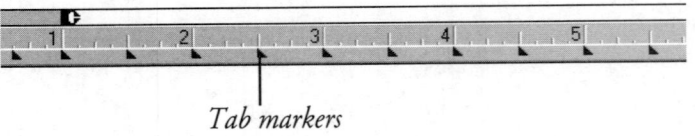

Tab markers

Figure 17. Underneath the ruler are the tab markers. These triangular markers denote the tab stops—that is how far the cursor moves when you press the tab key. By default, WordPerfect sets tabs at every half inch.

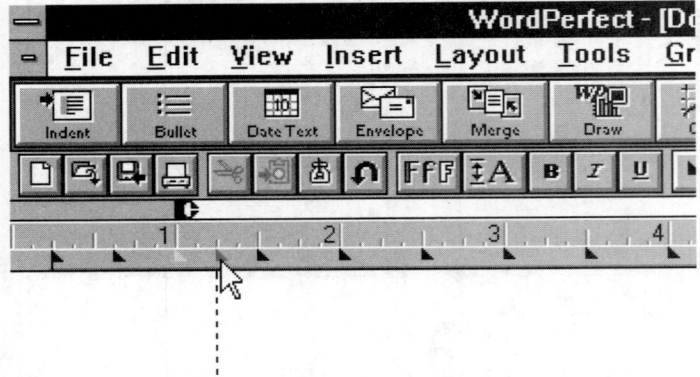

Figure 18. The tab markers not only show you each tab stop, but they also allow you to alter them. You do this by dragging the triangular tab markers to a new position on the ruler. You can also add or delete tabs with the mouse. To delete a tab marker from the ruler, simply drag it below the ruler and release the mouse button.

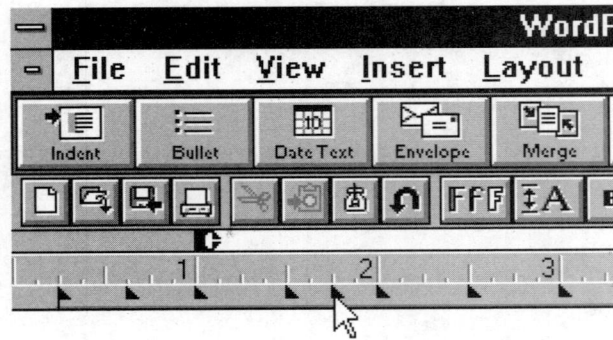

Figure 19. To add a tab to the ruler, simply click the mouse anywhere in the tab set section of the ruler. WordPerfect automatically inserts a tab marker in that position. To determine the type of tab that you want, click on the *Tab Set* button on the power bar and choose from the drop-down list that appears. For more information on setting tabs, see **Chapter 3**.

QUICKMENUS

Figure 20. QuickMenus are an easy way of accessing commands relevant to a particular feature. You can activate these pop-up menu lists by placing the mouse cursor over the relevant screen element and clicking the right mouse button. You can then select the command you want from the QuickMenu with the left mouse button. For example, to activate the QuickMenu for the button bar, position the mouse pointer over the button bar and click the right mouse button. The QuickMenu that appears gives you a list of commands specific to the button bar.

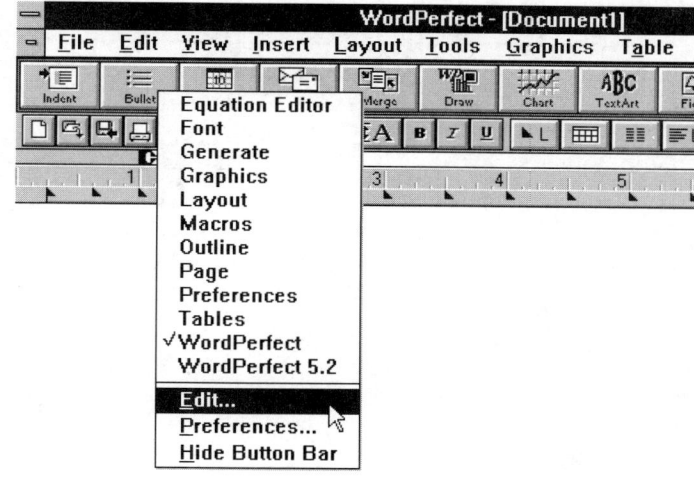

Figure 21. The table in this figure lists where you can click the right mouse button to get a QuickMenu.

Click the right mouse on these areas	Specific locations
Bars	The button bar, the power bar, the ruler bar, the status bar, feature bars, the menu bar and the scroll bars.
Customizing Editors	Button Bar Editor, Menu Editor, and Keyboard Editor dialog boxes.
Dialog boxes (list boxes only)	Open, Save, Save As, and WordPerfect Characters dialog boxes.
Document markers	Comments, sound annotations.
Document window	Text, columns, headers and footers, selected text and the left margin.
Graphics	Graphics, graphics lines, equations, and OLE objects.
Reveal codes	Reveal Codes screen.
WordPerfect Draw and Chart	WordPerfect Draw and Chart Windows.

FEATURE BARS

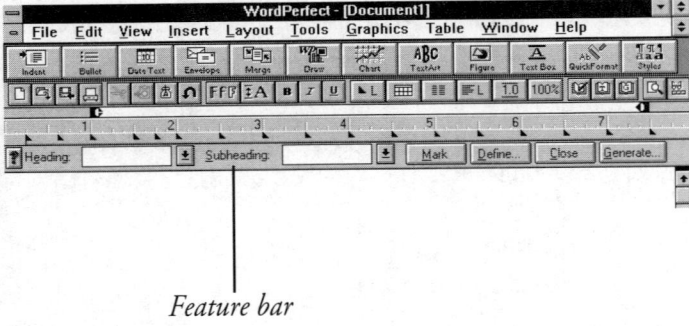

Feature bar

Figure 22. Another WordPerfect screen element is the feature bar. Feature bars operate in the same way as button bars and provide a quick and easy way for you to choose options for specific WordPerfect features.

Feature bars in WordPerfect are command specific and thus only appear when you use the relevant feature. For instance, selecting the *Index* command from the **Tools** menu displays the *Index* feature bar, offering you access to all of WordPerfect's indexing features.

We tell you about individual feature bars in the relevant sections of the book.

EDITING TEXT   2

INTRODUCTION

You can edit and format text in your WordPerfect documents in various ways. This chapter looks at simple editing and formatting of text, while **Chapter 3** looks at more complex page and paragraph formatting.

SIMPLE EDITING METHODS

MOVING THE INSERTION POINT

To reposition the insertion point within text using the mouse, put the I-beam where you want the insertion point and click the left mouse button. This puts the insertion point at the I-beam position.

Use the scroll bars to move to parts of your document that you can't see on your screen.

Figure 1. You can also reposition the insertion point in text using the arrow keys and the Home, End, Page Up, and Page Down keys on your keyboard. Using these keys in conjunction with the Ctrl and Alt keys also moves the insertion point by words, paragraphs, or whole lines at a time.

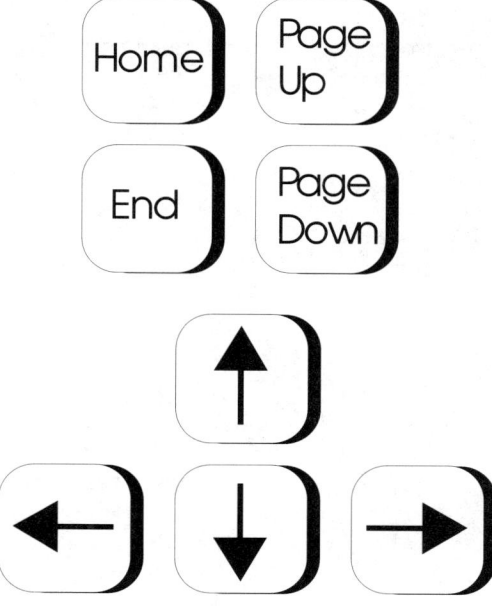

11

Figure 2. This table gives a summary of how to move the insertion point using the keyboard.

Press	To move	Press	To move
Up arrow	Up one line	Ctrl+left arrow	Left one word
Down arrow	Down one line	Ctrl+right arrow	Right one word
Left arrow	Left one character	Ctrl+down arrow	Down one paragraph
Right arrow	Right one character	Ctrl+up arrow	Up one paragraph
Page Up	To top of screen, then up one screen at a time	Ctrl+Home	To beginning of document (after formatting codes)
Page Down	To bottom of screen, then down one screen at a time	Ctrl+Home, Ctrl+Home	To beginning of document (before formatting codes)
Home	To beginning of line (after formatting codes)	Ctrl+End	End of document (after formatting codes)
Home, Home	To far left of line (before formatting codes)	Alt+Page Up	To first line on previous page
End	To end of line (after formatting codes)	Alt+Page Down	To first line on next page

INSERT AND TYPEOVER MODES

There are two typing modes that operate at the insertion point in WordPerfect, *Insert* and *Typeover*. By default, WordPerfect works in *Insert* mode. This means any text that you type into existing text forces the existing text to the right. This is the normal method of word-processing.

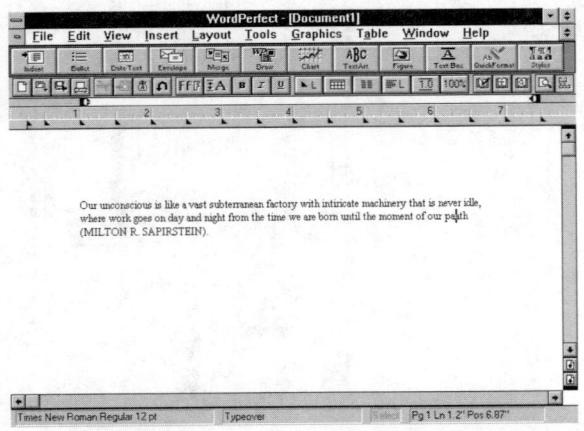

Figure 3. Pressing the Insert key on your keyboard activates *Typeover* mode. Existing text no longer moves to the right when you type, instead the new text types directly over the existing text. Turn *Typeover* mode off by pressing the Insert key again. The status bar indicates your current typing mode.

Note: When using Typeover mode, you cannot type over codes. If the text that you are typing over encounters a code, the code remains and the text is simply inserted at this point. (For an explanation of codes, see the **Codes** *section starting at Figure 16.)*

Chapter 2: Editing Text

EDITING KEYS

You use the Backspace and Delete keys for simple text editing in your document. The Backspace key moves the cursor one space to the left, removing characters as it goes. The Delete key removes the characters to the right of the cursor. The cursor remains where it is and the text moves towards the cursor.

UNDO AND UNDELETE

Figure 4. The *Undo* command from the **Edit** menu reverses the last change you made in WordPerfect. For instance, if the last thing you did was to change the page margins of your document, the *Undo* command changes the margins back to how they were. You can also undo your last action with the *Undo* button on the power bar.

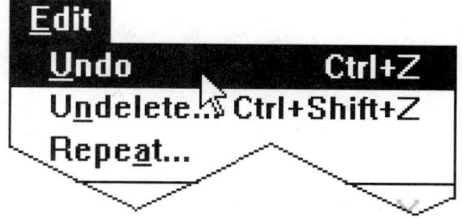

Figure 5. The *Undelete* command works in a slightly different way. Selecting *Undelete* from the **Edit** menu activates the *Undelete* dialog box.

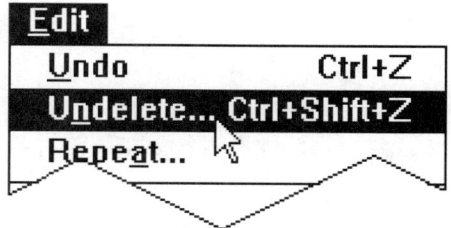

Figure 6. With the *Undelete* dialog box active, you can display the last three deletions you made, and restore them in your document.

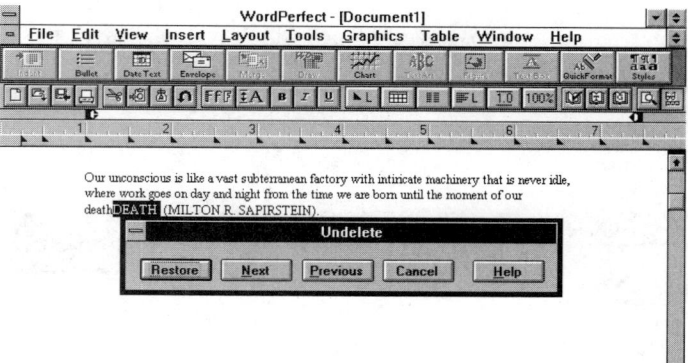

13

Chapter 2: Editing Text

SELECTING TEXT

To edit and format your documents effectively you need to be able to select text. There are a number of ways you can do this.

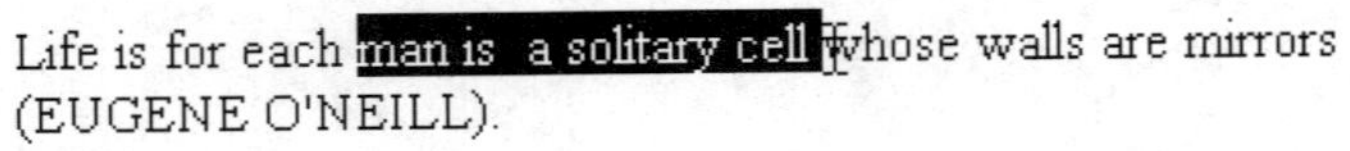

Life is for each **man is   a solitary cell** whose walls are mirrors (EUGENE O'NEILL).

Figure 7. The simplest way to select text is dragging. To do this, click and hold the left mouse button at the beginning of the text you want and then drag the mouse cursor to the end of the text you want. As you drag the mouse along, the text to the left of the I-beam is selected (selected text appears as white on black).

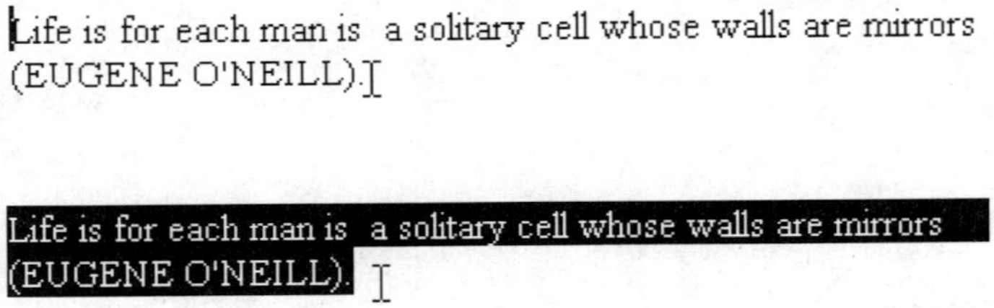

Life is for each man is   a solitary cell whose walls are mirrors (EUGENE O'NEILL).

Figure 8. Another way of selecting text is the shift-click method. Put the cursor at the beginning of the text you want to select, hold the Shift key down, and click the mouse at the end of the text you want. This selects everything between these two points.

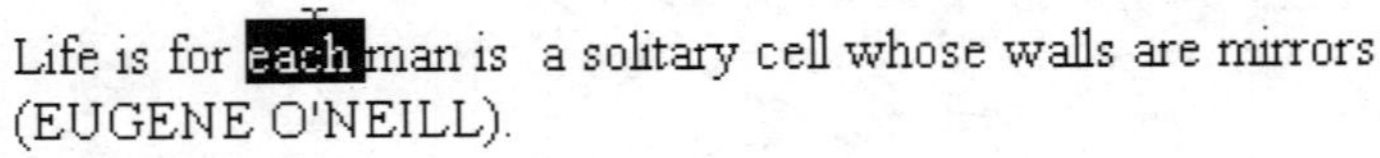

Life is for each man is   a solitary cell whose walls are mirrors (EUGENE O'NEILL).

Life is for **each** man is   a solitary cell whose walls are mirrors (EUGENE O'NEILL).

Double-click to select a word

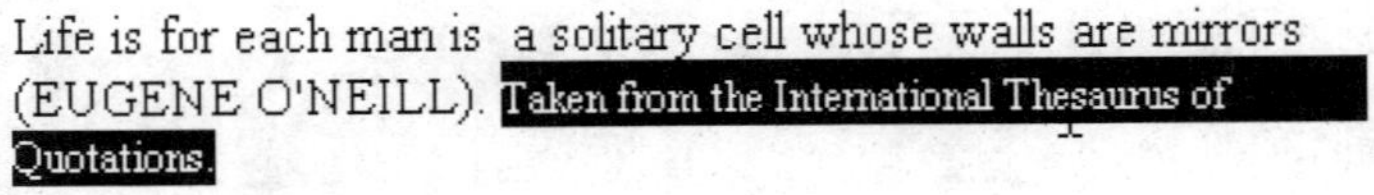

Figure 9. You can also use multiple clicks of the mouse to select words, sentences, and paragraphs. Double-click to select a word, triple-click to select a sentence, and quadruple-click to select a paragraph.

Life is for each man is   a solitary cell whose walls are mirrors (EUGENE O'NEILL). **Taken from the International Thesaurus of Quotations.**

Triple-click to select a sentence

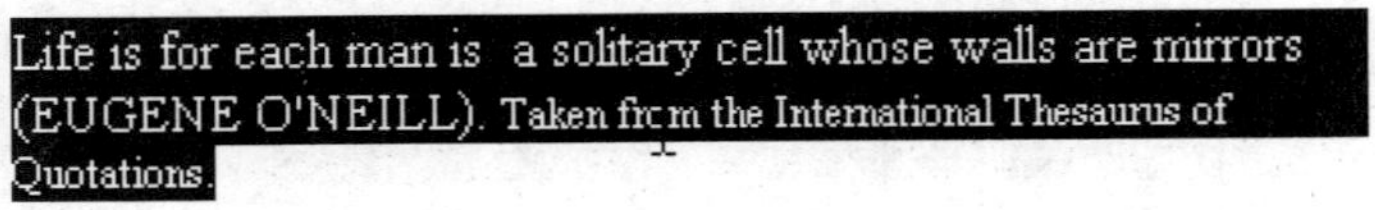

Life is for each man is   a solitary cell whose walls are mirrors (EUGENE O'NEILL). Taken from the International Thesaurus of Quotations.

Quadruple-click to select a paragraph

Chapter 2: Editing Text

Figure 10. The *Select* submenu from the **Edit** menu is another way you can select text. You have the option of selecting either the *Sentence, Paragraph,* or *Page* that the text cursor is in or you can select all of the text in your document.

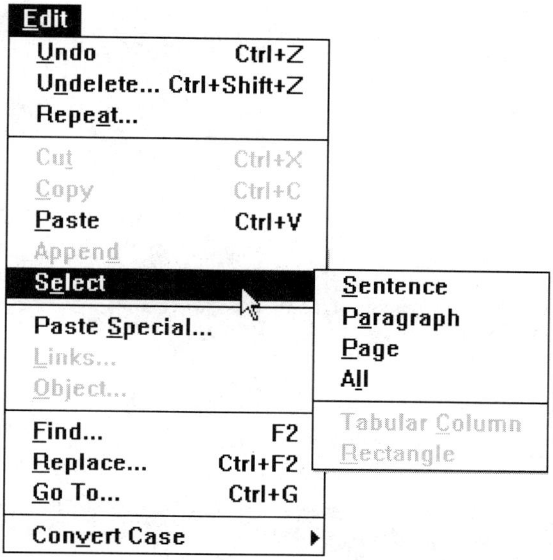

Another quick way of selecting text is to press the F8 key and use the arrow keys to highlight text from the cursor position.

CUT, COPY, PASTE, AND APPEND

Figure 11. The *Cut, Copy,* and *Paste* commands from the **Edit** menu are very useful editing tools. You can use *Cut* in conjunction with *Paste* to move selected material, or *Copy* in conjunction with *Paste* to copy selected material.

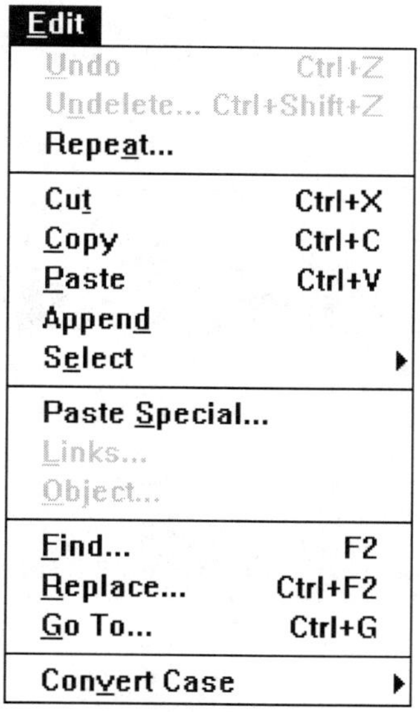

Selecting the *Cut* command removes the selected text or graphic from your document and puts it on the Windows clipboard. Selecting *Copy* leaves the selected text or graphic in your document and places a copy of it on the clipboard.

The *Paste* command inserts the contents of the clipboard at the cursor position.

The material on the clipboard remains there until it is replaced by other material through the Cut or Copy commands. You can paste material on the clipboard into your document as many times as you like.

15

The *Append* command lets you add text or graphics to what is already in the clipboard.

DRAG AND DROP

You can use the Drag and Drop feature of WordPerfect to move or copy text you have selected in your document without using the *Cut, Copy,* and *Paste* commands.

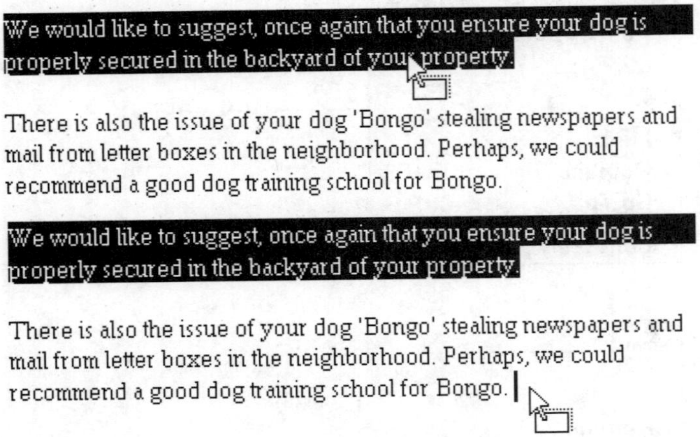

Figure 12. To move text you have selected, simply click on the text and drag the mouse to a new location. When you do this, the mouse pointer changes shape.

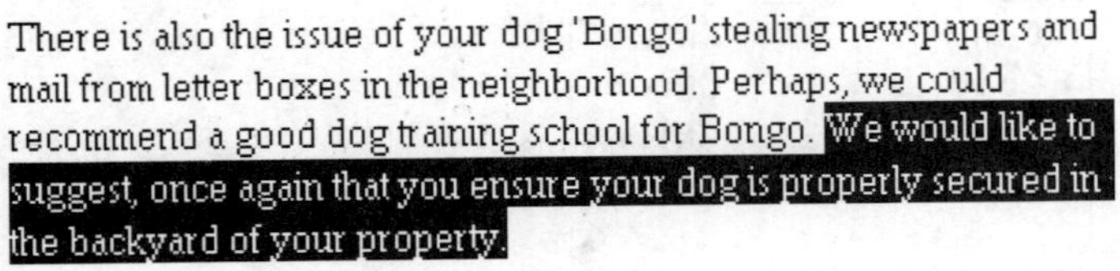

Figure 13. When you release the mouse button the selected text is automatically cut from its original position and pasted at the insertion point.

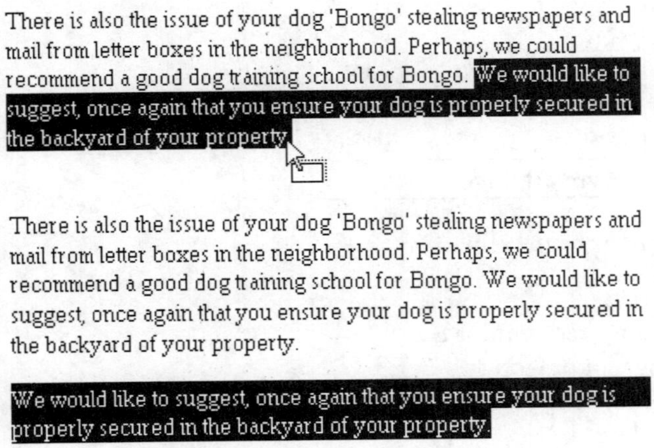

Figure 14. To copy selected text in this way, hold down the Ctrl key as you click and drag the selected text to a new location. Once again the mouse pointer changes shape, but this time the text is copied into its new location when you release the mouse button. The original text remains untouched.

CONVERT CASE

Figure 15. The *Convert Case* command from the **Edit** menu lets you convert selected text to either all uppercase or all lowercase characters and even to convert the first letter of each word into capitals. In any conversions the letter "I" remains in capitals when it appears as a word by itself and when it appears before an apostrophe.

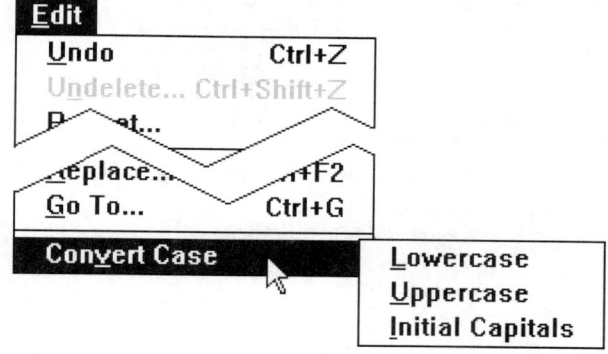

CODES

Figure 16. WordPerfect inserts formatting codes into your document every time you apply an attribute to it. These codes are not visible normally but if you activate the *Reveal Codes* screen, you can see them. To turn this screen on, select *Reveal Codes* from the **View** menu.

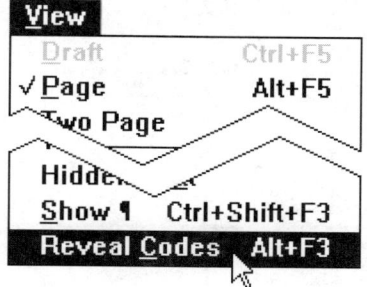

Figure 17. The *Reveal Codes* window appears at the bottom of the screen. This window is a direct reflection of the normal editing screen containing all text and graphics in your document, only the *Reveal Codes* screen also shows all of the formatting codes in your document.

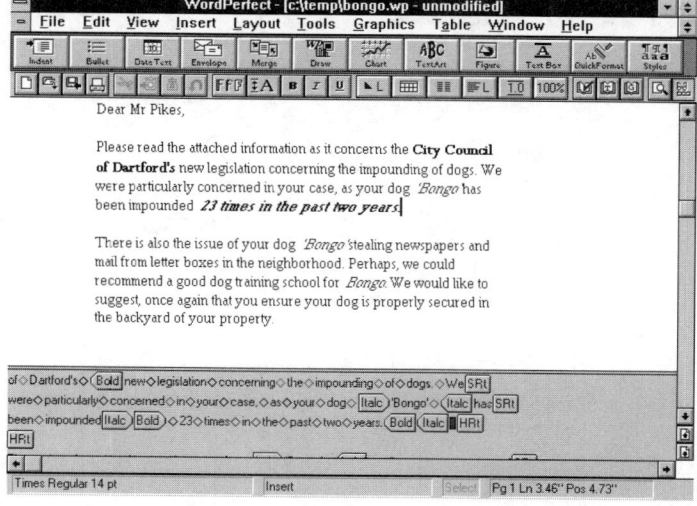

Chapter 2: Editing Text

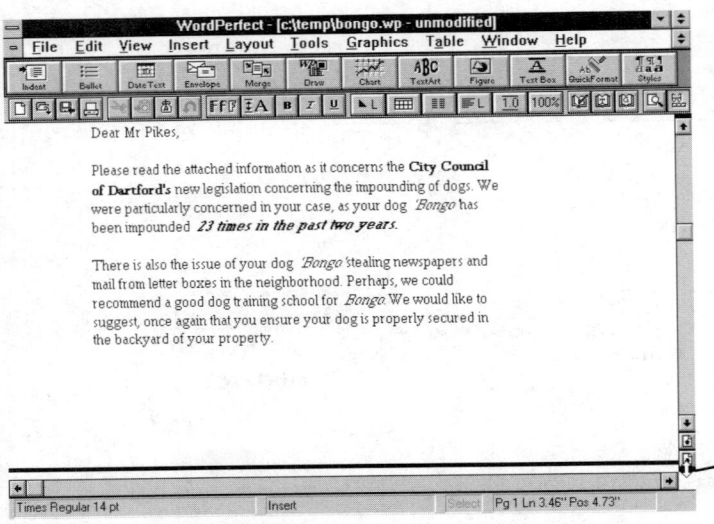

Figure 18. You can also activate the *Reveal Codes* screen by dragging the black section below the vertical scroll bar up to where you want the *Reveal Codes* screen to begin. Once you release the mouse button, WordPerfect activates the *Reveal Codes* screen.

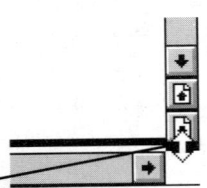

Figure 19. To resize the *Reveal Codes* screen, simply drag its border with the mouse.

Figure 20. Codes appear in brackets and indicate different formatting commands that relate to text, graphics and document layout. Some commands, such as italic, have a beginning and an end shown by the [Italc] and [Italc] codes. The italic text appears between these two codes. These are called *paired codes*.

Figure 21. There are two ways of applying paired codes. The first way is to select the text you want to affect and choose the required command. Note that when you select text, WordPerfect inserts a temporary [Select] code in the *Reveal Codes* screen and the word *Select* becomes active on the status bar.

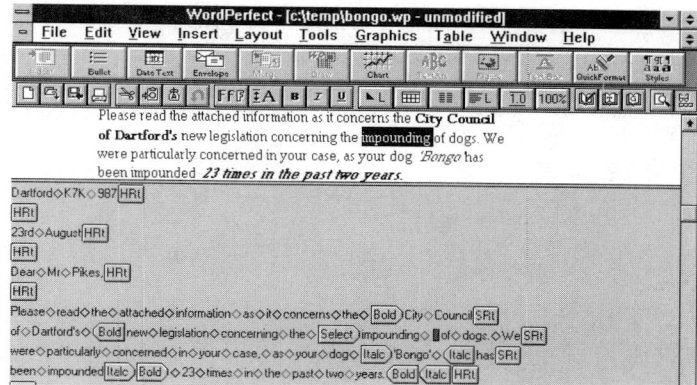

Figure 22. After you select *Bold* from the **Font** menu, the selected text becomes bold and WordPerfect inserts [Bold] and [Bold] codes in the *Reveal Codes* screen.

Alternatively, you can apply paired codes by selecting the *Bold* command to activate the [Bold] [Bold] codes with the cursor between them. Now type in the text you want before selecting the *Bold* command again to move you beyond the [Bold] code. Effectively you are selecting the *Bold* command to turn the bold typeface on and off like a switch as you type your text.

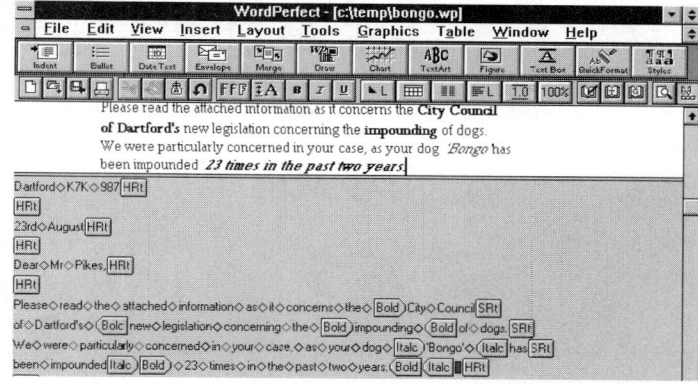

Figure 23. You can apply as many sets of paired codes to the same text as you want. Here we have applied the *Very Large* and *Bold* commands to the selected text. Note both sets of paired codes surround this text in the *Reveal Codes* screen.

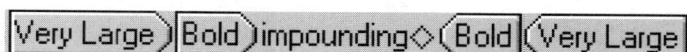

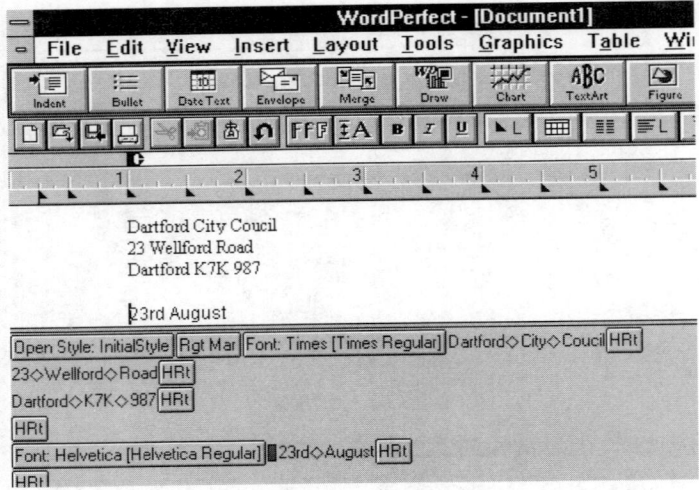

Figure 24. Another type of codes is known as *open codes*. These codes do not have an *On* and an *Off* code. Instead, open codes affect the text from where you first place them until you override them with another open code of the same type.

For example, the *Font* command inserts an open code. Inserting a font code affects all of the text following it to the end of the document unless you override it with another font code. In this example, the text is in Times until the Helvetica code replaces it. The Helvetica code now applies to the rest of the document (or until you insert another font code).

Each time you apply a command to either the text or the page layout, WordPerfect inserts a code. Where WordPerfect inserts this code depends upon the type of code you are adding. WordPerfect inserts paired codes directly to the text range that you specify, but many open codes need to take effect from the beginning of paragraphs or pages.

For commands such as *Columns, Margins (left and right), Paragraph Numbering,* and *Tab Set,* WordPerfect moves the codes to the beginning of the paragraph containing the insertion point. Other commands such as *Margins (top and bottom), Page (Center), Page Numbering, Page Size,* and *Suppress* move the code to the beginning of the current page.

Chapter 2: Editing Text

Figure 25. You can delete codes from the *Reveal Codes* screen by the normal text editing methods. Click on or directly before the code and press the Delete key. In this example, we clicked on the *Helvetica* code which now has a red rectangle before it. After you press the Delete key, the code disappears and WordPerfect reformats the text without the deleted formatting attribute.

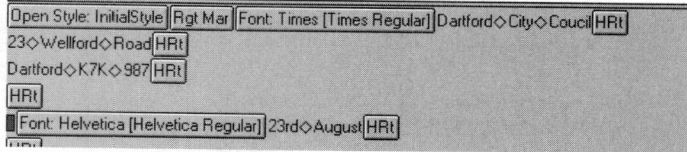

Figure 26. Alternatively, to delete a code, hold the mouse down on the code in the *Reveal Codes* screen and drag the code up into the document before you release the mouse. With a paired code, you can delete either the *On* or the *Off* code.

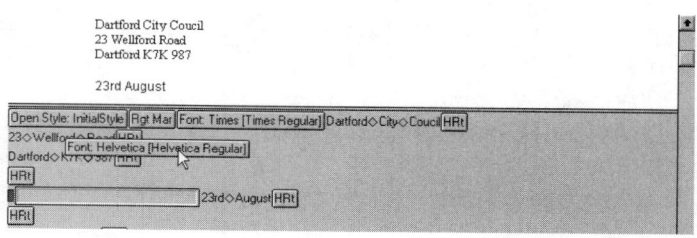

Figure 27. You can turn the *Reveal Codes* screen off by selecting *Reveal Codes* from the **View** menu or by dragging the window frame to the bottom of the screen.

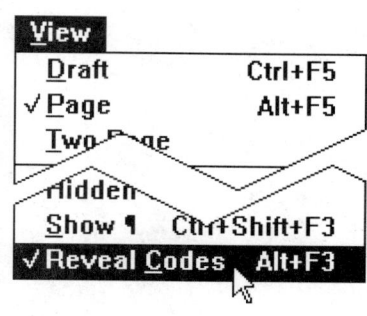

FIND AND REPLACE

Figure 28. The *Find* command from the **Edit** menu activates the *Find Text* dialog box where you can search for certain words in your document.

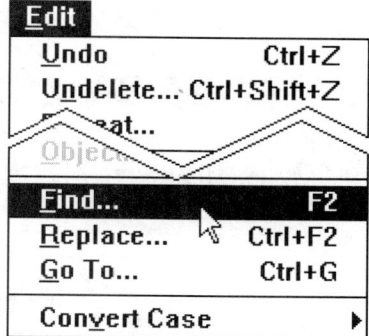

21

Chapter 2: Editing Text

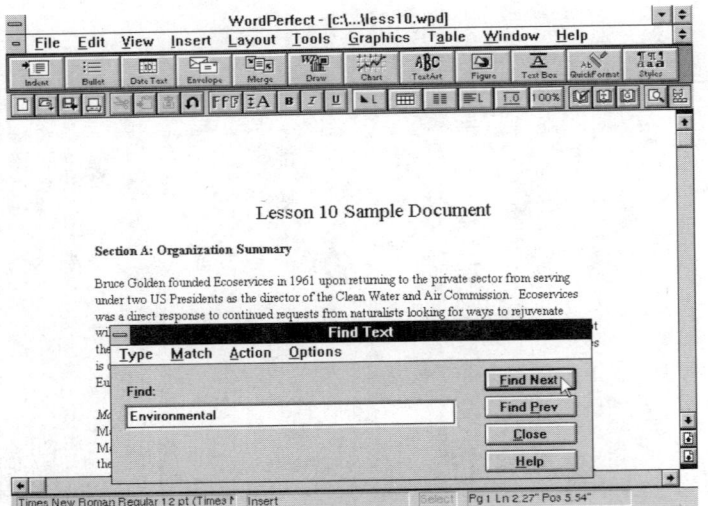

Figure 29. Type the words you want to find in your current document into the *Find* text box. Then click on the *Find Next* button.

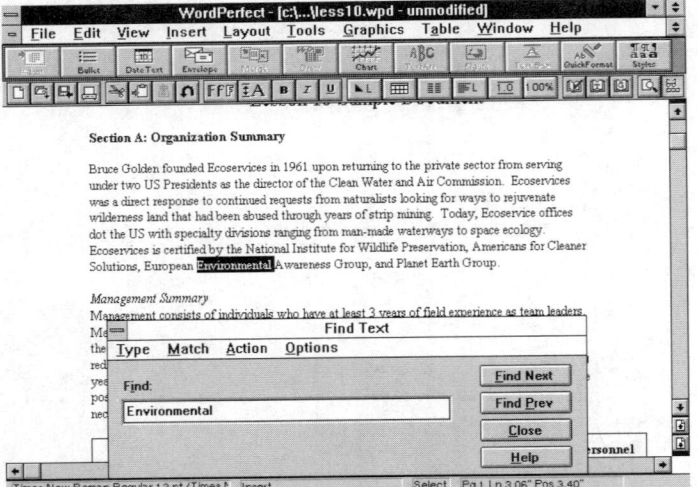

Figure 30. Once WordPerfect has found the specified text, it highlights it in your document. You can now edit this text directly and then click back in the *Find Text* dialog box to make it active again. To continue the search simply use the *Find Next* or *Find Previous* buttons to find the next or previous occurrence of the text in your document.

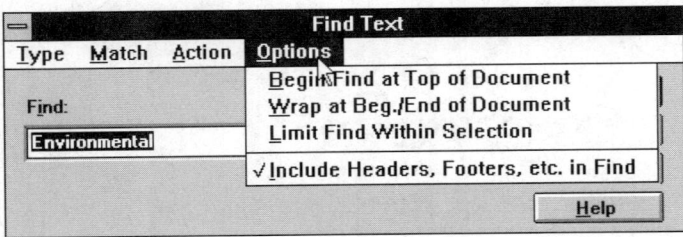

Figure 31. The **Options** menu in the *Find Text* dialog box allows you to determine the range of the text search and how WordPerfect performs the search.

22

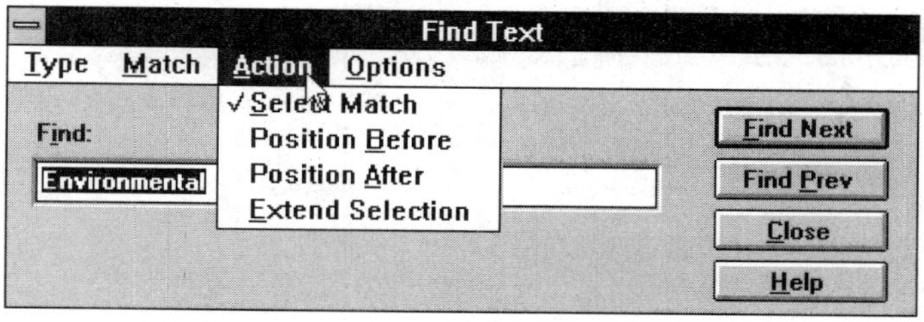

Figure 32. The **Action** menu in the *Find Text* dialog box determines what action WordPerfect takes once it has found the specified text. By default, WordPerfect highlights the text in your document.

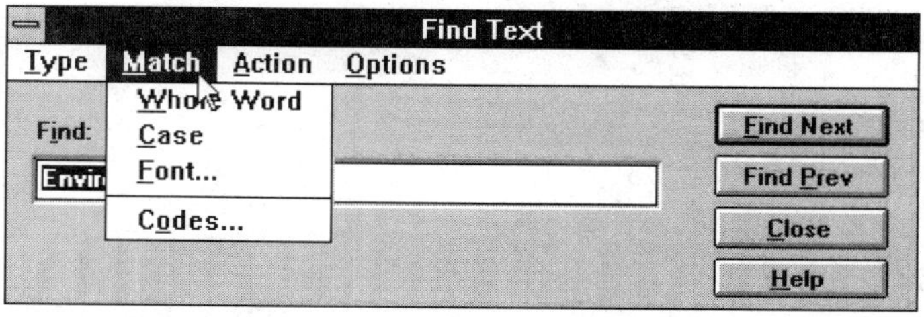

Figure 33. The **Match** menu in the *Find Text* dialog box lets you match the *Find* text exactly to text in the document that includes variations of case, font, and formatting codes.

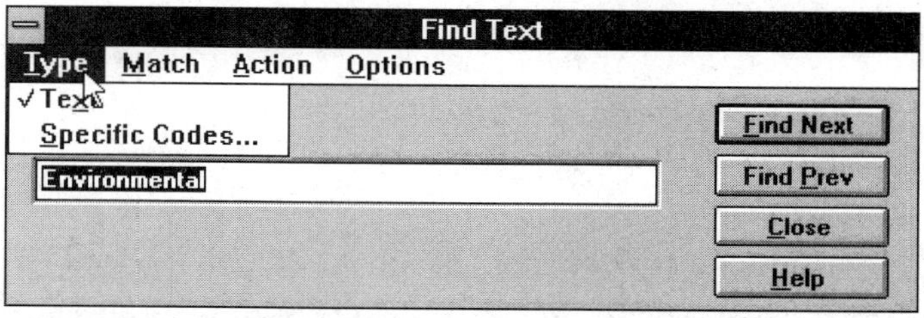

Figure 34. The **Type** menu allows you to specify the type of search you want to perform. Selecting *Specific Codes* here lets you search for codes specific to your document.

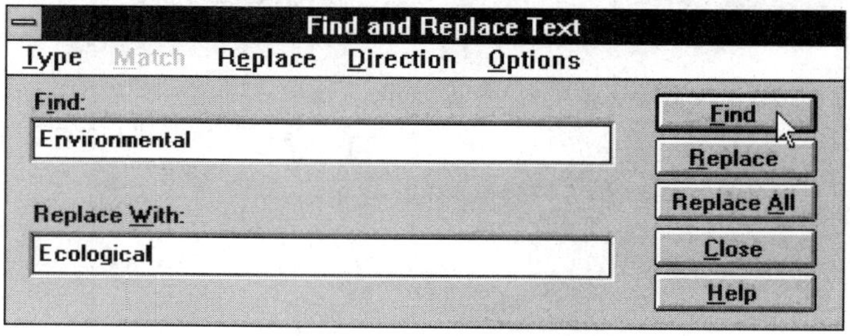

Figure 35. The *Replace* command in the **Edit** menu activates the *Find and Replace Text* dialog box. The *Find and Replace Text* dialog box lets you search for a word, as in the *Find Text* dialog box, but the options in this dialog box also let you replace the word with another. After typing the necessary text into the *Find* and *Replace With* text boxes, click on the *Find* button.

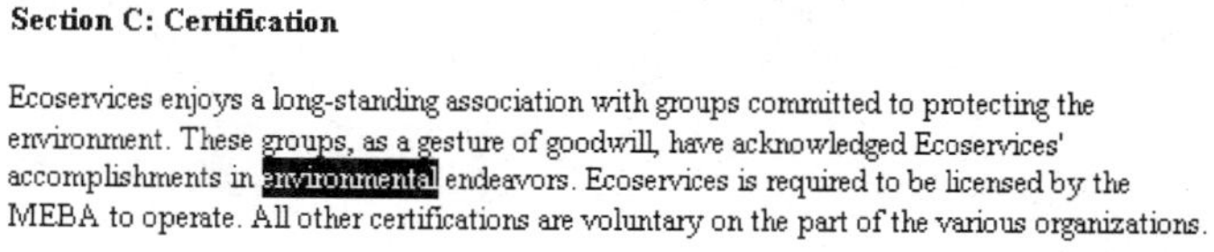

Figure 36. When WordPerfect finds the word you typed in the *Find and Replace Text* dialog box, it highlights it in the document.

Section C: Certification

Ecoservices enjoys a long-standing association with groups committed to protecting the environment. These groups, as a gesture of goodwill, have acknowledged Ecoservices' accomplishments in environmental endeavors. Ecoservices is required to be licensed by the MEBA to operate. All other certifications are voluntary on the part of the various organizations.

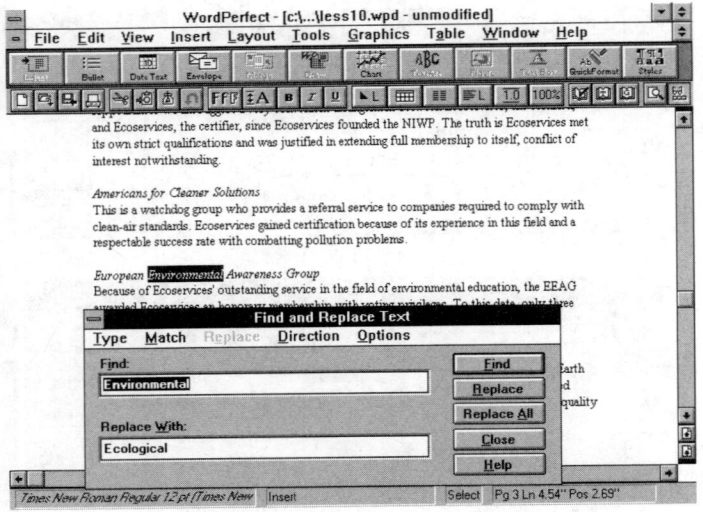

Figure 37. You can now decide if you want to replace this text, or skip this occurrence of the word and continue the search. If you do not want to replace the highlighted text, click on the *Find* button. WordPerfect moves to the next occurrence of the word.

If you want to replace the text, click on the *Replace* button. WordPerfect replaces the text and continues the search, highlighting the next occurrence of the word.

The *Replace All* option scans the whole document for all occurrences of the word in the *Find* text box and replaces them all with the word in the *Replace With* text box.

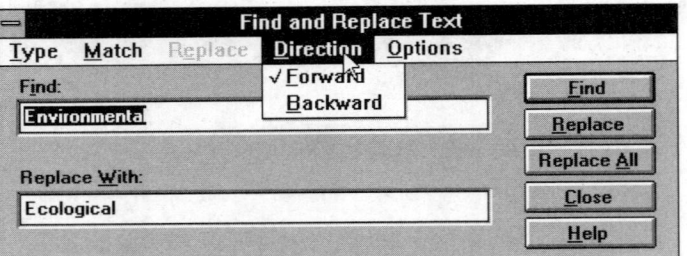

Figure 38. The **Direction** menu in the *Find and Replace Text* dialog box lets you determine the direction of the search.

The **Options**, **Type**, and **Match** menus are basically the same as in the *Find Text* dialog box.

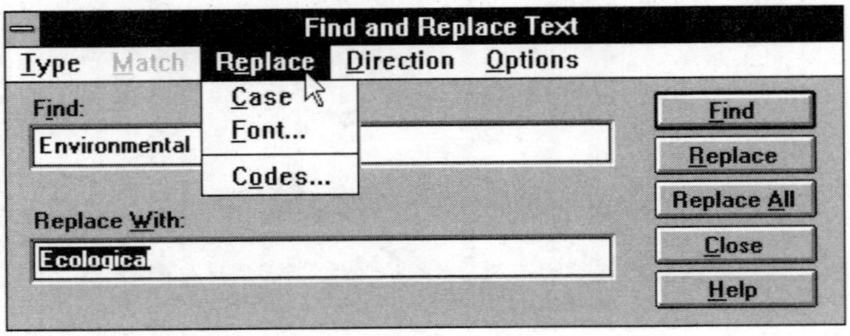

Figure 39. You use the **Replace** menu in the same way as the **Match** menu, except the commands available in the **Replace** menu apply to the *Replace With* text only. (You need to select the text in the *Replace With* text box to access the **Replace** menu.) For example, you can use the **Match** menu to

find text with specific case, font, and code formatting and then use the **Replace** menu to replace it with text containing specific case, fonts or codes. You can also select *Codes* from the **Match** and **Replace** menus to find and replace only the codes in your document (i.e. to change all bold text to italic text by replacing the codes).

ABBREVIATIONS

CREATING AN ABBREVIATION

Figure 40. You can use abbreviations in WordPerfect to abbreviate information that you often use into your document, and expand these abbreviations at a later date. To create an abbreviation, first select the text that you want to abbreviate and then select *Abbreviations* from the **Insert** menu.

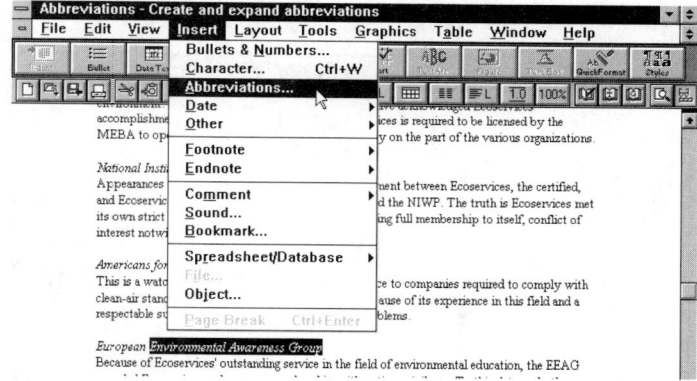

Figure 41. This opens the *Abbreviations* dialog box. Now click on the *Create* button to begin creating your abbreviation.

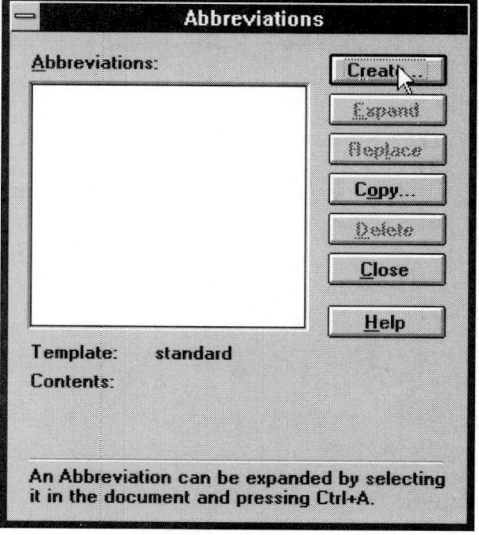

Chapter 2: Editing Text

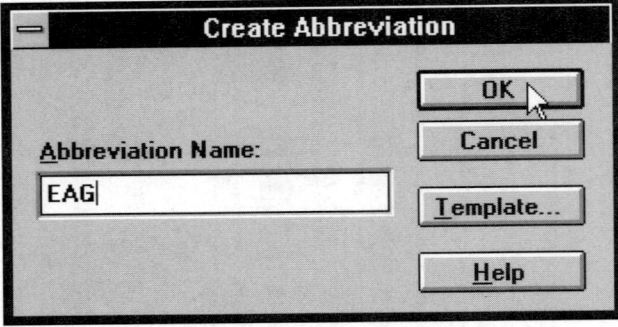

Figure 42. WordPerfect now opens the *Create Abbreviation* dialog box. Type an abbreviation for the text you selected earlier into the *Abbreviation Name* text box.

You can specify where this abbreviation is stored by selecting the *Template* button. Click on *OK* to accept your entry.

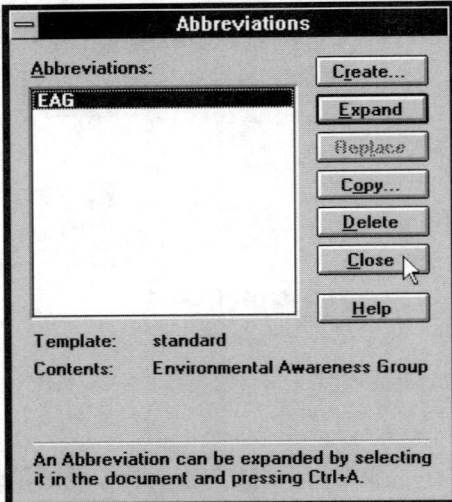

Figure 43. This returns you to the *Abbreviations* dialog box listing your new abbreviation. Now click on the *Close* button to return to your document.

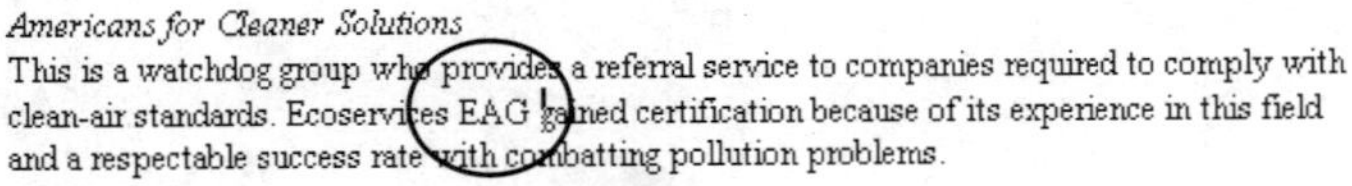

Americans for Cleaner Solutions
This is a watchdog group who provides a referral service to companies required to comply with clean-air standards. Ecoservices EAG gained certification because of its experience in this field and a respectable success rate with combatting pollution problems.

INSERTING AN ABBREVIATION

Figure 44. To insert an abbreviation into your text, simply type the abbreviation where you want the information represented by the abbreviation to appear.

Note: Abbreviations are case-sensitive, so if you create an abbreviation in lowercase letters, you must type it in lowercase for it to expand later.

Chapter 2: Editing Text

EXPANDING AN ABBREVIATION

Figure 45. You can expand abbreviations at any time. To do so, select the abbreviation in your document or place the insertion point in it and then select *Abbreviations* from the **Insert** menu. Click on the *Expand* button in the *Abbreviations* dialog box to expand the abbreviation into the original text.

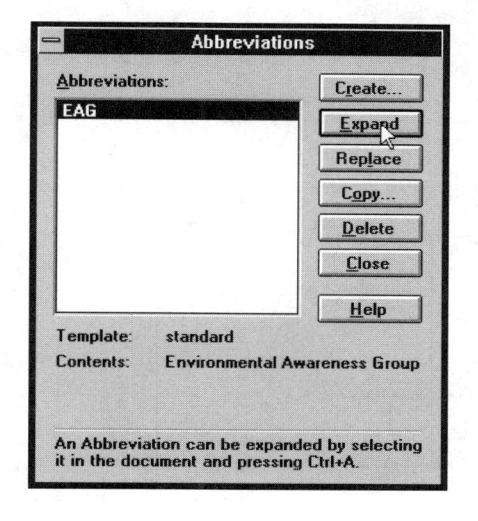

Figure 46. A quicker way of expanding abbreviations is to highlight the abbreviated text and then press Ctrl+A. This automatically expands the abbreviation for you. Repeat either of these processes for as many abbreviations as you have in your document.

FORMATTING

FONT

Figure 47. You can format text with different font options through the *Font* dialog box. To open the *Font* dialog box, select *Font* from the **Layout** menu or double-click on the *Font Face* button on the power bar.

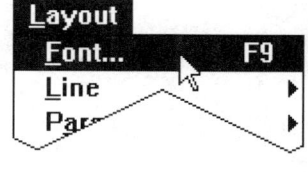

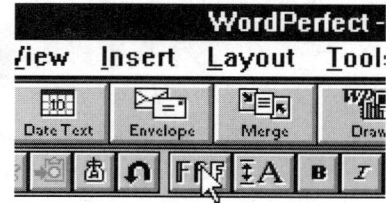

27

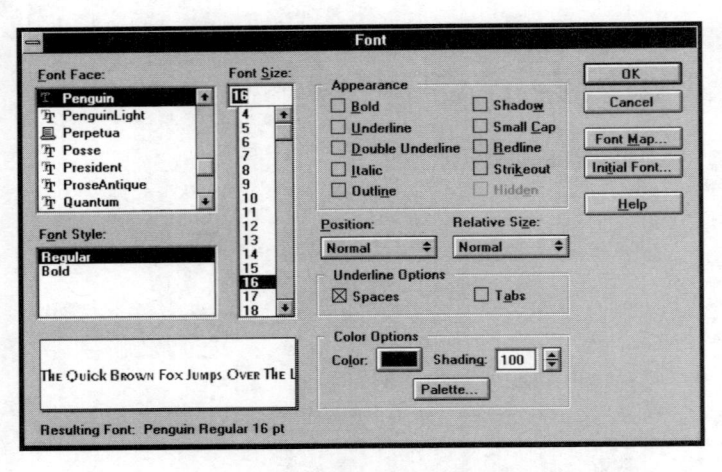

Figure 48. The *Font* dialog box gives you a range of options to change any of the font attributes of your text in WordPerfect. Any changes you make in this dialog box are reflected in the box below the *Font Style* list. You can select a new typeface from the *Font Face* list, and a new size for text from the *Font Size* list.

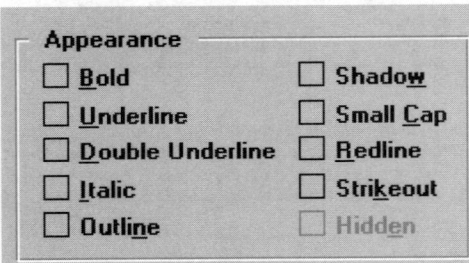

Figure 49. Most of the options in the *Appearance* section of the dialog box are self-explanatory and you can see their effect in the font sample box. The *Redline* option is usually used to highlight amendments that you have added to an existing document, so that it stands out from the original text. The *Strikeout* option is used to mark text to be deleted and places a line through the relevant text.

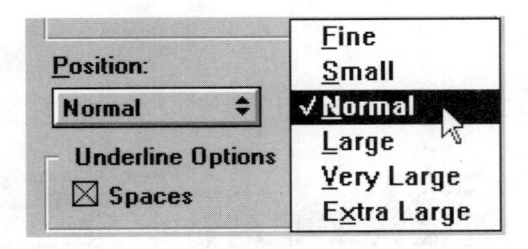

Figure 50. The *Relative Size* pop-up list contains options that let you vary the size of the text based on set percentages of the current point size.

Figure 51. The *Position* pop-up list allows you to set selected text above or below the natural line of text in your document.

Figure 52. Select the *Underline* options to determine whether WordPerfect underlines the spaces between words and tab spaces.

Figure 53. The *Color Options* section lets you change the color of text in your document. Clicking on the rectangle beside the *Color* section activates a pop-up list containing a number of colors already defined that you can apply to text.

Figure 54. You can also create your own colors by clicking on the *Palette* button to open the *Define Color Printing Palette* dialog box.

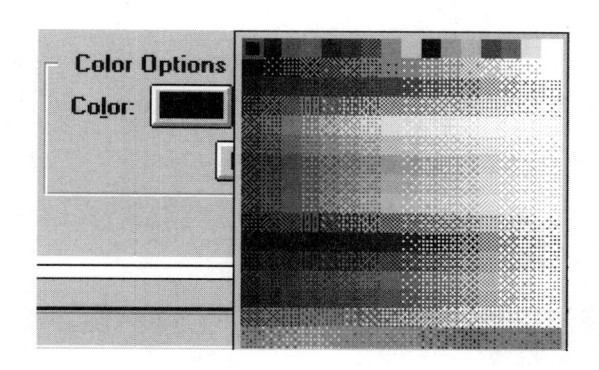

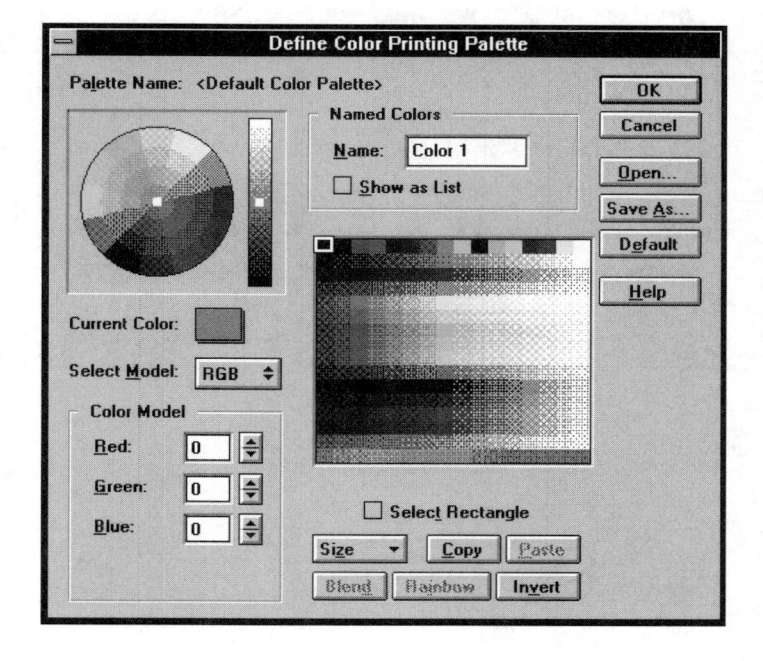

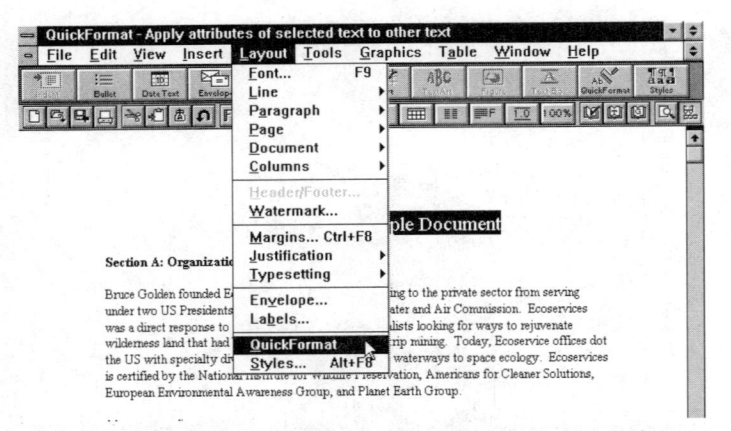

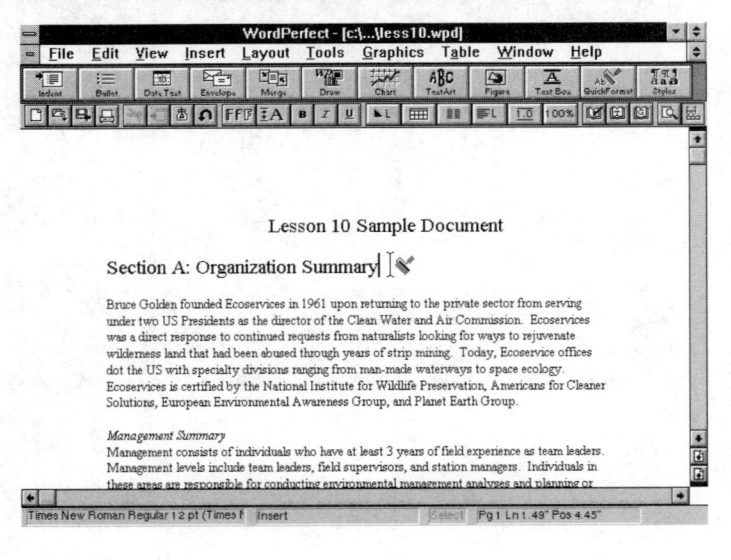

QUICKFORMAT

Figure 55. Use *QuickFormat* to copy text and paragraph formatting from one area of text to another. To do this, select the text containing the format you want to copy and select *QuickFormat* from the **Layout** menu.

Figure 56. If you insert the text cursor in the text, rather than highlighting it, and then select the *QuickFormat* command, the *QuickFormat* dialog box appears. Here, select whether you want to copy the *Fonts and Attributes*, the *Paragraph Styles* or both. Then click on *OK*.

Figure 57. The mouse pointer now changes. To format text in the new style, simply click and drag the changed mouse cursor over any text and WordPerfect formats it automatically into the original style.

Another way to use the QuickFormat feature is to position the cursor in the text you want to copy and click the right mouse button to activate a QuickMenu. Selecting *QuickFormat* from this menu changes the mouse cursor and allows you to QuickFormat selected text.

Choose *QuickFormat* from the **Layout** menu or the QuickMenu to turn the *QuickFormat* command off.

WORDPERFECT CHARACTERS

Figure 58. The *Character* command from the **Insert** menu activates the *WordPerfect Characters* dialog box. Here you can choose from more than 1500 characters to insert in your document. You can select the character from the *Characters* list box, or you can key in the relevant number into the *Number* text box.

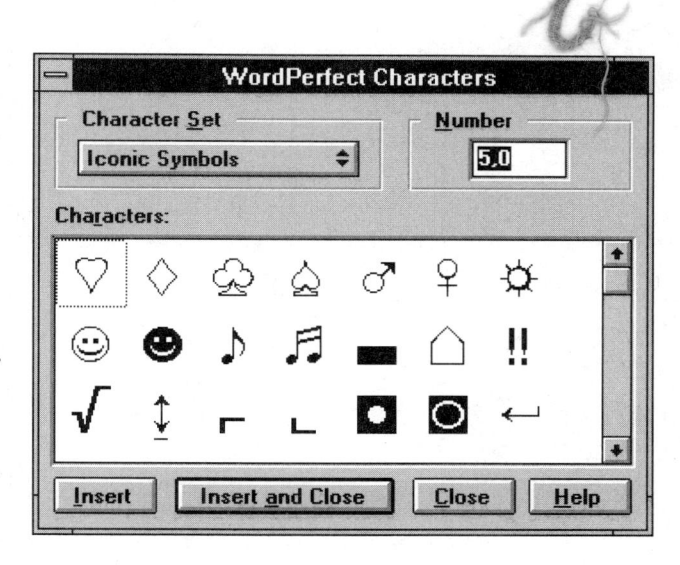

Figure 59. The *Character Set* pop-up list contains a range of character sets to display in the *Characters* list box.

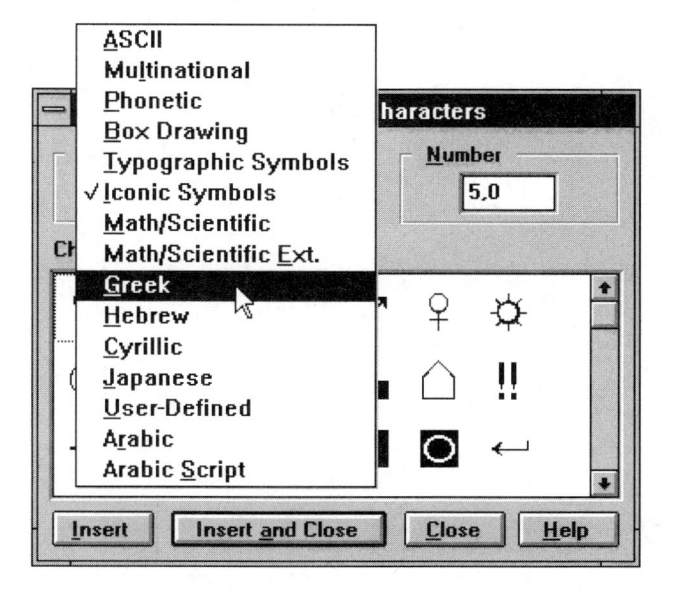

PAGE FORMATTING 3

PAGE VIEWS

You can change the way you view your document using the *Draft, Page,* and *Two Page* commands in the **View** menu. *Page* is the default view and displays headers and footers. *Draft* displays your page without headers and footers. *Two Page* displays two pages, side by side on your screen. *Draft* and *Two Page* views now allow you to edit your text as you do in *Page* view.

Figure 1. The *Draft, Page,* and *Two Page* commands are in the **View** menu. The command with the check mark next to it shows what view you are in.

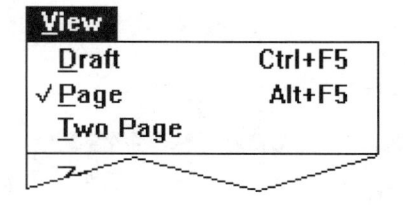

Figure 2. The screen with the *Page* command selected. In *Page* view you can view headers and footers, columns, footnotes, watermarks, and page and document formatting in general. Your page displays in the same proportions as it will print. You scroll through the pages. You can edit in *Page* view.

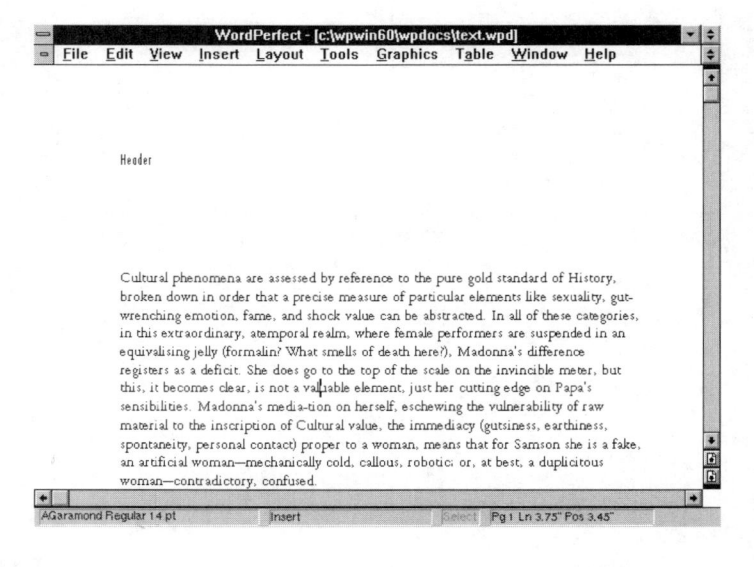

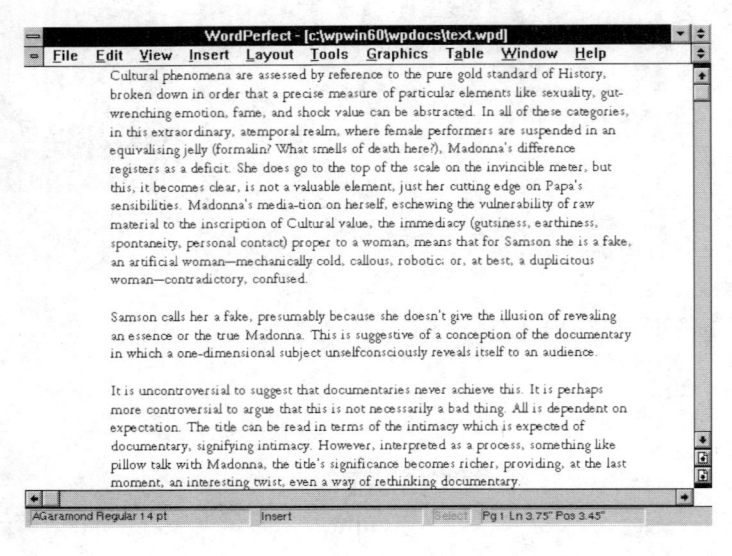

Figure 3. The screen with the *Draft* command selected. *Draft* view displays the screen in an imitation WYSIWYG environment. The screen appears close to how it will print but does not include things such as headers, footers and watermarks. Draft mode is faster to work in than Page and Two Page modes.

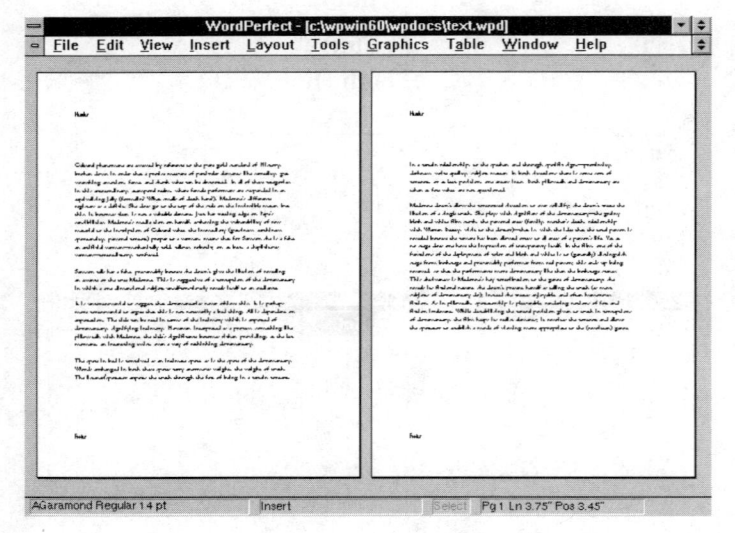

Figure 4. The screen with the *Two Page* command selected. *Two Page* view is similar to *Page* view except that two whole pages display side by side at the one time. This allows you to preview your document layout before printing. You can edit in *Two Page* view.

THE LAYOUT MENU

You can find most page formatting features in WordPerfect in the **Layout** menu. The term page formatting, in this case, includes *Page Size*, *Margins*, and *Columns*, as well as features such as *Tabs*, *Indents*, *Justification*, *Footnotes*, *Endnotes*, and *Typesetting*. The *Styles* command is discussed in **Chapter 10**. The *Font* command is discussed in **Chapter 2**.

LINE

Figure 5. The first page formatting option in the **Layout** menu is the *Line* option. Selecting this command activates the *Line* submenu.

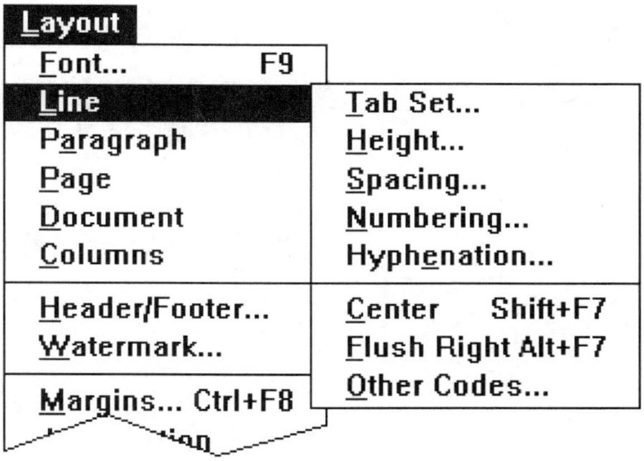

TAB SET

Figure 6. The *Tab Set* command in the *Line* submenu activates the *Tab Set* dialog box. This is an alternative method of setting up tabs, rather than using the ruler bar as described in **Chapter 1**.

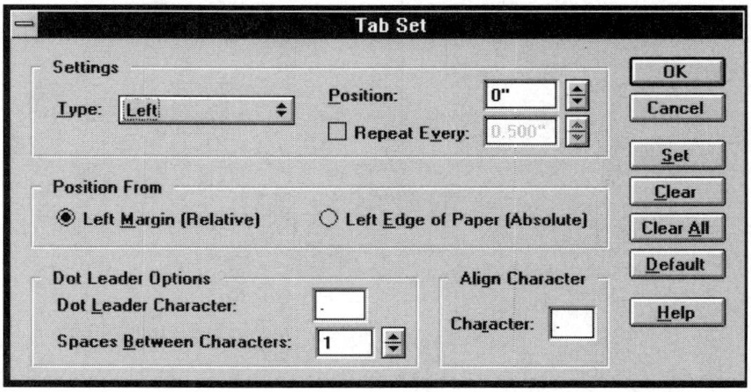

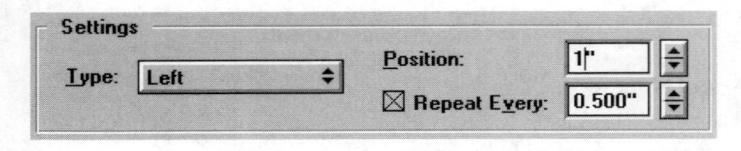

Figure 7. Use the *Settings* section of the *Tab Set* dialog box to set your tabs. First select a tab type from the *Type* drop-down list. Then enter a value in the *Position* text box.

If you want to place more tabs, you can position them relative to your initial tab location given in the *Position* text box. First click in the *Repeat Every* check box and in its text box give a value for the interval at which you want the tabs to occur.

Note: The changes you make in the Tab Set dialog box affect your document from the cursor onwards.

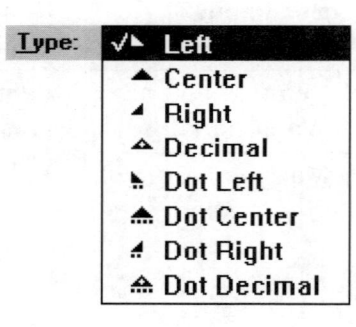

Figure 8. The *Type* drop-down list gives you access to the different tab types. *Left* forces the text to start to the right of the tab, similar to a left margin. *Center* centers the text on the tab, with equal amounts of text on either side of the tab. *Right* forces text to move to the left of the tab position.

The *Decimal* option aligns decimal points at the tab position, which is useful for entering columns of decimal values. The options *Dot Left*, *Dot Center*, *Dot Right*, and *Dot Decimal* place a row of dots between the previous tab location and the text at the next tab position.

Chapter 3: Page Formatting

Figure 9. You can also open the *Tab Set* dialog box by double-clicking on any one of the tabs on the ruler.

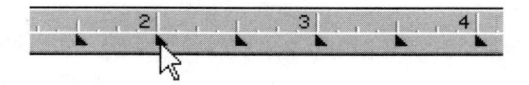

Figure 10. The *Clear* option removes an unwanted tab. First select the tab, then click on the *Clear* button to delete it.

The *Clear All* button removes all tab positions and the *Default* button returns the tab positions to the default setting of one every half an inch.

Figure 11. The *Position From* options in the *Tab Set* dialog box give you the choice of starting tabs from the edge of the page or the left margin. The *Left Edge of Paper* option starts tabs from the edge of the page no matter what margins you have set. The *Left Margin* option starts tabs from the left margin. With the latter option, tab positions move when you change the left margin setting.

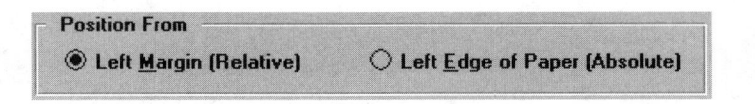

HEIGHT

Figure 12. The second command in the *Line* submenu is the *Height* command. This command activates the *Line Height* dialog box, which allows you to adjust the text measurement from baseline to baseline.

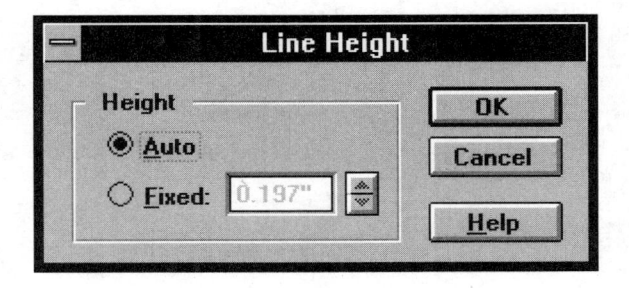

37

The distance between baselines, by default, is determined by the point size of the current text. Select the *Fixed* option if you want to type in your own measurement; this measurement remains constant even if you change the point size of the text. The *Auto* option is the default setting and the one you would normally use. The changes you make in this dialog box affect the selected text or all text from the insertion point onwards.

LINE SPACING

Figure 13. The third command in the *Line* submenu of the **Layout** menu is the *Spacing* command. This activates the *Line Spacing* dialog box. In this dialog box, you can increase or decrease the inter-line spacing of text in your document. You can also see how your text will appear. This option affects selected text or all text from the cursor onwards.

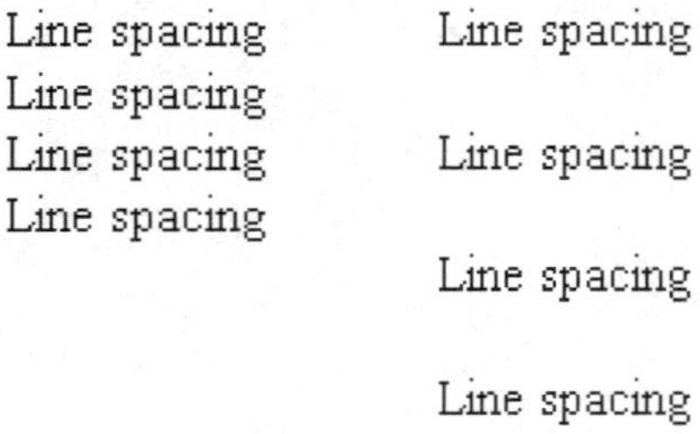

Figure 14. If you change the spacing to 2, for example, the selected text becomes double-spaced. WordPerfect accepts fractional line spacing, such as 1.75.

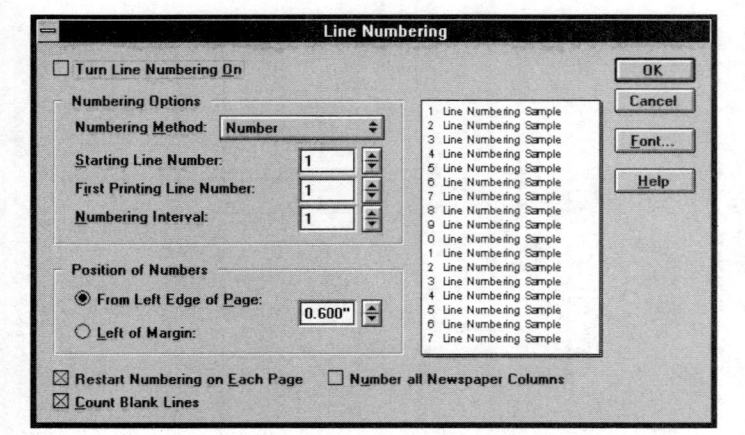

NUMBERING

Figure 15. The *Numbering* command from the *Line* submenu activates the *Line Numbering* dialog box. Here you can turn automatic line numbering on or off. If you have this command activated, WordPerfect places line numbers next to each line of the document of either the selected text or from the insertion point onwards.

Chapter 3: Page Formatting

Figure 16. Line numbering appears in all three views; *Draft*, *Page*, and *Two Page*.

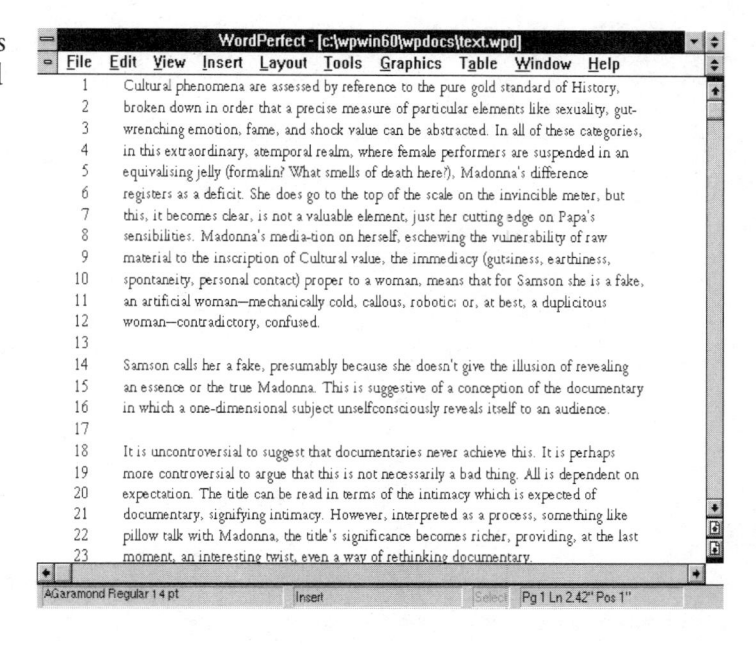

HYPHENATION

Figure 17. You open the *Line Hyphenation* dialog box by selecting *Hyphenation* from the *Line* submenu in the **Layout** menu. To turn hyphenation on, click in the *Hyphenation On* check box. This affects text from the insertion point onwards.

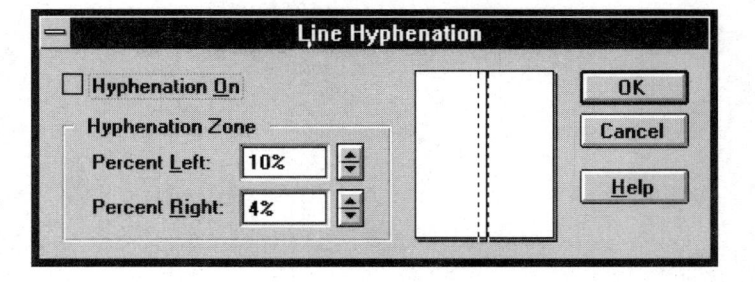

The *Hyphenation Zone* section determines when WordPerfect hyphenates a word. If a word falls within this zone, and you have checked *Hyphenation On*, the word is hyphenated. You can modify the options in the *Hyphenation Zone* if you need to, but the default settings are generally all you need. You can view your current hyphenation zone settings in this dialog box.

39

material to the inscription of Cultural value, the immediacy (gutsiness, earthiness, spontaneity, personal contact) proper to a woman, means that for Samson she is a fake, an artificial woman—mechanically cold, callous, robotic; or, at best, a duplicitous woman—contradictory, confused.

Text with the Center command applied

material to the inscription of Cultural value, the immediacy (gutsiness, earthiness, spontaneity, personal contact) proper to a woman, means that for Samson she is a fake, an artificial woman—mechanically cold, callous, robotic; or, at best, a duplicitous woman—contradictory, confused.

Text with the Flush Right command applied

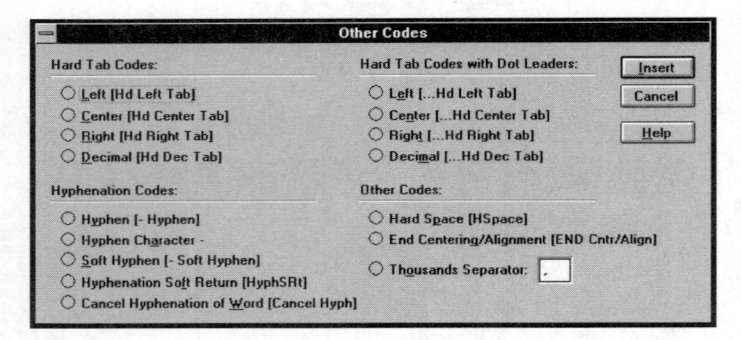

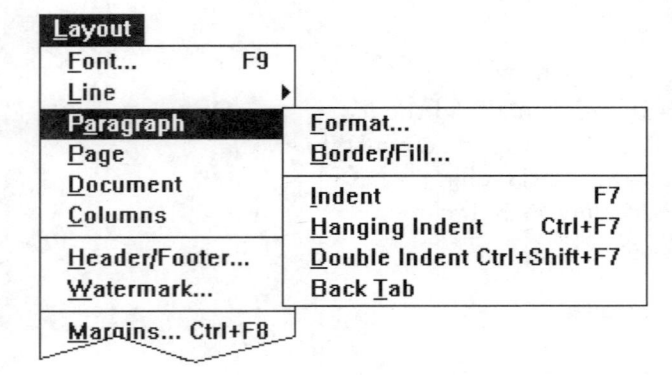

CENTER AND FLUSH RIGHT

Figure 18. The *Center* command in the *Line* submenu centers a line of text at a time. The insertion point must be at the beginning of the first word of the text to be centered. The *Flush Right* command right-justifies a line of text. You use these two commands for single lines of text and they are turned off when you insert a hard return. To center or right align larger blocks of text, use the *Justification* options in the **Layout** menu.

OTHER CODES

Figure 19. The *Other Codes* command in the *Line* submenu activates the *Other Codes* dialog box. You put these special codes into a document for ease of formatting. WordPerfect inserts the code you select into the document wherever the insertion point is, when you click on the *Insert* button.

PARAGRAPH

Figure 20. The *Paragraph* command in the **Layout** menu opens this submenu for you to format paragraphs. These commands affect selected paragraphs or the paragraph containing the cursor.

FORMAT

Figure 21. The options in the *Paragraph Format* dialog box affect all paragraphs following the insertion point. To restrict the formatting to apply to a single paragraph only, first select that paragraph.

The formatting aspects in the *Paragraph Format* dialog box allow you to indent the first line in the paragraph, adjust paragraph margins, and adjust spacing between paragraphs. The sample page in the dialog box shows the effects of your formatting changes.

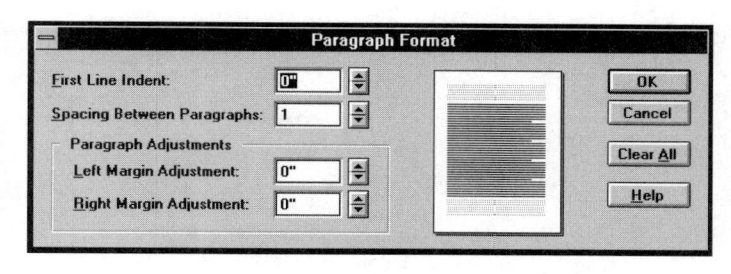

BORDER/FILL

Figure 22. The *Border/Fill* command opens the *Paragraph Border* dialog box. Use the options in the *Border Options* section of the dialog box to create a border around your paragraph. Select a border style from the *Border Style* drop-down list. Click on the *Customize Style* button for further border style formatting options.

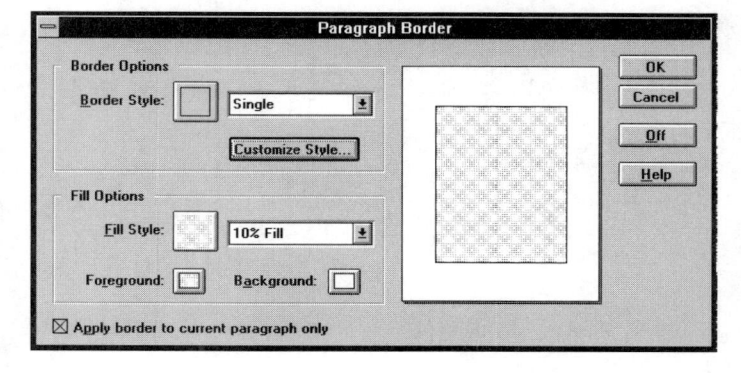

If you want to fill your border with a pattern fill or gradient fill, select one from the *Fill Style* value set and give it a fill density in the adjacent text box. You can choose a background as well as a foreground color.

The *Apply border to current paragraph only* check box restricts your border formatting to the current paragraph. The sample page demonstrates your border and fill formatting.

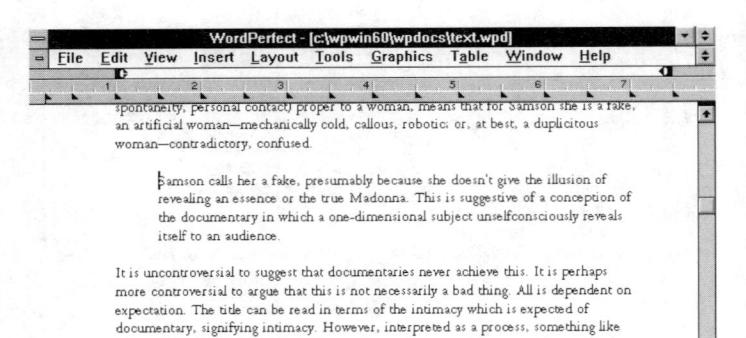

INDENT

Figure 23. The *Indent* command indents the full paragraph to the first tab position on the ruler. You can adjust this distance by changing the tab settings. For multiple indents, select the command as many times as you need to. The first paragraph in this example has been indented to the first tab stop.

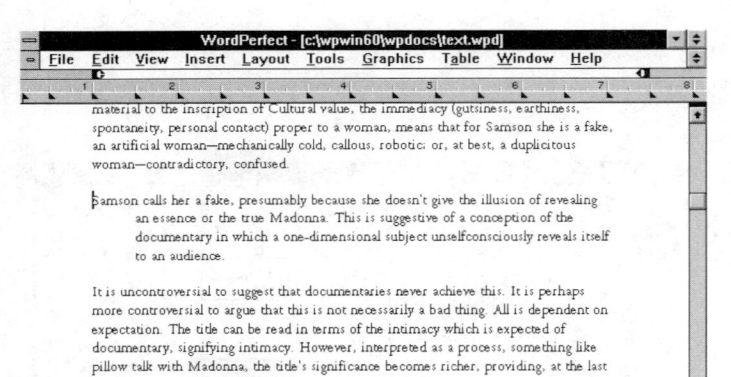

HANGING INDENT

Figure 24. The *Hanging Indent* command from the *Paragraph* submenu keeps the first line of the paragraph in its original position and indents the rest of the paragraph to the next tab stop.

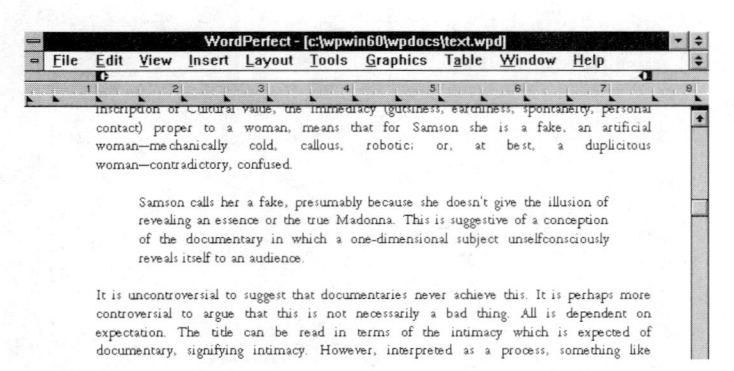

DOUBLE INDENT

Figure 25. Select the *Double Indent* command from the *Paragraph* submenu to indent the text from both the left and right margins by one tab stop.

BACK TAB

Figure 26. The *Back Tab* command in the *Paragraph* submenu moves the cursor to the preceding tab setting. This command can also move the insertion point to the tab that is to the left of the left margin.

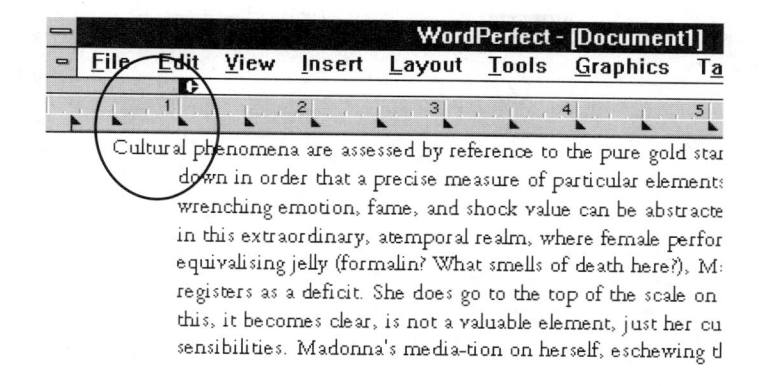

COLUMNS

Figure 27. There are two ways of defining columns. The first way is by selecting *Define* from the *Columns* submenu in the **Layout** menu. This activates the *Columns* dialog box.

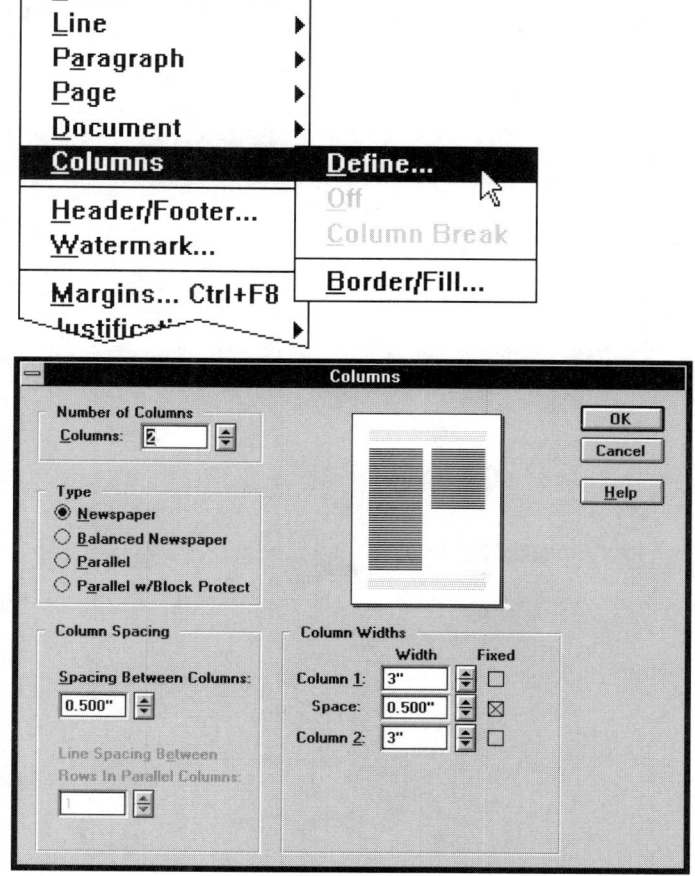

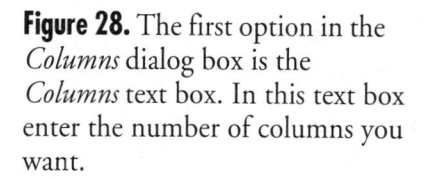

Figure 28. The first option in the *Columns* dialog box is the *Columns* text box. In this text box enter the number of columns you want.

In the *Type* section, the *Newspaper* option is for columns that flow from the bottom of one column to the top of the next, such as in a newspaper or newsletter.

The *Balanced Newspaper* option gives you newspaper columns of equal length.

The *Parallel* option is used for columns that run side by side. The text is grouped across the page in rows. Pressing hard page (Ctrl+Enter) moves the cursor to the next column. The *Parallel w/Block Protect* option is the same as *Parallel*, except that the rows stay together. If one column moves over the page, the whole row of columns moves with it.

The next section available in the *Columns* dialog box is the *Column Spacing* section. The *Spacing Between Columns* option controls the spacing (or gutters) between columns for evenly spaced columns.

The *Column Widths* section allows you to set individual widths for your columns and inter-column spacing. You use the *Fixed* check boxes to keep the width of the current column or space regardless of width or margin changes in other columns.

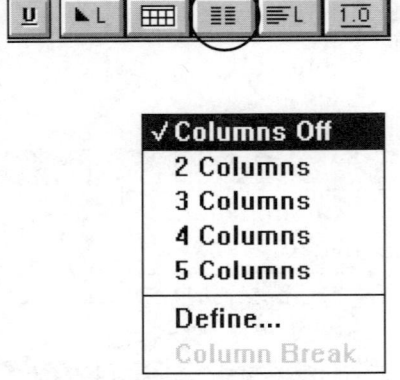

Figure 29. The second way to create columns is to click on the *Columns* icon on the power bar. This activates a drop-down list that contains the options shown here. Select the *Define* command to open the *Columns* dialog box of Figure 28.

For more information on the power bar, see **Chapter 1**.

PAGE

Figure 30. Most page formatting features can be found in the *Page* submenu of the **Layout** menu.

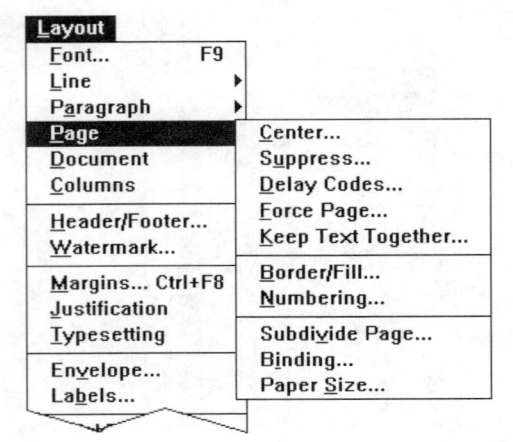

CENTER

Figure 31. The *Center* command opens the *Center* dialog box. The *Center Page* command centers text vertically between the top and bottom margins. Select *Current Page* to center the current page. Select *Current and Subsequent Pages* to center the current page and the pages following it. *Turn Centering Off* turns the centering off.

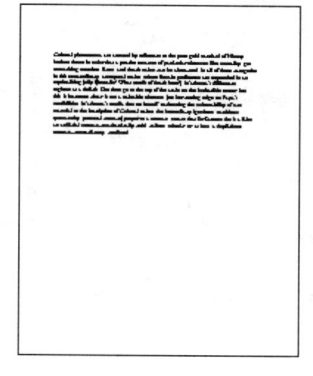

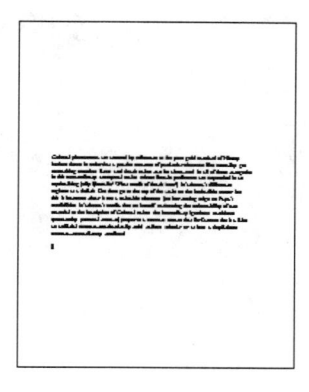

Normal page   *Centered page*

SUPPRESS

Figure 32. The *Suppress* command opens the *Suppress* dialog box. This dialog box lets you turn off headers, footers, page numbering, and watermarks for the current page. It gives you the further option of printing the page number at the bottom center on the current page.

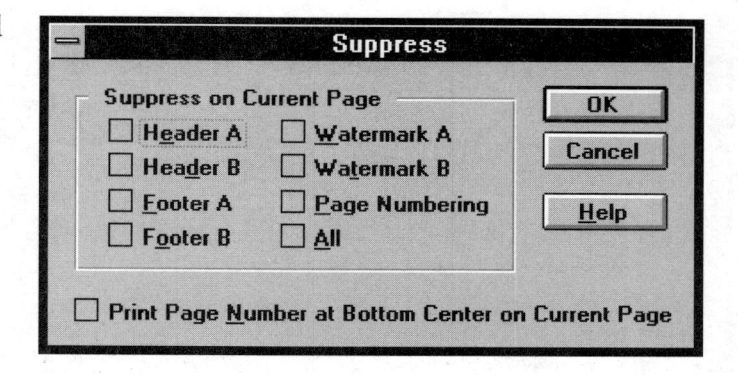

DELAY CODES

Delay Codes lets you insert features, like formatting options, into your document before the page that you want them to take effect.

Figure 33. Select *Delay Codes* from the *Page* submenu to open the *Delay Codes* dialog box. Enter the number of pages you want the codes inactive in the *Number of Pages* text box. In the *Define Delayed Codes* screen, choose the features you want from the menus and feature bar. Click on *Close* to return to your document.

You edit delay codes through the *Reveal Codes* screen.

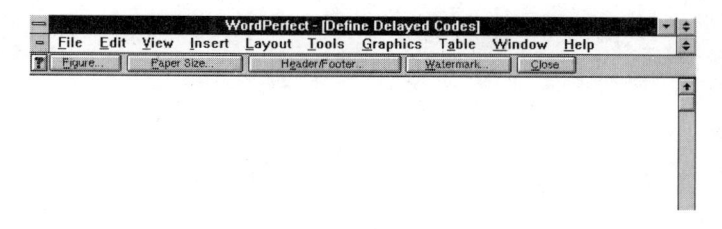

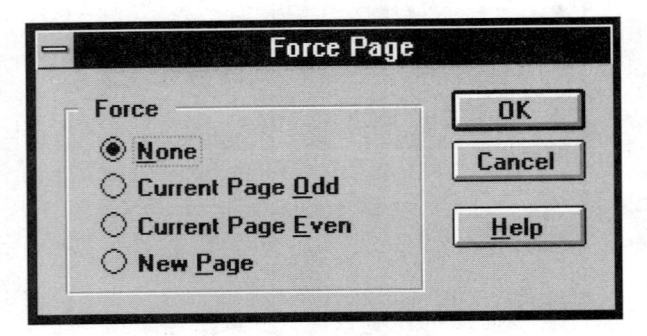

FORCE PAGE

Figure 34. The *Force Page* command opens the *Force Page* dialog box. You use the options in this dialog box to ensure that a certain page always has an odd or an even page number.

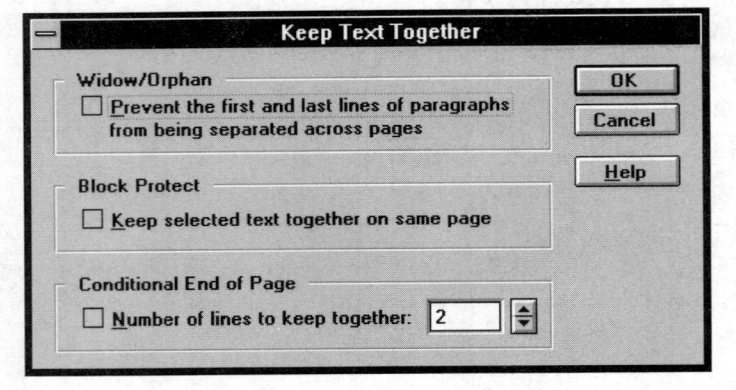

KEEP TEXT TOGETHER

Figure 35. The *Keep Text Together* command opens the *Keep Text Together* dialog box.

The first section of this dialog box is the *Widow/Orphan* section. Select the check box in this section to prevent the first and last lines of paragraphs in your document being separated and placed on different pages. This option is effective from the insertion point onwards.

The next section is the *Block Protect* section. Use this option to keep selected text together on the one page.

The *Conditional End of Page* section lets you nominate a number of lines to keep together at the bottom of your page.

BORDER/FILL

Figure 36. Select *Border/Fill* from the *Page* submenu to activate the *Page Border* dialog box. The options in this dialog box are the same as those in the *Paragraph Border* dialog box of Figure 22. The border and fill options you select in this dialog box apply from the current page onwards. To restrict your border and fill formatting to the current page, select the *Apply border to current page only* check box.

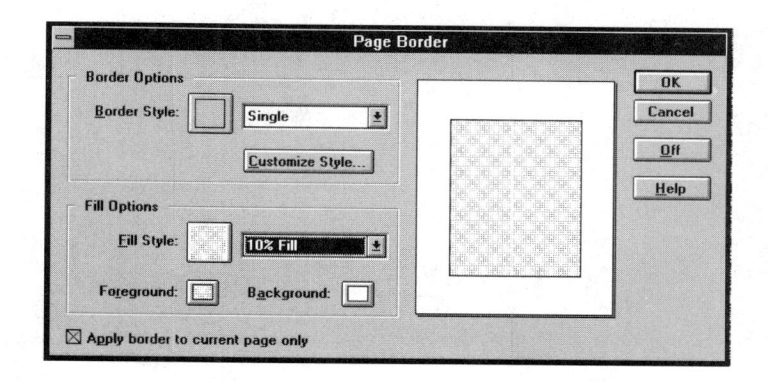

NUMBERING

To insert page numbers, but not as part of a header or footer, use the *Numbering* command from the *Page* submenu of the **Layout** menu. First position the insertion point on the page where you want page numbering to begin.

Figure 37. The *Numbering* command opens the *Page Numbering* dialog box.

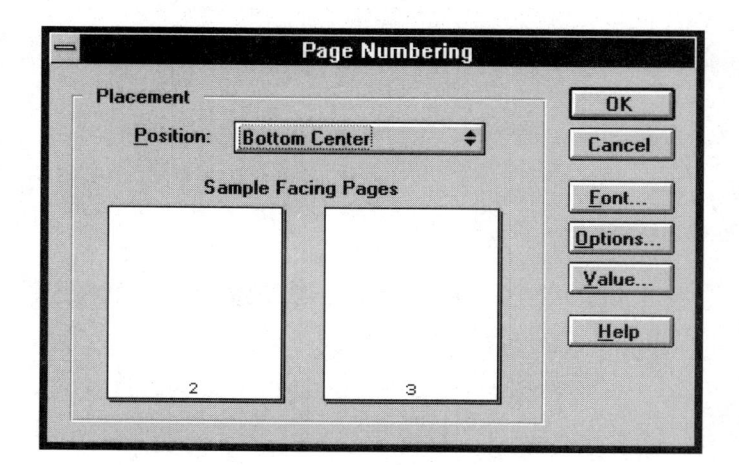

Chapter 3: Page Formatting

Figure 38. In the *Page Numbering* dialog box, choose where your numbers appear on the page from the *Position* drop-down list.

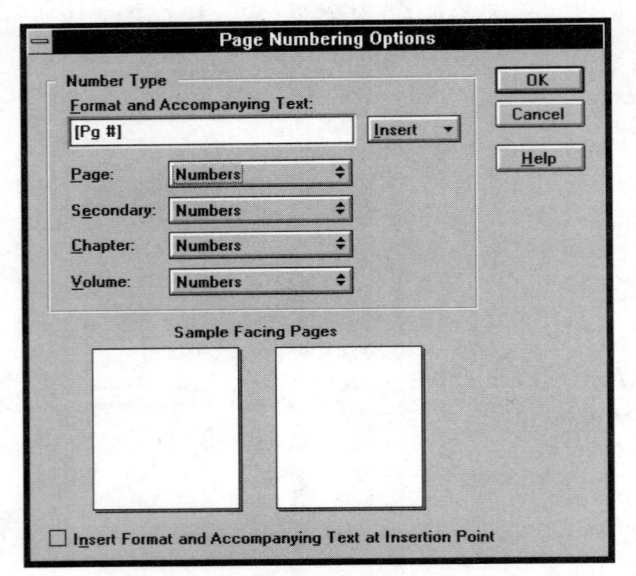

Figure 39. The *Options* button in the *Page Numbering* dialog box opens the *Page Numbering Options* dialog box. In the *Number Type* section of this dialog box you can enter text to accompany your page numbering, for example the word "Page."

Figure 40. The *Number Type* section of the dialog box also gives you five choices of numbering style, including both arabic and roman numerals.

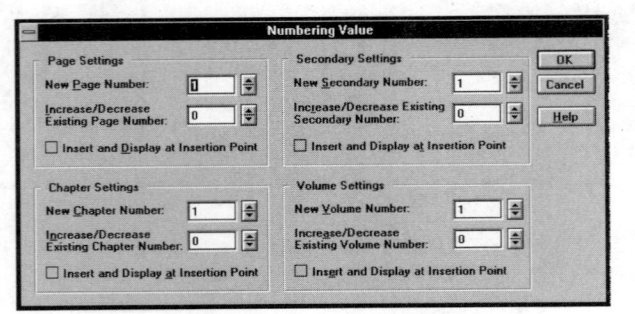

Figure 41. Use the options in the *Numbering Value* dialog box to change page numbers, secondary numbers, chapter numbers, and volume numbers.

48

Chapter 3: Page Formatting

Figure 42. The *Font* button in the dialog box opens the *Page Numbering Font* dialog box. Here you can format your page numbers.

SUBDIVIDE PAGE

Figure 43. The *Subdivide Page* command in the *Page* submenu opens the *Subdivide Page* dialog box. The options in this dialog box let you divide your page up into sections, known as "logical pages," which you can then enter text in as you would for normal pages.

Use Ctrl+Enter to move to a new logical page and begin entering text. Use Alt+PgDn to move to the next logical page, and Alt+PgUp to move to the previous logical page.

BINDING

Figure 44. The *Binding* command in the *Page* submenu opens the *Binding Options* dialog box. Use the options in this dialog box to create additional space on one margin for binding. In the *Binding Width* section, choose the margin you are binding on, then enter the amount you want the margin space increased by in the *Amount* text box.

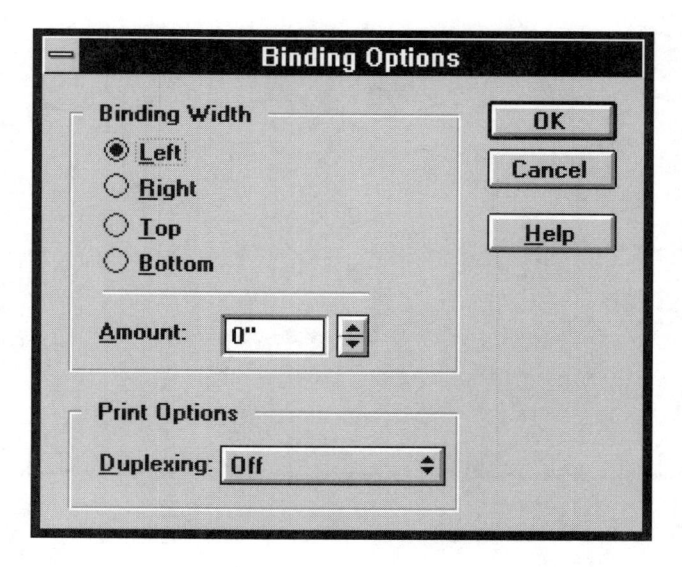

49

PAPER SIZE

The *Paper Size* command is the next command in the *Page* submenu in the **Layout** menu. Selecting this command activates the *Paper Size* dialog box. This command is useful only if you have selected a WordPerfect printer driver. See **Chapter 7** for more details on Windows and WordPerfect printer drivers.

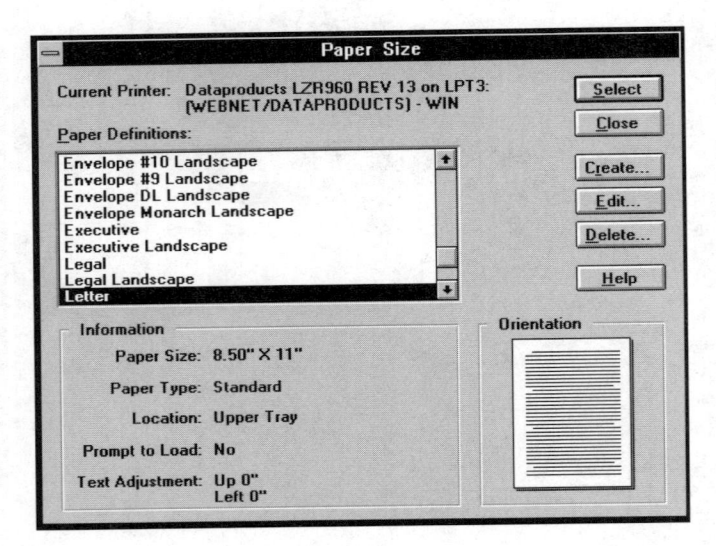

Figure 45. The changes you make in the *Paper Size* dialog box affect the document from the insertion point onwards. This dialog box also shows the currently selected printer. To change the current paper size, choose an option from the list available and click on the *Select* button.

If you have a Windows printer driver selected, activating this command shows the current paper size only.

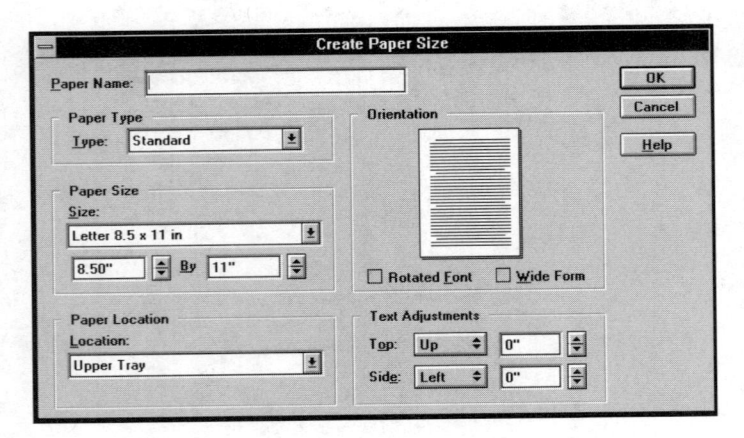

Figure 46. To create a new paper size, click on the *Create* button in the *Paper Size* dialog box to activate the *Create Paper Size* dialog box. The paper size you create is added to the *Paper Definitions* list box in the *Paper Size* dialog box. Enter the name you want the paper to have in the *Paper Name* text box.

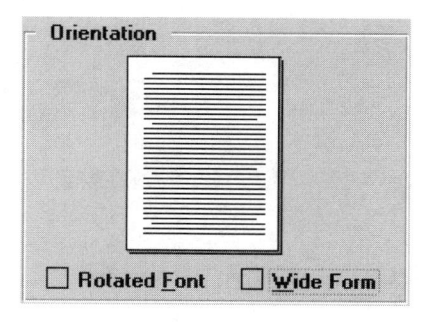

Figure 47. The *Paper Type* drop-down list in the *Create Paper Size* dialog box lets you name the paper type. Select an option from the list.

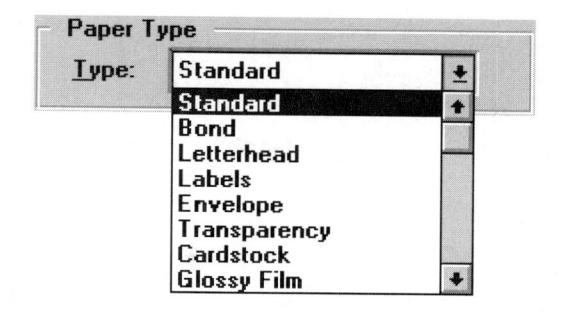

Figure 48. The *Paper Size* drop-down list lets you select a paper size from the options listed.

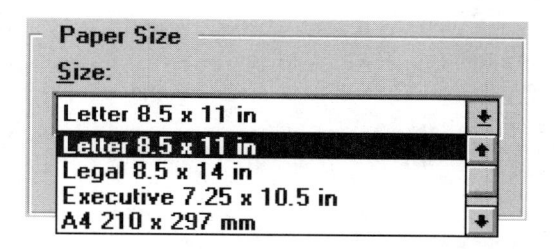

Figure 49. The *Text Adjustments* options let you tell WordPerfect where on the page to print the text in relation to the top and the side of the page. You can use these options if you are not happy with the current position of the text, or if you plan to bind the document at the top or side of the page.

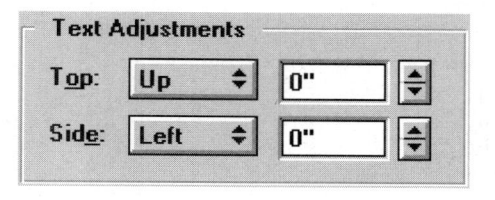

Figure 50. The *Paper Orientation* options let you specify which way you want your document printed (portrait or landscape).

Figure 51. The *Paper Location* drop-down list of the *Add Paper Size* dialog box lets you determine where the paper is in the printer.

Once you have set up the paper size options in the *Add Paper Size* dialog box, click on the *OK* button.

The new size option appears in the list in the *Paper Size* dialog box. To make this new listed size the current paper size for the open document, make sure it is highlighted, and click on the *Select* button. This exits from the dialog box and takes you back to your document.

If you want to edit a paper size, highlight it in the list in the *Paper Size* dialog box, and click on the *Edit* button. This activates the *Edit Paper Size* dialog box (which is the same as the *Create Paper Size* dialog box shown in Figure 46).

The *Delete* button in the *Paper Size* dialog box allows you to delete a selected paper size from the list.

The *Close* button lets you exit from the dialog box without activating the currently selected paper size.

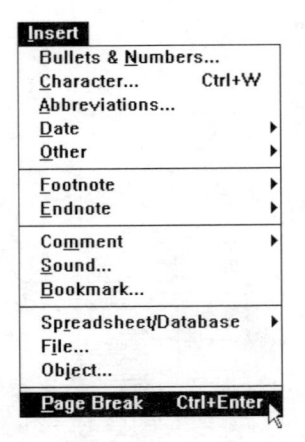

PAGE BREAK

Figure 52. You use the *Page Break* command in the **Insert** menu to insert a page break in your document at the insertion point.

WordPerfect automatically inserts a "soft" page break when text or graphics naturally reach the end of a page. The *Page Break* command gives you the option of manually determining where a page ends. This is known as a "hard" page break.

Chapter 3: Page Formatting

Figure 53. The way your hard page break appears on screen changes depending on your current page view.

In *Page* view your whole page always displays. This means that when you insert a hard page break your page displays partially blank in *Page* view.

In *Draft* view a hard page break displays as a double line. A soft page break places only one line across the page break position. The code for a soft page break in *Reveal Codes* is [SPg] while the hard page break inserts an [HPg] code.

You can also insert a page break at the insertion point by pressing Ctrl+Enter. Delete a page break by putting the insertion point directly before the page break and pressing Delete. You can do this in all three views.

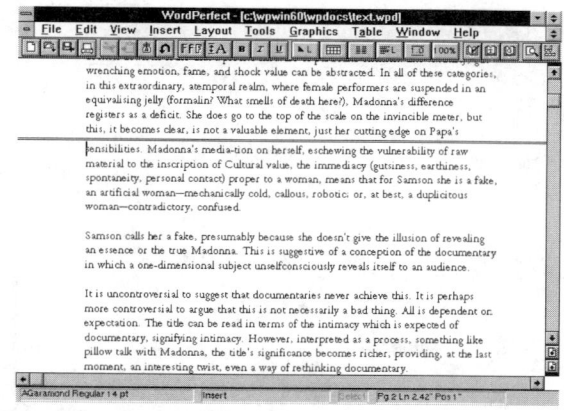

Page break in Draft view

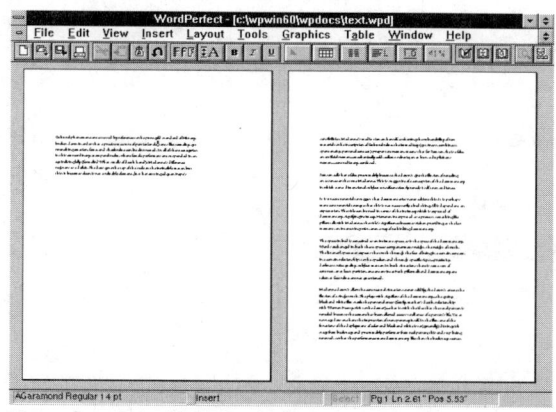

Page break in Two Page view

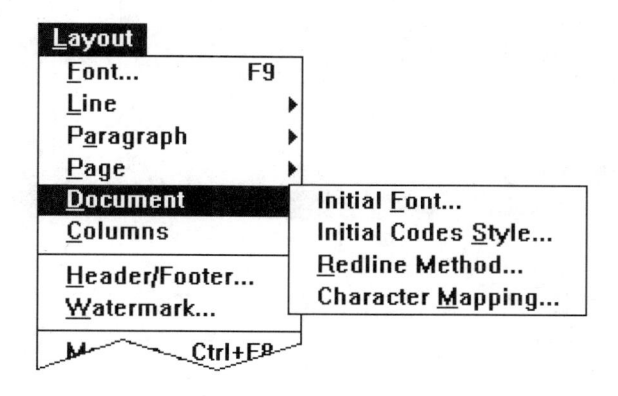

DOCUMENT FORMATTING

Figure 54. The *Document* submenu in the **Layout** menu contains some commands you can use to format your document.

53

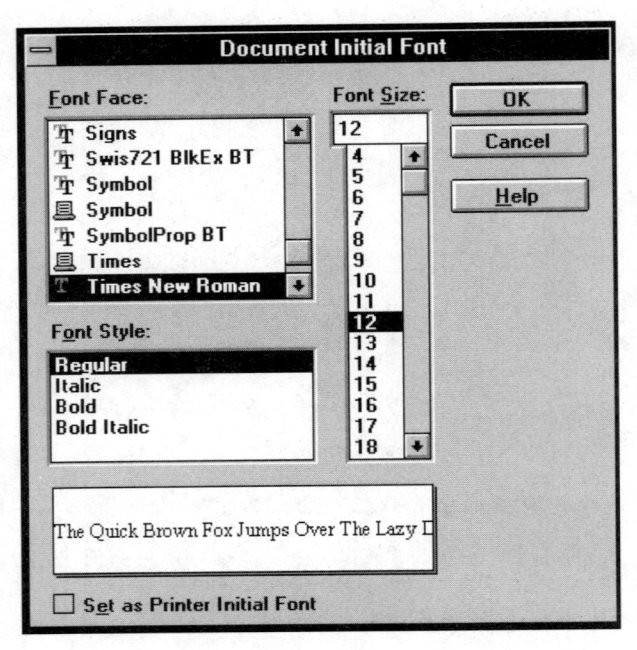

Figure 55. The *Initial Font* command in the *Document* submenu in the **Layout** menu lets you change the default font and point size setting for the current document. Selecting this command activates the *Document Initial Font* dialog box shown here. Choose the new font and size, and click on *OK*.

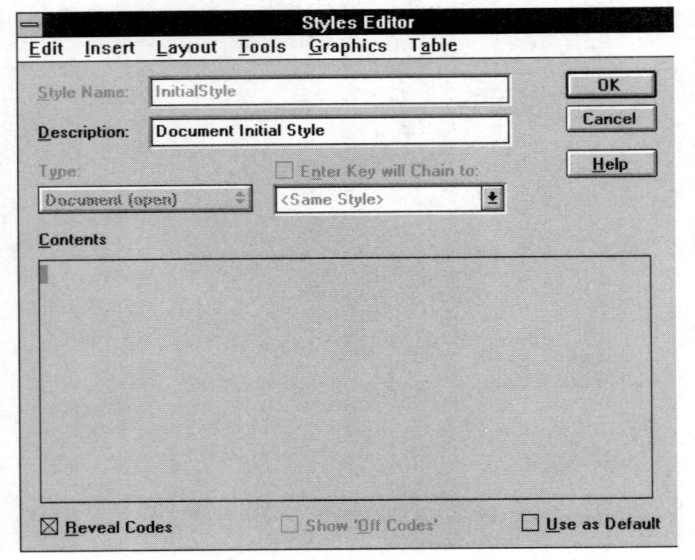

Figure 56. Selecting *Initial Codes Style* from the *Document* submenu activates the *Styles Editor* dialog box. In this dialog box you can set up text and page formatting attributes to become the default settings for the current document.

Figure 57. The *Redline Method* option in the *Document* submenu activates the *Redline* dialog box. This provides a number of options to determine how the *Redline* feature (in the **Font** menu) prints.

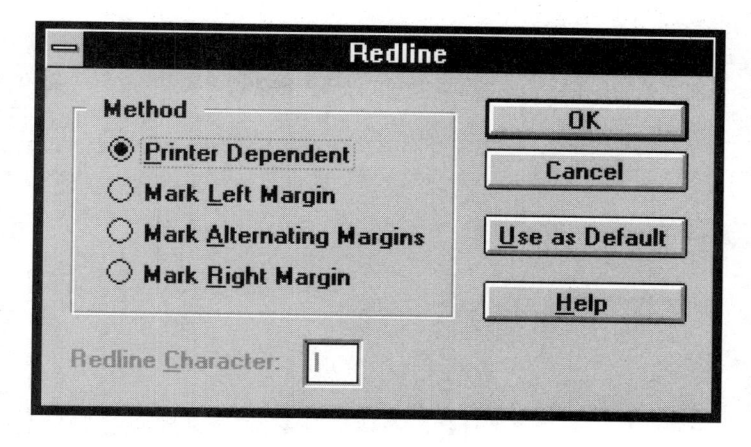

If the *Printer Dependent* option is selected, the printed appearance of redline depends on your printer. Most laser printers print redlined text with a shaded background. Use *Mark Left Margin, Mark Alternating Margins,* and *Mark Right Margin* to mark redline text in the margin with a redline character. You can specify the character you want to use in the *Redline Character* text box.

Use *Remove Markings* from the *Document Compare* submenu of the **Tools** menu to delete the markings.

Figure 58. You can use the *Character Mapping* command in the *Document* submenu to reduce the size of your document if you are typing in a language with a non-Roman writing system.

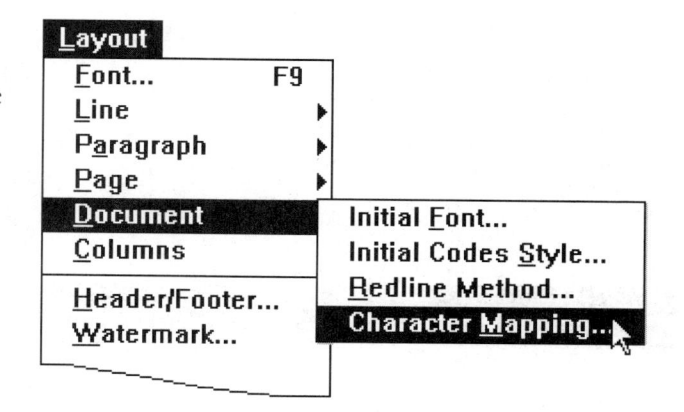

HEADERS AND FOOTERS

Headers and footers insert information at the top and bottom of each page in your document. Headers appear at the top of the page and footers at the bottom. You create headers and footers in the same way, so Figures 59 through 63 discuss the creation, editing, and placement of headers only.

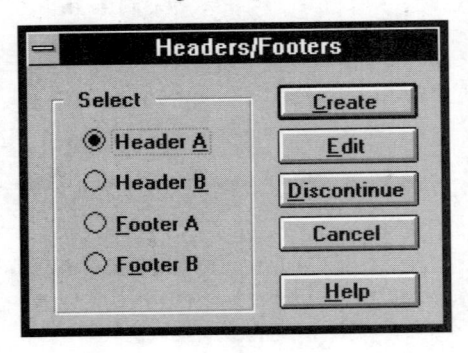

Figure 59. Select the *Header/Footer* command from the **Layout** menu to activate the *Headers/Footers* dialog box. In this dialog box, select the *Header A* option if you need only one piece of information at the top of the page. You can select the *Header B* option if you want to put two pieces of information at each side of the top of a page.

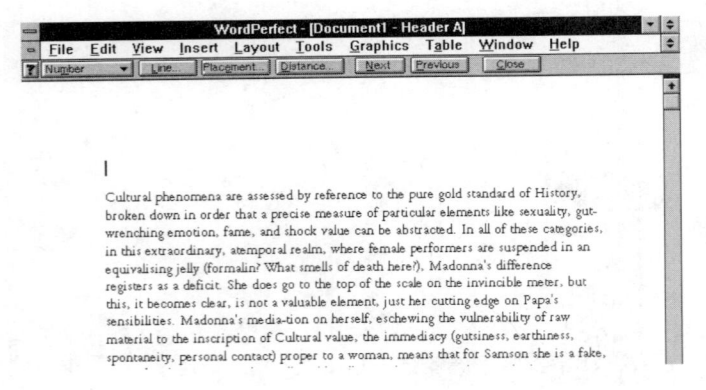

Figure 60. For this example, we left the setting on *Header A*. Next, click on the *Create* button to activate the *Header/Footer* feature bar. In Draft mode this takes you to a *Header A* editing window.

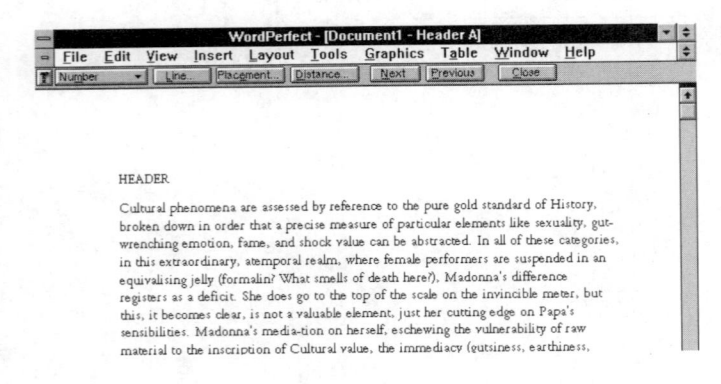

Figure 61. Type in the text you want as your header. You can format this text normally. You can enter a page, section, chapter, or volume number in your header by selecting the corresponding option from the *Number* drop-down list.

Chapter 3: Page Formatting

Figure 62. The *Placement* button on the feature bar lets you choose whether this header appears on all pages, odd pages only, or even pages only. (This lets you create alternate headings.)

Once you have created your header, click on the *Close* button in the *Header* window to return to your document.

Figure 63. You can view the header in both *Page* view and *Two Page* view but not in *Draft* view.

The *Edit* button in the *Headers* dialog box lets you edit an existing header. You edit a header in the same way that you create one.

When you click on the *Discontinue* button, WordPerfect discontinues the header or footer from the page that the insertion point is currently on to the end of the document.

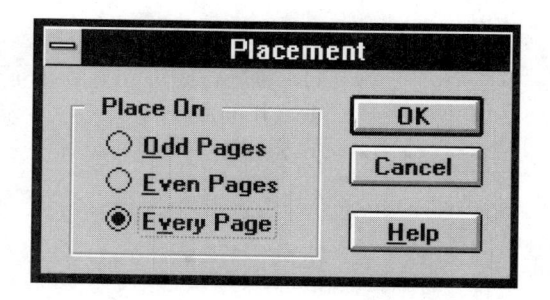

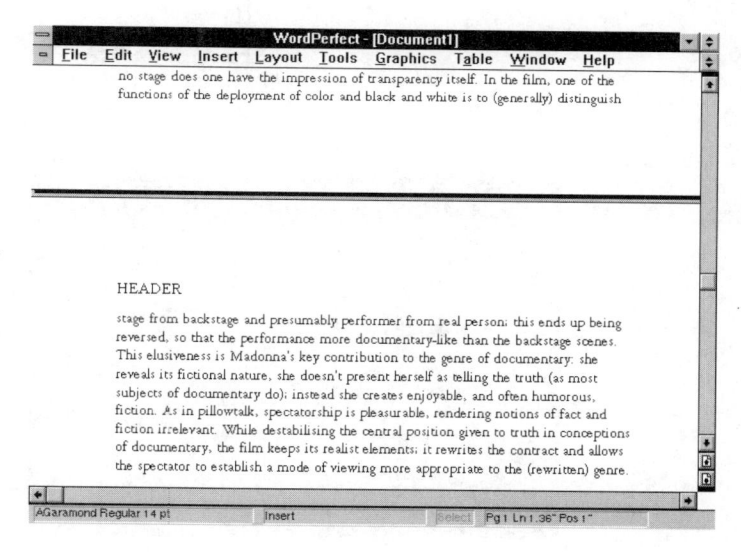

Header in Page view

You can set up a new header or footer part-way through a document. Place the insertion point on the page where you want to begin the new header and create it using the method just described (Figures 59 through 63). A header or footer continues in a document until you either create another header or footer, or you insert a *Discontinue* code.

To remove a header/footer from a document, delete the code from the *Reveal Codes* screen.

The position of headers and footers is at the top and bottom of the text area. They do not print in the margins.

WATERMARKS

Use watermarks to add graphics or text behind printed document text.

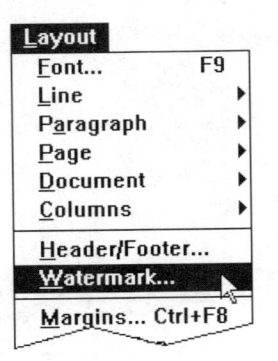

Figure 64. In *Page* view, position the insertion point in the first paragraph on the page where you want the watermark to begin. Select *Watermark* from the **Layout** menu.

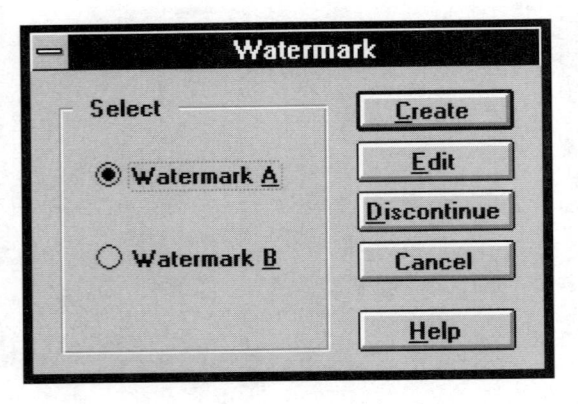

Figure 65. This opens the *Watermark* dialog box. Choose either *Watermark A* or *Watermark B* then click on *Create*.

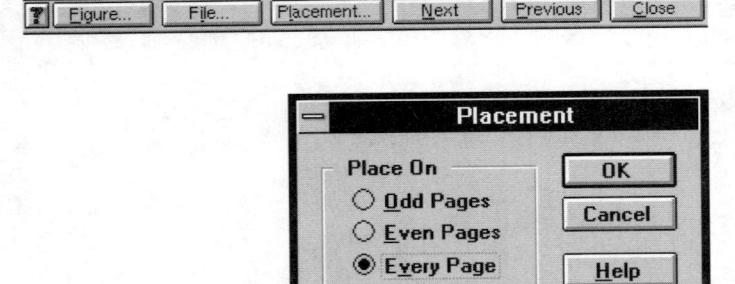

Figure 66. WordPerfect opens a new window which contains a *Watermark* feature bar. Select the *Placement* button on this feature bar and then select the pages you want your watermark to appear on in the dialog box that appears. If you want to use text as your watermark, type your text at the insertion point.

Chapter 3: Page Formatting

Figure 67. If you want a graphic as your watermark, click on the *Figure* button on the feature bar to open the *Insert Image* dialog box. Select a graphic and click on *OK*.

This activates the *Graphics Box* feature bar and inserts the image in the watermark editing screen. You can size and position your watermark and give it a caption and a border and fill. Click on *Close* when you have finished to return to the Watermark feature bar.

Figure 68. Click on *Close* again to return to your document where the watermark then appears.

You can delete watermarks in the *Reveal Codes* screen.

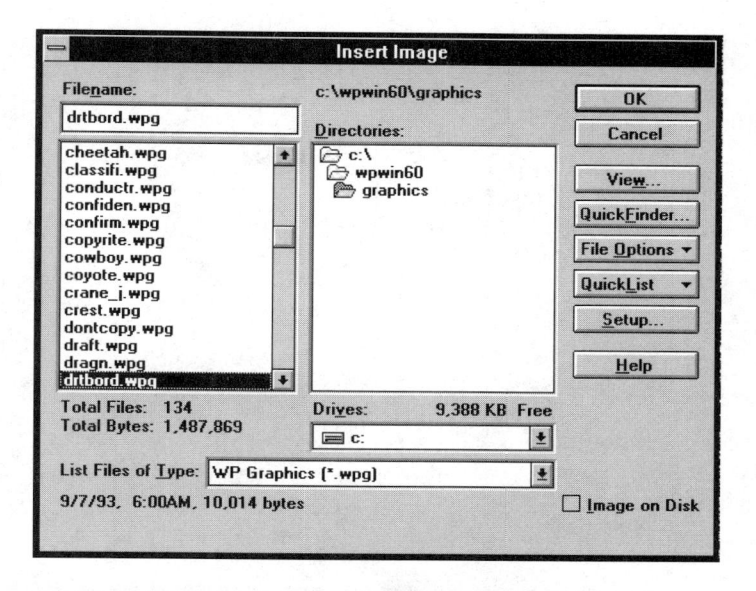

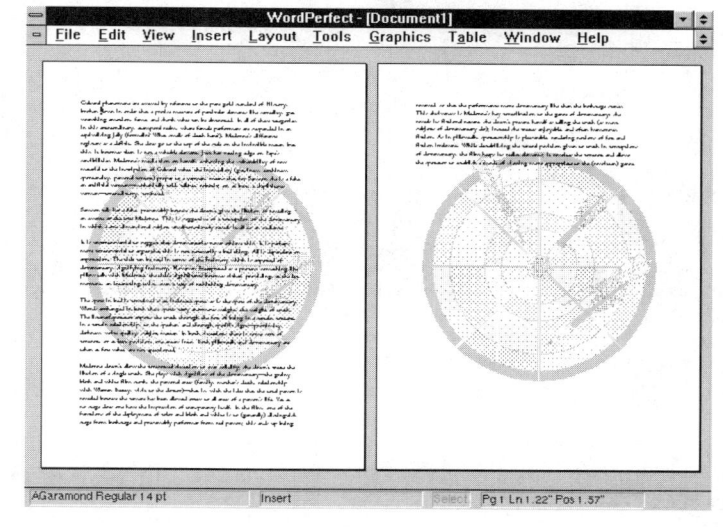

TYPESETTING

Figure 69. The *Typesetting* submenu in the **Layout** menu contains typesetting features.

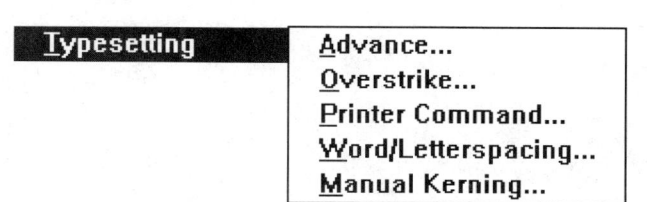

59

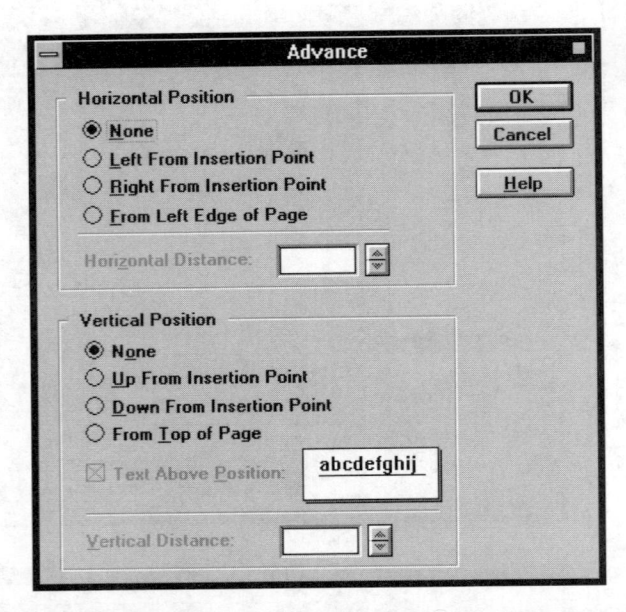

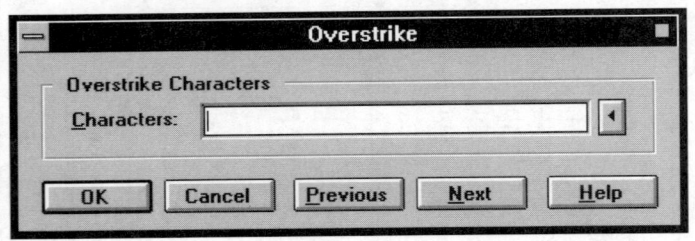

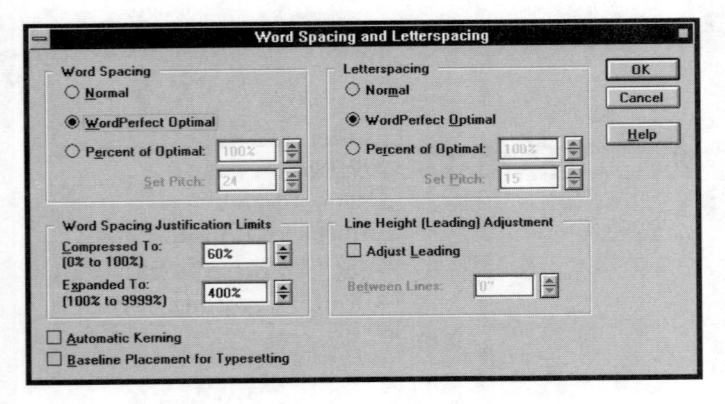

ADVANCE

Figure 70. The *Advance* command in the **Layout** menu activates this dialog box. In the *Advance* dialog box you can specify a distance and direction you would like to reposition the line of text containing the insertion point on the page.

OVERSTRIKE

Figure 71. To create overstrike characters, select *Overstrike* from the *Typesetting* submenu in the **Layout** menu. This activates the *Overstrike* dialog box. Here you designate characters that WordPerfect places on top of one another; simply type them into the *Characters* text box and click on *OK*.

WORD/LETTERSPACING

Figure 72. The options in the *Word Spacing and Letterspacing* dialog box, which you open with the *Word/Letterspacing* command, control spacing in your document. *Word Spacing* adjusts spacing between words and *Letterspacing* adjusts spacing between letters.

You can also control the limits of your justification, adjust the leading and change kerning and placement of baseline options from this dialog box.

PLACEMENT OF TEXT

JUSTIFICATION

Figure 73. The *Justification* submenu in the **Layout** menu lets you alter the way text lines up on the page.

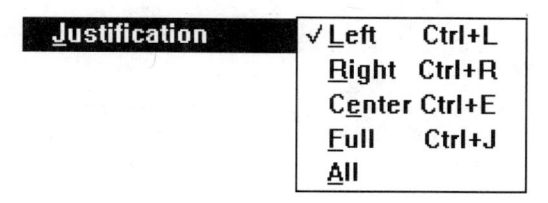

Justification	
√ **L**eft	Ctrl+L
Right	Ctrl+R
C**e**nter	Ctrl+E
Full	Ctrl+J
All	

Figure 74. These examples show the four types of text justification you can use.

The *Full* option wraps text onto the next line at the same position for each line, thus providing perfectly straight left and right margins.

This text is left justified

This text is right justified

This text is centre justified

This text is full justified This text is full justified This text is full justified This text is full justified This text is full justified This text is full justified This text is full justified This text is full justified This text is full justified

T h i s   t e x t   i s   a l l   j u s t i f i e d

MARGINS

Figure 75. You can modify margins in a number of ways. One way is to select *Margins* from the **Layout** menu, and modify the values within the *Margins* dialog box shown in Figure 76.

Layout	
Font...	F9
Line	▶
Paragraph	▶
P**a**ge	▶
Document	▶
Columns	▶
Header/Footer...	
Watermark...	
Margins...	Ctrl+F8
Justification	

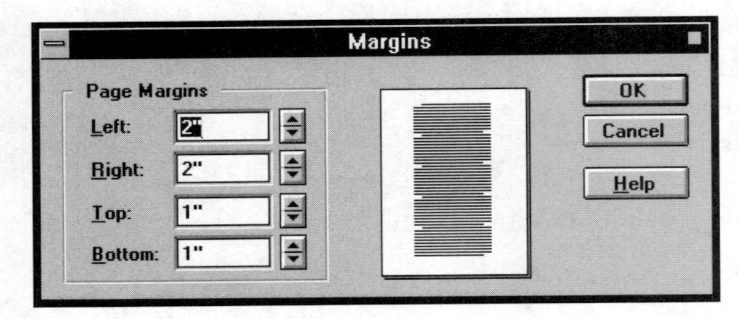

Figure 76. The changes you make in the *Margins* dialog box affect selected text, or text from the insertion point onwards, until WordPerfect comes across another margin code in the document.

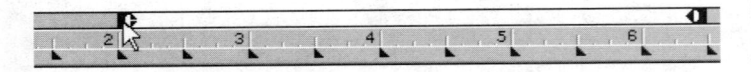

Figure 77. Another way to change margin settings for the right and left margins is to move the margin markers on the ruler.

See **Chapter 1** for more information on adjusting margins with the ruler.

CREATING AND MANAGING FILES   4

WORDPERFECT FILES

Creating new files in WordPerfect is a simple process. WordPerfect also has many features that help you manage these files. This chapter describes the various **File** menu commands associated with creating and managing new files. It also looks at manipulating multiple documents through the **W**i**ndow** menu and how to work with QuickLists.

ACCESSING FILES

NEW

Figure 1. The first option available in the **File** menu is the *New* command. When you start WordPerfect you are in a new, empty document. If you have not made any changes, the title bar reads **WordPerfect - [***Document1 - unmodified***]**. If you select the *New* command again, it opens a new document that reads **WordPerfect - [***Document2 - unmodified***]**. *Document1* is still open but not active.

At any time, you can select the *New* command to start a new document (you can have a maximum of nine files open at once).

File	
New	Ctrl+N
Template...	Ctrl+T
Open...	Ctrl+O
Close	Ctrl+F4
Save	Ctrl+S
Save **A**s...	F3
QuickFinder...	
Master **D**ocument	▶
Compa**r**e Document	▶
Document Summar**y**...	
Document **I**nfo...	
P**r**eferences...	
Print...	F5
Se**l**ect Printer...	
E**x**it	Alt+F4

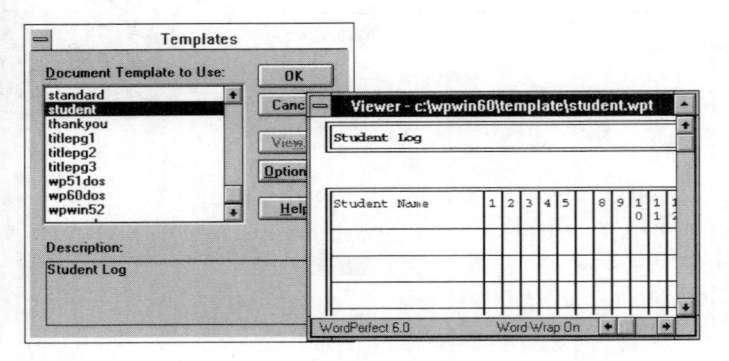

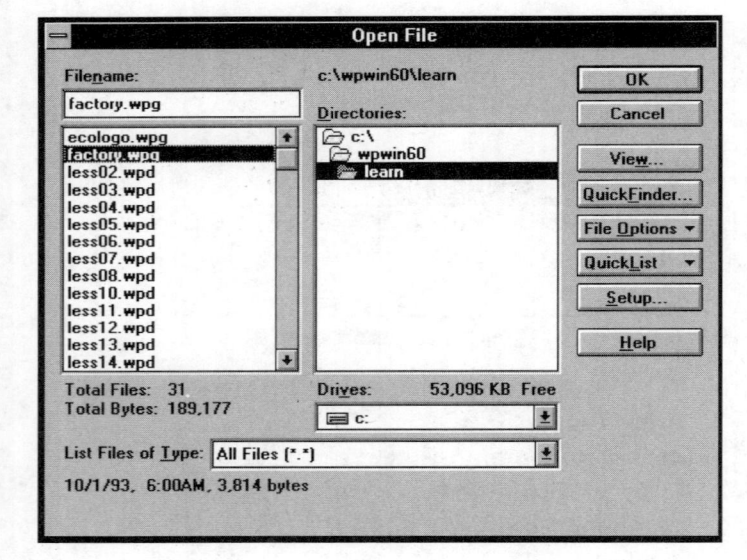

TEMPLATE

Figure 2. The *Template* command in the **File** menu is similar to the *New* command except that the new file has a predetermined structure. Using a template is similar to using a stencil and can make creating and formatting your documents far quicker and easier.

OPEN

Figure 3. The *Open* command in the **File** menu or the *Open* button on the power bar activates the *Open File* dialog box. From this dialog box you can access any of the WordPerfect file management functions. The primary purpose for the *Open* dialog box is to retrieve files from the directories and disks you saved them in.

The *Filename* text box in this dialog box displays the name of the file currently selected in the *Files* list box, or the range of files displayed if no file is selected.

Beside the *Files* list box is the *Directories* list box. You can change directories by double-clicking on any of the directories listed here. The *Current Dir* line above this list box indicates the currently open directory.

Figure 4. You can change the active disk drive through the *Drives* list box immediately below the *Directories* list box. Clicking on the arrow activates a drop-down list displaying the available drives that you can choose from.

Figure 5. The *List Files of Type* box lets you determine what type of files you want to display in the *Files* list box. Clicking on the arrow activates another drop-down list of the available file types that you can display.

Directly under this list box is the *File Info* line. This line displays the size of the selected file and when it was last modified.

Figure 6. After using the available options to list the files you want in the *Files* list box, you can use the *View* button to see which files you want to open. Selecting the *View* button displays the selected file in a separate window. This *View* window lets you see the full document. You can look at any WordPerfect text or graphic file in this way.

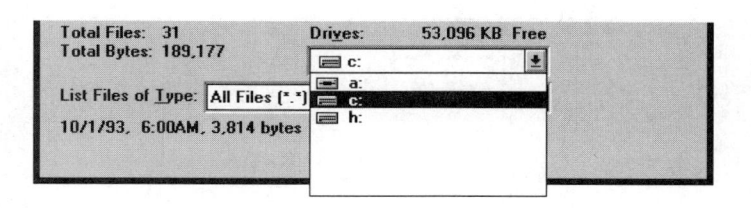

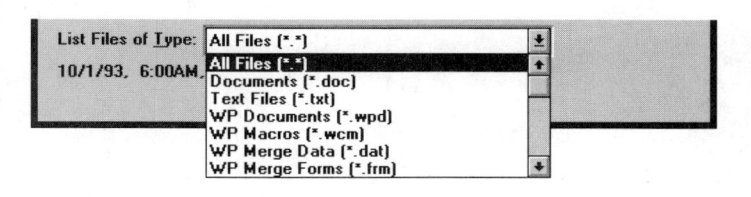

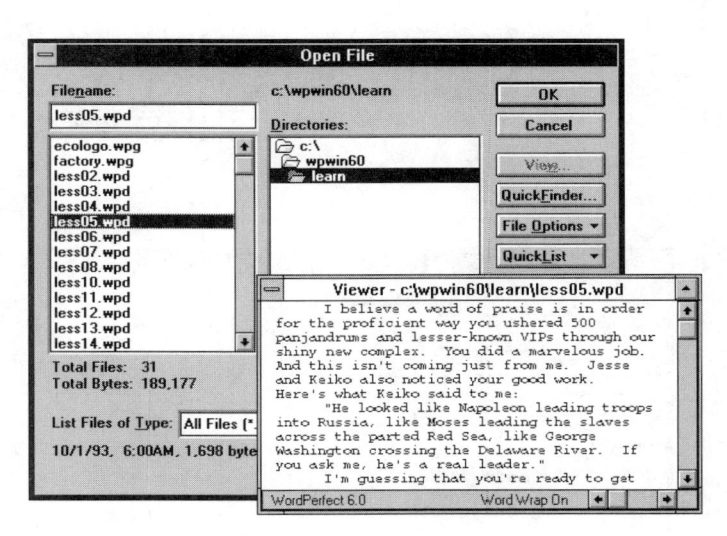

Once you have selected the file you want to open, click on *OK*. (The *Cancel* button exits from the dialog box without opening a file.) Alternatively, double-click on the filename to open it.

The remaining options in this dialog box are discussed in the **File Management** section of this chapter.

Chapter 4: Creating and Managing Files

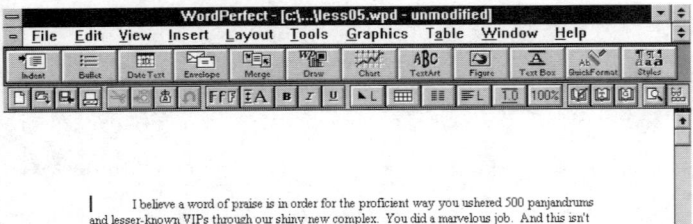

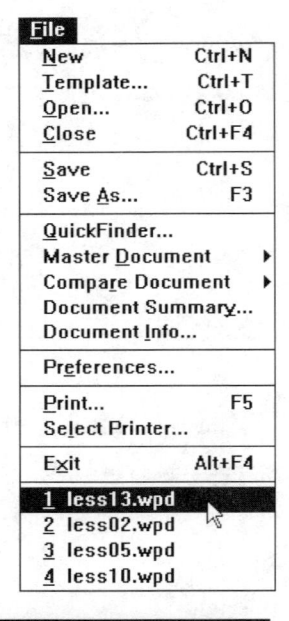

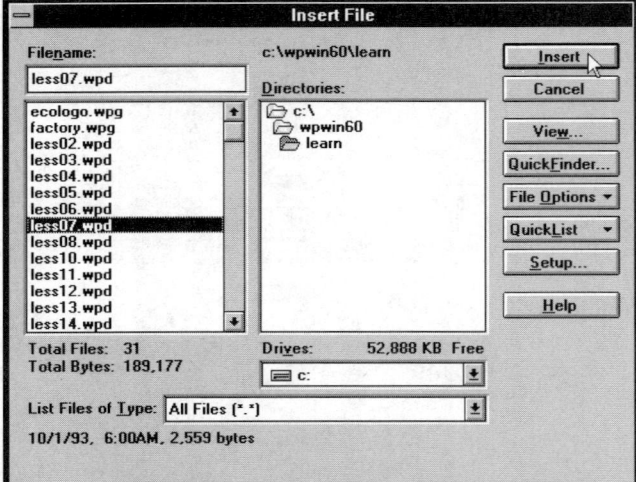

Figure 7. After clicking on the *Open* button in the *Open File* dialog box, the file you selected appears in the current document window with its title in the title bar. Until you make changes to the file, the title bar also says *unmodified*.

Figure 8. At the bottom of the **File** menu WordPerfect lists the last four documents you have opened. You can open any of these four documents by simply selecting the filename from the menu.

INSERT FILE

Figure 9. Another option for accessing files in WordPerfect is to insert them into existing document windows. You can insert a file at any time at the current insertion point. To do this, select *File* from the **Insert** menu. This opens the *Insert File* dialog box. The options available in this dialog box are exactly the same as in the *Open File* dialog box, only you click on the *Insert* button after selecting the file from the *Files* list box.

If you insert a file into a new document window, the document title bar takes on the name of the file as it does when you open a file. However, inserting a file into an existing document does not change the document name. The inserted file simply becomes part of that document's text.

WordPerfect displays a warning dialog box if you try to insert a file into an existing document. Clicking *Yes* inserts the file at the current insertion point.

SWITCHING BETWEEN DOCUMENTS

Because WordPerfect allows you to open more than one file at once (you can open up to nine), you can move between the currently open files. This feature lets you quickly and easily cut, copy, and paste information between documents.

Each time you select the *New* command, or open another document without selecting the *Close* command, these documents become part of the list of open documents.

Figure 10. To view the list of all currently open files, activate the **Window** menu. In this example there are two documents open. The check mark next to the second document indicates that this is the currently active file. To make the other document in this list active, simply select it from the menu.

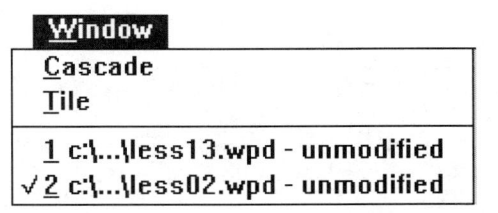

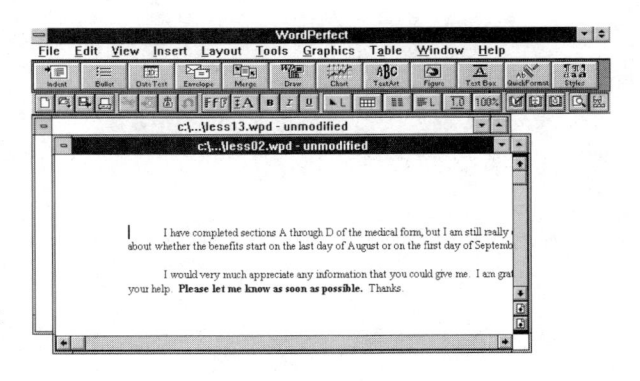

Figure 11. Selecting *Cascade* from the **Window** menu arranges the documents so that they overlap, with the title bar of each document showing. The active document is the one at the front. By clicking on one of the other document windows, you make that document active and bring it to the front of the cascade stack.

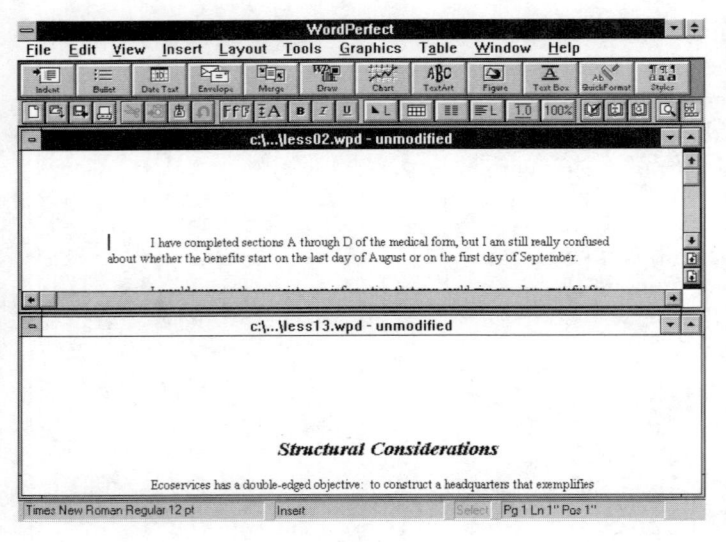

Figure 12. The *Tile* command in the **Window** menu arranges the documents so that you can see them all at once in a tiled formation. Again, simply clicking in a document window makes that document active (denoted by a highlighted title bar). In this figure, the top document is the active one. Any commands you select from the menu bar affect only this document.

You can cancel the Tile or Cascade view of your documents at any time by maximizing one of your documents.

FINALIZING

SAVE AND SAVE AS

Figure 13. If you haven't saved the document before, selecting the *Save* or *Save As* commands from the **File** menu, or clicking on the *Save* button on the power bar, activates the *Save As* dialog box. Here WordPerfect asks you to name your document and decide where you want to save it. Choose the directory you want to save the file in from the *Directories* list box.

To change the drive that you want to save your file to, click on the arrow in the *Drives* list box and choose from the available drives in the drop-down list that appears.

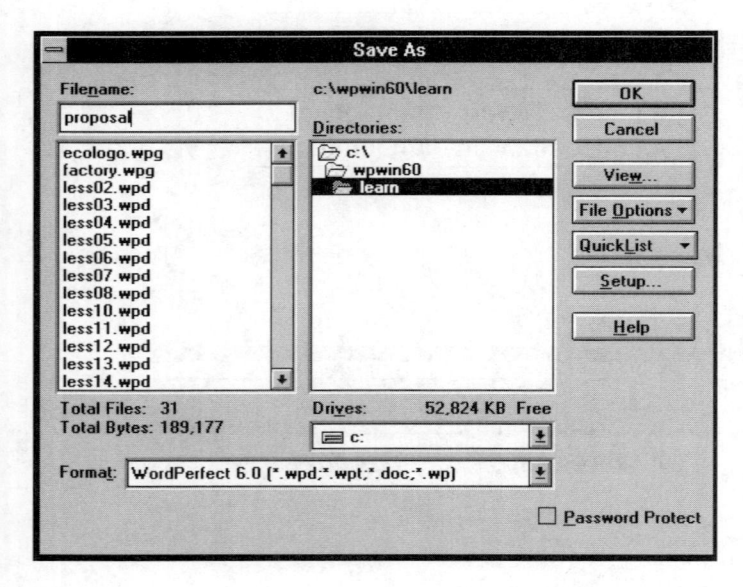

To name your file, type its name into the *Filename* text box at the top of this dialog box.

The *Format* drop-down list lets you save your WordPerfect document in different formats so you can use them in other programs.

Once you have found the drive and directory you need and named your file, click on the *OK* button. The new file name appears in the document window title bar.

Choosing the *Save* command for a file you've already named saves any changes you've made since you last used the *Save* or *Save As* command.

Choosing the *Save As* command for a file you've already named also activates the *Save As* dialog box. This command allows you to make a copy of the file by saving it with a different name.

The other buttons in this dialog box act in the same way as in the *Open* dialog box described earlier in this chapter.

CLOSE

Figure 14. The *Close* command from the **File** menu closes the active document window without exiting from WordPerfect. If you have made any changes to the current document, then WordPerfect asks if you want to save these changes. Clicking on *Yes* saves changes to an already named document, or activates the *Save As* dialog box if it is a new document. If you have another document open, it becomes active after the current document closes. If there are no other documents open, WordPerfect reverts to a clear editing screen—*Document 1 - unmodified.*

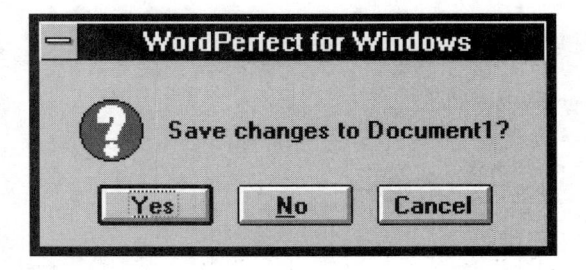

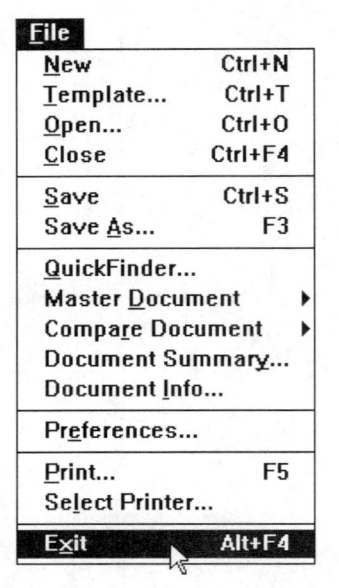

EXIT

Figure 15. The *Exit* command in the **File** menu shuts down WordPerfect. If you have not saved any of your open documents since making changes to them, WordPerfect asks if you want to do this before closing the application.

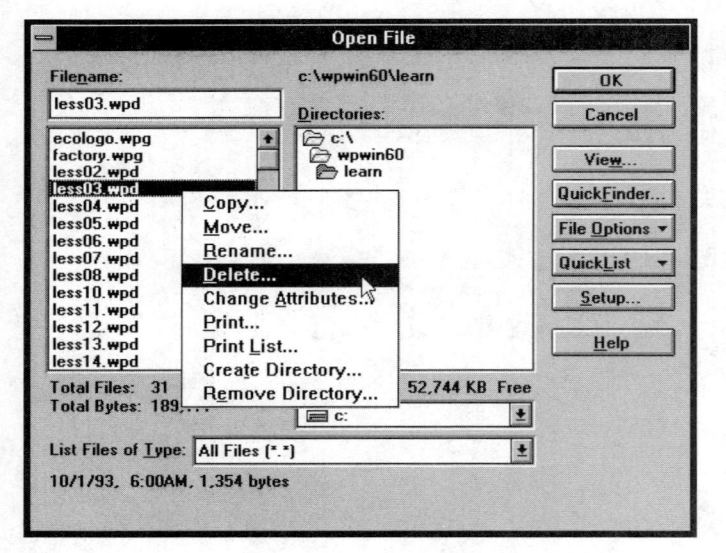

FILE MANAGEMENT

Figure 16. The WordPerfect file management system now operates entirely from any of the directory dialog boxes (most commonly the *Open File* dialog box). To perform any file management operations such as copying, moving, renaming, deleting, and printing files, or creating and deleting directories, simply select *Open* from the **File** menu.

In the *Open File* dialog box you can access the file management functions through the buttons available, or through QuickMenus. To use the QuickMenus, click the right mouse button on either of the list boxes to activate the QuickMenu relevant to that area of the dialog box.

Chapter 4: Creating and Managing Files

FILE OPTIONS

Figure 17. Selecting the *File Options* button from the *Open File* dialog box activates its drop-down list. To copy, move, rename, delete, or print a file, simply select it from the *File* list and then select one of these commands.

The *Change Attributes* command lets you change the Hidden, Read Only, Archive, and System attributes of selected files.

The *Print List* command prints the list of files currently displayed in the *Files* list. You can also use this command to print only the selected files in this list.

The *File Options* drop-down list also enables you to create and delete directories to help you organize and store your files.

QUICKLIST

WordPerfect lets you group similar files into what are called *QuickLists*. This feature provides an easier way of accessing and changing directories.

Figure 18. Select the *QuickList* button to activate its drop-down menu. To work with QuickLists, select *Show QuickList* from this drop-down list.

71

Chapter 4: Creating and Managing Files

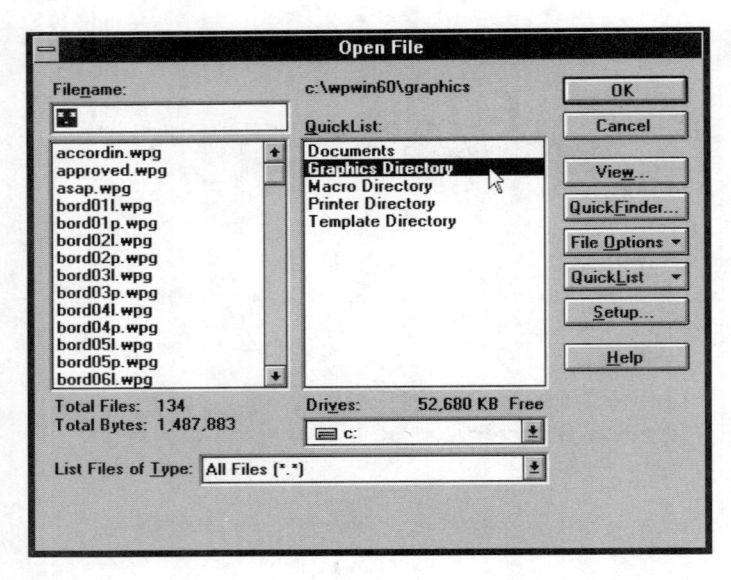

Figure 19. The *Directories* list is now replaced by the *QuickList* list. A group of default WordPerfect QuickLists appear for you to choose from. Working with QuickLists is basically the same as working with normal directories except QuickLists group files into descriptive groups.

Double-click on any of the available QuickLists to list their files in the *Files* list box. You can then select and work with the files as you normally would.

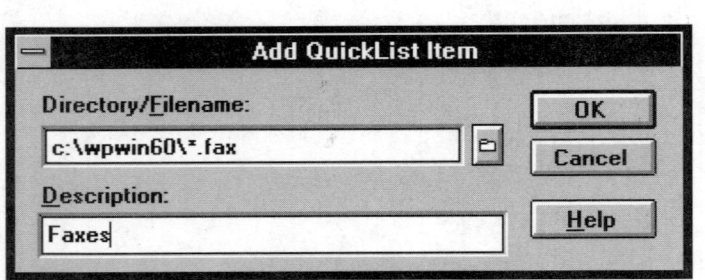

Figure 20. To create a QuickList, select *Add Item* from the *QuickList* drop-down list. This opens the *Add QuickList Item* dialog box where you can create a new QuickList.

To create a QuickList you need to specify a directory and filenames for the descriptive group that you want your QuickList to include. For instance, if you saved all of your fax files in the *wpwin60* directory with a *.fax* extension you could create a "Faxes" QuickList to contain only these files.

Type the directory and filename of the files you want to include in your QuickList into the *Directory/Filename* section of the dialog box. In this case we have used the * wildcard to specify all files with a *.fax* extension in the *wpwin60* directory.

Now click in the *Description* text box of the dialog box and enter a descriptive name that will remind you of what the QuickList contains, in this case "Faxes." Click on *OK* to create this QuickList.

Figure 21. WordPerfect now displays the QuickList in the *Open File* dialog box. To edit or delete any QuickList entry, select it and choose the appropriate command from the *QuickList* drop-down list.

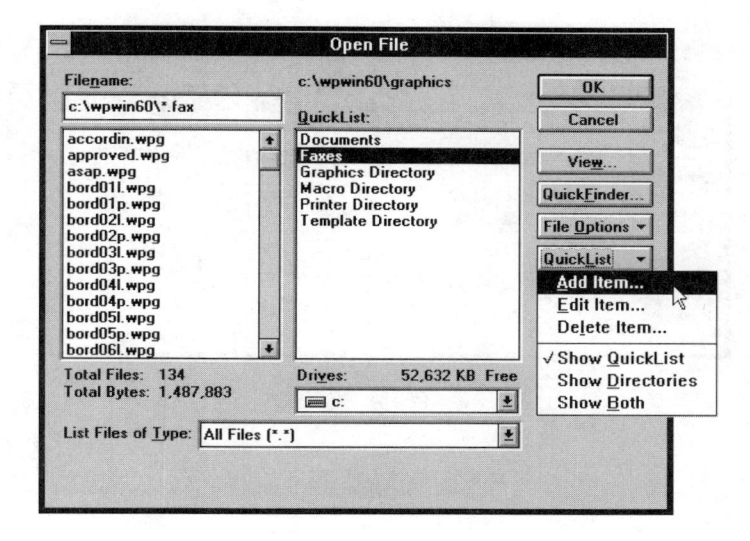

Figure 22. You can switch back to displaying the *Directories* list by selecting *Show Directories* from the *QuickList* drop-down list. You can also display both the *Directories* list and the *QuickList* list at the same time.

SETUP

Figure 23. Selecting the *Setup* button opens the *Open/Save As Setup* dialog box where you can specify how you want to display your file lists. This dialog box also lets you select or deselect the *Change Default Directory* option. If this option is selected, WordPerfect uses the last directory that you worked in as the default for when you next open a directory dialog box.

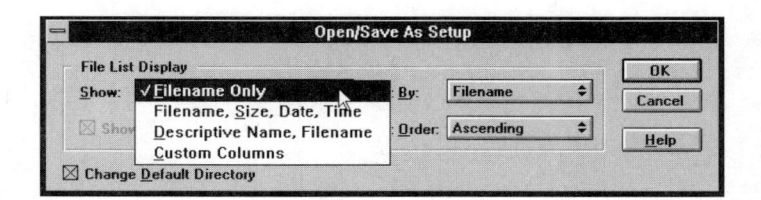

Chapter 4: Creating and Managing Files

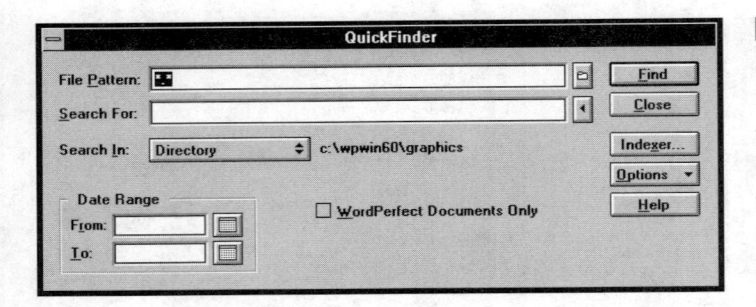

QUICKFINDER

Figure 24. Selecting the *QuickFinder* button opens the *QuickFinder* dialog box. You can use this dialog box to activate the QuickFinder indexing feature that lets you search and retrieve text within files in specific directories, subdirectories, or disks.

74

SETTING PREFERENCES 5

THE PREFERENCES DIALOG BOX

The *Preferences* command in the **File** menu lets you customize the way WordPerfect runs. This command opens the *Preferences* dialog box where you can select from a range of preference areas. The changes you make in the dialog boxes associated with the *Preferences* dialog box affect all future documents, until you modify the settings again.

Figure 1. To open the *Preferences* dialog box, select the *Preferences* command from the **File** menu.

Figure 2. This dialog box contains a variety of icons that activate further dialog boxes where you can select a range of default settings. Double-click any of these icons to open its corresponding dialog box.

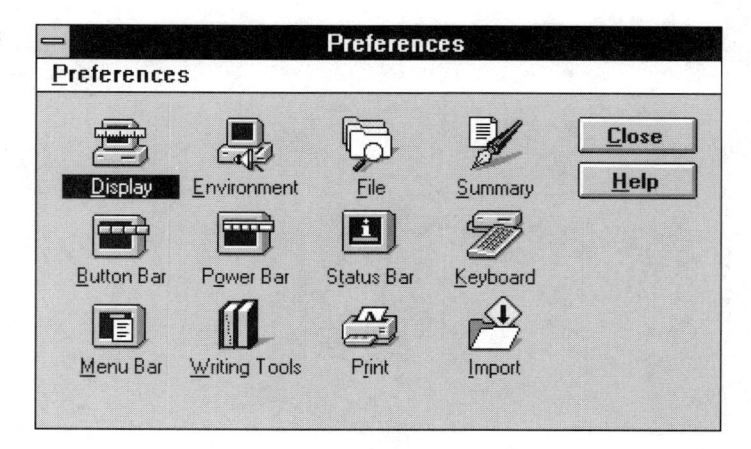

75

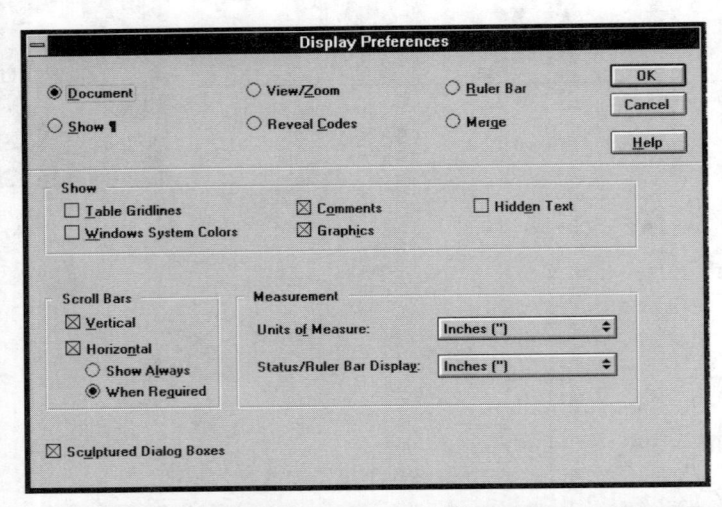

Figure 3. The *Display Preferences* dialog box lets you change certain elements of WordPerfect's display to suit your needs. Selecting the different radio buttons at the top of the dialog box enables different display choices.

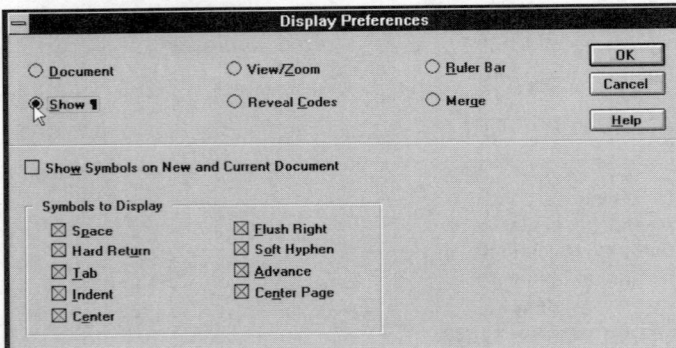

Figure 4. For example, selecting the *Show* radio button displays the *Show* options. In this way, each radio button at the top of the dialog box activates the display options for that element of the WordPerfect program.

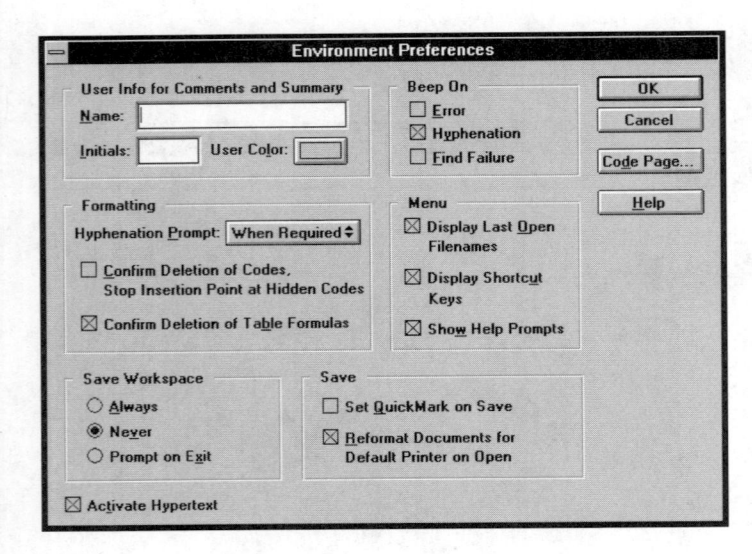

Figure 5. The *Environment Preferences* dialog box offers a range of choices that affect the operating environment of WordPerfect, such as what to include in menu displays and how certain formatting functions operate.

Figure 6. The *File Preferences* dialog box lets you determine where certain file types are stored when using WordPerfect. You can also use this dialog box to set backup options. Selecting the radio buttons at the top of the dialog box activates a new set of choices in the bottom of the dialog box.

For instance, selecting the *Templates* radio button changes the file location options specific to the templates file type.

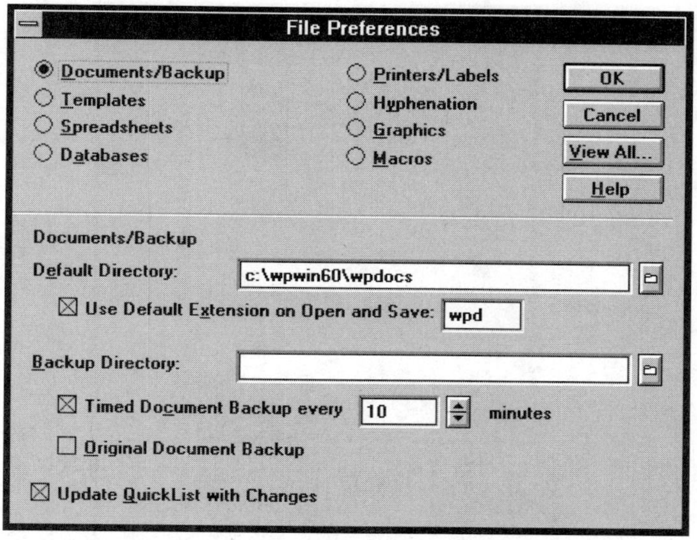

Figure 7. In the *Document Summary Preferences* dialog box you can set your preferences to automate certain document summary tasks.

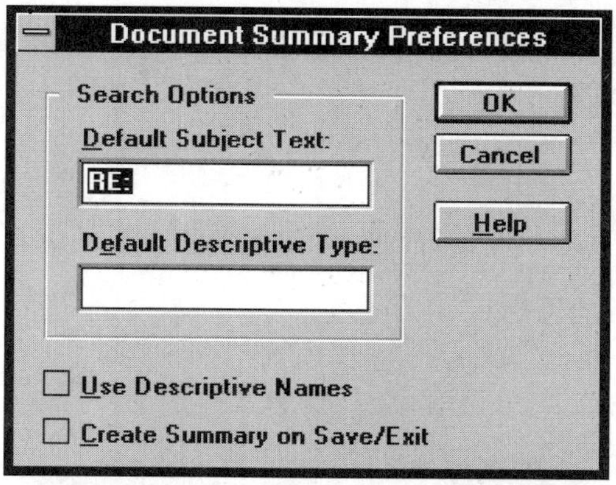

Figure 8. The *Button Bar Preferences* dialog box lets you select, create, edit, copy, and delete button bars and button bar items. You can also customize the position and display of the button bar. This dialog box is discussed in greater detail in **Customizing the Screen** later in this chapter.

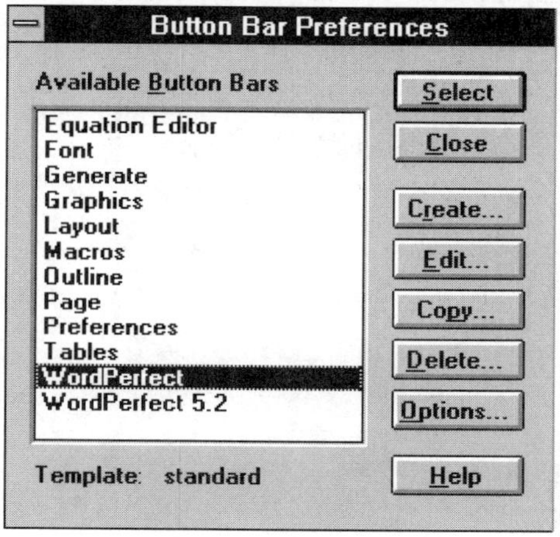

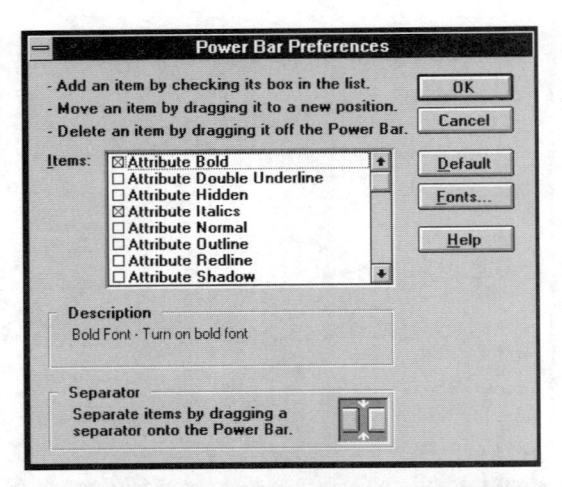

Figure 9. In the *Power Bar Preferences* dialog box you can edit and customize the power bar to include the commands you use most in WordPerfect. You can also reorganize the display of the power bar by moving items to new locations. This dialog box is discussed in greater detail in **Customizing the Screen** later in this chapter.

Figure 10. The *Status Bar Preferences* dialog box allows you to customize the display of the status bar. Unlike previous WordPerfect versions, you can now specify what information you want displayed on the status bar and where on the status bar you want the information displayed. This dialog box is discussed in greater detail in **Customizing the Screen** later in this chapter.

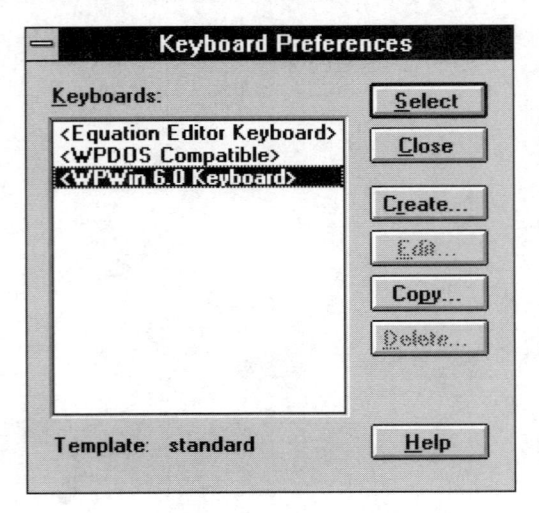

Figure 11. You can customize the function key layout of your keyboard in WordPerfect to suit you with the *Keyboard Preferences* dialog box. You can either select a keyboard type from the list, or create your own keyboard layout.

Chapter 5: Setting Preferences

Figure 12. In the *Menu Bar Preferences* dialog box you can customize the menu type and display what you want in WordPerfect. You can select an existing menu, edit a menu, or even create your own menu display.

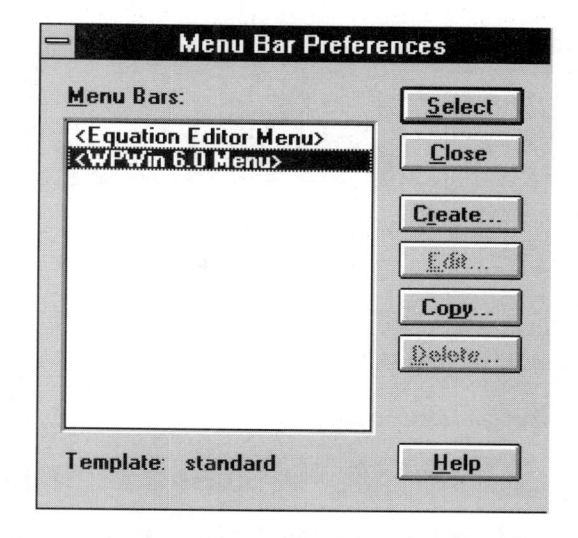

Figure 13. The *Writing Tools* dialog box lets you specify which writing tools you want to display in the **Tools** menu and in what order WordPerfect displays them.

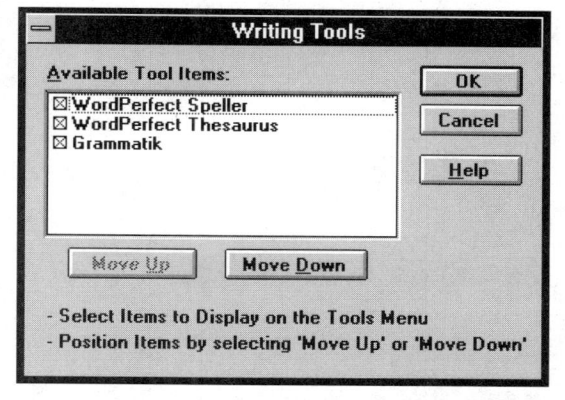

Figure 14. The *Print Preferences* dialog box allows you to set default print settings for your WordPerfect documents. These print settings take effect every time you print, until you change them in this dialog box again.

79

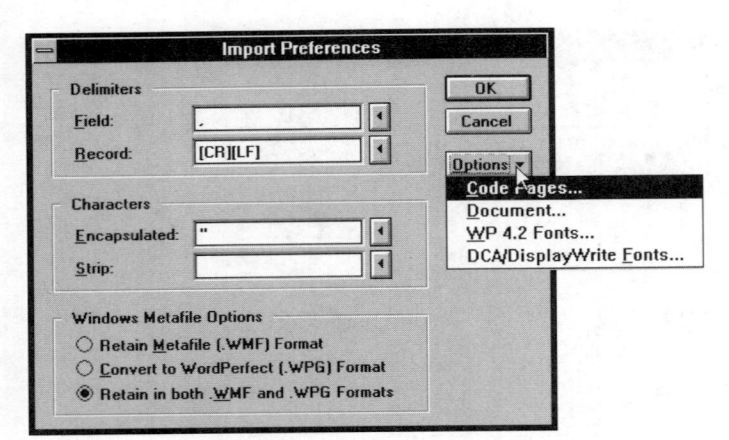

Figure 15. In the *Import Preferences* dialog box you can customize the way WordPerfect imports different types of files into your documents. Selecting the *Options* button activates a drop-down list so you can set import and conversion preferences.

Selecting Printers

Another important command to examine is *Select Printer* from the **File** menu. This command determines the default printer for your documents and in turn, it affects the whole format of your documents.

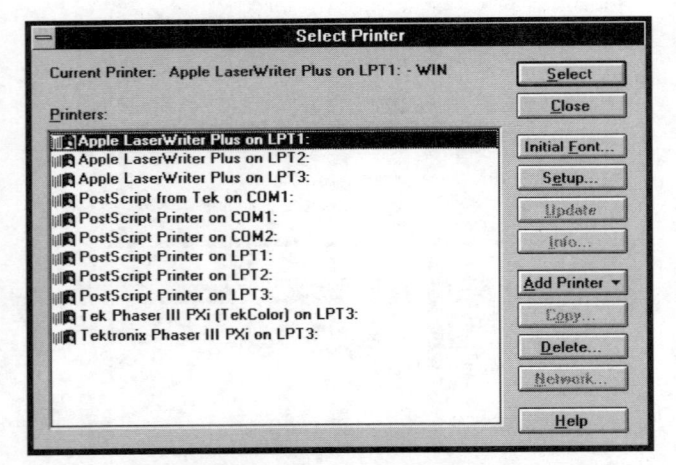

Figure 16. Selecting this command opens the *Select Printer* dialog box. The first line of the dialog box lists the current printer that you are using. Below this is a list of available printers for you to choose from as the default printer for your WordPerfect documents.

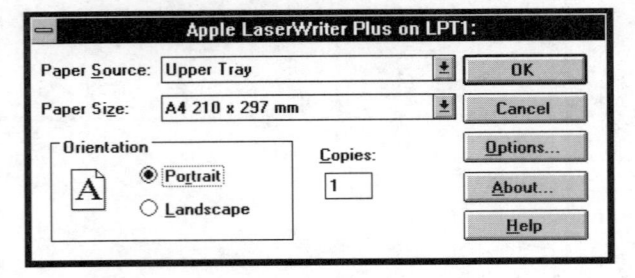

Figure 17. Selecting the *Setup* button allows you to determine the paper size and source, and the orientation of your printing. The other commands in the dialog box let you control which printers you can use.

Customizing the Screen

WordPerfect now allows you to customize almost all of the default screen elements to suit your individual preferences. You can do this using either the *Preferences* command from the **File** menu, or by using QuickMenus for the specified screen elements.

THE BUTTON BAR

Figure 18. To customize the button bar, activate its QuickMenu by clicking the right mouse button anywhere on it. The QuickMenu offers a variety of default button bars to choose from, as well as options to edit, set preferences for, and hide the button bar.

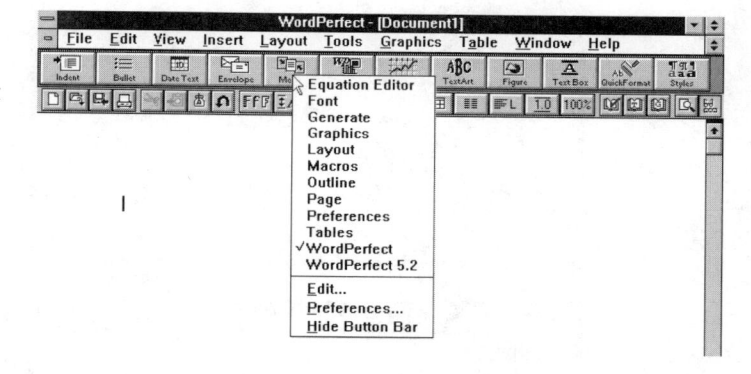

SELECTING BUTTON BARS

Figure 19. Selecting any of the default button bars replaces the current button bar. The default button bars offer a range of task specific buttons for the most commonly used commands for that task.

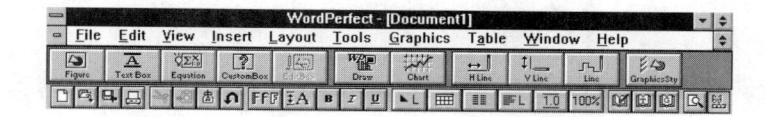

For example, the **Graphics** button bar contains buttons for the most common functions used when creating or manipulating graphics.

Chapter 5: Setting Preferences

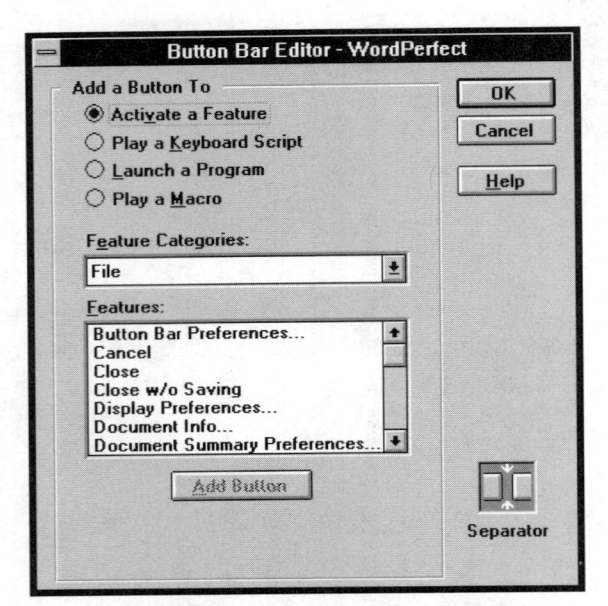

EDITING BUTTON BARS

Figure 20. You can edit the current button bar by selecting *Edit* from the **Button Bar** QuickMenu. This opens the *Button Bar Editor* dialog box.

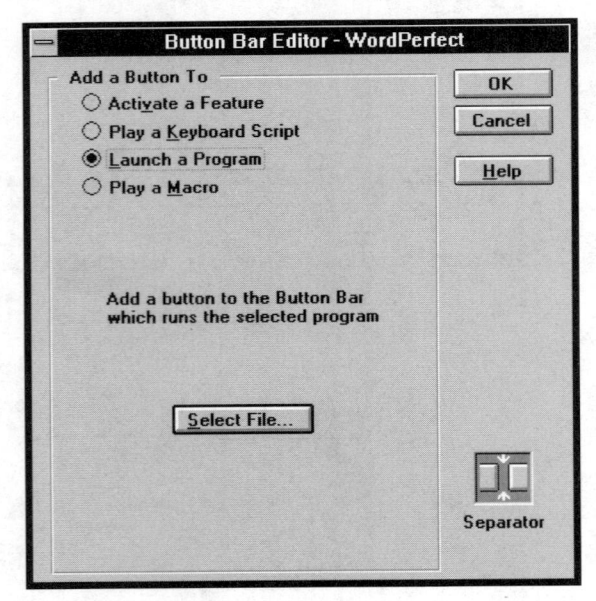

Figure 21. The radio buttons in this dialog box let you select the function of the buttons that you add to the button bar. Selecting each radio button affects the choices available in the dialog box.

Chapter 5: Setting Preferences

Figure 22. To add a button that activates a WordPerfect feature or command, first select the relevant menu from the *Feature Categories* drop-down list. Then select the feature you want from the *Features* list box. As you select a feature the *Add Button* button becomes active and a brief explanation of the button appears below it. Click on *Add Button* to add this button to the button bar.

Alternatively, you can add a button to the button bar by simply selecting a command from the menu bar while the *Button Bar Editor* dialog box is open.

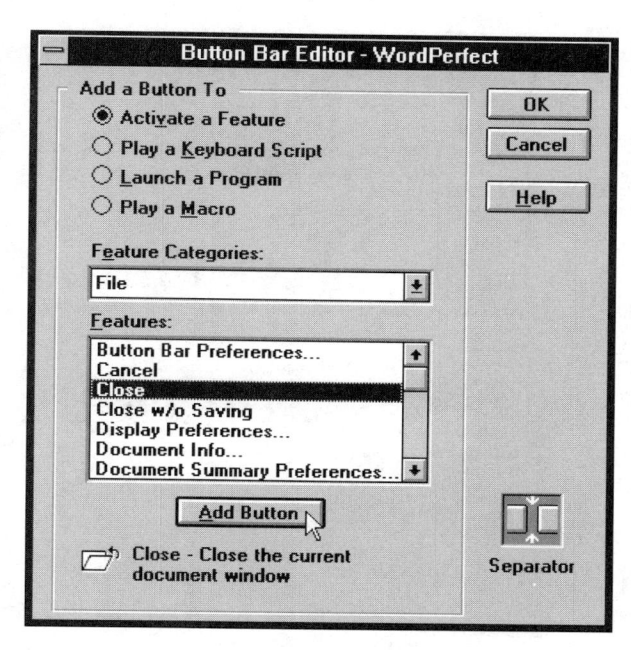

Similarly, to remove a button from the button bar, simply drag it from the bar with the mouse with the *Button Bar Editor* dialog box open. When you have finished editing the button bar, click on *OK* to accept the changes you have made.

CREATING BUTTON BARS

Figure 23. To create a button bar, select the *Preferences* command from the **Button Bar** QuickMenu. This opens the *Button Bar Preferences* dialog box where you can create, edit, copy, or delete the available button bars. To perform any of these functions, select a button bar and click on the appropriate button. To create a button bar, simply click on the *Create* button from this dialog box.

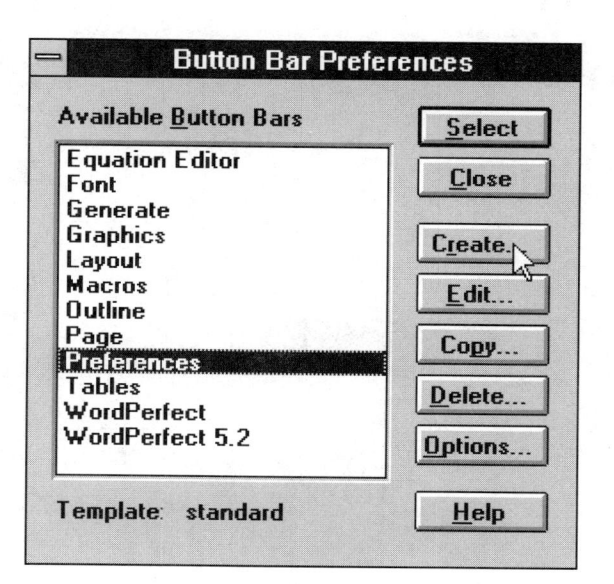

83

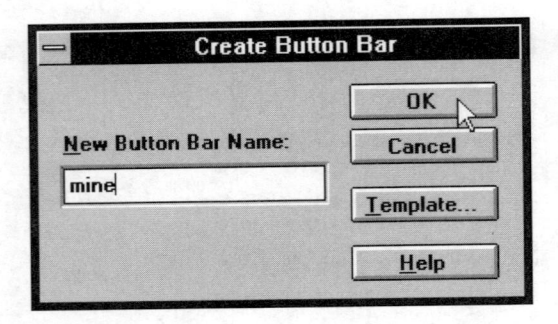

Figure 24. This opens the *Create Button Bar* dialog box where you are asked to name the button bar you are creating so that you can identify it later. Type the name of your button bar here and click *OK*.

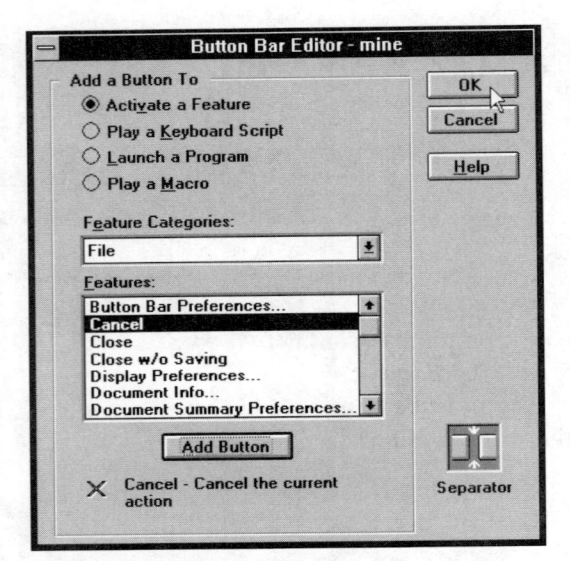

Figure 25. WordPerfect now opens the *Button Bar Editor* dialog box with the name of your button bar displayed on its title bar. Add buttons to your button bar as you would when editing a button bar (described earlier in this chapter). When you have finished adding buttons to your button bar, click *OK*.

Figure 26. WordPerfect highlights your new button bar in the *Available Button Bars* list box ready for you to select it at any time in the future.

Chapter 5: Setting Preferences

BUTTON BAR DISPLAY OPTIONS

Figure 27. Selecting the *Options* button from the *Button Bar Preferences* dialog box opens the *Button Bar Options* dialog box where you can set the display options for your WordPerfect button bars.

Select from the *Font* and *Font Size* options to change the size and type of the font on your button bars.

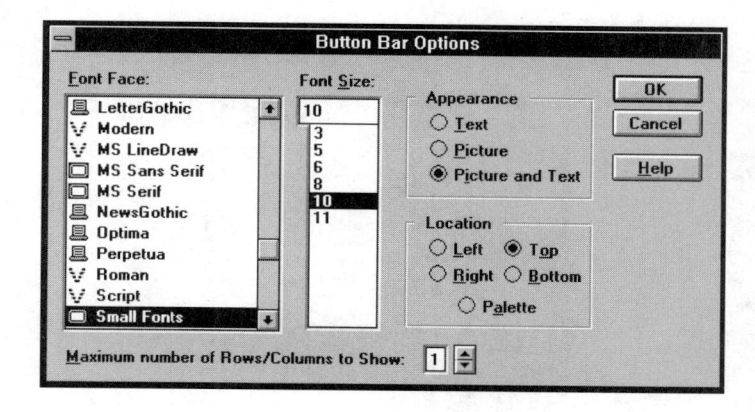

The *Appearance* section of this dialog box lets you display buttons as text only, pictures only, or both text and pictures.

The *Location* section allows you to put the button bar on any edge of the WordPerfect screen or as a floating palette.

Click *OK* to accept any changes as the default display for your button bars.

THE POWER BAR

Figure 28. To customize the power bar, activate the **Power Bar** QuickMenu by clicking the right mouse button anywhere on the bar. Then select the *Preferences* command.

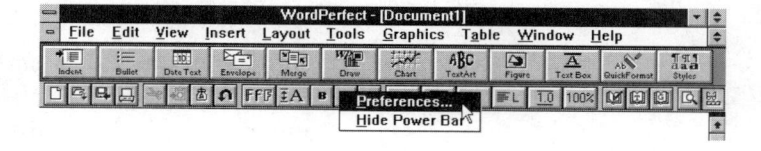

85

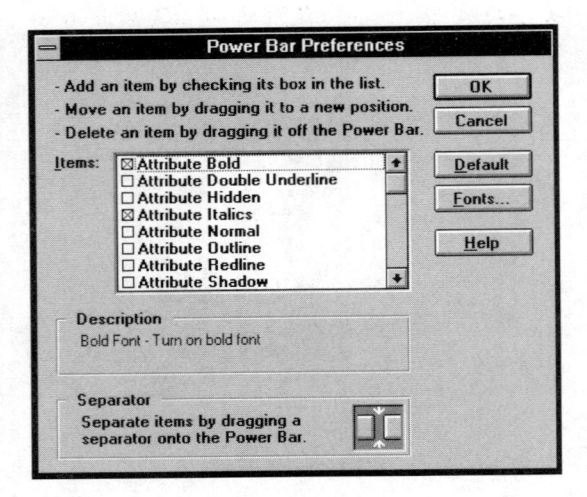

EDITING THE POWER BAR

Figure 29. The *Power Bar Preferences* dialog box allows you to customize the power bar to include the commands that you use most often.

The *Items* list displays everything you can include as buttons on the power bar. The check marks beside the items indicates that the power bar currently has a button for that item.

Figure 30. To remove an item's button from the power bar, simply deselect its check box from the *Items* list. You can also remove a button by dragging it off the power bar with the mouse.

To add a button to the power bar you must first remove a button to make room for it. Once you have made room for the new button, simply select an item's check box from the *Items* list. WordPerfect then automatically includes that button on the power bar.

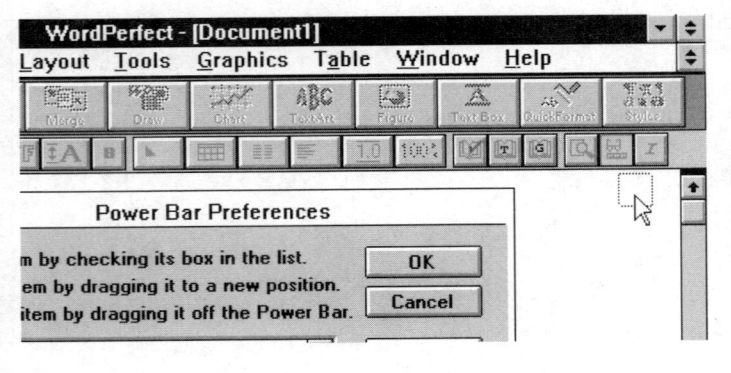

Figure 31. You can move a button on the power bar by dragging it to a new location with the mouse. When you release the mouse button, WordPerfect inserts the button into its new position on the power bar.

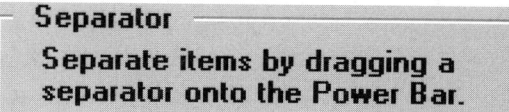

Chapter 5: Setting Preferences

Figure 32. You can also separate items on the power bar into logical groups using a power bar separator. To do this, position the mouse pointer over the box in the *Separator* section of the dialog box. As you do so the mouse pointer changes into a hand icon. You can now click and drag a separator onto the power bar using this hand cursor. When you release the mouse button on the power bar, WordPerfect inserts the separator.

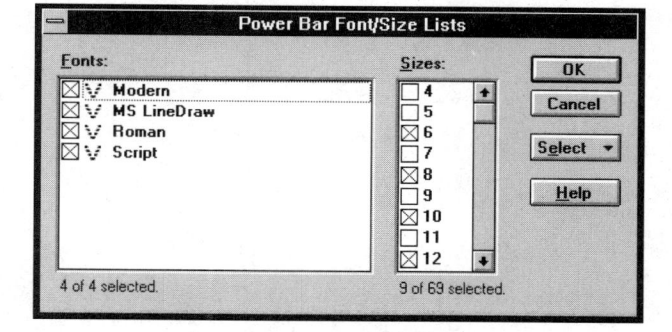

Figure 33. Select the *Fonts* button to open the *Power Bar Font/Size Lists* dialog box where you can specify what fonts and font sizes to include in the *Font Face* and *Font Size* button lists on the power bar. The check boxes indicate which fonts or sizes will be included in the power bar lists.

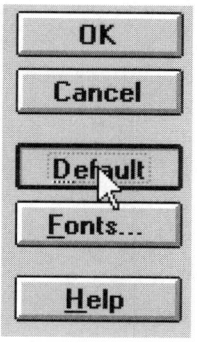

Figure 34. You can revert to the power bar's default settings at any time by selecting the *Default* button. Click on *OK* to accept any changes you make to the power bar.

87

Chapter 5: Setting Preferences

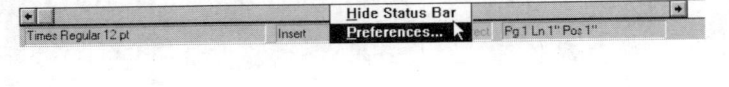

THE STATUS BAR

Figure 35. To customize the status bar, activate the **Status Bar** QuickMenu by clicking the right mouse button anywhere on it and then select the *Preferences* command.

EDITING THE STATUS BAR

Figure 36. The *Status Bar Preferences* dialog box is very similar to that for the power bar. The *Status Bar Items* list includes everything you can display on the status bar. Check marks beside items indicate that they are already on the status bar.

Figure 37. To remove an item from the status bar, simply deselect its check box from the *Status Bar Items* list. You can also remove an item by dragging it off the status bar directly with the mouse.

To add an item to the status bar display simply select its check box from the *Status Bar Items* list. WordPerfect then automatically includes it on the status bar.

88

Figure 38. You can move an item on the status bar by dragging it to a new location.

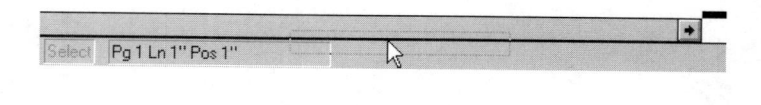

Figure 39. You can also resize the display window of items by dragging its edge with the mouse.

Figure 40. You can revert to the status bar's default settings at any time by selecting the *Default* button. Click on *OK* to accept any changes you make to the status bar.

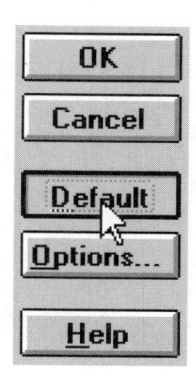

Speller, Thesaurus, and Grammatik   6

The Speller

The spell checking feature is common to most word processing programs. It scans your documents for any misspelled words and offers suggestions for you to replace them with. However in WordPerfect the Speller is actually a separate program that can also run on its own.

USING THE SPELLER

Figure 1. To spell check an open document, select *Speller* from the **Tools** menu or click on the *Speller* button on the power Bar. This activates the *Speller* window.

To start spell checking, simply click on the *Start* button. When WordPerfect begins spell checking, the spell checker starts looking for words that may be spelled incorrectly.

Figure 2. Once Speller finds a word, it highlights it in the document and shows it in the *Speller* window. The words *Not found* refer to the fact that the spell checker has not found a match for this word in its dictionaries.

In the *Suggestions* area of the *Speller* window, the spell checker usually makes some suggestions as to how the selected word

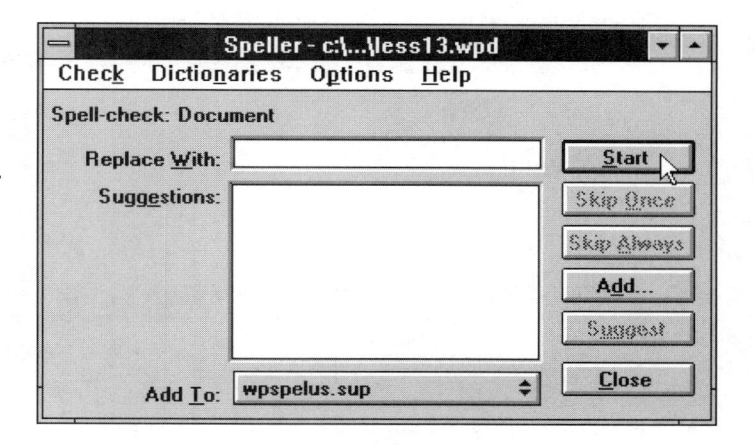

91

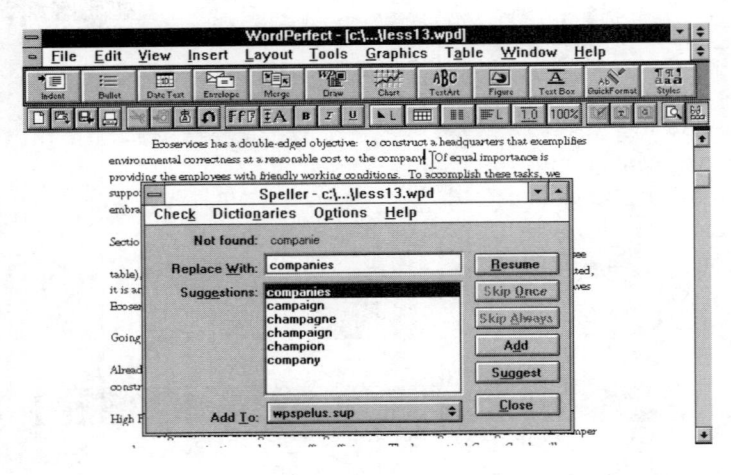

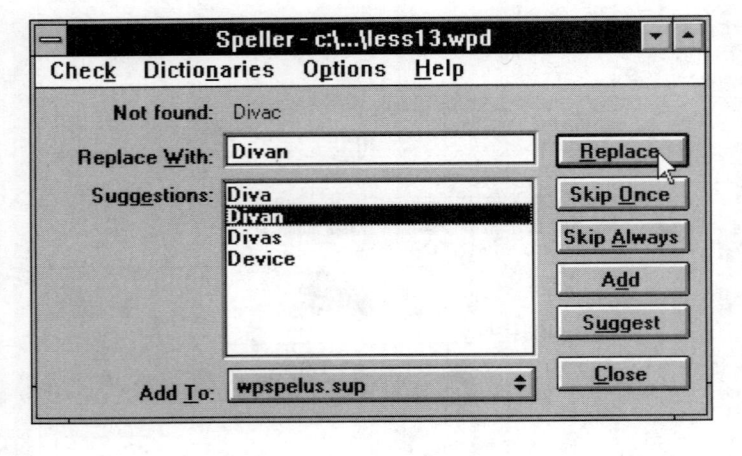

should be spelled. You can select any of these suggestions to replace a misspelled word or you can correct it yourself.

Figure 3. To correct a word yourself, click the insertion point in your document and edit the word directly as you normally would. Once you have corrected the word, click back in the *Speller* window to make it active again. The *Replace* button is replaced by the *Resume* button so that you can resume your spell check.

Another way of correcting a word yourself is to make a correction or type a new word in the *Replace With* text box. You can then replace the misspelled word with your correction by clicking on the *Replace* button.

Figure 4. If one of the WordPerfect suggestions is the correct spelling of the word that you want, select the appropriate word from the *Suggestions* list. The word you select in the *Suggestions* list then appears in the *Replace With* text box. To replace the incorrectly spelled word with the new word, click on the *Replace* button. WordPerfect replaces the word in the document, and Speller moves on to find other incorrectly spelled words.

Chapter 6: Speller, Thesaurus, and Grammatik

Occasionally you may decide that the word highlighted by the Speller is in fact correctly spelled. This is because a misspelled word to the Speller is any word that is not found in its dictionaries. However, like any ordinary dictionary, the Speller's dictionary does not contain every possible word. You may decide the misspelled word is the name of a person or company, or a word or acronym which is used in your particular industry.

Select *Skip Once* to ignore this word once, *Skip Always* to ignore this word for the rest of the document, or you can add this word to the WordPerfect dictionary by clicking on the *Add* button.

Figure 5. The WordPerfect Speller also highlights words that may not have a space between them. If this happens, place the cursor in the *Replace With* text box and add the space yourself. Click on the *Replace* button so your correction replaces the mistake. Alternatively you can make the correction directly in your document.

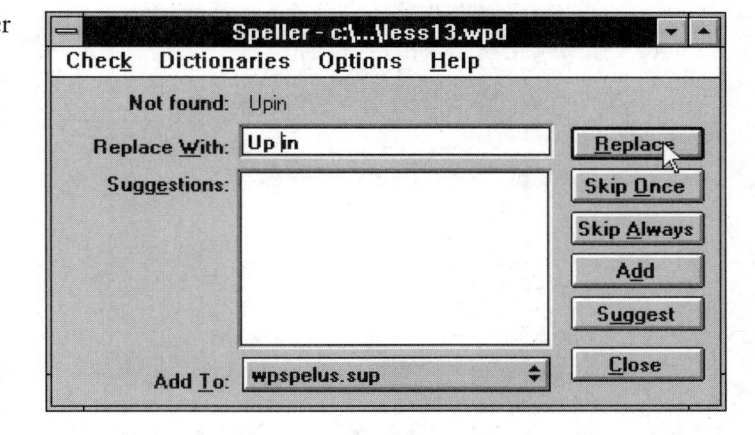

Figure 6. When the Speller finds two occurrences of a word in a row, such as "the the," it highlights the words and identifies them as *Duplicate words*. In these instances WordPerfect suggests replacing the duplicate words with just one occurrence of the word, listing it in the *Replace With* text box. Make the choices from the Speller as you normally would to continue.

93

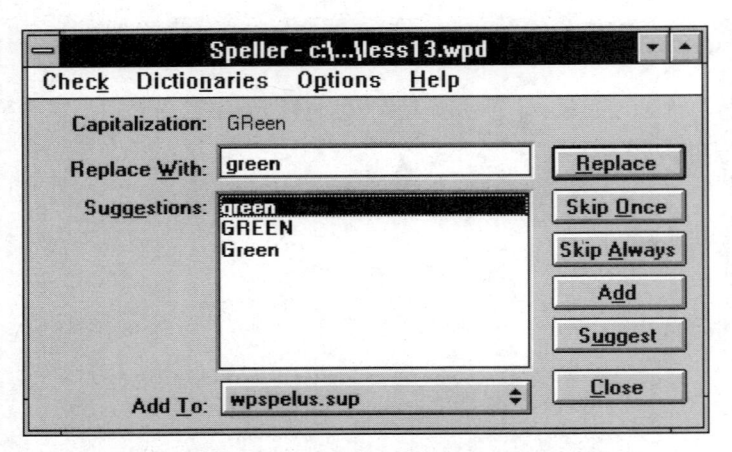

Figure 7. Speller may also pick up an error that it identifies as a capitalization error such as "GReen." In these instances it lists the capitalization possibilities "green," "Green," and "GREEN" in the *Suggestions* list for you to choose from.

Figure 8. Sometimes the Speller finds words containing numbers like "low2er". Simply correct these as you normally would and continue with the spell check.

Figure 9. If you click on the *Suggest* button after entering a word, whether it is spelled incorrectly or not, you get a list of phonetic matches. This is a list of words that sound similar to the found word.

Note: If you key a word into the Speller Word text box, the Start button doesn't have the same effect, however the Suggest button displays a list of phonetic matches for this word. To spell check an individual word in WordPerfect, select the word in the document before activating the Speller. Once you have started the Speller, the Selected Text option appears automatically in the Check pop-up list; just click on the Start button.

THE CHECK MENU

Figure 10. The Speller contains a variety of menus that allow you to control how it checks your documents. The options you have in the **Check** menu of the *Speller* window refer to which part of the current document you want to check. The options such as *Word, Sentence, Paragraph, Page,* and *Document* refer to text ranges that contain the cursor. The *Selected Text* and *Text Entry Box* options only become active when you have selected the appropriate text to check. The *Number of Pages* option allows you to check a specified number of pages from the current page.

THE DICTIONARIES MENU

Figure 11. The options available in the Speller **Dictionaries** menu let you choose different dictionaries from the one currently loaded. The *Main* dictionary is the dictionary to which WordPerfect first refers, while the *Supplementary* dictionary is the dictionary that contains any words you have added to the Speller.

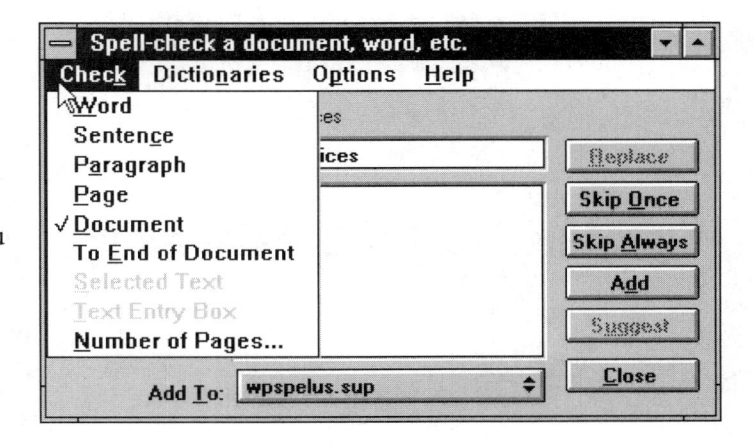

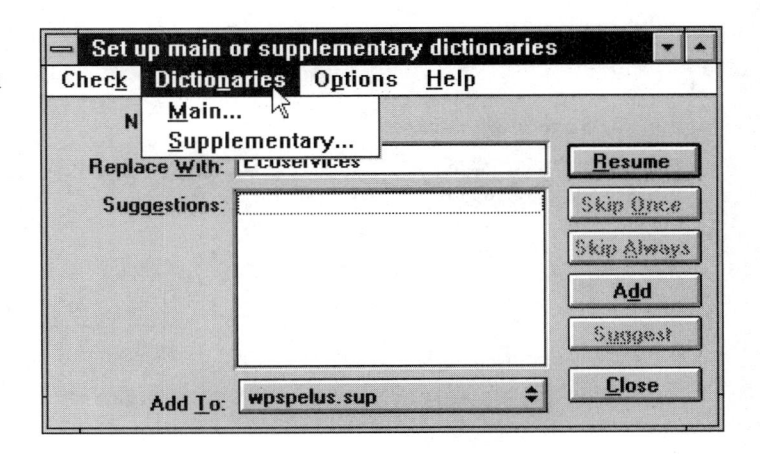

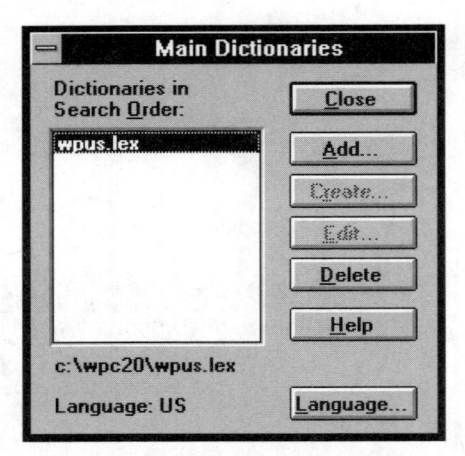

Figure 12. Selecting one of these options from the **Dictionary** menu takes you to a dialog box, where you can select another dictionary you want to load.

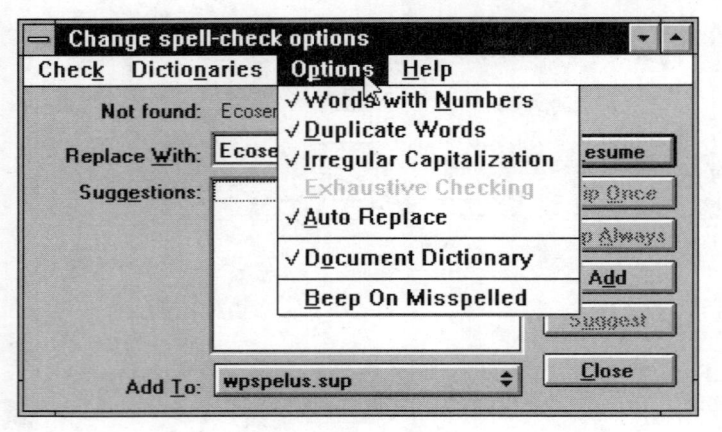

THE OPTIONS MENU

Figure 13. By default, the first three commands in the **Options** menu are active. To turn them off, select them from this menu and the check mark disappears.

The *Auto Replace* option automatically makes replacements in your document that you have defined in selected supplementary dictionaries. The *Document Dictionary* option turns the document specific dictionary on or off and the *Beep On Misspelled* option makes the Speller beep whenever it finds a possible error.

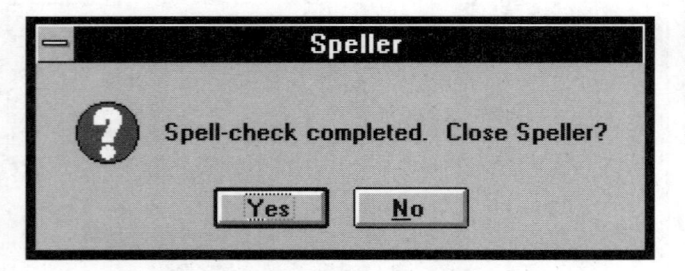

Figure 14. Whenever spell checking is complete, a message box appears. Click on *Yes* to return to your document.

USING THE SPELLER IN STAND-ALONE MODE

Figure 15. You can use the Speller outside WordPerfect. Simply double-click on the Speller icon in the Windows Program Manager.

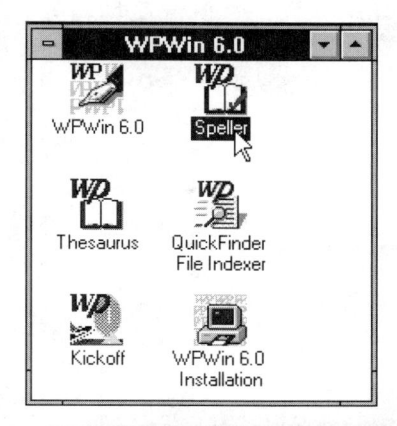

Figure 16. You can now enter individual words into the *Word* text box and spell check them one at a time.

Once you have entered the word you want, click on the *Start* button, and a list of possible alternative spellings for this word appears in the *Suggestions* list box. If the word is spelled correctly, it appears in the *Suggestions* list box.

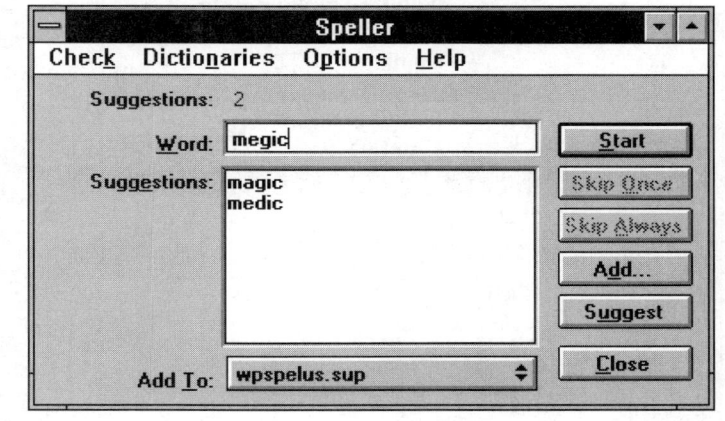

THESAURUS

The Thesaurus feature of WordPerfect is designed to be used as a writers' tool. Like a printed thesaurus, the Thesaurus program lists synonyms and antonyms for selected words. The WordPerfect Thesaurus, however, lets you view synonym listings for up to three words at a time and can update your document directly. The Thesaurus, like the Speller, is a separate program and can also run in stand-alone mode.

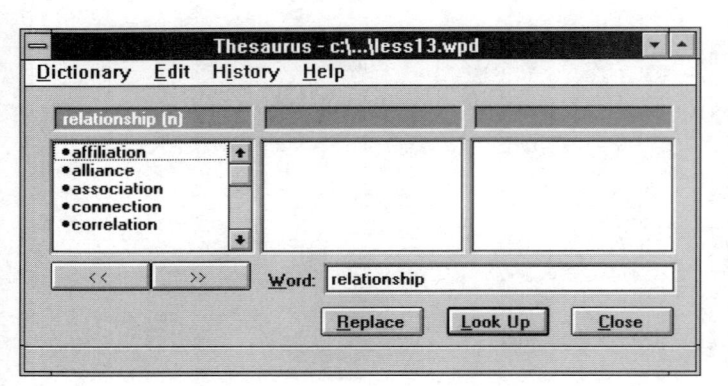

USING THE THESAURUS

Figure 17. To see a list of synonyms for a word, place the cursor within that word and select *Thesaurus* from the **Tools** menu or click on the *Thesaurus* button on the power Bar.

This opens the *Thesaurus* window with the selected word listed in both the *Word* text box and above the first column. The word above the first column is known as the headword and the letter in parentheses tells us what kind of word it is (e.g. noun, adjective). A list of synonyms and antonyms for this word appear in the column below it. If the list of synonyms and antonyms is larger than the list window, scroll bars appear.

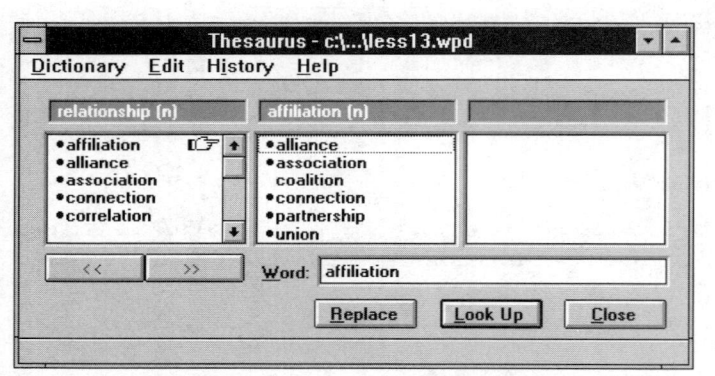

Figure 18. You can double-click on any word listed in a column to view synonyms and antonyms for that word.

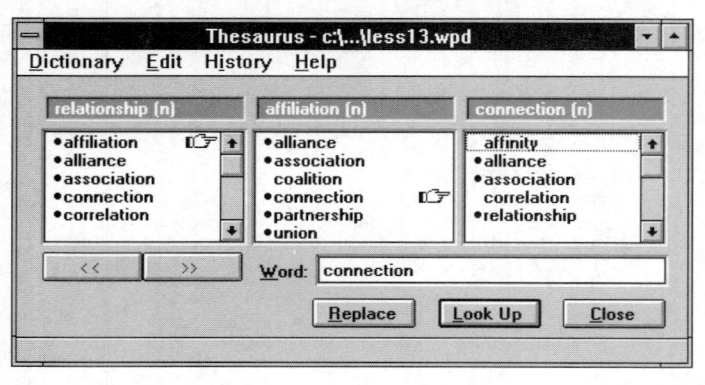

Figure 19. This process, called "reference chaining," can continue on for additional columns. For example, double-clicking a word in the second column lists a new set of synonyms and antonyms for that word in the third column.

Figure 20. If you have double-clicked on more than three words, the scrolling buttons below the first column give you access to words in earlier or later columns.

Figure 21. Whenever you highlight a word in the synonym list, the Thesaurus puts it in the *Word* text box. If you select or type a new word in the *Word* text box and click on the *Look Up* button, the Thesaurus reveals a new list of words. This word appears as the headword for column one and any words previously listed disappear.

Figure 22. If the word you have typed in the *Word* text box is not in the Thesaurus, the Thesaurus tells you in the bottom-left of the window.

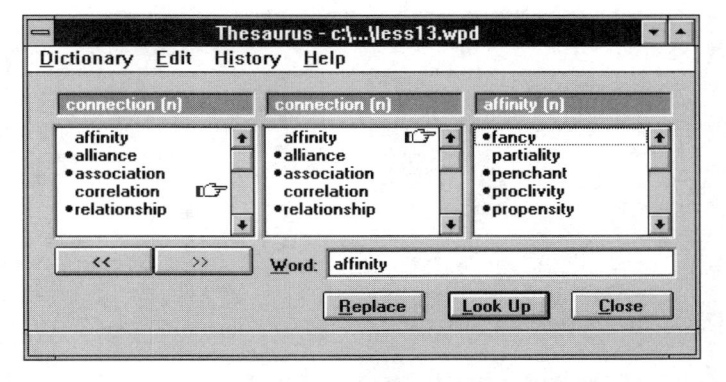

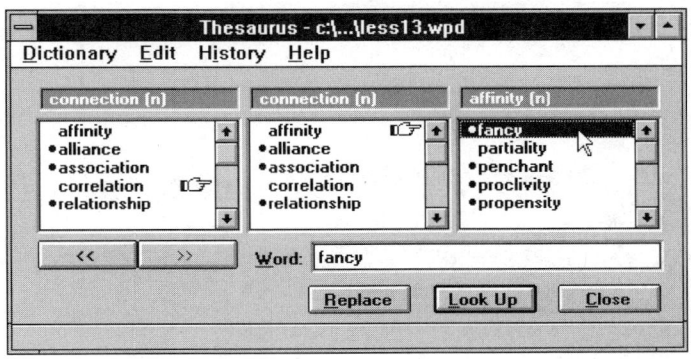

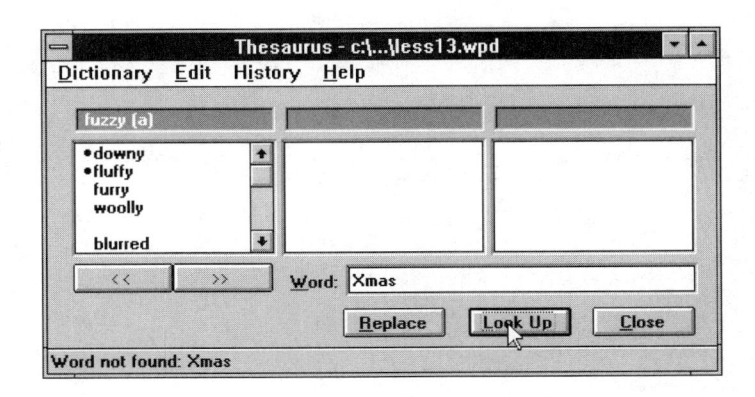

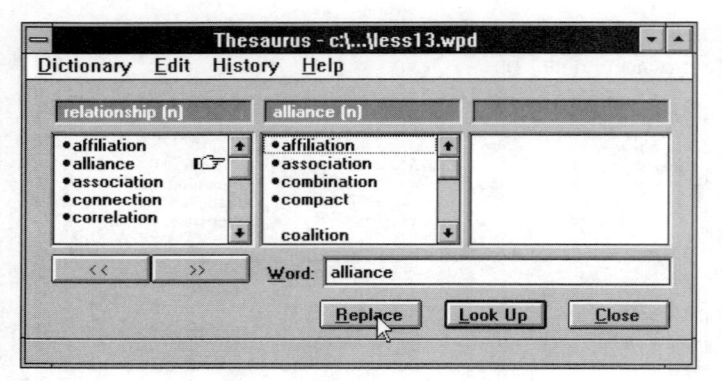

Chapter 6: Speller, Thesaurus, and Grammatik

Figure 23. Click on the *Replace* button to replace the word in the document with whatever is in the *Word* text box. Once you select the *Replace* button the Thesaurus disappears, and you return to the document with the new word replacing the original. If the original word was capitalized, the new one is also capitalized. If you wish to return to the text without making any changes, click on the *Close* button in the *Thesaurus* window.

THE DICTIONARY MENU

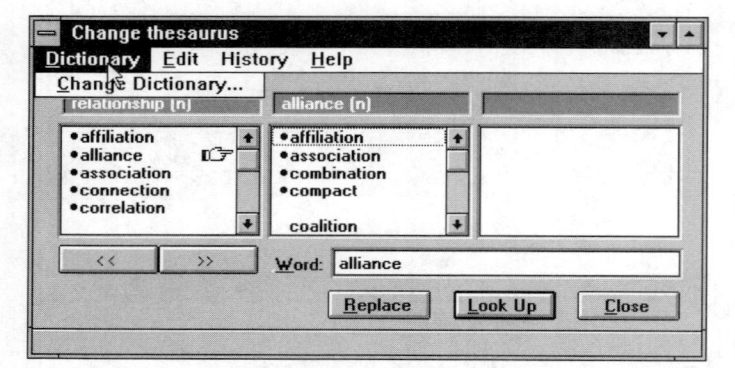

Figure 24. The Thesaurus **Dictionary** menu loads a new language dictionary as the current dictionary. Select *Change Dictionary* to activate the *Select a WordPerfect Thesaurus* dialog box. Choose the new thesaurus dictionary file and click on *Select* to load it.

THE EDIT MENU

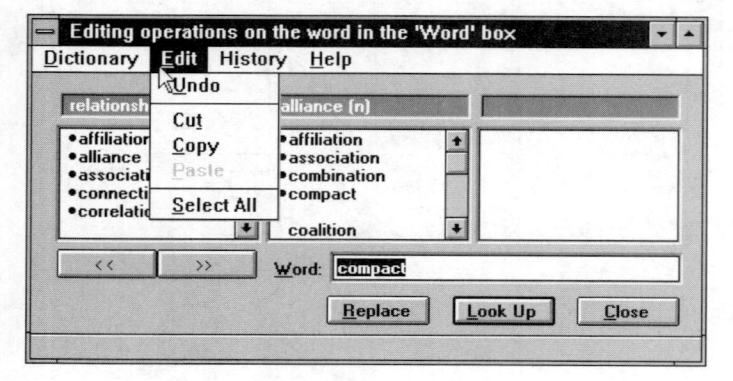

Figure 25. The first command in the **Edit** menu is the *Undo* command. On selecting this command, any changes you have just made in the *Word* text box are deleted. The *Cut* command cuts whatever is in the *Word* text box and places it in the Windows clipboard. The *Copy* command makes a copy of whatever is in the *Word* text box for the clipboard, as well as leaving the original behind. You must select the text in the *Word* text box

before you *Cut* or *Copy*. The *Paste* command places a copy of whatever is in the clipboard into the *Word* text box.

The *Select All* command highlights whatever is in the *Word* text box, so you can use the *Cut* or *Copy* command.

THE HISTORY MENU

Figure 26. The **History** menu contains a list of all words that you have looked up since starting the Thesaurus. If you select a word from this menu, it appears as the headword for column one with its synonyms below it, replacing the previous contents of this column.

USING THE THESAURUS IN STAND-ALONE MODE

Figure 27. You can use the Thesaurus outside WordPerfect. Simply double-click on the Thesaurus icon in the Windows Program Manager.

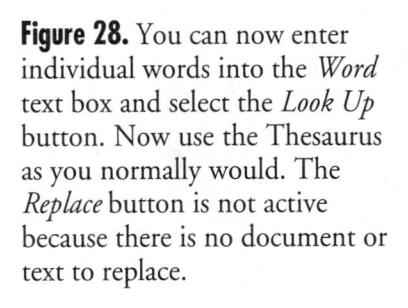

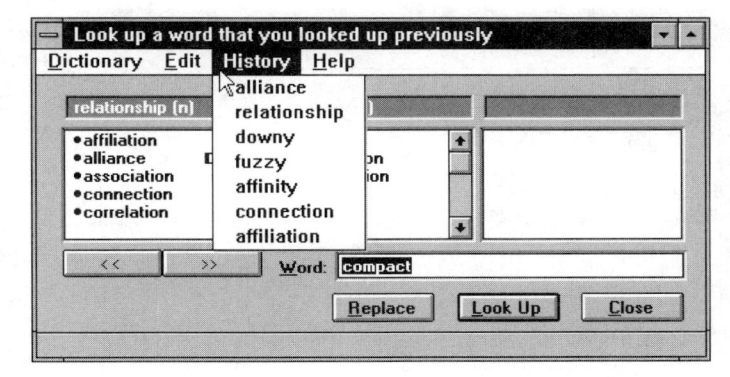

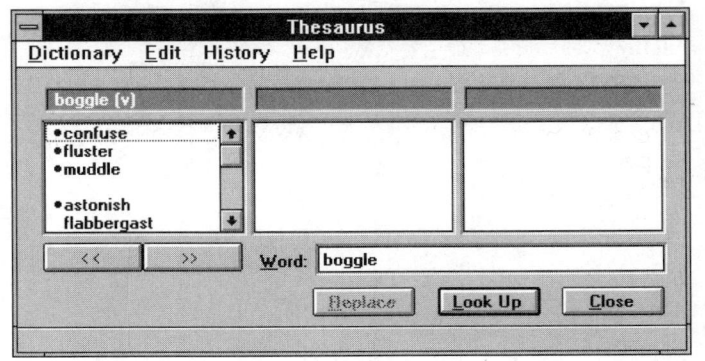

Figure 28. You can now enter individual words into the *Word* text box and select the *Look Up* button. Now use the Thesaurus as you normally would. The *Replace* button is not active because there is no document or text to replace.

GRAMMAR CHECKER

WordPerfect 6.0 comes with its own grammar checker, Grammatik V. You can use this to check the grammar, style, punctuation, and spelling of your entire document, or just a specific section.

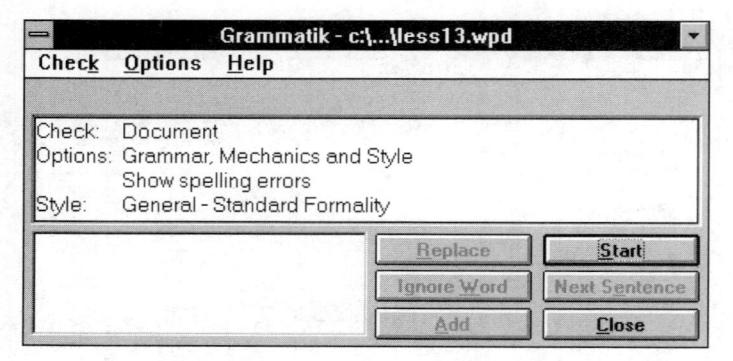

Figure 29. When in your WordPerfect document, select *Grammatik* from the **Tools** menu or click on the *Grammatik* button on the power bar to open the *Grammatik* window where you can begin checking your document.

The *Grammatik Advice Box* displays the current menu settings of how it will check your document. The text beside *Check* and *Options* display the current settings from the **Check** and **Options** menus. The text beside *Style* refers specifically to the *Writing Style* selected from the **Options** menu.

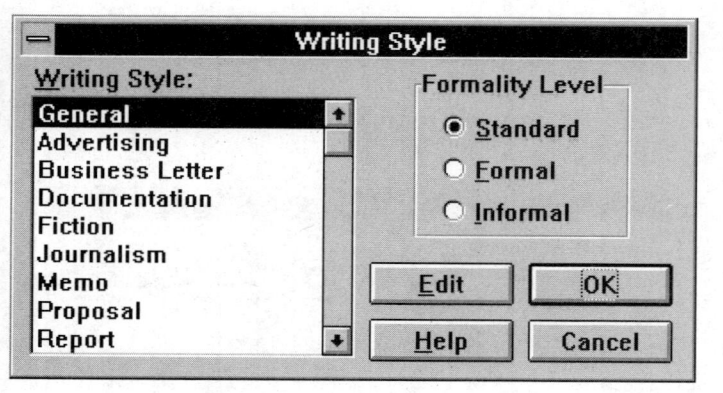

Figure 30. To change the style, select *Writing Style* from the **Options** menu. In the *Writing Style* dialog box, select a style that best describes your document. The *Formality Level* options change automatically, depending on which *Writing Style* you select.

Click on the *Help* button if you want more information about the *Writing Style* options.

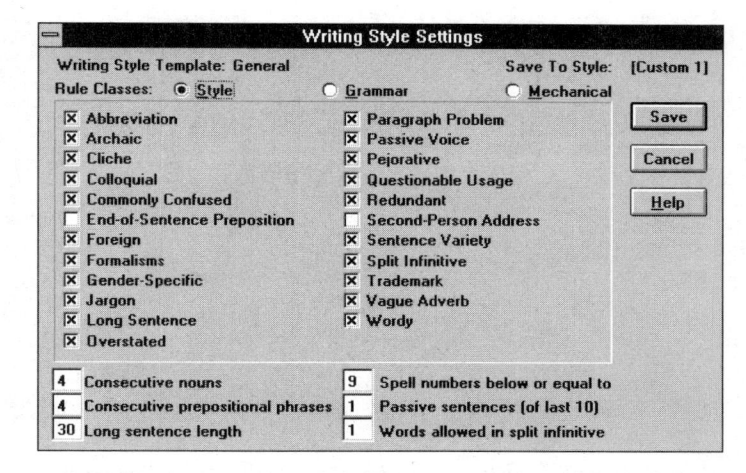

Chapter 6: Speller, Thesaurus, and Grammatik

Figure 31. To get a better idea of what a specific writing style is based on, select one of the options from the *Writing Style* list, and click on the *Edit* button. This activates the *Writing Style Settings* dialog box which shows you the characteristics of that style.

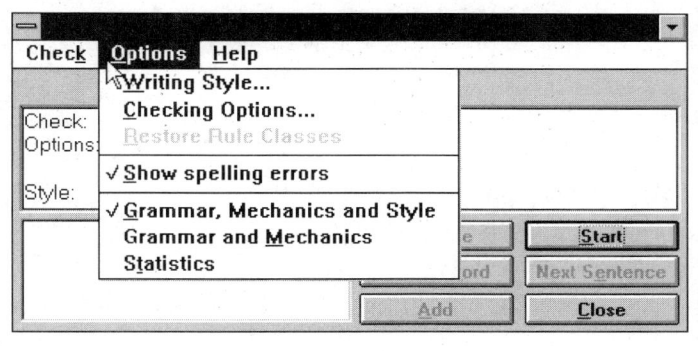

Figure 32. To view some of the default options for Grammatik click on the **Options** menu. The *Checking Options* command lets you determine how Grammatik proofreads your document. The *Restore Rule Classes* command restores any rules that you have turned off during a proofreading session. *Show spelling errors* means that Grammatik will display any spelling errors that it finds when proofreading. The *Grammar, Mechanics and Style* and *Grammar and Mechanics* commands determine what type of check Grammatik performs, and the *Statistics* command displays statistics for your document.

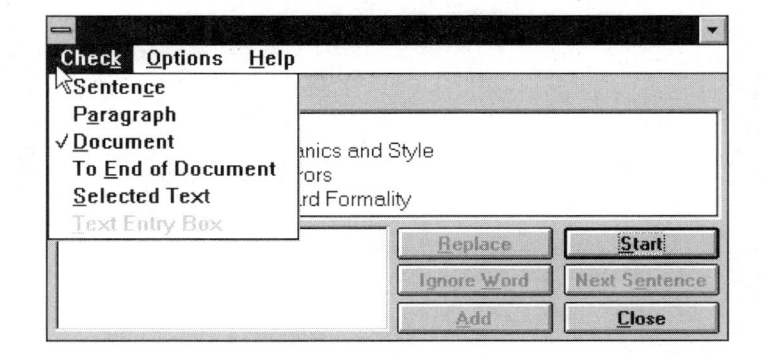

Figure 33. You can change the level of the document that Grammatik checks through the **Check** menu. A check mark indicates the current level of the document.

103

Chapter 6: Speller, Thesaurus, and Grammatik

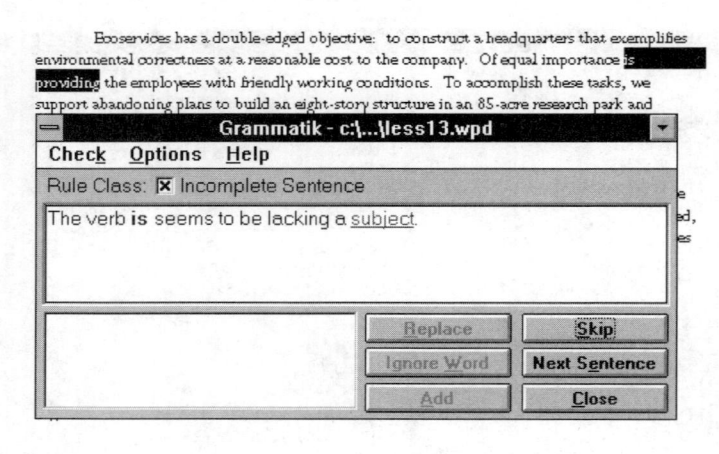

Figure 34. Once you have determined all of the menu settings that you want (displayed in the *Advice* Box) click on the *Start* button to start the proofreading session.

Grammatik now begins proofreading your document. Whenever it finds a possible problem, it displays it in the *Advice Box*. You can now choose from the available buttons.

Clicking the *Ignore Word/Phrase* button ignores the specific word or phrase for the rest of the proofreading session. The *Add* button allows you to add a word to the user dictionary so that WordPerfect no longer identifies it as an error.

The *Skip* button tells Grammatik to ignore this problem and skip to the next one. Selecting the *Next Sentence* button moves Grammatik to check the next sentence in your document.

The *Replace* button replaces the problem Grammatik finds in your document with any selected suggestions it offers.

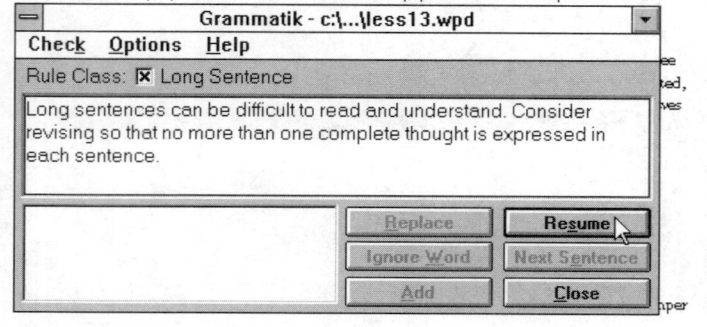

Figure 35. If Grammatik identifies a problem but does not offer any suggestions, then you can edit the problem manually. To do this, simply click in the text in the document window that Grammatik has identified, and edit it as you normally would. As you do this, the *Skip* button in the *Grammatik* window changes to become a *Resume* button. When you have made the changes you want, click on the *Resume* button to continue the proofreading session.

104

Chapter 6: Speller, Thesaurus, and Grammatik

Figure 36. The explanations in the *Advice Box* often contain underlined terms in green type. As the mouse pointer passes over these terms it changes into a question mark, indicating that you can access an explanation for that term. This also happens when you put the mouse cursor over the *Rule Class* explanation. To access an explanation for any of these terms, simply click on them with the mouse.

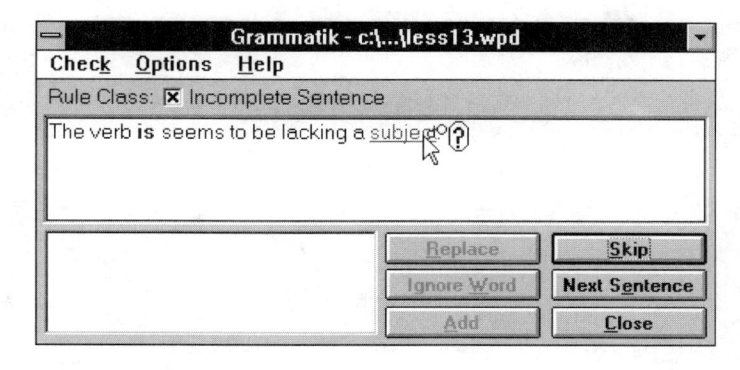

Figure 37. WordPerfect then displays their explanations in the *Help* dialog box.

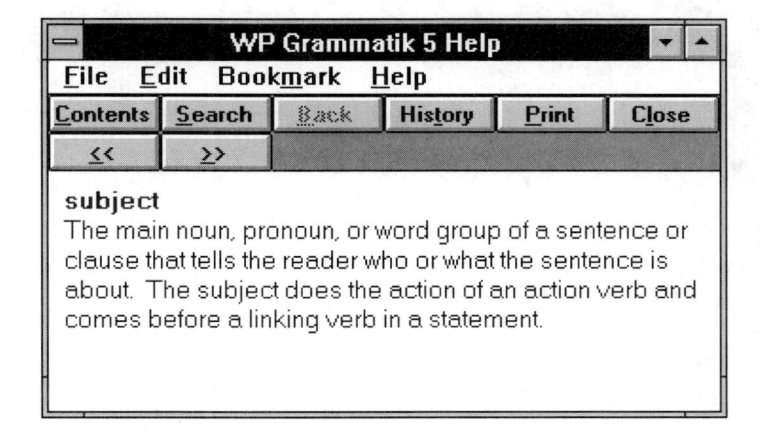

Figure 38. At any time you can also select the *Rule Class* command from the **Help** menu if you want an involved explanation of the rule class that Grammatik is listing as a problem in your document. WordPerfect then displays the rule class explanation in the *Help* dialog box.

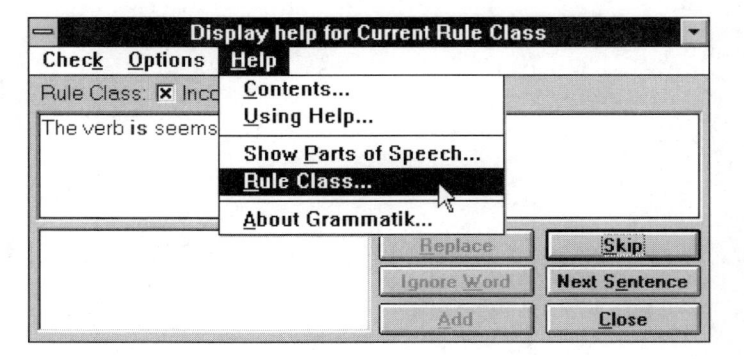

105

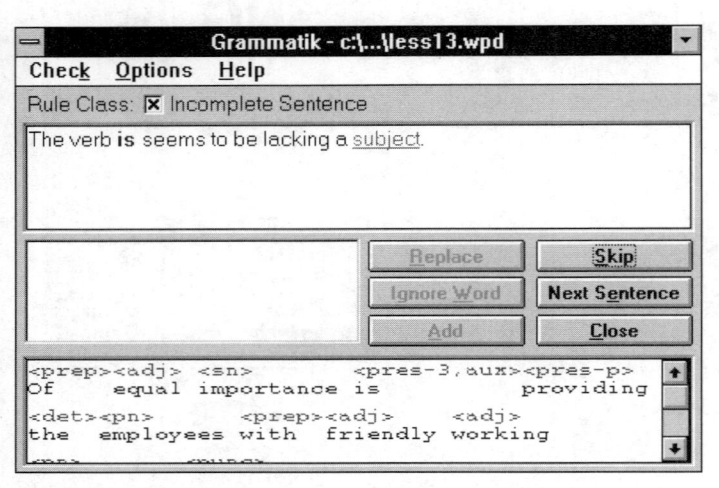

Figure 39. Choose *Show Parts of Speech* from the **Help** menu if you want to see how Grammatik analyses the current sentence that it is checking. This activates a new window at the bottom of the *Grammatik* window. Select *Hide Parts of Speech* to close this window again.

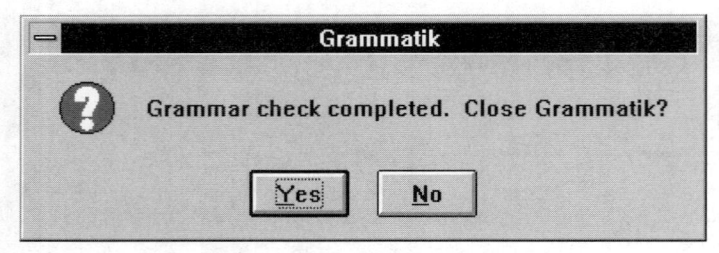

Figure 40. When Grammatik is finished, a prompt box appears. Click on *Yes* to close Grammatik and return to your document.

PRINTING 7

PREVIEWING DOCUMENTS

Figure 1. It is often a good idea to preview your documents before you print to make sure that the page layout is exactly how you want it. However, WordPerfect no longer has a specific print preview command. This is because the various page and zoom views now allow you to preview your document exactly as it will print.

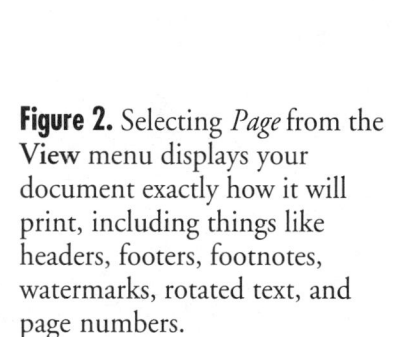

Figure 2. Selecting *Page* from the **View** menu displays your document exactly how it will print, including things like headers, footers, footnotes, watermarks, rotated text, and page numbers.

If you want to preview the overall layout of your document you can select *Two Page* from the **View** menu. This displays your document in a zoomed out view with two consecutive pages of your document side by side. This allows you to see the overall effect of the facing pages in your

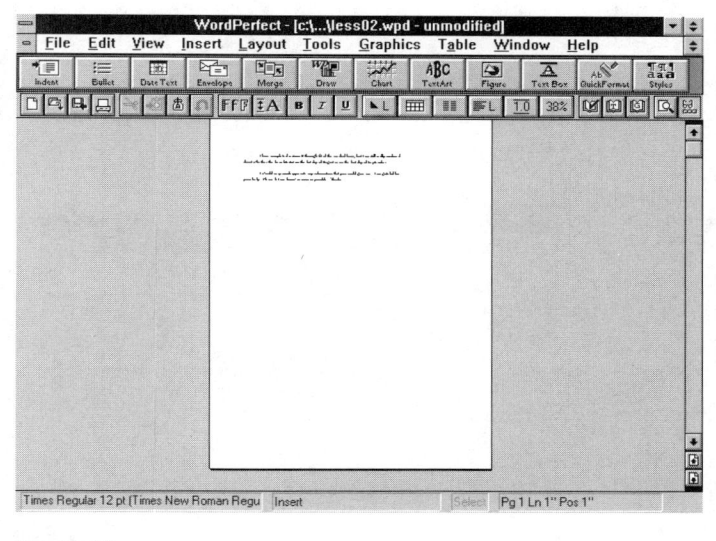

107

document and how page elements such as graphics and text interact on the page.

You can also use the *Zoom* button on the power bar to zoom your document to different magnifications to view your layout changes.

Printing Documents

You can print your documents in WordPerfect with either the *Print* command in the **File** menu or the *Print* button on the power bar. The options connected with printing from WordPerfect are extremely varied, allowing you to customize the way you print the document.

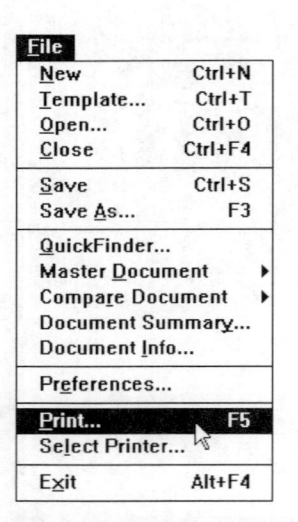

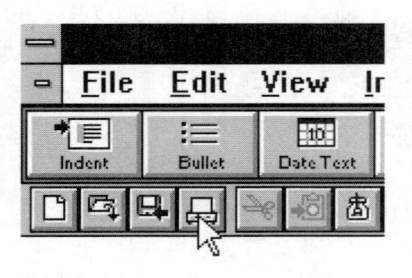

Figure 3. Selecting *Print* from the File menu, or clicking on the *Print* button on the power bar activates the *Print* dialog box.

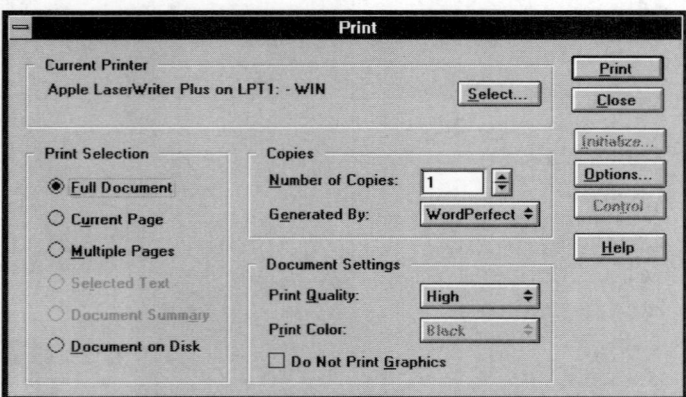

Figure 4. The *Print* dialog box gives you access to a variety of printing functions to help you print your document, or parts of your document, exactly as you want.

Chapter 7: Printing

SELECTING PRINTERS

Figure 5. The *Current Printer* section of this dialog box lists the currently selected printer that WordPerfect will print to. Clicking on the *Select* button in this section of the dialog box invokes the *Select Printer* dialog box.

In this dialog box you can modify the printer settings. To change the printer, select a different printer name from the *Printers* list box.

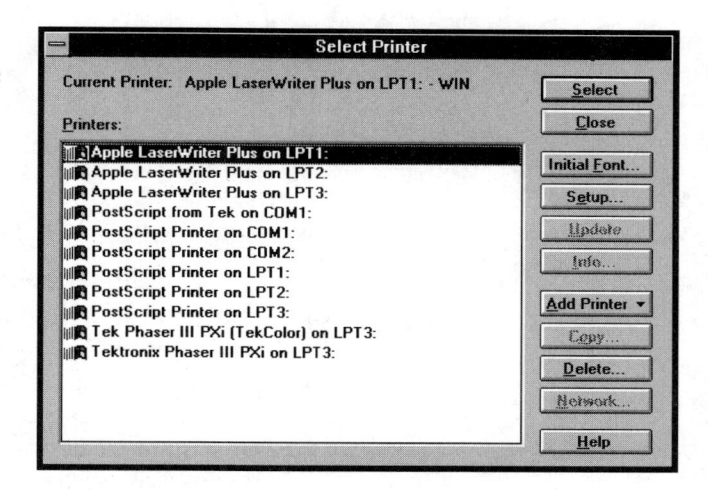

This dialog box also gives you access to many printer functions including setting the initial printer font, the printer setup, the ability to add and delete printers and to use network printing. To accept any changes you make in this dialog box, click on *OK*.

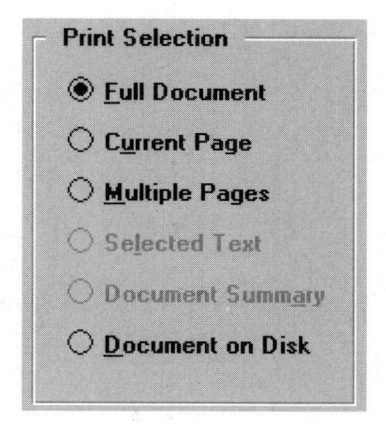

Figure 6. The *Print Selection* section of the *Print* dialog box allows you to decide what portion of your document you want to print.

Selecting *Full Document*, *Current Page* or *Selected Text* prints the ranges of text specified in relation to the cursor position.

Multiple Pages allows you to select the pages, or page range that you want to print.

Selecting *Document Summary* allows you to print only the document summaries of selected files and *Document on Disk* lets you print a file on a disk without opening the file first.

109

Chapter 7: Printing

Figure 7. The *Copies* section of the *Print* dialog box allows you to specify how many copies of your document you want to print, and where they will be generated from.

Increase or decrease the number of copies of your document you want to print using the arrows shown.

You can also decide where multiple copies are generated, in WordPerfect or in the printer. If WordPerfect is selected from the *Generated By* pop-up list, WordPerfect creates multiple copies of your document and sends these to the printer. These will print as collated sets. If *Printer* is selected, the printer simply generates multiple copies of each page that it receives from WordPerfect.

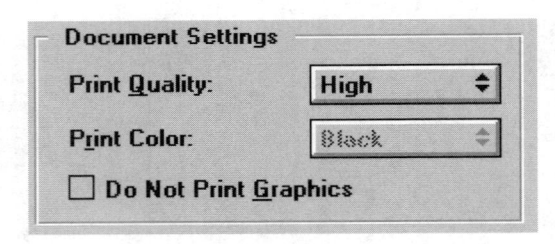

Figure 8. The *Document Settings* section of the dialog box allows you to select print settings for your entire document.

Print Quality lets you determine the overall quality of the printout. The lower the print quality, the less time it takes to print. You can also specify print colors and whether you want to print graphics in your document from here.

Figure 9. The *Initialize* button in the *Print* dialog box allows you to download soft fonts to your printer before the print job starts.

Figure 10. The *Options* button allows you to access the *Print Output Options* dialog box. Here you can choose options like reverse order printing, odd/even page printing, and more. You can even specify how the copies will come out of the printer.

When you have set all of the printing options as you want them, the *Print* button starts the print job and sends it to the printer.

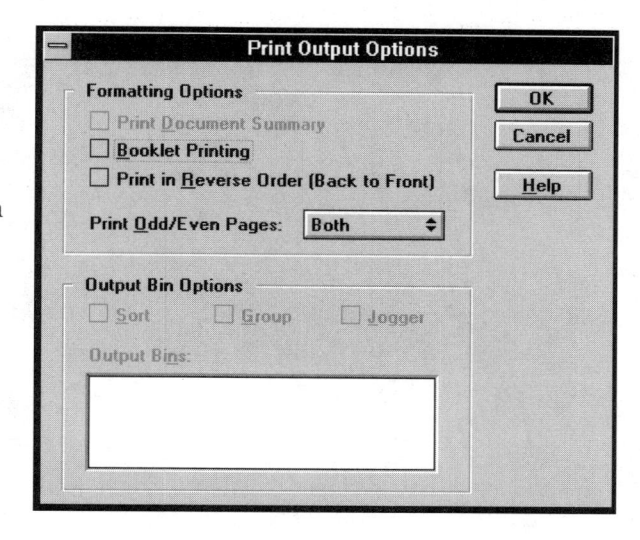

TABLES 8

WORDPERFECT TABLES

The table features of WordPerfect lets you create professional-looking tables, schedules, worksheets, calendars, and other tabular layouts as well as giving you access to spreadsheet capabilities. Tables allow you to arrange information into multiple rows and columns that are specific to your needs. You can manipulate this information in various ways using the range of commands available through the **Table** menu.

CREATING TABLES

Figure 1. You can create tables in WordPerfect by selecting the *Create* command from the **Table** menu.

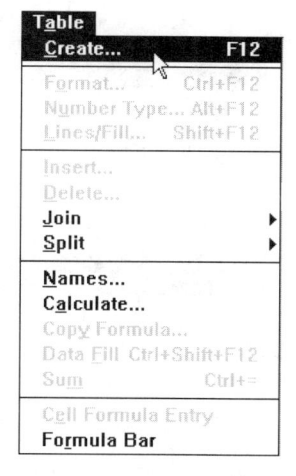

Figure 2. This is the *Create Table* dialog box that you activate through the *Create* command.

113

Chapter 8: Tables

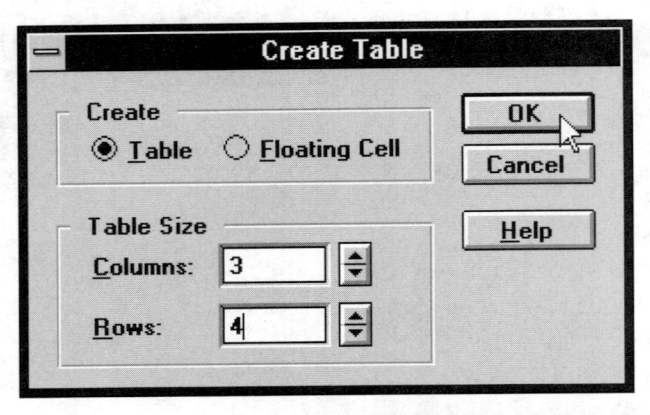

Figure 3. In the *Create Table* dialog box, key in the number of columns and rows you want into the appropriate boxes and click on *OK*.

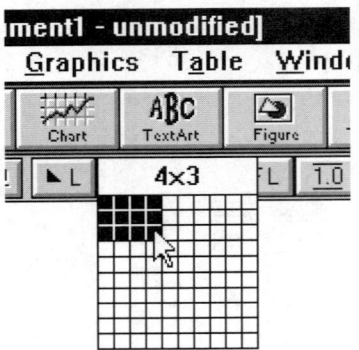

Figure 4. Alternatively, to create a table, you can click on the *Table Quick Create* button on the power bar. This activates a grid representing the number of rows and columns you want to include in your table. Simply drag the cursor to highlight table settings that you want.

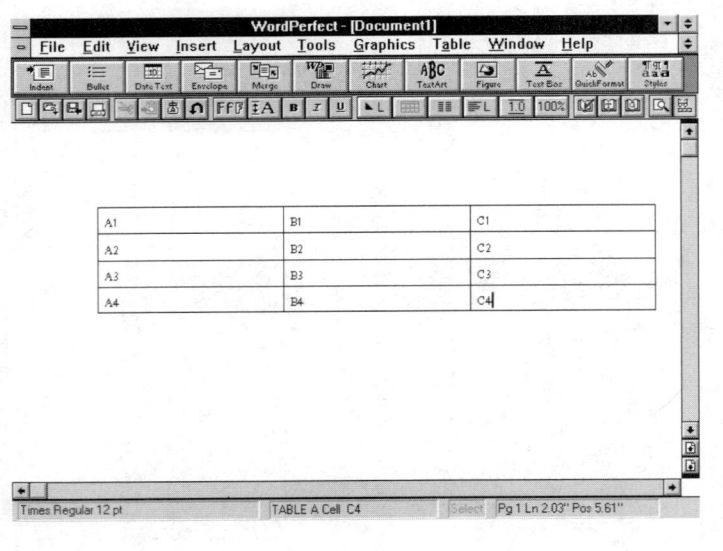

Figure 5. The table is now displayed on screen. A table consists of intersecting rows and columns that form cells. Each cell can contain text, graphics, numbers, or formulas. To type text into a cell, put the insertion point inside the required cell and start typing. Use the Tab key to move to the next cell, and the Shift+Tab keys to return you to the previous cell. This allows you to move around the table without using the mouse. Alternatively, the arrow keys on your keyboard also move you between cells in the table.

114

The text we typed into this table shows how WordPerfect references individual cells within a table. Columns are referenced by letters and rows by numbers. Thus the cell created by the intersection of column A with row 3 is called cell A3. When the cursor is inside a cell, its reference is shown in the status bar.

SELECTING CELLS

Figure 6. To select individual cells, move the mouse to the left-hand side of a cell until you see a left arrow, then click the mouse. Double-click to select the full row.

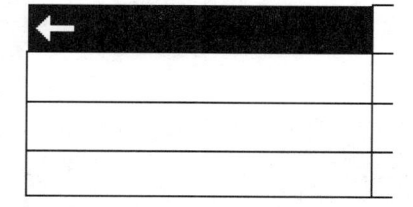

Figure 7. You can also select a cell by moving the mouse to the top of a cell until it becomes an upward arrow, then click the mouse. Double-click to select the full column.

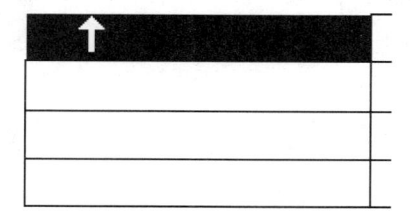

Figure 8. To select the whole table, click and drag the mouse from the top-left cell to the bottom-right. When the entire table is highlighted, release the mouse button. Using this approach, you can select as many adjoining cells as you like.

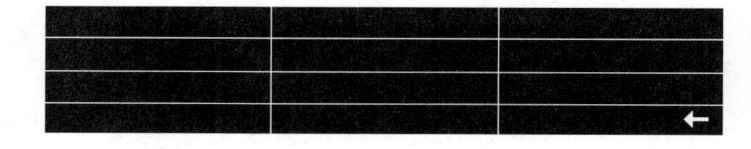

Alternatively, you can select the full table by triple-clicking when either the vertical or horizontal mouse pointer arrows are visible.

Chapter 8: Tables

SELECTING TEXT IN CELLS

Figure 9. You select text inside individual cells as you would normally select text in WordPerfect. That is, by either dragging over text with the mouse or by double-clicking. You edit text in the table the same way you would edit text in your document.

Figure 10. To select all text in a table, click and hold down the mouse button in the top-left cell and drag it down and to the right. As you move down, all cells you drag over become highlighted. Keep dragging the cursor past the table so that the highlighting of the cells switches to the text. You can now change or delete the text attributes.

THE TABLE MENU

Figure 11. Once you have created your table, you can edit its structure and contents through the various commands in the **Table** menu.

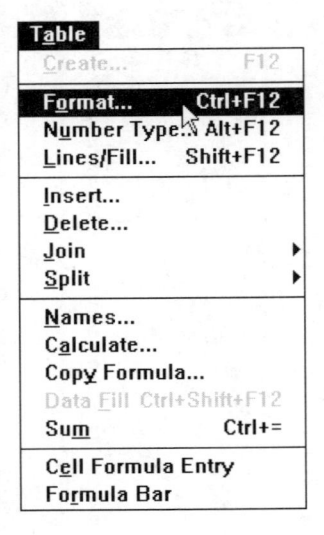

116

FORMATTING TEXT IN TABLES

Figure 12. To format the text in your table, insert the text cursor somewhere in the table and select the *Format* command from the **Table** menu. This opens the *Format* dialog box. Here you can format the contents of cells, columns, rows, or the entire table.

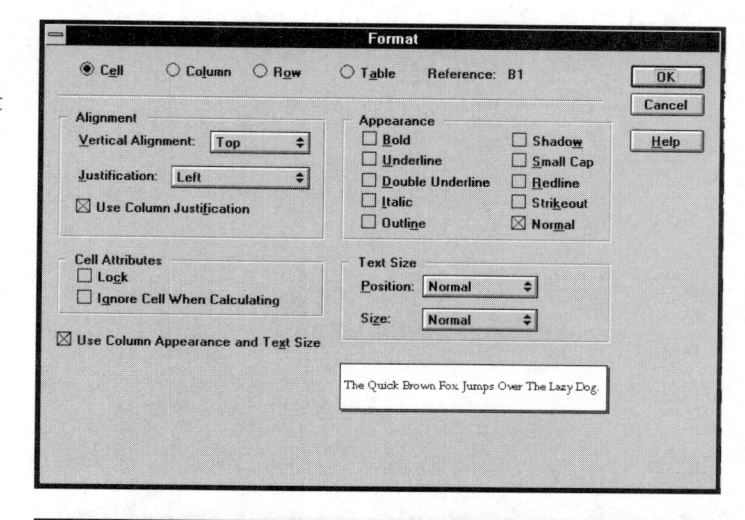

Figure 13. Selecting a radio button activates the dialog box choices for that table element. For instance, selecting the *Column* radio button activates a set of choices specific to formatting entire columns in your table.

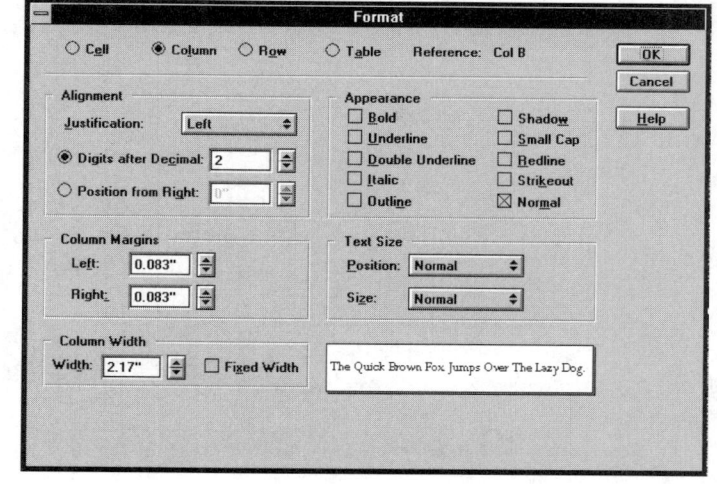

Figure 14. Choices made for cells, columns, and rows affect the cell ranges in relation to the "reference." "Reference" refers to the current cursor location in your table or any cells you selected before activating the *Format* dialog box.

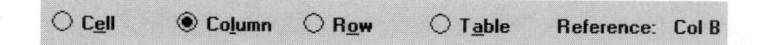

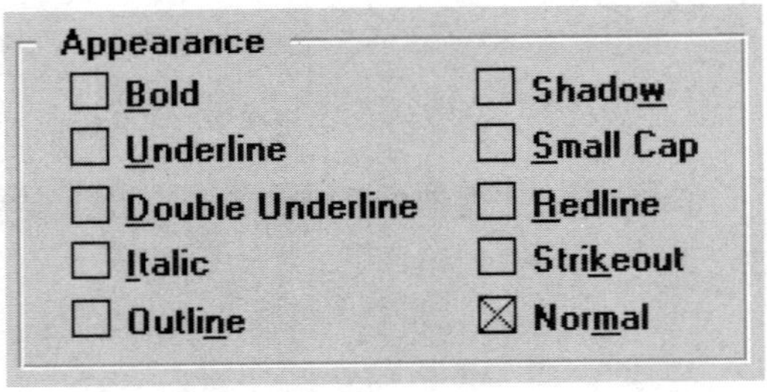

Figure 15. Use the *Appearance, Text Size,* and *Alignment* sections of the dialog box to change the appearance, size, and alignment of text for cells, columns, or the entire table. The remaining choices are specific to which radio button you select and these let you format your table contents exactly as you wish.

CELLS

Figure 16. The remaining choices available for the *Cell* radio button affect the text in the selected cells. The first option available in the *Cell Attributes* section of the dialog box is the *Lock* option. This protects the contents of selected cells so that you can't change the information until you deselect this option.

If you select *Ignore Cell When Calculating* for a selected cell, WordPerfect ignores this cell when calculating a formula. (See the **Formula Bar** section from Figure 42 onwards for using formulas within tables.)

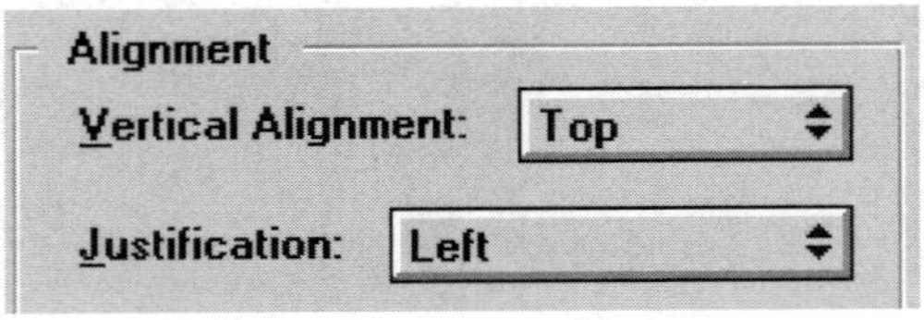

Figure 17. The *Alignment* section of the dialog box lets you select how the text sits in each selected cell. The options available in the *Justification* pop-up list apply to the horizontal positioning of text within cells.

The *Vertical Alignment* options determine the vertical alignment of text. The changes you make to the alignment of text don't appear in the document, but do display in the *Print Preview*.

Figure 18. When you select the *Use Column Justification* option, WordPerfect allows the *Justification* settings of the *Column* choices to override the cell's justification settings. Column justification normally applies to all cells in that column.

Figure 19. The *Use Column Appearance and Text Size* option works in the same way and applies to the choices available in the *Appearance* and *Size* sections of the dialog box.

COLUMNS

Figure 20. Selecting the *Column* radio button in the *Format* dialog box activates different options. These options affect the whole column that the cursor is in.

The *Digits after Decimal* option in the *Alignment* section of the dialog box lets you determine the number of digits that appear after a decimal point for numbers within the column. The *Position from Right* option determines the distance the decimal point is from the right of the cells in a column.

The *Column Margins* section of the dialog box allows you to set the left and right margins for the current column whereas the *Column Width* option allows you to change the width of selected columns.

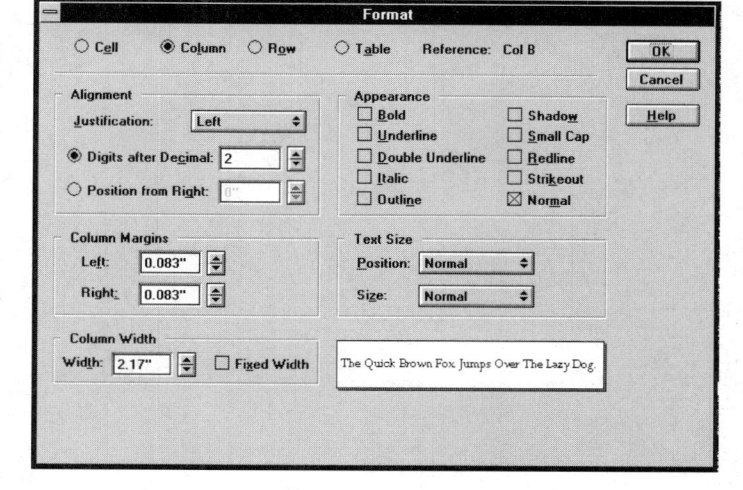

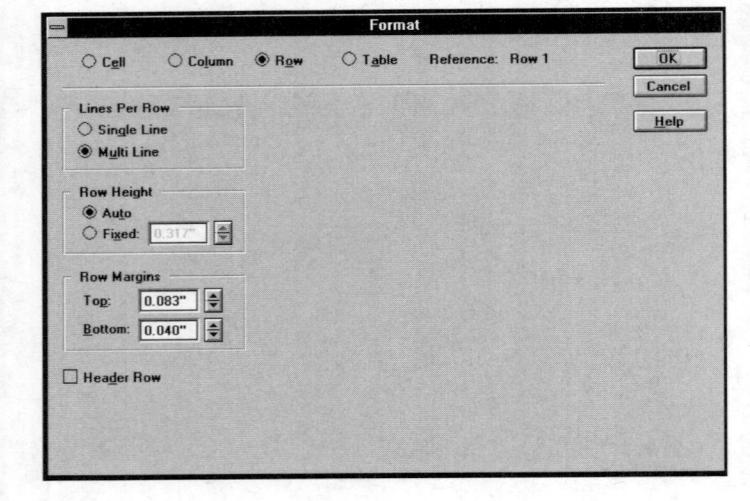

Figure 21. You can also adjust the width of a column directly in the table. If you position the cursor over a column divider in the table, it changes to a two way arrow. When this occurs you can click and drag the column divider to a new width.

If you hold the Ctrl key down while you reposition one of these markers, the right margin of the document also moves.

ROWS

Figure 22. Selecting the *Row* radio button activates these choices in the *Format* dialog box.

The *Single Line* option in the *Lines Per Row* section ensures that only one line of text appears in a cell. The *Multi Line* option allows more than one line of text and "wraps" the contents within the cell.

If you select the *Auto* option in the *Row Height* section, WordPerfect automatically adjusts the height of the row according to the current font. If you have the *Fixed* option selected, you can type in the height you want.

The *Row Margins* section allows you to determine the margins for text in your rows in relation to the top and bottom of cells.

TABLES

Figure 23. Selecting the *Table* radio button activates the options shown here. The choices combine many of the choices from the *Cell*, *Column*, and *Row* options. However, these choices apply formatting to the entire table.

The *Table Position* section of this dialog box lets you position the table horizontally on the page or to specify a measurement from the left edge of the page. The rest of the choices in this dialog box act in the same way as the other radio buttons' choices described earlier.

NUMBER TYPES

Figure 24. You can also determine the format for the type of numbers you want to include in your table through the *Number Type* command in the **Table** menu. Selecting this command opens the *Number Type* dialog box.

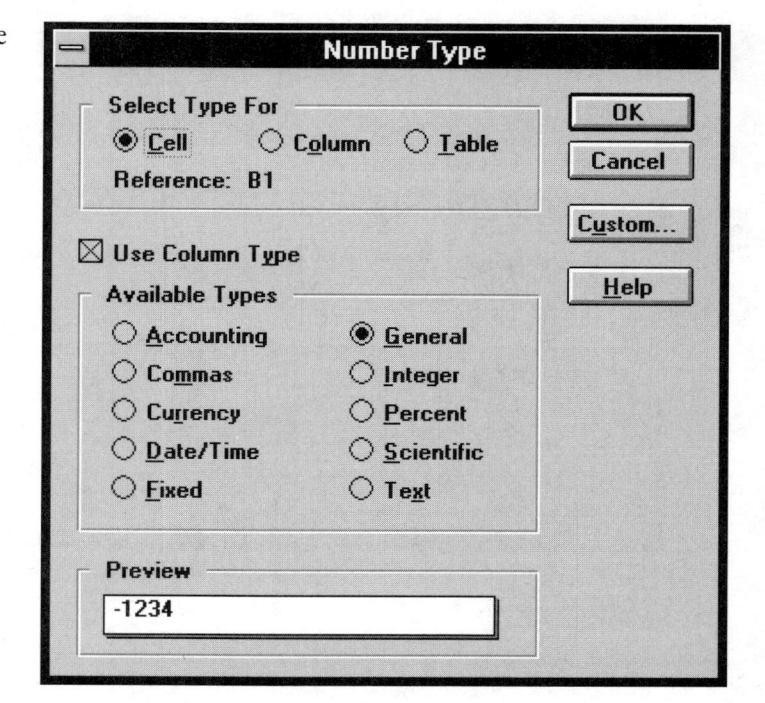

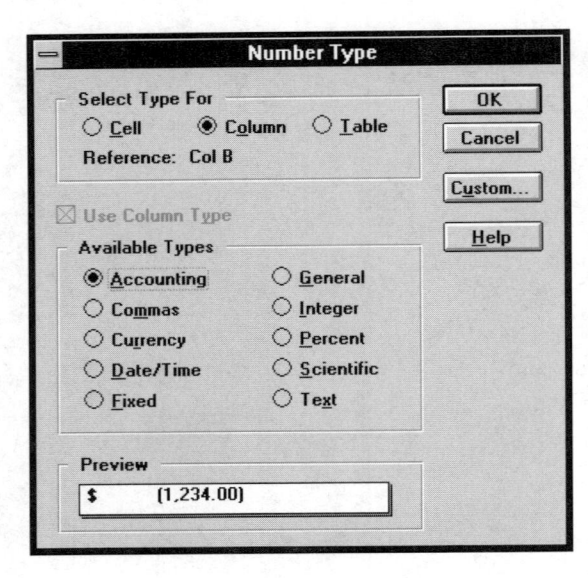

Figure 25. Select the radio buttons in the *Select Type For* section of this dialog box to determine the cell range of the number type that you set. Then select a radio button from the *Available Types* to apply that number type. The *Preview* window displays the format for the number type that you select.

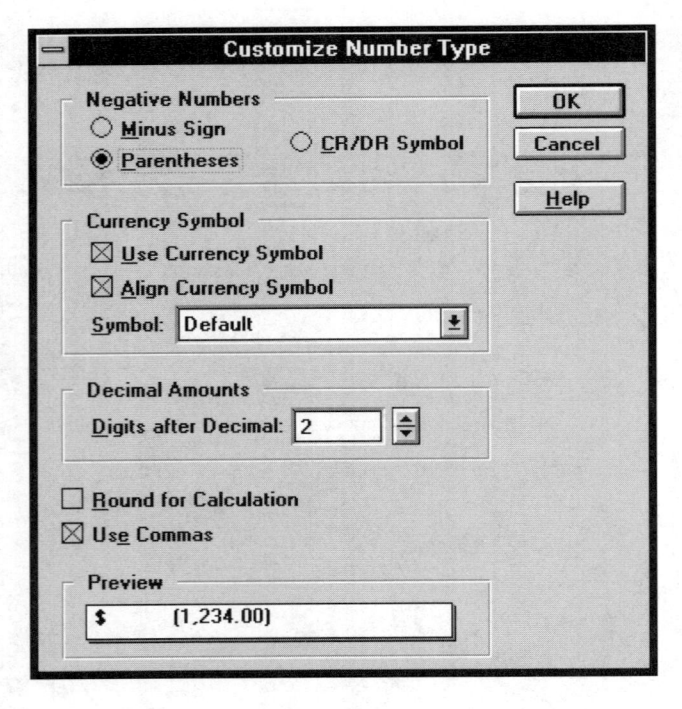

Figure 26. The *Custom* button in the *Number Type* dialog box opens the *Customize Number Type* dialog box. Here you can change settings of the different number type to suit your needs.

Chapter 8: Tables

EDITING THE TABLE STRUCTURE

There are a variety of commands in the **Table** menu that let you edit the structure of your table as you work with it.

LINES/FILL

Figure 27. Select *Lines/Fill* from the **Table** menu to open the *Table Lines/Fill* dialog box. Use the radio buttons at the top of this dialog box to specify whether you are editing the selected cells or the entire table.

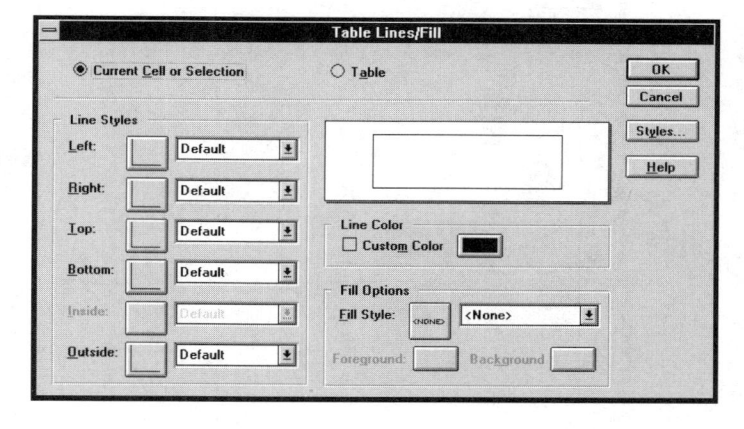

Figure 28. You can then click on the buttons available to change the line, color, and fill options for your table.

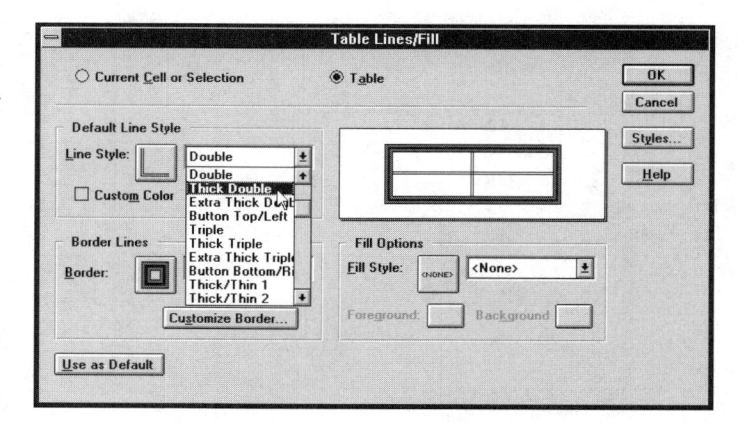

123

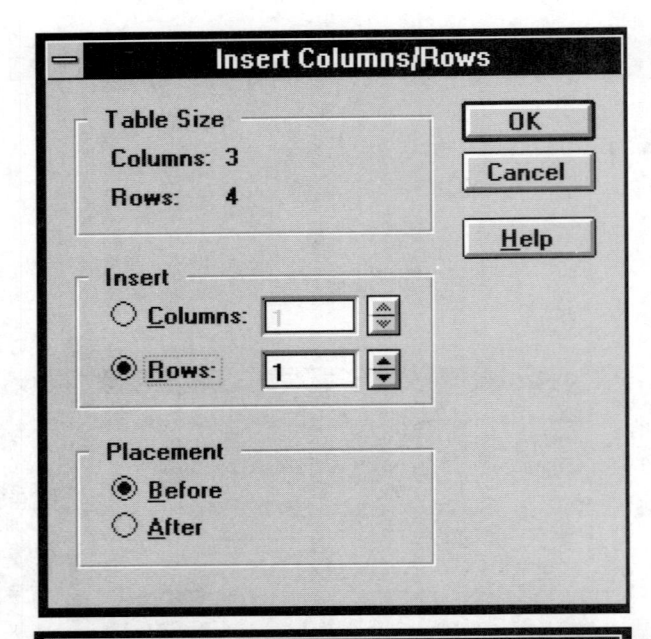

INSERT

Figure 29. Use *Insert* from the Table menu to add new columns and rows into your table. In the *Insert Columns/Rows* dialog box, select a radio button in the *Insert* section to insert either columns or rows. Then use the arrows, or type in the number of columns or rows you want. The *Placement* section of the dialog box allows you to specify if you want to insert the columns or rows before or after the current cursor position.

Figure 30. In this example, we put the cursor in the last column of the table and entered 2 in the *Columns* text box. We then selected the *Before* radio button in the *Placement* section of the dialog box before selecting *OK*.

Figure 31. Note that in this figure, WordPerfect has added two columns to the table in front of the original third column.

DELETE

Figure 32. To delete a row or column, insert the cursor in the column or row you want to remove. Then select *Delete* from the *Tables* submenu in the **Layout** menu. This activates the *Delete* dialog box. Choose the *Columns* or *Rows* radio button (you can't delete both at once), and type in the number of rows or columns you want to delete, then click on *OK*. You can also choose the *Cell Contents* radio button if you want to delete the contents of a cell or selected cells without deleting the structure of the table.

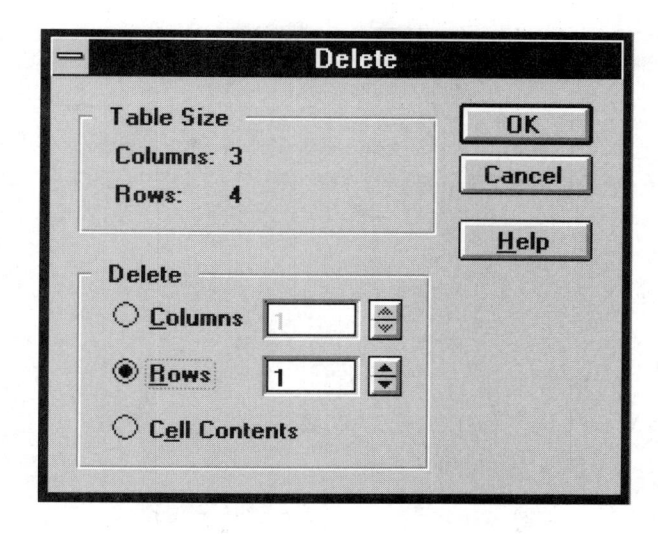

If you highlighted multiple cells, columns, or rows before selecting *Delete*, you don't need to type in a number.

An alternative way of deleting the contents of a row or column without deleting the actual structure of the table is to select the rows or columns and press Backspace or Delete on the keyboard.

Figure 33. If you press the Delete key when you have the whole table selected, you activate the *Delete Table* dialog box. In this case, you have the option of deleting the whole table, just the text, the table structure without deleting the text, or of converting the table to a merge data file (see **Chapter 14**).

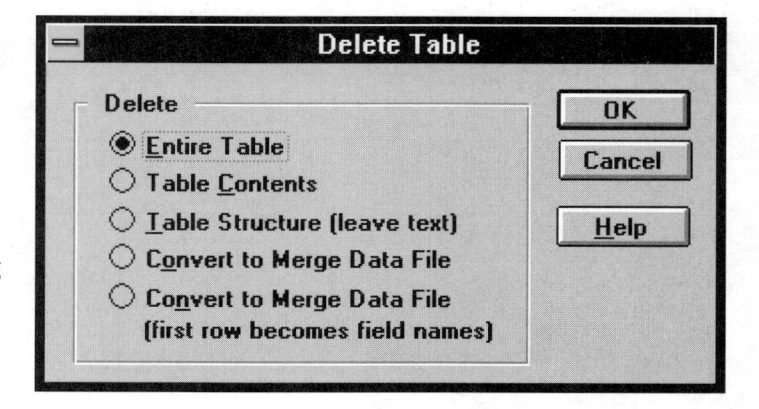

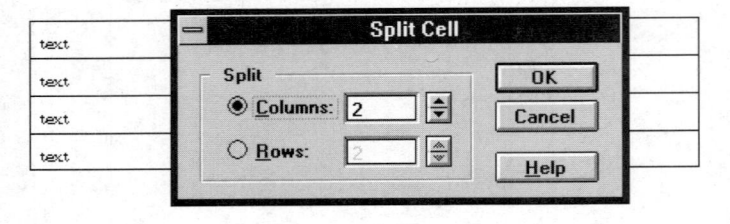

JOIN

Figure 34. The next option in the **Table** menu is the *Join* command. This command joins any cells you have selected so that they become one larger cell or alternatively it lets you join two tables with the same number of columns. Here we selected the first and second cells of row one and then we chose the *Cell* option from the *Join* submenu. They are now one cell.

SPLIT

Figure 35. The *Split* command in the **Table** menu can split any selected cells into a number of smaller cells or split the table itself into two parts. In this example we placed the cursor in the top-left cell of the table and selected *Cell* from the *Split* submenu. In the *Split Cell* dialog box, we placed a "2" in the *Columns* text box.

Figure 36. After you select *OK*, WordPerfect splits the top-left cell into two columns.

WORKING WITH TABLES

WordPerfect also offers a range of ways for you to manipulate and work with the contents of your tables.

CUTTING, COPYING, AND PASTING

Figure 37. You can cut and copy text in cells and then paste it from cell to cell, or even to other sections of your document outside the table. To do this, you must first select the text inside the cell.

Once you select the text, choose either *Cut* or *Copy* from the **Edit** menu.

Figure 38. Insert the cursor where you want the text from the clipboard to go and select *Paste* from the **Edit** menu. WordPerfect pastes the text at the insertion point.

Figure 39. You can also copy and paste certain sections of the table to form another table. If you select the cells of a table and then choose *Copy* or *Cut* from the **Edit** menu, the *Table Cut/Copy* dialog box is activated.

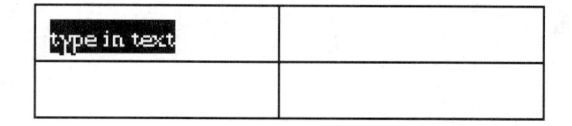

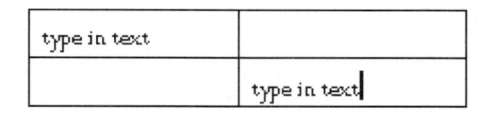

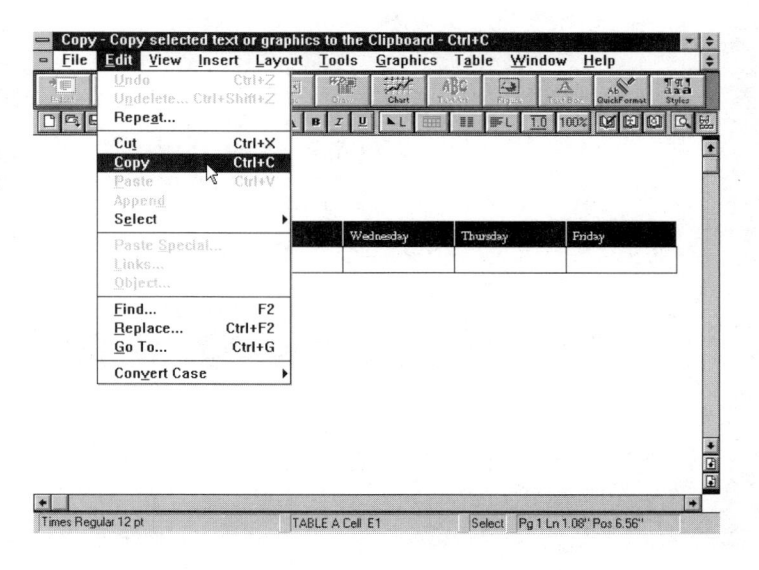

Chapter 8: Tables

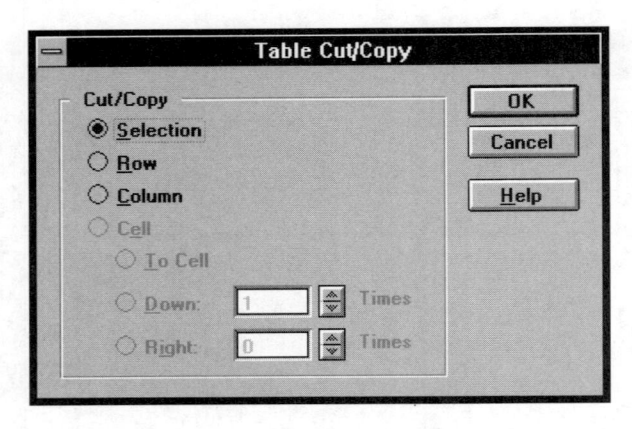

Figure 40. In the *Table Cut/Copy* dialog box, you can cut or copy the selection of cells, or the rows or columns that the selected cell or cells are in.

Figure 41. If you choose the *Selection* option before clicking on *OK*, put the cursor outside the table and select *Paste*. The new table appears at the insertion point.

THE FORMULA BAR

Figure 42. Choose *Formula Bar* from the **Table** menu to activate the *Table Formula* feature bar. This gives you access to powerful spreadsheet capabilities in WordPerfect.

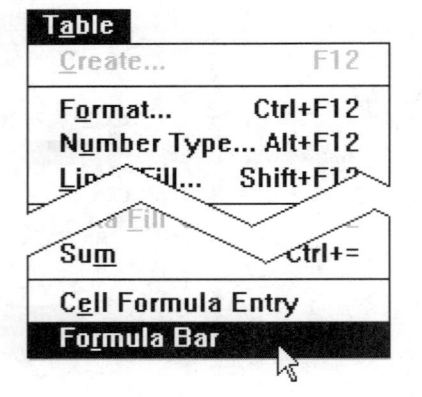

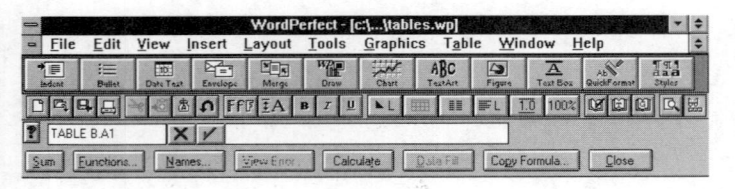

Figure 43. The *Table Formula* feature bar appears at the top of the editing window with a number of buttons that allow you to create and insert formulas into your tables.

INSERTING FORMULAS

Insert a formula into a cell by clicking in the *Formula Edit* text box on the *Table Formula* feature bar. The bar then displays "Formula Edit Mode Is On." You can enter formulas that include cell names, formula functions, and mathematical operations such as "A1+A3" to add the values in cells A1 and A3. (For more information see your *WordPerfect Reference Manual*).

Turn the formula edit mode off and return to your cell by clicking the *Cancel* button ⊠, or click on the *Insert* button ✓ to insert the formula into the cell.

Note: A cell containing a formula displays the result of the formula only. A cell's formula displays in the feature bar for you to edit.

Figure 44. The *Table Formula* feature bar contains buttons for accessing spreadsheet functions. The *Sum* button allows you to calculate the sum of the cells above or to the left of the current cell. If there are values above and to the left of the current cell, highlight the current cell and the cells of the values you want to add and then click the *Sum* button.

Figure 45. The *Functions* button activates the *Table Functions* dialog box listing the available functions that you can include in your formulas.

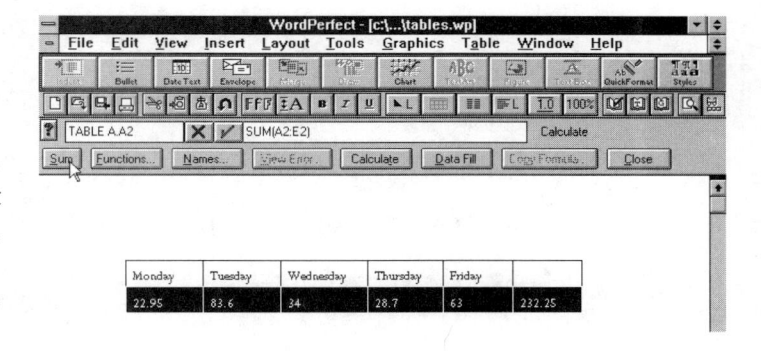

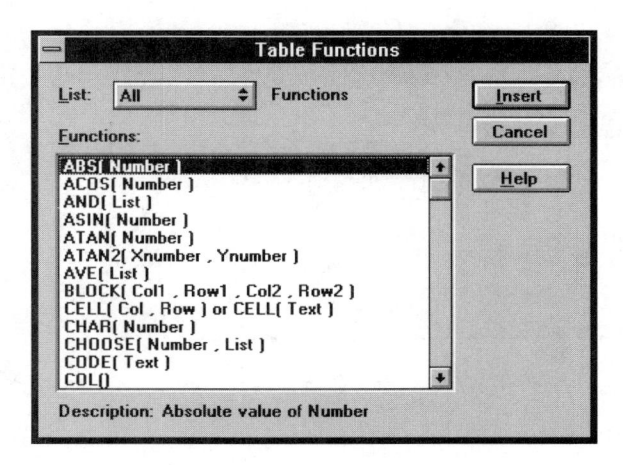

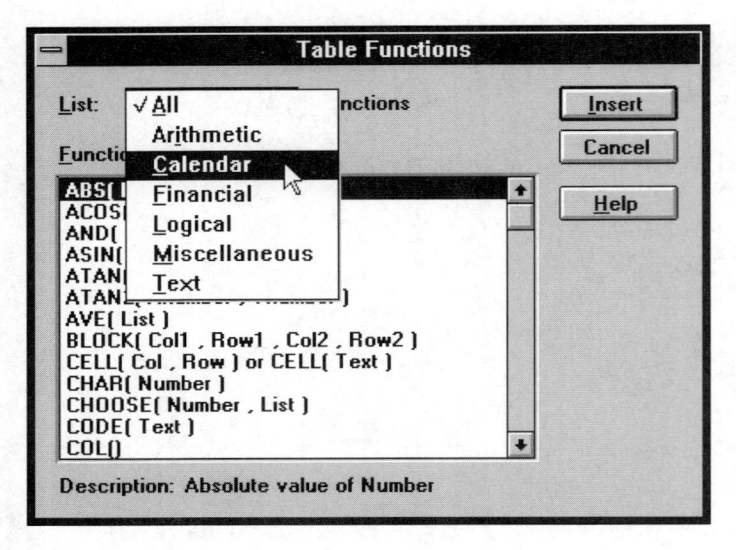

Figure 46. The *List* drop-down list allows you to display different function lists in the *Functions* list box. To insert a function into a cell's formula, select it from the list and click the *Insert* button. This inserts the function into the *Formula Edit* text box on the *Table Formula* feature bar (see your *WordPerfect Reference Manual* for the meanings and use of the available functions).

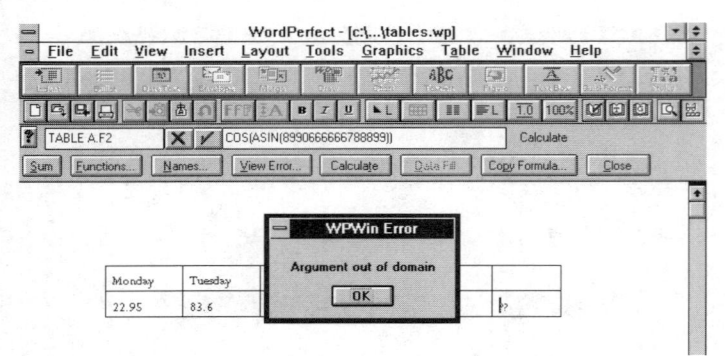

Figure 47. Occasionally when you insert a formula into a cell, the cell displays a double question mark "??." This means that the formula contains an error and WordPerfect cannot determine the formula's value. To see an explanation of the formula error, click on the *View Error* button.

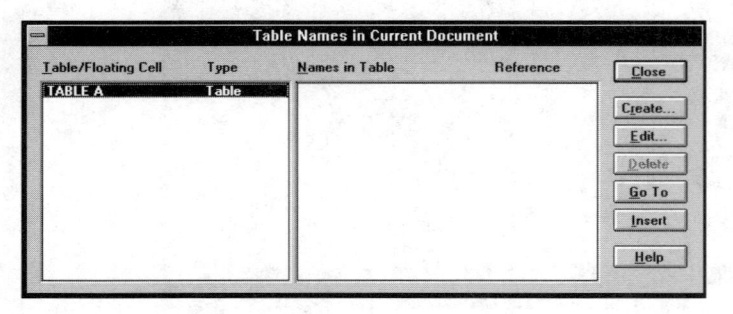

NAMING TABLES

Figure 48. The *Names* button opens the *Table Names in Current Document* dialog box where you can create or edit names for your tables, cells, or cell ranges. You can then use these descriptive names to help organize and simplify your formulas.

Figure 49. To create names for your cells or cell ranges, click on the *Create* button in the *Table Names in Current Document* dialog box. This opens the *Create Name* dialog box where you can type a name for a cell, cell range, column, or row. You can also decide to name the cells using the contents of the cell or surrounding cells. Click on *OK* to accept the name you specify and to list it in the *Names in Table* section of the *Table Names in Current Document* dialog box.

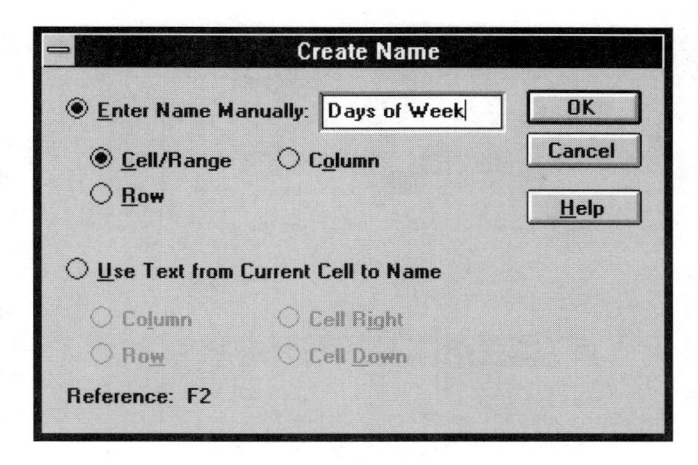

You can also access any cell or table that you have named by clicking on the *Go To* button in the *Table Names in Current Document* dialog box. Also, you can insert a name into a formula using the *Insert* button.

CALCULATING FORMULAS

The *Calculate* button is used to calculate all of the table formulas in your current document. This can be important when you are changing values in cells that are used in formulas because the formula value is not updated when you change the cell's value.

DATA FILL

The *Data Fill* button allows you to continue a pattern of values across rows or down columns. For instance, if you enter "Mon" and "Tue" in consecutive cells of a row, you can fill the entire row beyond them with the remaining days of the week using the *Data Fill* button.

Chapter 8: Tables

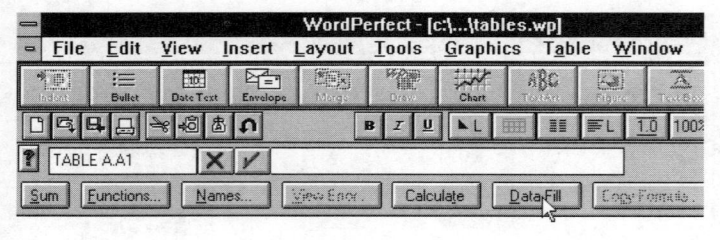

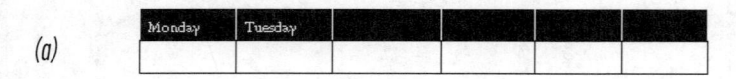

Figure 50. To do this, highlight the first two cells and extend the highlight to the end of the row. Then click on the *Data Fill* button (a). WordPerfect automatically fills the row with the incrementing value (b). You can also do this with numbers, roman numerals and months, as long as there is a pattern that WordPerfect can recognize and continue.

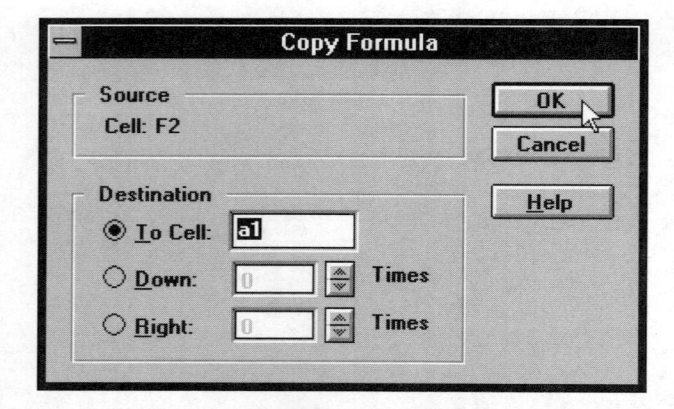

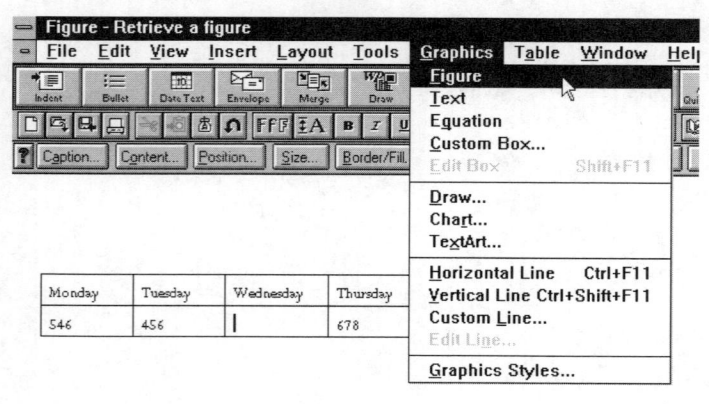

COPYING FORMULAS

Figure 51. The *Copy Formula* button allows you to copy formulas from one cell to another. In the *Copy Formula* dialog box, specify a destination cell and click on *OK* to copy the current cell's formula.

PUTTING GRAPHICS IN TABLES

Figure 52. To place a graphic inside a table, insert the cursor in the cell where you want the graphic to appear, and retrieve the graphic in the normal way (see **Chapter 11**).

Chapter 8: Tables

Figure 53. Once you've retrieved a graphic into the table the *Graphics Box* feature bar appears, allowing you to work with it as you would work with a normal graphic.

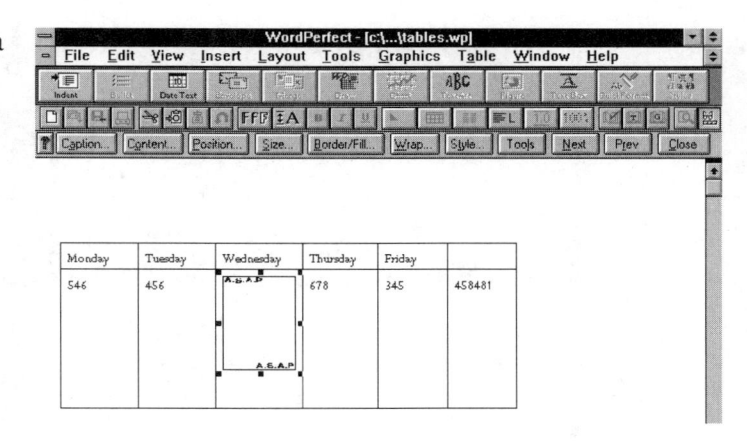

Figure 54. You can move a graphic to other cells in your table, or out of the table completely by dragging it with the mouse. You can also drag a graphic into the table with the mouse.

CREATING TABLES FROM EXISTING TEXT

Figure 55. You can convert text that is already on the page in a table. Select the text you want included in the table and then select *Create* from the **Table** menu.

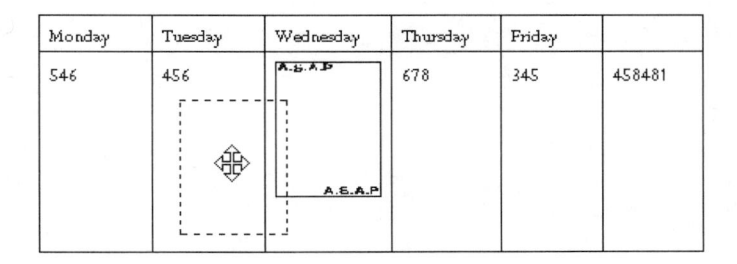

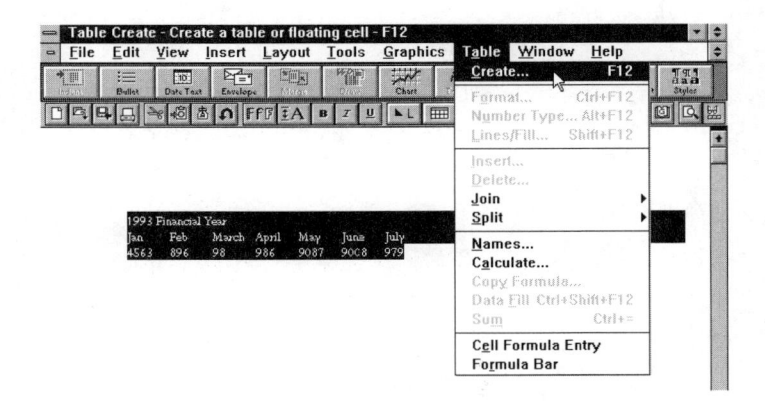

133

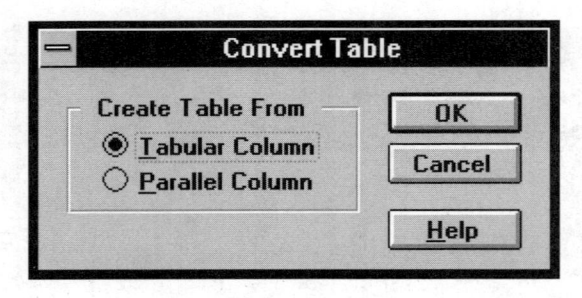

Figure 56. The *Convert Table* dialog box that WordPerfect displays gives you two choices. If the sections of the text are separated with tabs, select the *Tabular Column* option. If the text is arranged in parallel columns, select the *Parallel Column* option and click on *OK*.

Figure 57. This is the result of selecting the *Tabular Column* option. The text is now in a table that you can edit with the commands from the **Table** menu.

CHARTS 9

WORDPERFECT CHART

WordPerfect now includes a powerful charting feature that provides an easy, visual way of displaying information.

CHARTING YOUR TABLES

The quickest and possibly most useful way of using the *Chart* feature is to chart information in tables you have created in your document.

Figure 1. To chart the information in your tables you first have to select the table, or the portion of the table, that you want to chart. To do this, click and drag the mouse pointer from the first to the last cell in your table, highlighting the information that you want to include in your chart (for more information on tables, see **Chapter 8**).

Once you have done this, select *Chart* from the **Graphics** menu or click on the *Chart* button on the button bar.

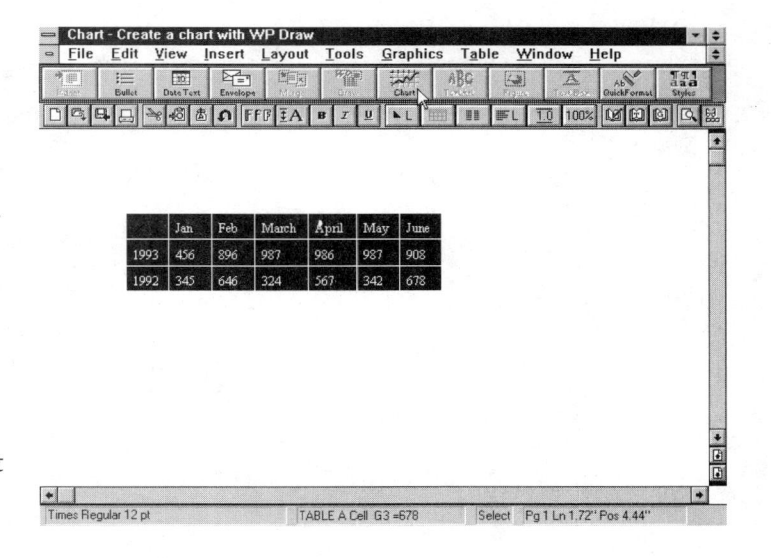

135

Chapter 9: Charts

THE CHART EDITOR

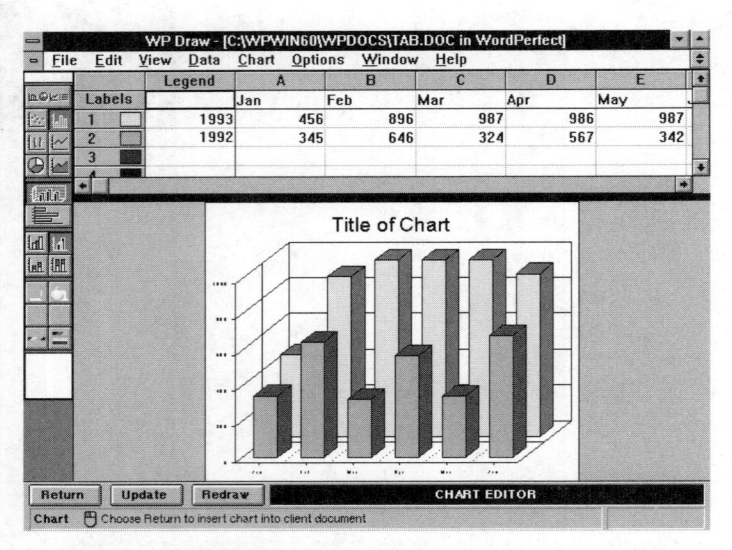

Figure 2. Selecting the *Chart* command opens the Chart Editor in the WP Draw application (see **Chapter 12** for more information on WP Draw).

The Chart Editor is divided into two sections, the chart section and the data section.

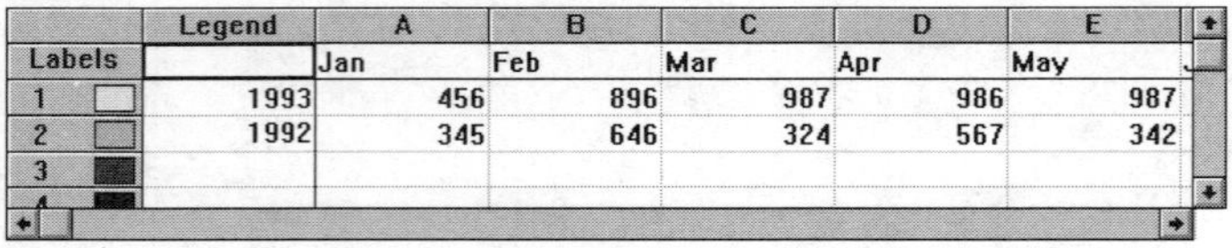

Figure 3. The data section of the Chart Editor displays your table information in a new table setup. You can now select and edit any cells in this table to suit your needs.

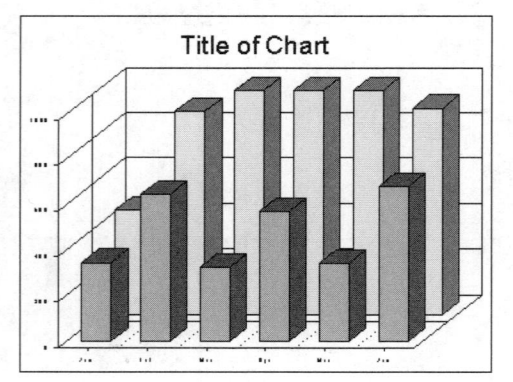

Figure 4. Below the data section of the Chart Editor is the chart itself. This chart displays the information contained in the table above. Currently the information in the table is displayed as a three-dimensional bar chart.

Figure 5. You can redraw the chart to include any changes that you make to the data section of the Chart Editor by clicking on the *Redraw* button.

Chapter 9: Charts

CHANGING CHART TYPES AND STYLES

Figure 6. You can display your table information as different types of charts through the **Chart** menu. Selecting this menu gives you a choice of six basic chart types, as well as allowing you to access the Chart Gallery.

Select *Gallery* from the **Chart** menu to open the *Chart Gallery* dialog box.

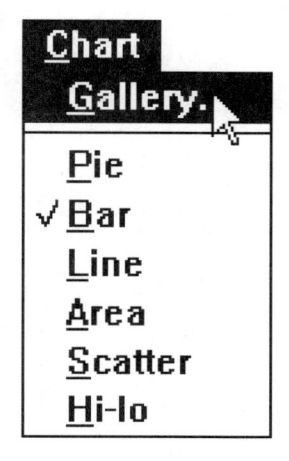

Figure 7. In the *Chart Gallery* dialog box you can choose from a variety of chart types and styles. The current display gives you access to different chart styles for bar charts. To change the type of chart, click on the *Chart Types* button.

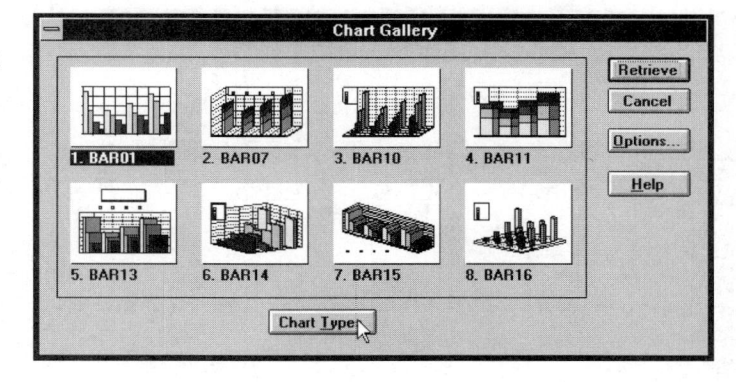

Figure 8. The *Chart Gallery* dialog box now displays the various chart types that you can choose from. The currently active chart type has its title highlighted in the dialog box. To select another chart type, simply click on it with the mouse. For example, to display your table as a line chart, click on the *Line Chart* icon or its title.

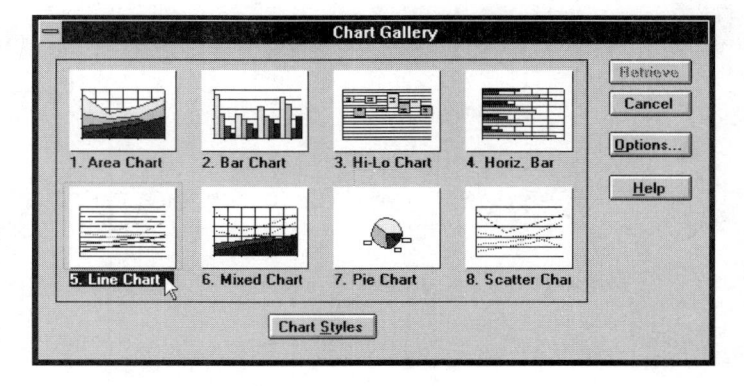

137

Chapter 9: Charts

Figure 9. You can now choose between a variety of line chart styles by clicking on the *Chart Styles* button.

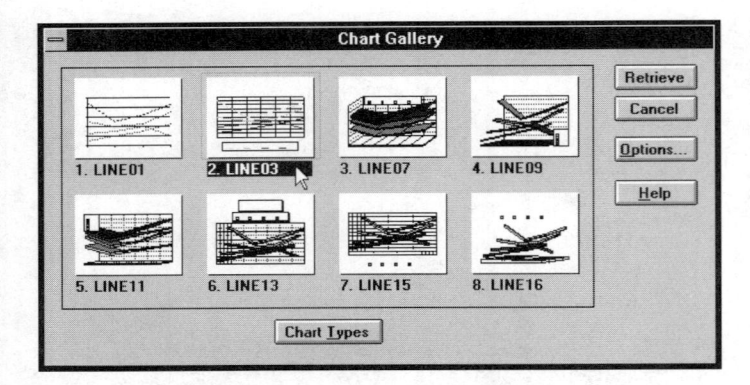

Figure 10. The dialog box now displays the various styles of line charts that you can choose. To select a chart style and return to your document, simply double-click on one of the available options.

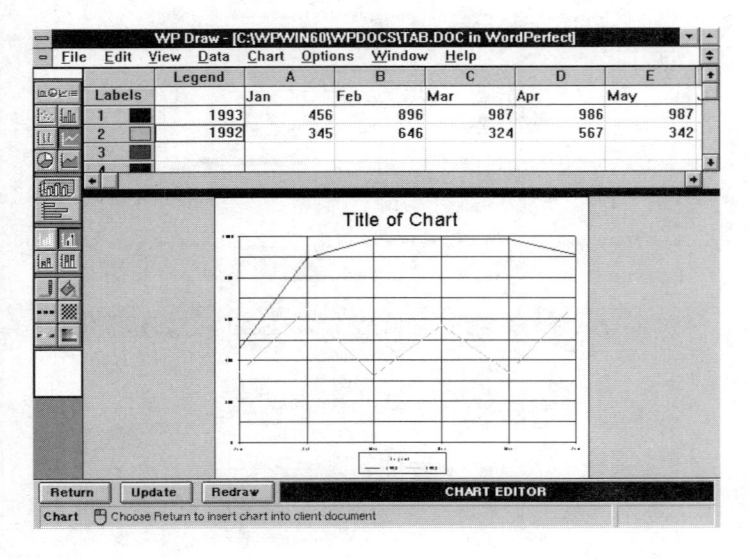

Figure 11. In this example we double-clicked on the second chart style option "LINE03." The *Chart Editor* now redraws the chart to display your information as a line chart.

138

Chapter 9: Charts

CHART TITLES

Figure 12. You can add a title to your chart at any time by selecting *Titles* from the **Options** menu.

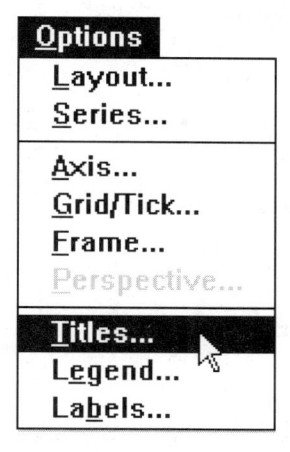

Figure 13. This opens the *Titles* dialog box with "Title of Chart" highlighted in the *Titles* text box.

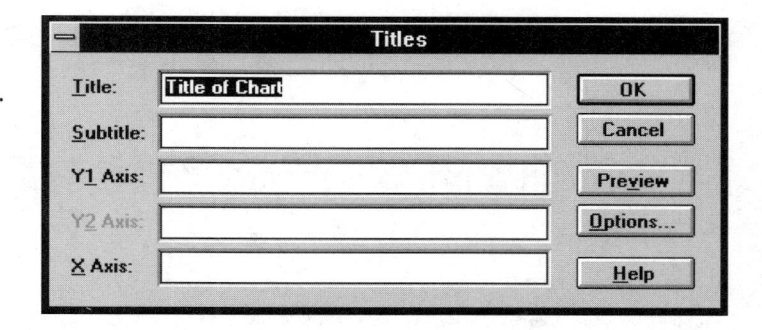

Figure 14. To add a title to your chart, simply enter it here. You can also add a subtitle and label the *X* and *Y* axis in this dialog box. Click *OK* to accept any changes you make and return to the Chart Editor.

139

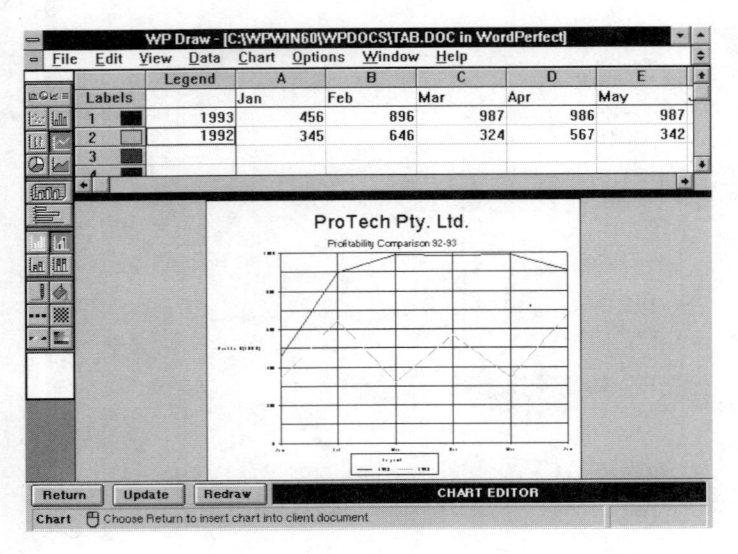

Figure 15. The Chart Editor now redraws the chart to include the title changes that you have made.

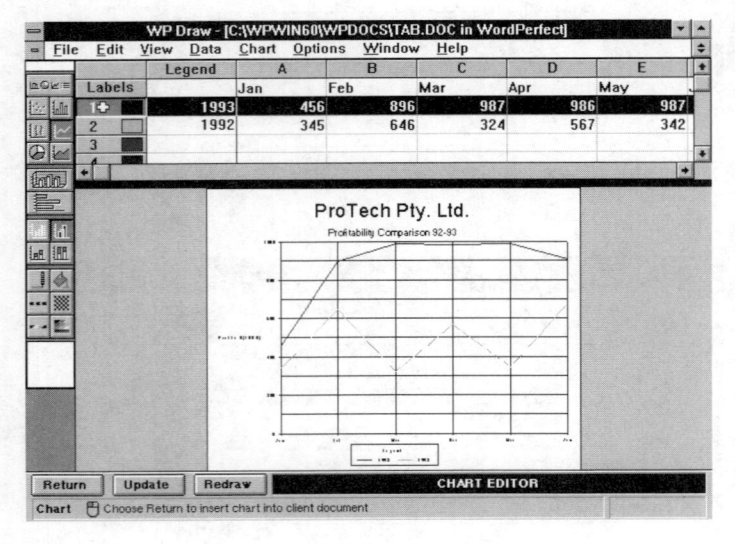

DISPLAY OPTIONS

Figure 16. You can change the color and type of the lines in your chart by double-clicking on the relevant row's label button in the data section of the Chart Editor.

For example, if you wanted to change the color or type of the line represented by the first row of your table, you would double-click on the first row's button.

Figure 17. This opens the *Series Options* dialog box. You can now change the color and type of the line through the *Attributes* section of this dialog box.

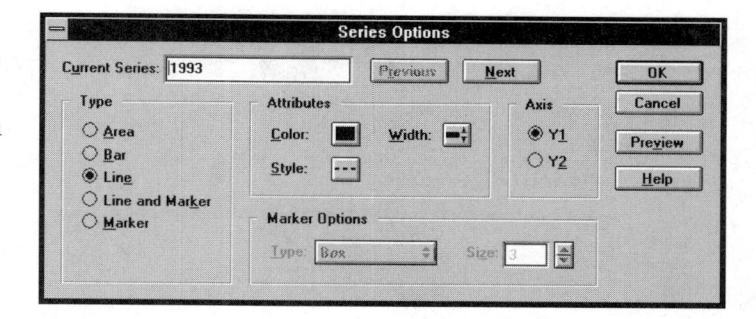

Figure 18. To change the color of the line, click on the *Color* button and select the color you want from the palette that appears.

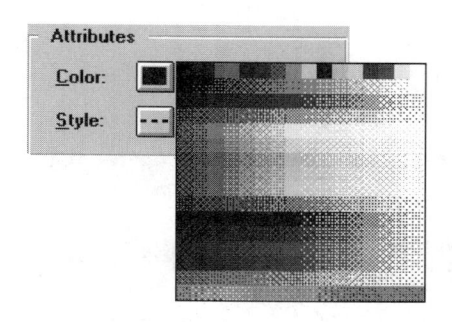

Figure 19. To change the width of the line, click on the *Width* button and select a new width from the value set that appears.

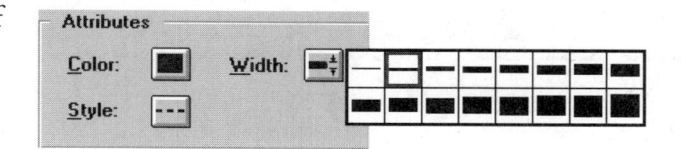

Figure 20. You can also change the style of the line through the *Style* button. Click on this button and choose the line style that you want from the options that appear.

After you have selected the options that you want, click on *OK* to return to the *Chart Editor* and redraw the chart to include your changes.

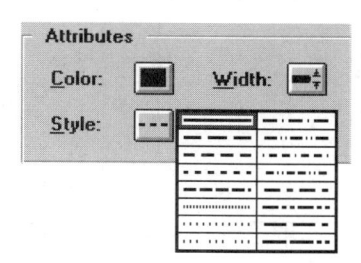

Chapter 9: Charts

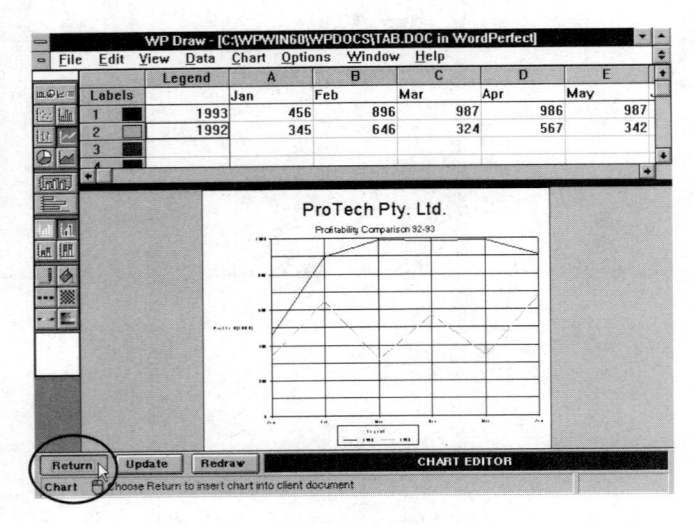

PLACING CHARTS

Figure 21. When your chart is ready, you can close the Chart Editor and insert your chart in your document by clicking on the *Return* button in the bottom-left corner of the Chart Editor.

Figure 22. This activates a prompt box asking if you want to save changes to your document.

Click *Yes* to close the Chart Editor and insert your chart into your document. Clicking *No* closes the Chart Editor but does not insert the chart into your document, and *Cancel* returns you to the Chart Editor.

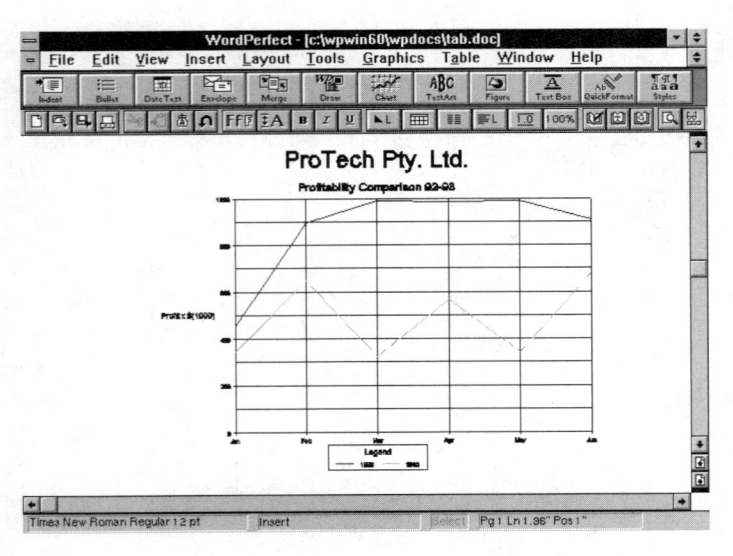

Figure 23. WordPerfect inserts your chart into the document. You can now manipulate your chart like a normal WordPerfect graphic (see **Chapter 11** for more information).

STYLES AND OUTLINES 10

STYLES

You can set up styles in WordPerfect to make formatting of a document quicker and easier. Each style can have a variety of formatting instructions which you can apply to a document in one operation.

CREATING STYLES

BASED ON EXISTING TEXT

You can create styles based on existing text that you have already formatted, or you can create a style from scratch.

Figure 1. To create a style from existing text, you first need to format some text in the way you want. For example, you can format one heading the way you want all of your document headings to look and then create a style based on that heading.

With the cursor positioned in the text you have formatted for your style, select *Styles* from the **Layout** menu.

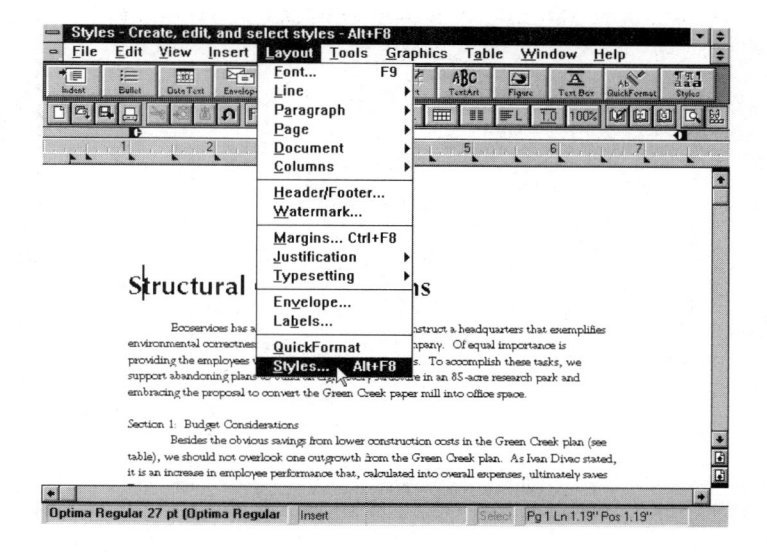

Chapter 10: Styles and Outlines

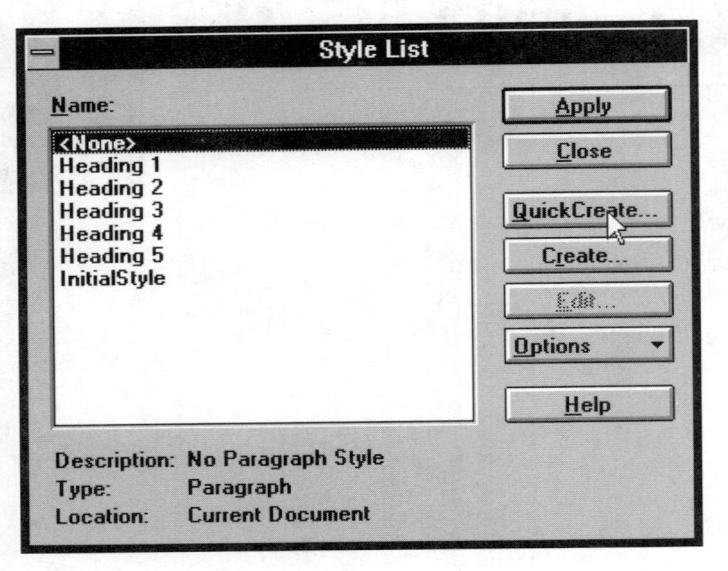

Figure 2. This activates the *Style List* dialog box which lists any styles that come with WordPerfect, or any styles you have created. To create your style based on the text where the insertion point is, click on the *QuickCreate* button.

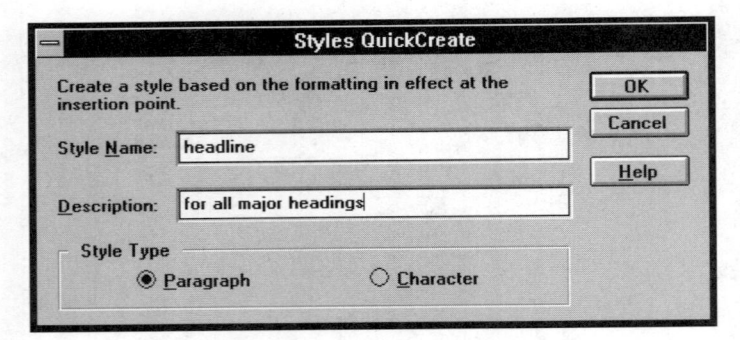

Figure 3. The *Styles QuickCreate* dialog box appears where you can assign a name and description for your style. The radio buttons in the *Style Type* section of this dialog box affect the way the style is applied. Selecting the *Paragraph* radio button applies the style to the entire paragraph containing the cursor, where selecting *Character* applies the style to selected text or text you are about to type (see **Applying Styles** later in this chapter).

Click on *OK* to create your style and WordPerfect lists it in the *Style List* dialog box.

CREATING A NEW STYLE

Figure 4. You can also create a style from scratch from the *Style List* dialog box. To do this, click on the *Create* button to create a new style.

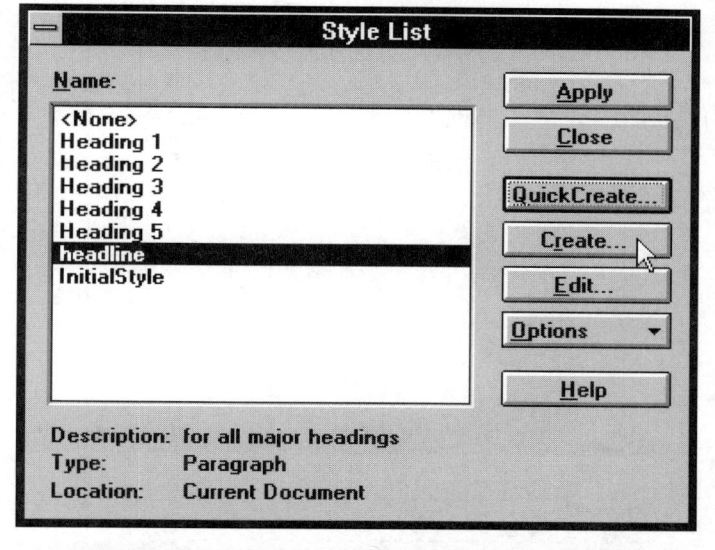

Figure 5. WordPerfect then displays the *Styles Editor* dialog box. Once again you can type a name and description for your style.

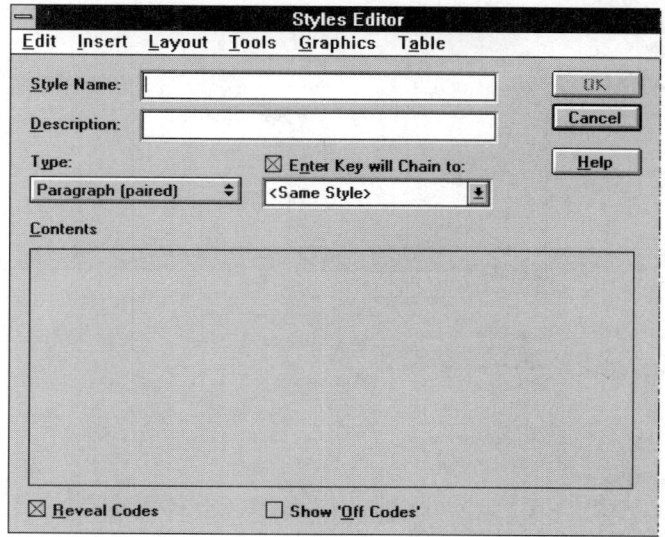

Figure 6. The *Type* drop-down list in the *Styles Editor* dialog box gives you two basic options relating to styles: paired and open.

With one of the paired options selected, WordPerfect puts a *Style On* and a *Style Off* code before and after the group of codes that make up your style. This ensures that once a paired style is turned off, its attributes don't affect any following text.

The *Type* drop-down list contains choices for paragraph and character paired styles. Choosing *Paragraph (paired)* applies the style to the entire paragraph containing the cursor or selected text, whereas choosing *Character (paired)* styles affects selected text or text you are about to type. The *Document (open)* option affects all text following the cursor, until modified by other codes.

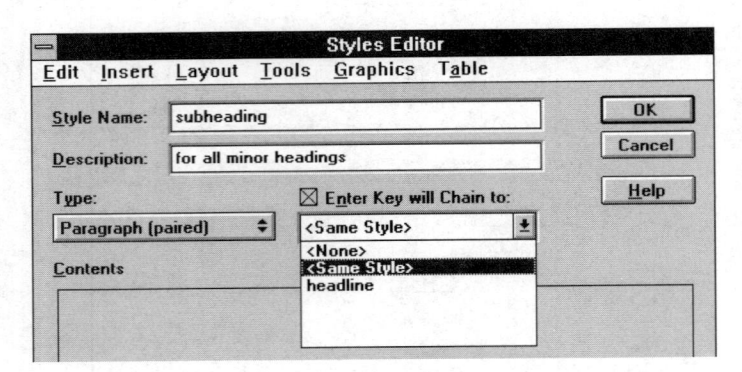

Figure 7. The *Enter Key will Chain to* option in the *Styles Editor* dialog box specifies how hard returns affect any paired style. The choices in the drop-down list control what style is activated when you press the *Enter* key.

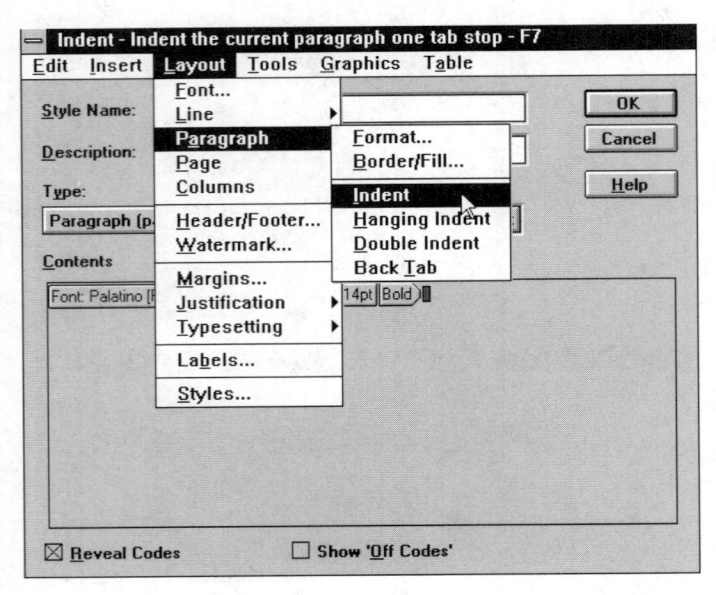

Figure 8. To create your style, use the *Styles Editor's* menus to select commands that you want to include in your style. As you do this, WordPerfect lists the command's codes in the *Contents* box. You can continue selecting the formatting commands you want in your new style until you have set it up, or you can include text, graphics, and many other elements as parts of your style by entering them in the *Contents* box.

Chapter 10: Styles and Outlines

Figure 9. When you have finished creating your style, click on *OK* to include it in the *Style List* dialog box.

You can now click on *Close* to return to your document.

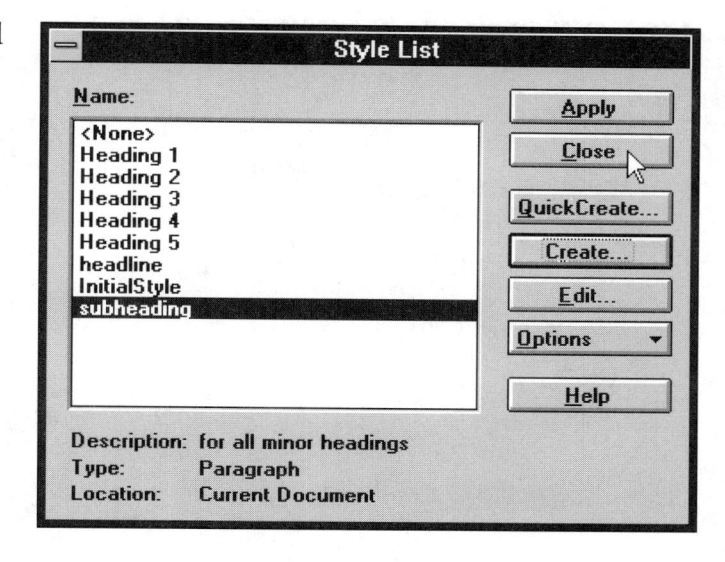

APPLYING STYLES

Figure 10. To apply a style to text, highlight the text or position the cursor in the text range you want to affect, and click the *Styles* button on the button bar.

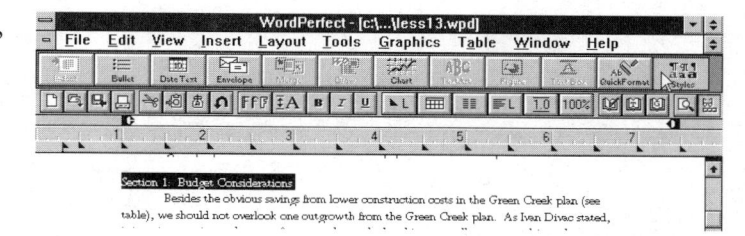

Figure 11. This activates the *Styles List* dialog box where you can choose from one of the available styles. Select the style you want to apply and click the *Apply* button. Alternatively you can double-click on the style name.

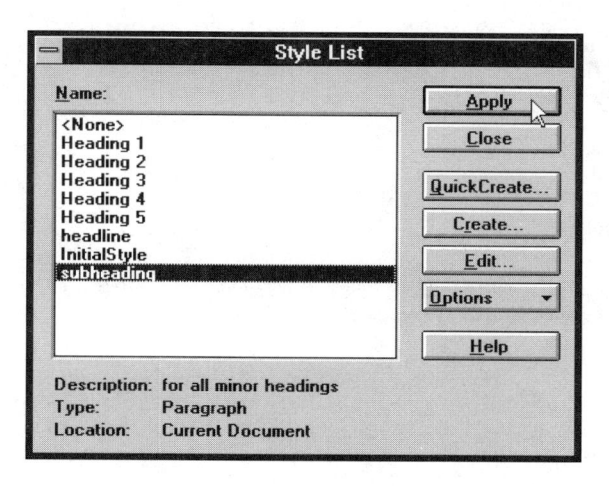

147

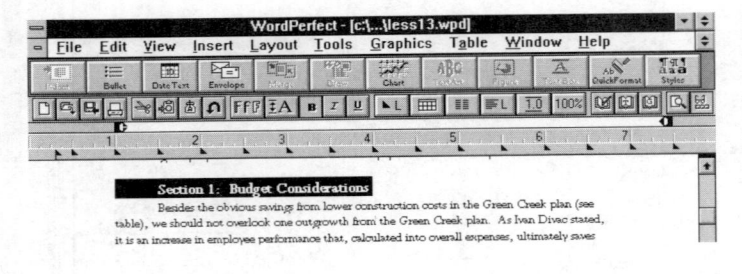

Figure 12. The text we selected in Figure 10 now takes on the attributes of that style.

To apply a character style to a character, select the text you want to format and apply the style to it. Alternatively you can activate the style, type the text you want, and turn the style off again.

If you are applying a paragraph style, simply position the cursor in the paragraph that you want the style to affect before selecting the style, and to apply a document style, position the cursor where you want the style to start and select the style from the *Style List*.

Note: If you paste some text into a section of a document where a paired style is active, all text takes on the attributes of that style.

EDITING STYLES

Figure 13. Choose *Styles* from the **Layout** menu or double-click on the *Styles* button on the button bar to activate the *Style List* dialog box. From the list of styles in this dialog box, select the style you want to edit and click on the *Edit* button.

Figure 14. The *Styles Editor* dialog box appears, showing all the codes that belong to the style. You can now add or remove any features of this style. If you want to change a code, simply delete it from the *Contents* box. You can also add new formatting codes in the same way as when you create a new style (see Figures 4 through 9). You can change the *Name, Description, Type,* and *Enter Key will Chain to* options for the style in the *Styles Editor* dialog box. When you have finished editing your style, click on *OK* to return to the *Style List* dialog box listing your modified style.

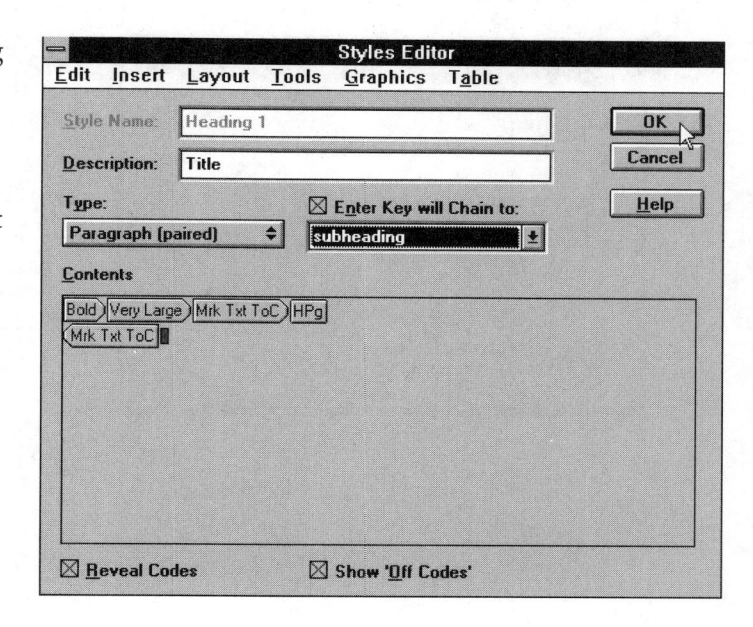

SAVING STYLES

Unless you save styles as a file on your hard disk, they are only available in the document that you created them in. Saving these styles as a file allows you to use them in other documents.

Figure 15. To save the styles of a current document, click on the *Options* button in the *Style List* dialog box. This activates a drop-down list of options for working with your documents styles. Now select *Save As* from this list.

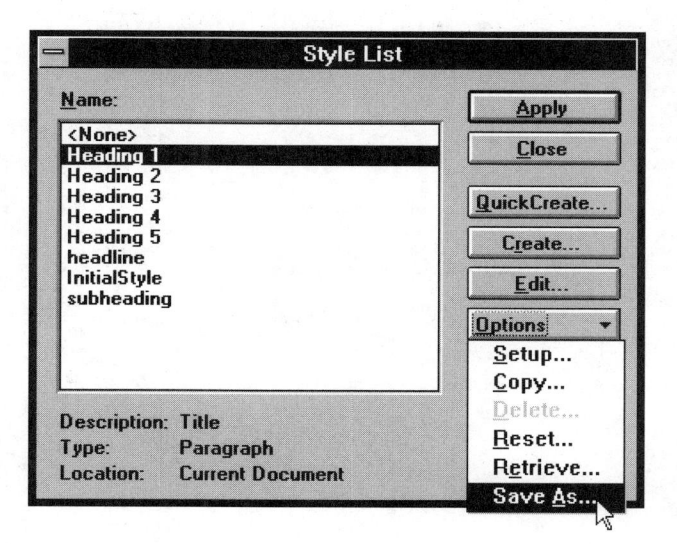

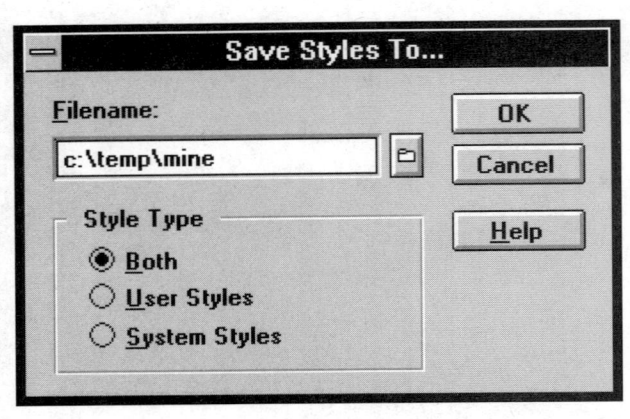

Figure 16. This activates the *Save Styles To* dialog box. This dialog box lets you save styles anywhere on your hard disk.

Type a name for your styles into the *Filename* text box, it is a good idea to give your styles a *.sty* extension to avoid confusing them with other WordPerfect files.

Select which styles you want to save through the *Style Type* section of the dialog box or select *Both* to save all styles in the current document in your file. Click on the *OK* button after naming the style file.

RETRIEVING STYLES

If you have saved styles from another document as a style file you can retrieve them into your current document's *Style List* dialog box at any time.

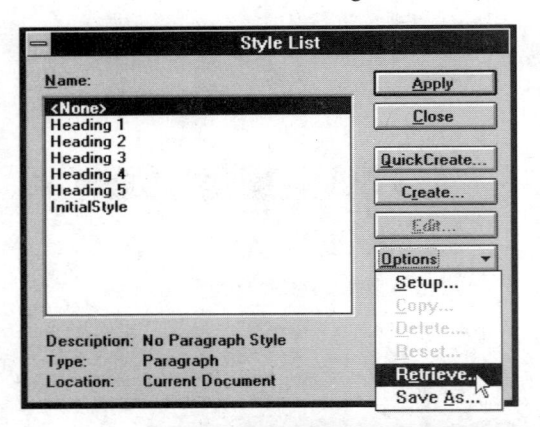

Figure 17. Select *Retrieve* from the *Options* drop-down list in the *Style List* dialog box.

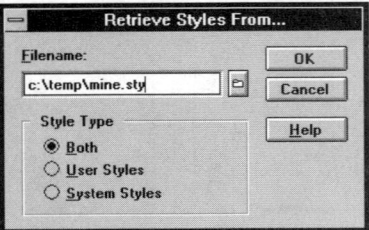

Figure 18. This activates the *Retrieve Styles From* dialog box. Enter the filename of the required style's file into the *Filename* text box. Alternatively, search for the file by clicking on the list button at the end of the

Filename text box and double-clicking the required file. Specify the *Style Type* that you want to retrieve and then select *OK*.

Figure 19. If any styles in the document have the same name as any of the styles you are retrieving, WordPerfect asks if you want to replace them.

Any changes you make to a style that you retrieve affect only the current document.

DELETING STYLES

Figure 20. To delete a style, select it from the list of styles in the *Style List* dialog box and select *Delete* from the *Options* drop-down list.

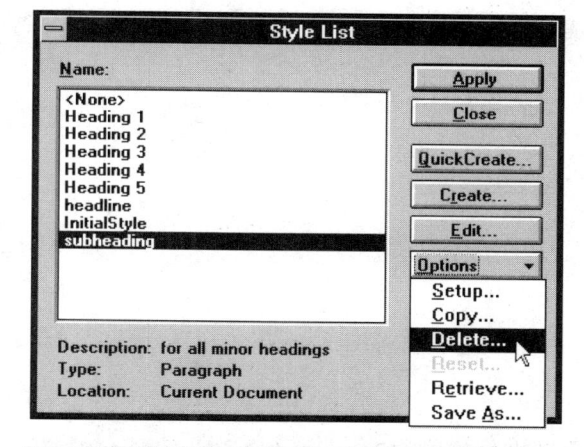

Figure 21. This activates the *Delete Styles* dialog box. If you select the *Include Codes* option, this deletes the style and the relevant codes from the document. You can no longer use the style in the current document. If you select *Leave Codes,* you delete the style from the list but all the formatting codes connected with the style remain.

Chapter 10: Styles and Outlines

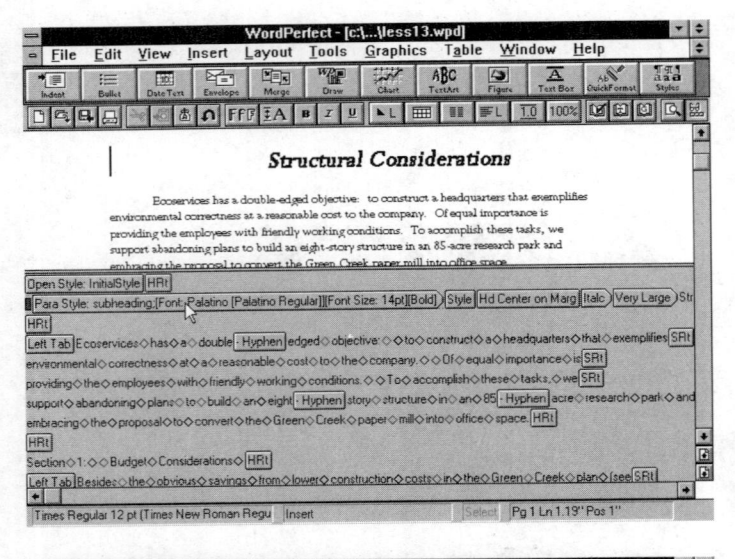

Figure 22. If you need to remove a style from text, select the style code in the *Reveal Codes* screen and then press the Delete key to delete it.

GRAPHICS, TABLES, AND TEXT IN STYLES

Figure 23. You can include graphics, tables, and text in styles. You do this by adding them to the *Contents* section of the *Styles Editor* dialog box when you are creating the style.

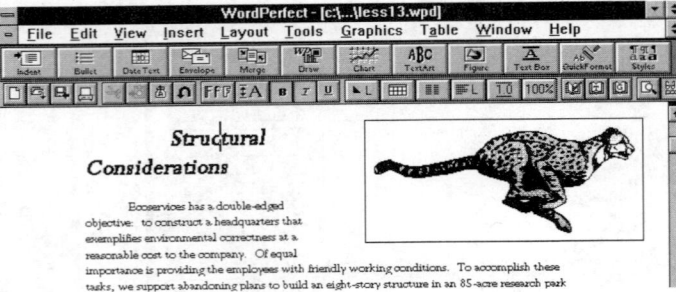

In this figure, we have added a graphic to this style. Every time you apply this style, the graphic appears. If you add a table, retrieve a graphic, or add text to a style, you must return to the *Styles Editor* window to edit it.

USING OUTLINES

The outline feature of WordPerfect allows you to create outlines with different levels and numbered paragraphs to help you structure and organize your documents. It is easier to start using the outline feature before you start typing your text.

Figure 24. Select *Outline* from the **Tools** menu to activate the *Outline* feature bar and start the outline feature. By default a first level entry number appears as "1." if the insertion point is on a new line. Any text already in your document appears with a "T" to the left of each paragraph which represents text that is not part of the outline.

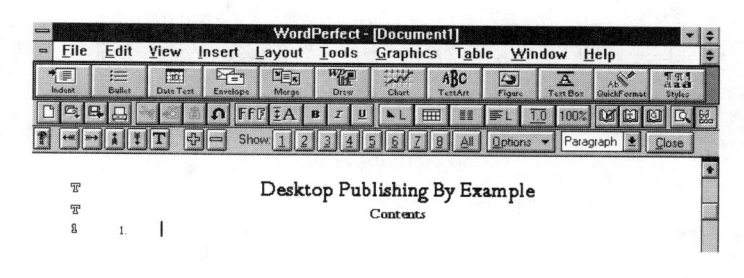

Figure 25. Each time you press the Enter key after adding text, another first level entry appears. The entry value increases each time but the level number of your outline stays at "1." In this example, we have added text to create chapters.

Figure 26. To get a second-level entry, press enter after a current first level entry and then click on the right pointing arrow on the left-hand side of the feature bar. The new entry in this figure is represented by an "a." with the number "2." on the left-hand side denoting the entry as second level.

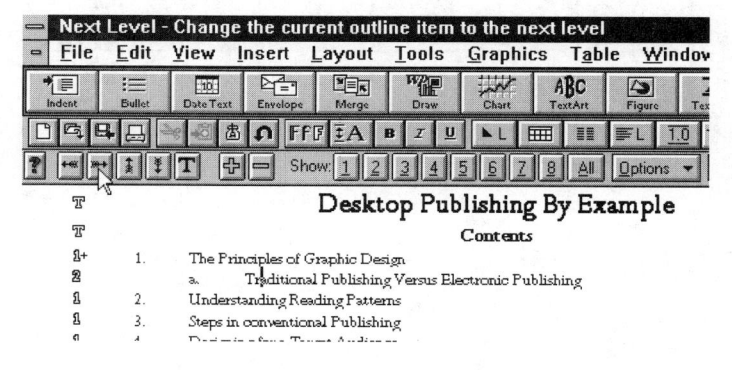

You can continue to add levels in this way to include up to eight subordinate levels, each identified by a different number or letter. To change the level of any entry back and forth, simply click on either of the first two arrows on the *Outline* feature bar.

Chapter 10: Styles and Outlines

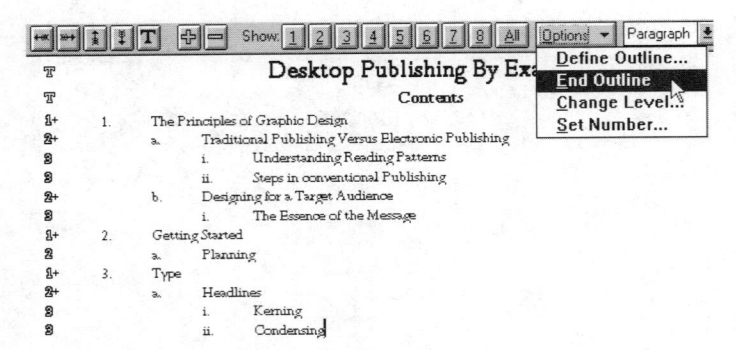

Figure 27. To finish creating your outline, position the cursor at the end of the outline text and choose *End Outline* from the *Options* drop-down list on the *Outline* feature bar.

MOVING FAMILIES

Figure 28. A family in outlines refers to any paragraph number and its associated text plus any subordinate levels. You can select an outline item, family, or paragraph of body text simply by clicking its symbol.

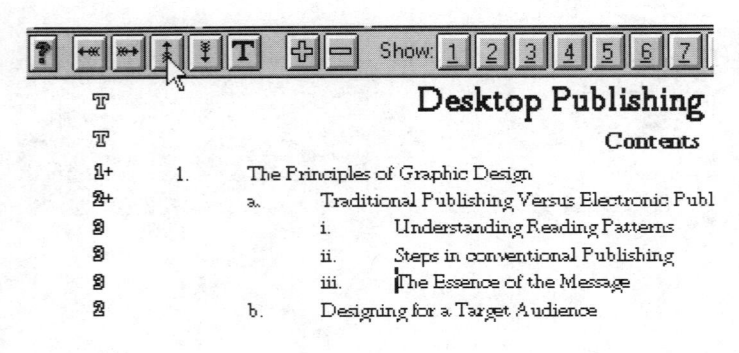

Figure 29. You can move an outline family or item by selecting it and clicking on the *Move Up* or *Move Down* arrows on the *Outline* feature bar. This repositions the selected paragraphs up or down, keeping the outline levels the same.

The outline numbering system updates automatically when a family changes position.

OUTLINE DISPLAYS

There are a number of ways of changing the display of your outline levels and level numbering.

Figure 30. You use the *Show Family* and *Hide Family* buttons to display and hide outline families. For example, you can hide all but the current level of a family by selecting the *Hide Family* button. In this example, we selected all the outline text and clicked on the *Hide Family* button to view only the level one structures. Click on the *Show Family* button to redisplay the hidden levels of the current outline family.

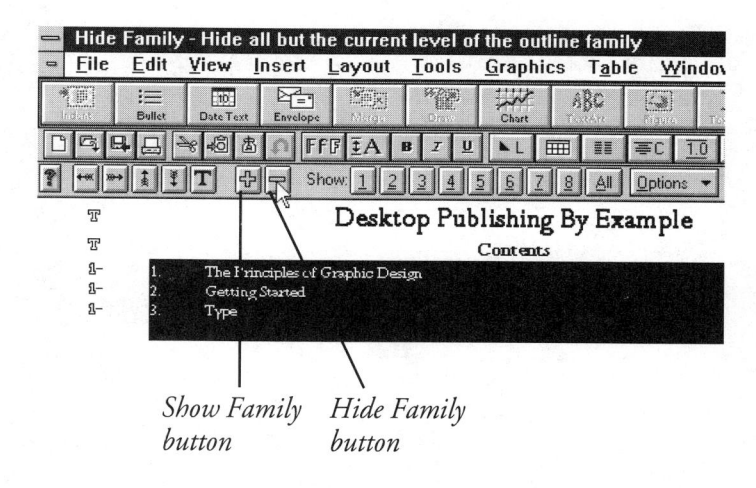

Figure 31. You can also use the *Show* buttons on the *Outline* feature bar to view only certain levels of your outline. This lets you display different levels of your structure. For instance, clicking on the *Show 2* button displays the first and second level entries. You can then work on the structure of these level entries.

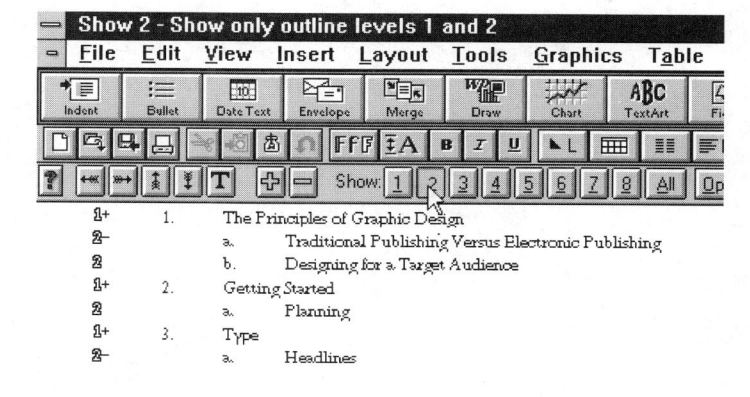

Clicking on the *Show 3* button displays the first, second, and third level entries only, allowing you to work on these levels of your outline and so on. Any other text in your document also disappears when you view your outline this way. The *Show All* button displays all the levels of your outline and any other text.

Chapter 10: Styles and Outlines

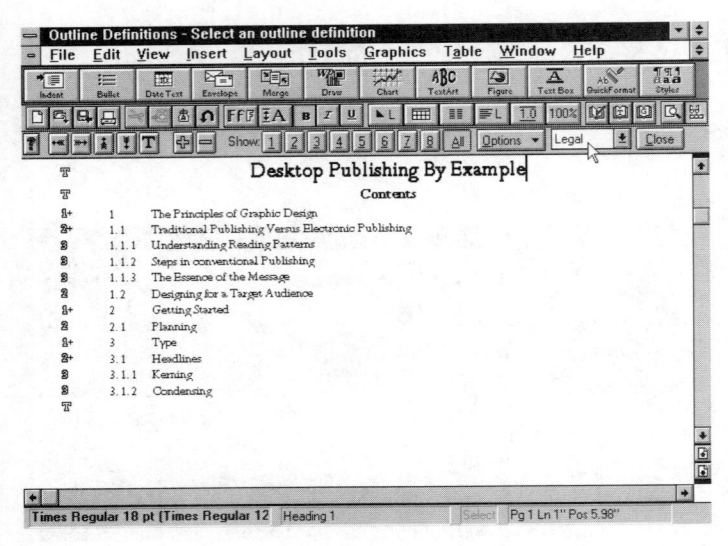

Figure 32. To change outline levels structure and numbering, click on the down arrow in the *Outline Definitions* section on the right-hand side of the *Outline* feature bar. This activates a drop-down list where you can select from a variety of predefined outline definitions.

For example, we have changed the current outline numbering to a legal numbering system by selecting the *Legal* option from the drop-down list. WordPerfect automatically changes the current outline to a legal format.

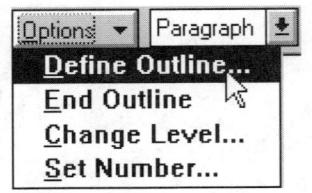

OUTLINE OPTIONS

Figure 33. The *Options* button gives you control over a number of further outline features. To access the outline options, click the *Options* button on the *Outline* feature bar to activate its drop-down list.

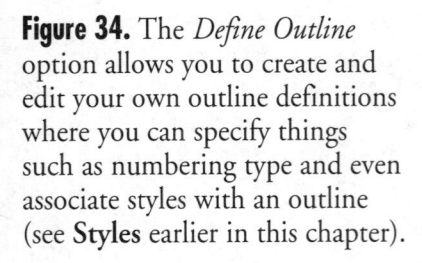

Figure 34. The *Define Outline* option allows you to create and edit your own outline definitions where you can specify things such as numbering type and even associate styles with an outline (see **Styles** earlier in this chapter).

The *End Outline* option ends the current outline session and returns you to normal editing in your document.

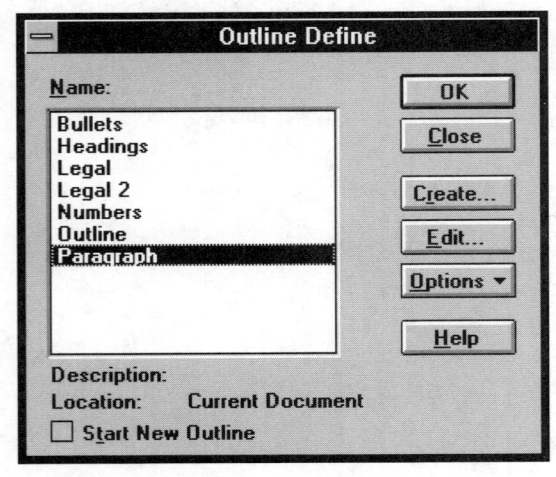

156

Figure 35. Choose the *Change Level* option to change the level of the current item in your outline.

Figure 36. Select the *Set Number* option to activate the *Set Paragraph Number* dialog box. Here you can determine the first number of an outline. This is useful if you turn on a second outline further on in a document and you want it to run in numeric order with any previous outlines.

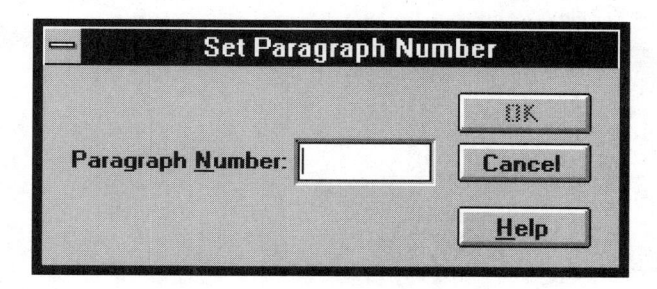

GRAPHICS 11

GRAPHICS

WordPerfect is compatible with most graphics file formats. You can import any graphic files from programs with WordPerfect compatible formats into your documents. You can then alter the way an imported graphic looks, as well as create and modify graphics through WordPerfect Draw.

RETRIEVING GRAPHICS

Figure 1. To import a graphic into your document, select *Figure* from the **Graphics** menu.

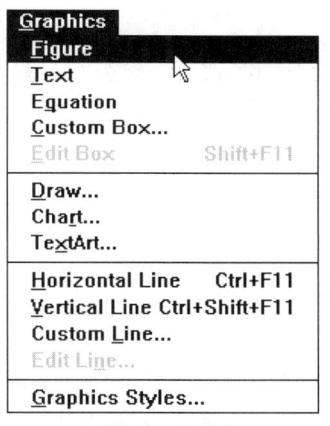

Figure 2. WordPerfect displays the *Insert Image* dialog box, where you can move to any drive or directory. You can also use any of the File Management features described in **Chapter** 4.

WordPerfect has a graphics directory containing graphics files you can use in your documents. To import one of these graphics, open the graphics directory from the *Directories* list box. This lists the graphics directory's contents in the *Files* list box.

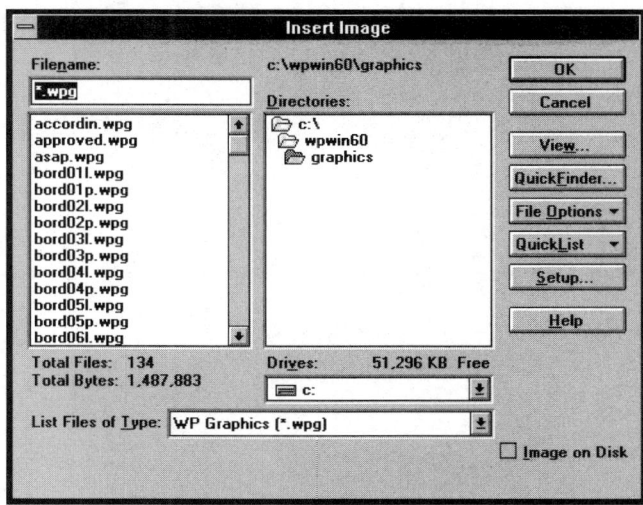

159

Chapter 11: Graphics

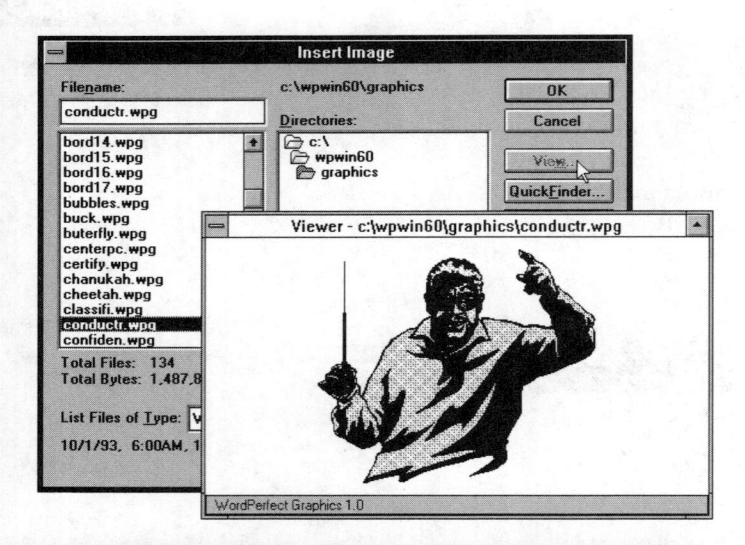

You can also list graphics with other file formats through the *List Files of Type* drop-down list box.

Figure 3. Click on the *View* button to see what a selected file looks like before you import it into your WordPerfect document.

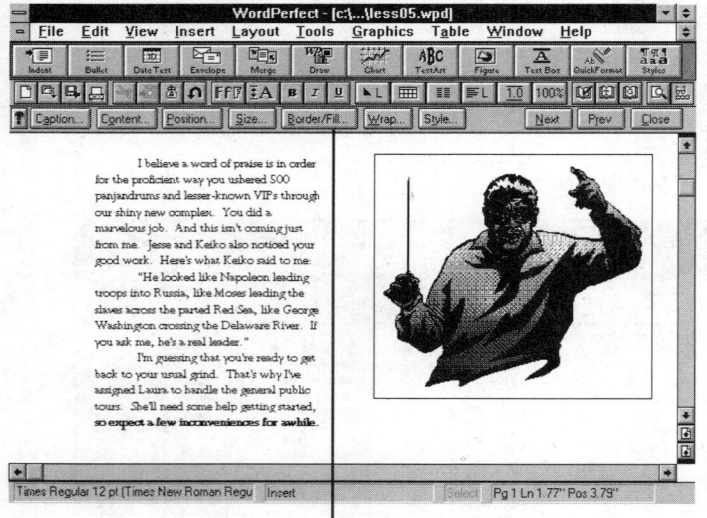

Figure 4. Once you have selected a graphic, click on the *OK* button, or double-click its filename to insert it into your document at the insertion point.

If there is any text in the document, by default the text wraps around the graphic box.

When WordPerfect inserts the graphic into your document it activates the *Graphics Box* feature bar. This feature bar gives you access to all of the WordPerfect graphics features.

Graphics Box feature bar

Chapter 11: Graphics

MOVING GRAPHICS

Figure 5. You can select a graphic by clicking on it with the mouse. Eight black handles appear around its border after you have selected it.

Figure 6. When you move the mouse cursor over a selected graphic the mouse cursor changes to a four-headed arrow. To move the graphic, click and drag it to a new position. When you release the mouse, any text in the document reformats around the newly positioned graphic.

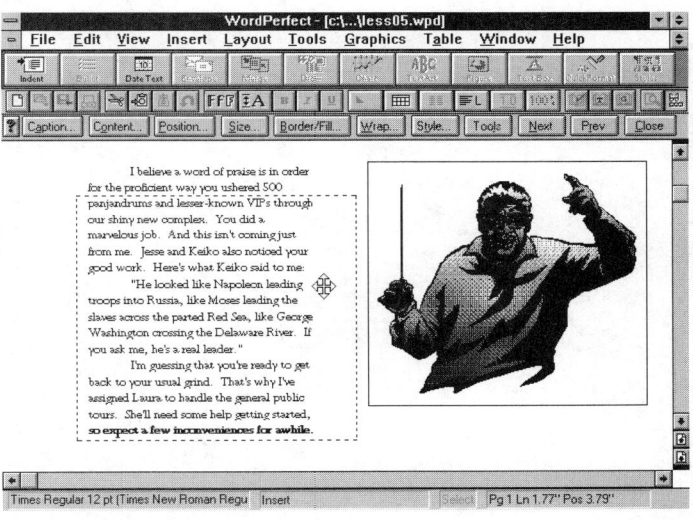

Figure 7. Another way of determining a graphic box's position is through the *Position* command. To do this, click on the *Position* button on the *Graphics Box* feature bar.

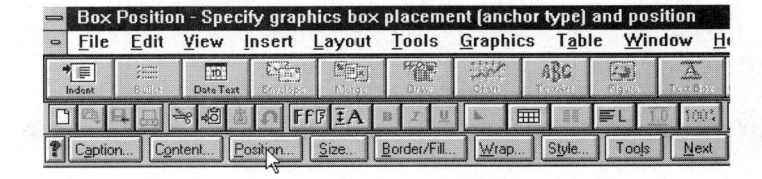

161

Chapter 11: Graphics

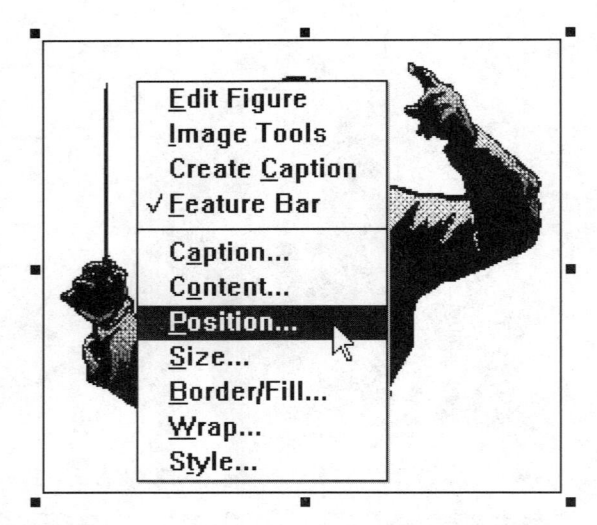

Figure 8. You can also select this command from a graphic's QuickMenu. To do this, move the mouse over the graphic and press the right mouse button. You can then select *Position* from the QuickMenu that appears.

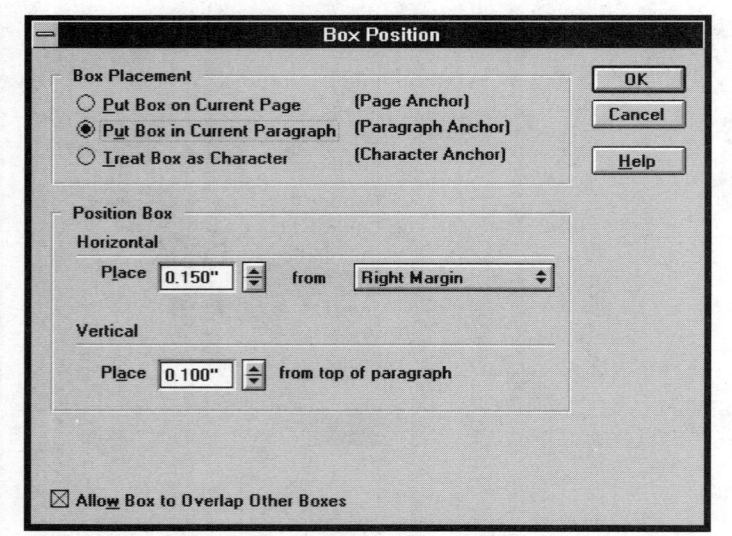

Figure 9. WordPerfect now opens the *Box Position* dialog box. In this dialog box you can anchor the graphic to a specific page, paragraph, or character in the *Box Placement* section of the dialog box. The *Put Box on Current Page* option ensures the graphic remains on the current page.

The *Put Box in Current Paragraph* option keeps the graphic with its paragraph, even if you later move this paragraph and the *Treat Box as Character* option treats the graphic as part of the text.

The *Vertical* and *Horizontal* options in the *Position Box* section of the dialog box let you determine the position of the graphic on the page. Selecting one of the *Box Placement* options, other than the *Put Box on Current Page* option, affects your vertical and horizontal selections in the *Position Box* section.

Chapter 11: Graphics

RESIZING GRAPHICS

Figure 10. You can resize a graphic by dragging one of its black handles. As you position the mouse on top of a black handle, the cursor changes to a two-headed arrow. When this happens, simply click and drag the handle to change the size of the graphic. Once you release the mouse, the graphic redraws at the new size.

Figure 11. You can also resize a graphic by clicking the *Size* button on the *Graphics Box* feature bar, or by selecting *Size* from a graphic's QuickMenu.

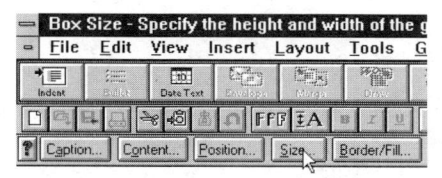

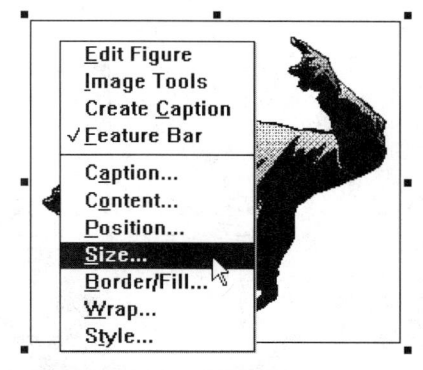

Figure 12. In the *Box Size* dialog box you can determine the size of your graphics box. Selecting the *Set* radio button for either the *Width* or *Height* sections allows you to set a specific measurement for the graphics box. The *Full* radio button forces the graphics box to fill the width or height of the page from margin to margin. The *Size to Content* radio button adjusts the width or height of the graphics box to the width or height of its contents.

163

EDITING GRAPHICS

You can now edit your graphics at two levels in WordPerfect. You can edit an image in a graphics box using the image tools, or you can edit or create an image directly through WP Draw.

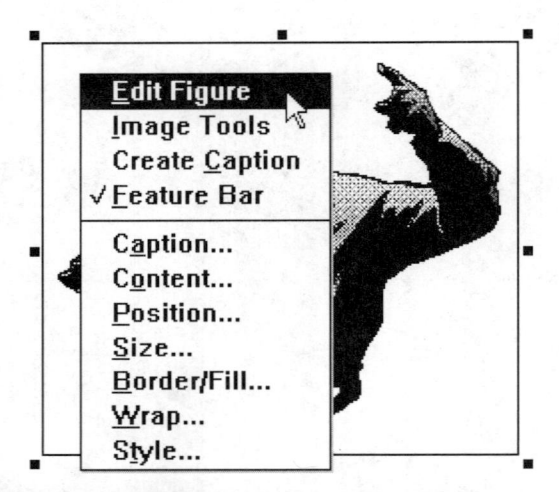

EDITING/CREATING GRAPHICS

Figure 13. To edit or create a graphic directly in WordPerfect select *Edit Figure* from a graphic's QuickMenu, or double-click on the graphic itself. If you want to create a graphic from scratch, select *Draw* from the **Graphics** menu or click on the *Draw* button on the button bar.

Figure 14. This opens WP Draw. If you are editing a figure directly, WordPerfect displays it in the drawing window. You can now use the WP Draw features to edit or create your graphic (for more information on using WP Draw, see **Chapter 12**).

IMAGE TOOLS

Figure 15. To edit an image within a graphics box, select *Image Tools* from its QuickMenu or click on the *Tools* button on the *Graphics Box* feature bar.

Figure 16. This activates the *Image tools* palette where you can crop, scale, flip, and rotate your image. You can also make color, contrast, and brightness adjustments and change the fill type of the image.

You can either use the individual buttons on the *Image tools* palette, or access them all at once by clicking on the *Image Settings* button in the bottom-right corner of the *Image tools* palette.

Figure 17. This opens the *Image Settings* dialog box. The *Modify Image Appearance* section of this dialog box contains radio buttons for all of the *Image tools* options. Selecting any of these radio buttons activates a corresponding set of choices at the bottom of the dialog box.

The preview window in this dialog box contains a sample of your graphic. This window redraws your graphic every time

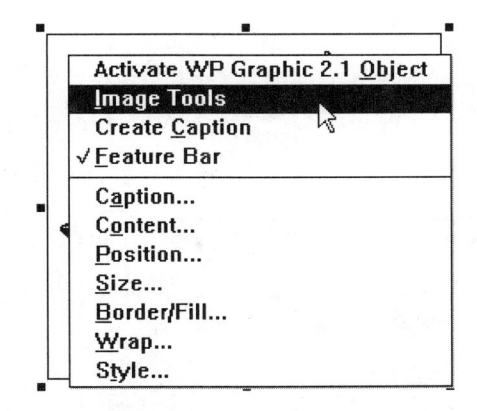

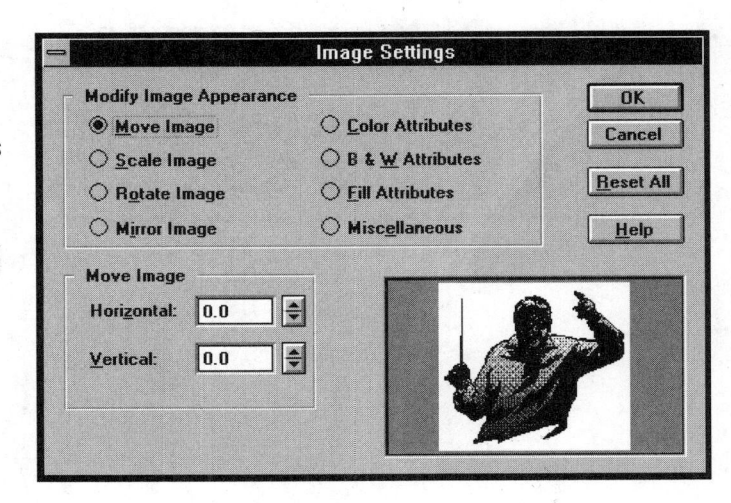

165

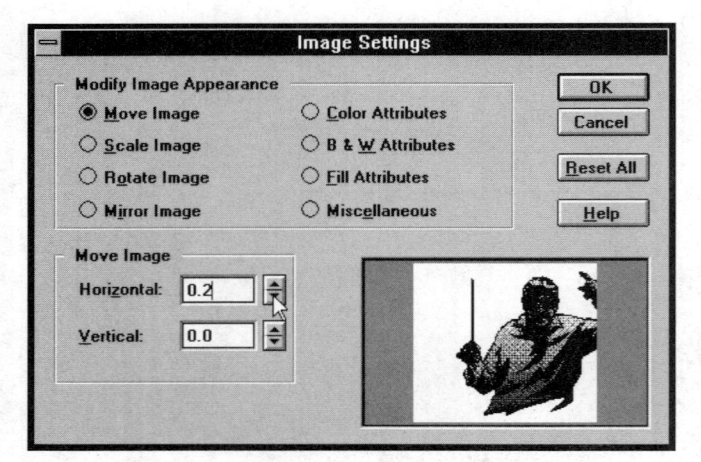

you make changes in this dialog box. This lets you see the result of any changes before you apply them. To reset the image to its original form click on the *Reset All* button.

Figure 18. Select the *Move Image* radio button to activate the *Move Image* choices. Here you can use the arrows to move your image vertically and horizontally by a specified amount.

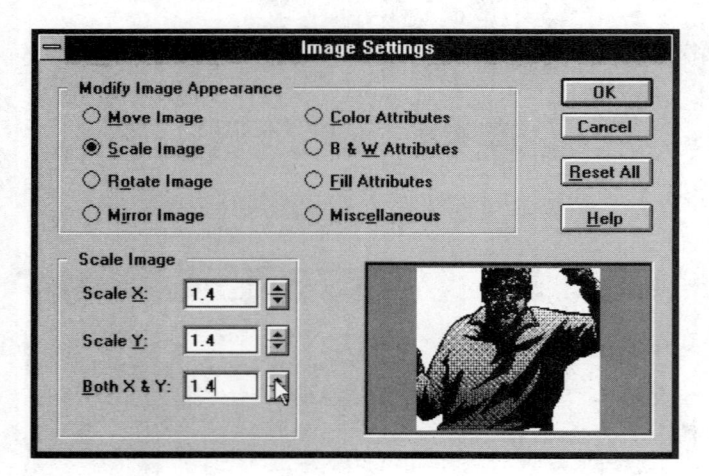

Figure 19. Selecting the *Scale Image* radio button allows you to scale your image's height, width, or both at once.

Chapter 11: Graphics

Figure 20. The *Rotate Image* radio button allows you to use the arrows or enter a value to rotate your image through 360 degrees. The image rotates anti-clockwise for positive degree values that you specify in the *Amount* box.

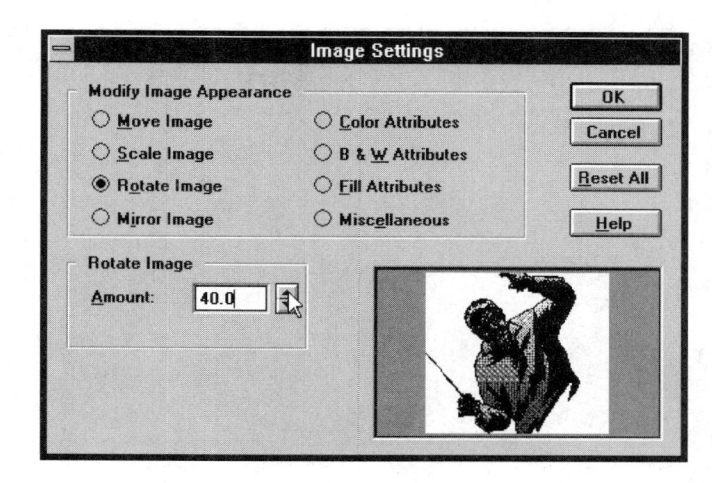

Figure 21. Selecting the *Mirror Image* radio button allows you to flip your image horizontally or vertically.

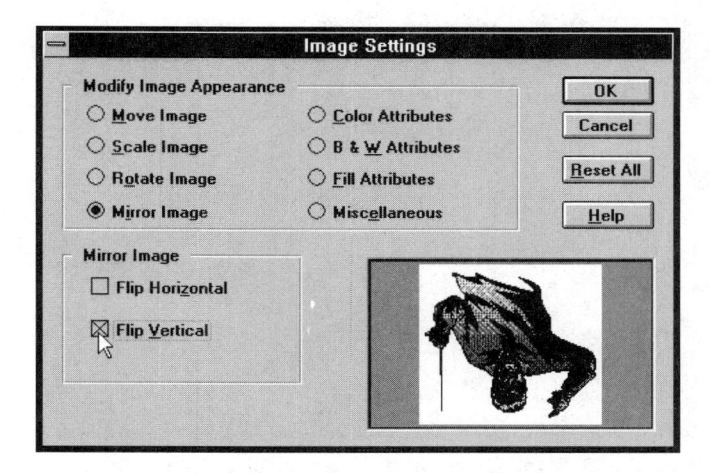

Figure 22. The *Color Attributes* radio button lets you invert the colors of the image and set the *Contrast* and *Brightness* levels. To change the *Contrast* and *Brightness*, either click on the relevant button and select a predefined level, or use the arrows to change the value.

167

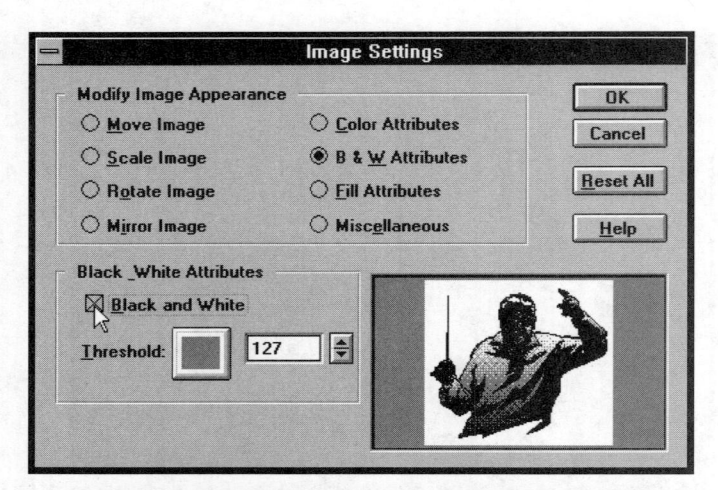

Figure 23. The *B & W Attributes* radio button allows you to change your image to a black and white display. To do this, click in the check box and then adjust the threshold by clicking on the available button and choosing a level, or use the arrows to change the value shown.

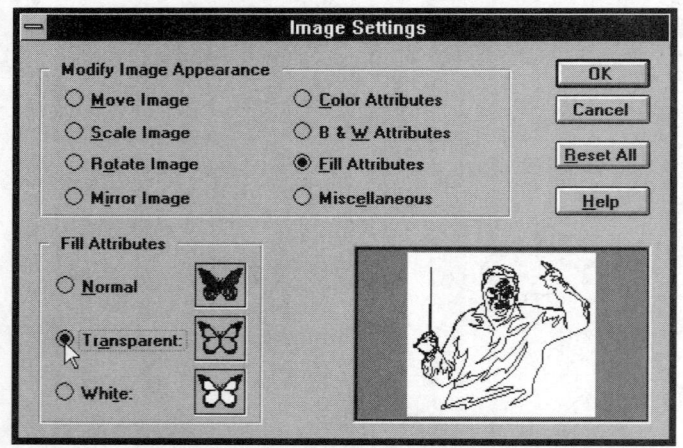

Figure 24. The *Fill Attributes* radio button allows you to make your image transparent so that the background shows through the image, or to give your image a black outline with a white fill.

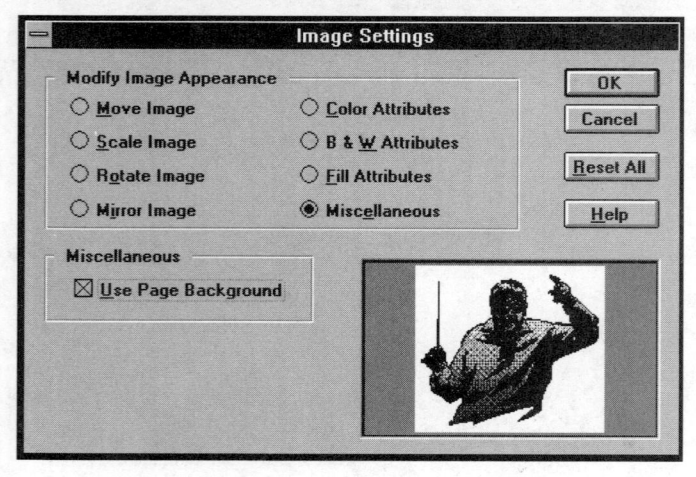

Figure 25. The *Miscellaneous* radio button allows you to use the page background for your graphic if the graphic image file contains predefined background colors or fills.

Chapter 11: Graphics

CREATING A CAPTION

Figure 26. To create a caption for a graphic, select the graphic and then click on the *Caption* button on the *Graphics Box* feature bar. Alternatively you can activate a graphic's QuickMenu and select the *Caption* command.

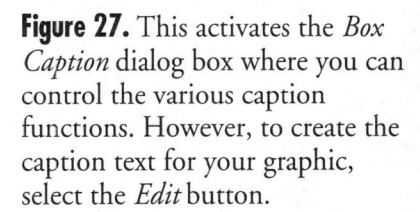

Figure 27. This activates the *Box Caption* dialog box where you can control the various caption functions. However, to create the caption text for your graphic, select the *Edit* button.

Alternatively, you can select the *Create Caption* command from the QuickMenu to get the same result.

Figure 28. WordPerfect places the caption "Figure 1" below your graphic, followed by a text cursor. Edit the caption as you normally would using any of the various WordPerfect text formatting commands.

When you have finished editing, click outside the graphics box to return to your document. WordPerfect automatically numbers any following figure numbers in other captions.

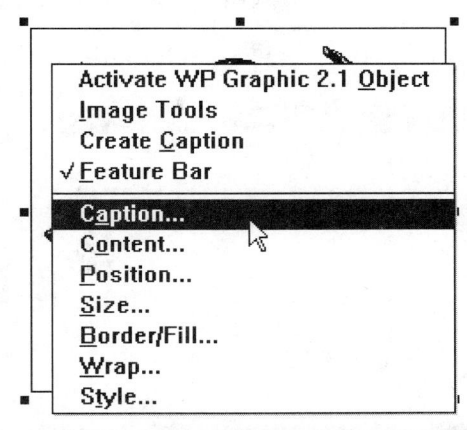

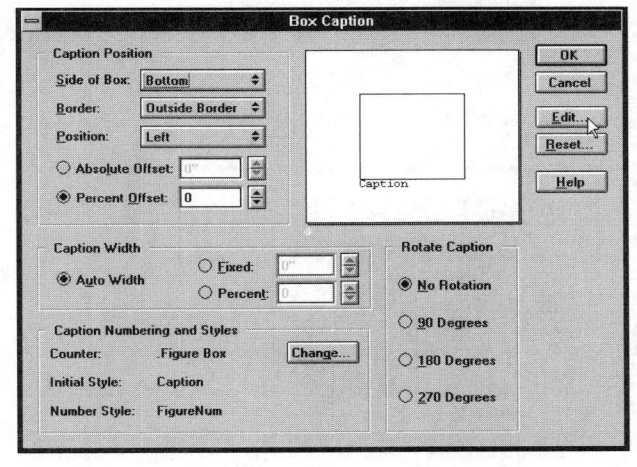

By default, the caption appears below the graphic and moves with the graphic. You can now edit this caption by clicking on the *Caption* button or selecting *Caption* from the graphic's QuickMenu.

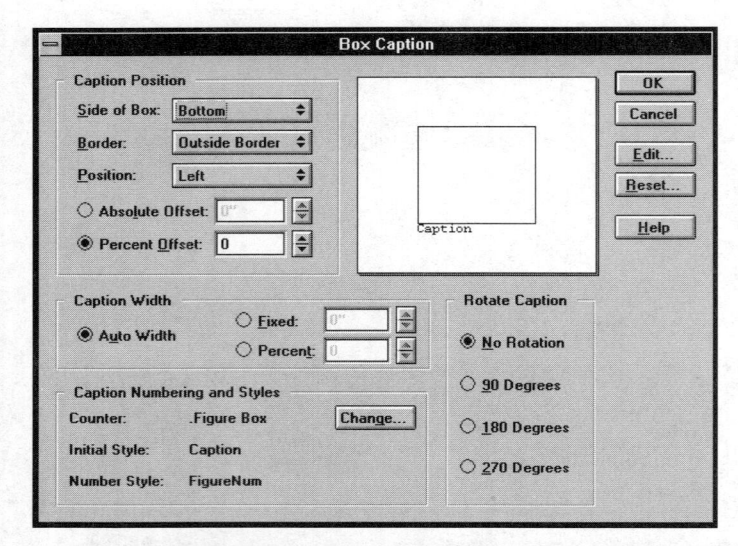

Figure 29. The *Box Caption* dialog box allows you to change the caption's position in relation to the graphics box, its width and rotation, and also the numbering and styles. You can delete a caption by selecting the *Reset* button.

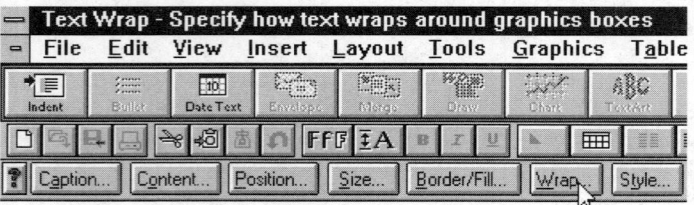

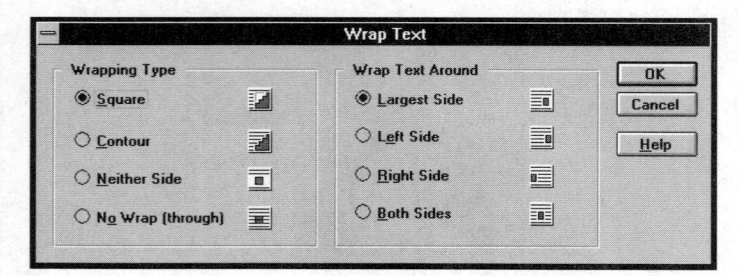

TEXT WRAP

Figure 30. To change how text wraps around your graphic, click on the *Wrap* button on the *Graphics Box* feature bar, or by selecting *Wrap* from a graphic's QuickMenu.

Figure 31. This opens the *Wrap Text* dialog box. Select an option from the *Wrapping Type* section to determine how the text flows around your graphics box. If you want to contour text around a graphic, first remove the border from the graphics box.

The *Wrap Text Around* section allows you to determine which side of a graphic the text will contour around. The *Largest Side* option wraps text to the side of the graphic with the most white space.

BORDERS AND FILLS

Figure 32. You can apply a variety of borders and fills to your WordPerfect graphics boxes through the *Border/Fill* button on the *Graphics Box* feature bar or by selecting the *Border/Fill* command from a graphic's QuickMenu.

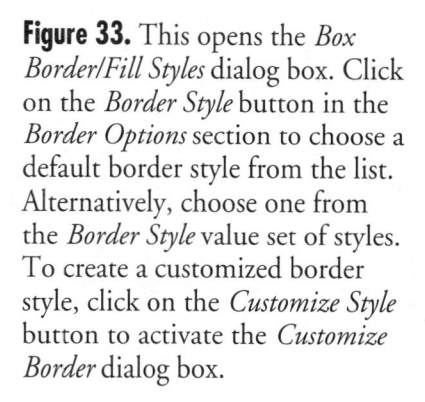

Figure 33. This opens the *Box Border/Fill Styles* dialog box. Click on the *Border Style* button in the *Border Options* section to choose a default border style from the list. Alternatively, choose one from the *Border Style* value set of styles. To create a customized border style, click on the *Customize Style* button to activate the *Customize Border* dialog box.

Figure 34. Use the *Fill Options* section of the dialog box to specify a fill type and color for your graphics boxes. Click on the *Fill Style* button and select a fill style from the list that appears, or click on the down arrow in the *Fill Style* entry box to activate a value set of styles to choose from.

You can also click on the *Foreground* and *Background* buttons to activate a color palette to specify your fill colors. If the fill style is a solid shade, only the *Foreground* colors will display.

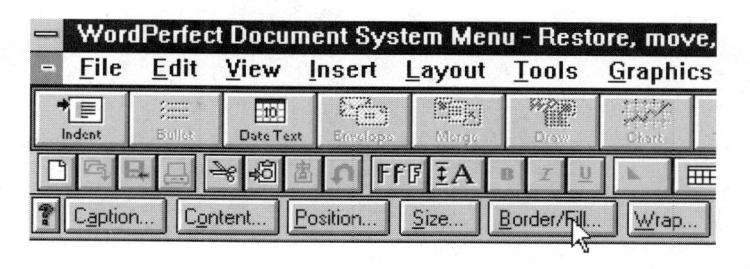

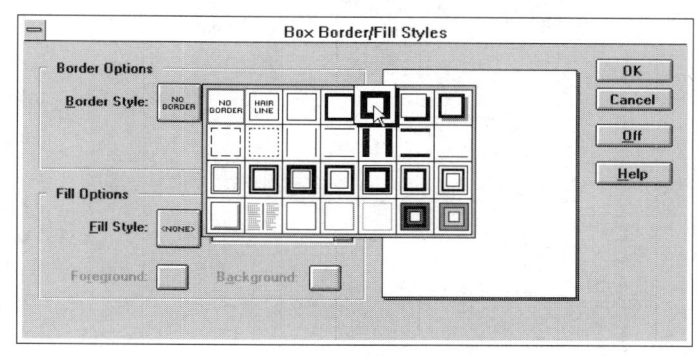

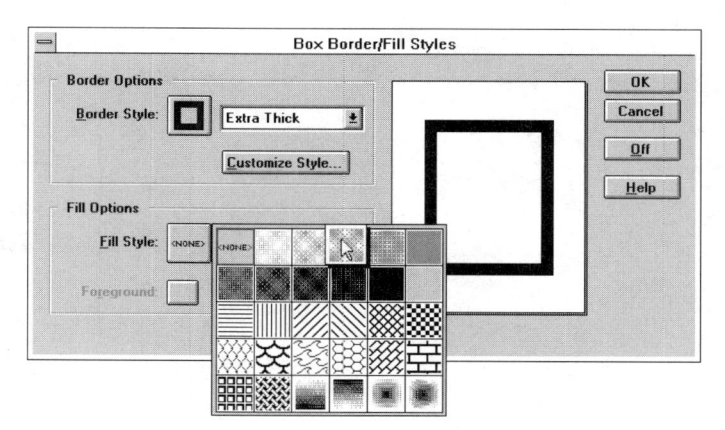

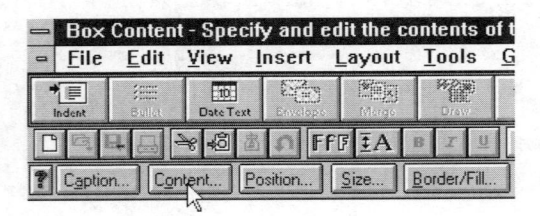

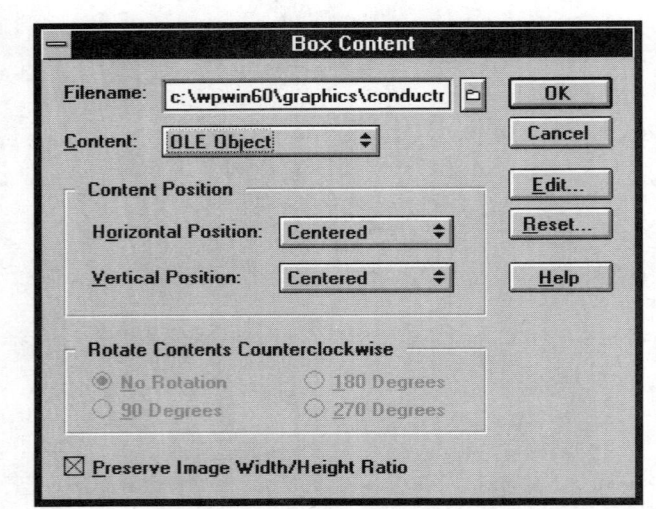

GRAPHICS BOX CONTENTS

Figure 35. You can alter the contents of a graphics box through the *Content* button on the *Graphics Box* feature bar, or through *Content* from a graphics box's QuickMenu.

Figure 36. This opens the *Box Content* dialog box. In the *Filename* section of this dialog box you can specify which file will be in the graphics box. Click the list button to open the *Select File* dialog box where you can retrieve a graphic file from any directory or disk.

The *Content* pop-up list allows you to specify or change the type of graphic and the *Content Position* allows you to align the box contents within the graphics box.

Select an option in the *Rotate Contents Counterclockwise* to rotate the box contents through 90 degree increments. The *Preserve Image Width/Height Ratio* option lets you keep a graphics box's contents in proportion when resizing.

To edit the contents of any graphics box directly, click on the *Edit* button. Click on the *Reset* button to revert to the default box content and delete all current settings.

PUTTING TEXT IN BOXES

Figure 37. You can insert text into a graphics box to make quotes or other important information stand out from the rest of your document. To do this, choose *Text* from the **Graphics** menu to create a new graphics box for text.

Alternatively, you can change an existing graphics box's contents to text and then edit the box contents to add your text (see **Graphics Box Contents** earlier in this chapter).

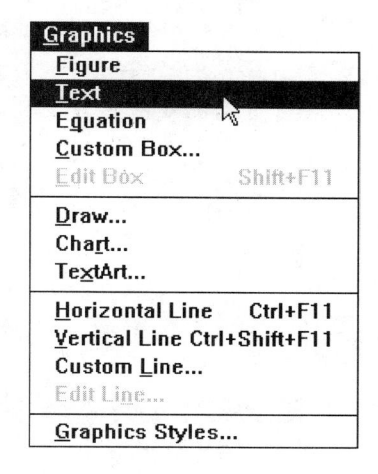

Figure 38. WordPerfect now positions a graphics box containing the insertion point in your document. Simply type in the text you want for the text box, applying any formatting attributes as you normally would.

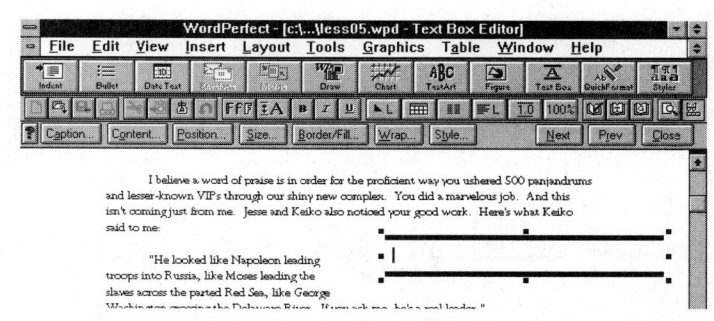

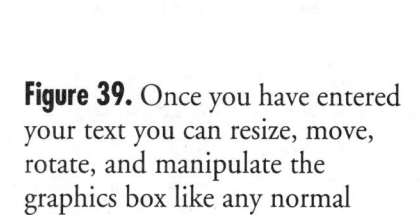

Figure 39. Once you have entered your text you can resize, move, rotate, and manipulate the graphics box like any normal graphic.

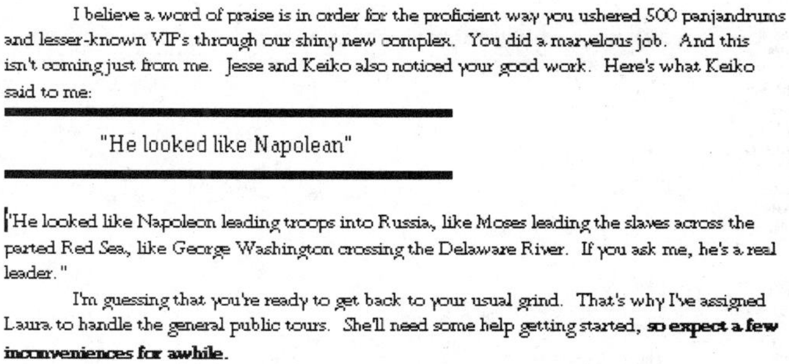

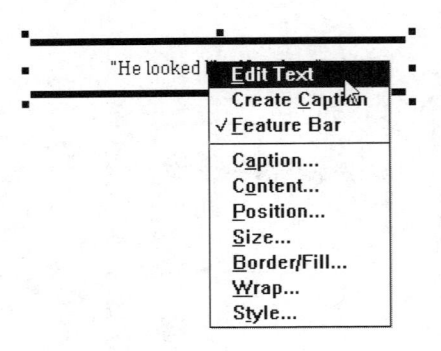

Figure 40. To edit the text in the text box once it is on the page, activate its QuickMenu and select the *Edit Text* command.

EQUATIONS

You can also make equations appear in graphics boxes, and edit them in similar ways.

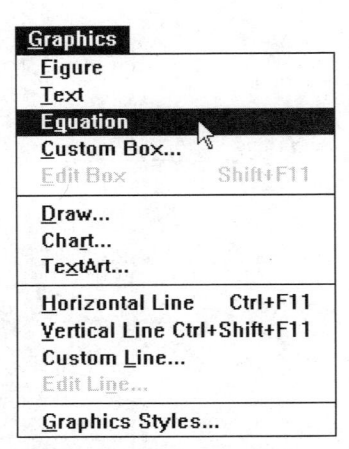

Figure 41. To do this, select the *Equation* command from the **Graphics** menu.

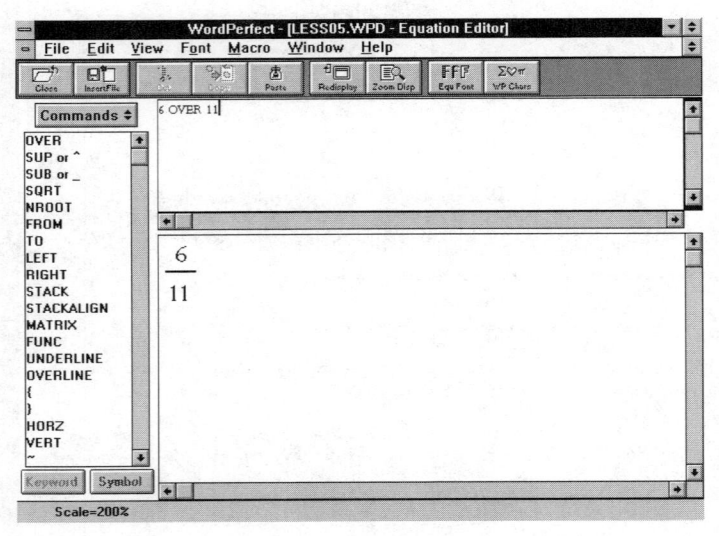

Figure 42. WordPerfect displays the *Equation Editor* screen. Here you can create (but not calculate) mathematical and scientific equations. The list box to the left of the screen contains a variety of symbols and commands you can use in your equations.

The drop-down list above this contains options that display different choices below. Make a selection from the list box, then click on the *Keyword* or *Symbol* button to insert it on the screen. Type numbers and insert the commands and symbols that you need to create your equation.

Click on the *Redisplay* button to display your equation in the preview window and click on *Close* to insert the equation into your document.

Figure 43. Once an equation box appears in the document you can move, resize, and edit it like other WordPerfect graphics boxes. To edit the equation, select *Edit Equation* from the graphics box's QuickMenu.

CREATING LINES

You can create horizontal and vertical lines in WordPerfect and insert them anywhere in your document. You can then resize, move, and edit the lines in your document similarly to a standard graphics box.

Figure 44. To insert a horizontal or vertical line into your document, select either the *Horizontal Line* or the *Vertical Line* command from the **Graphics** menu.

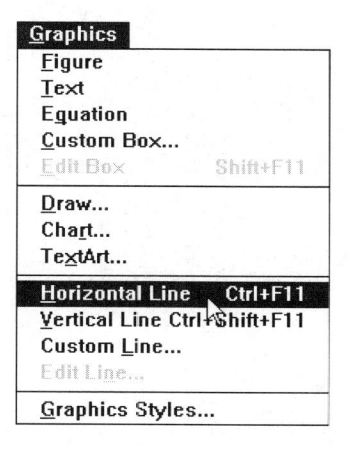

Figure 45. WordPerfect automatically inserts the specified line on your page at the insertion point.

175

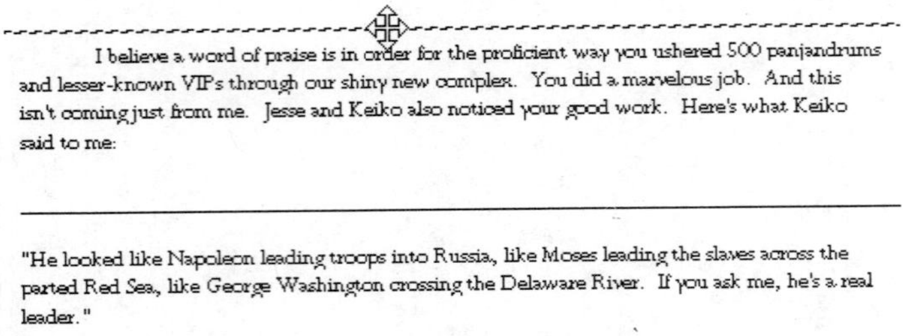

Chapter 11: Graphics

Figure 46. To move a line to a new position, simply click and drag it to the desired location with your mouse.

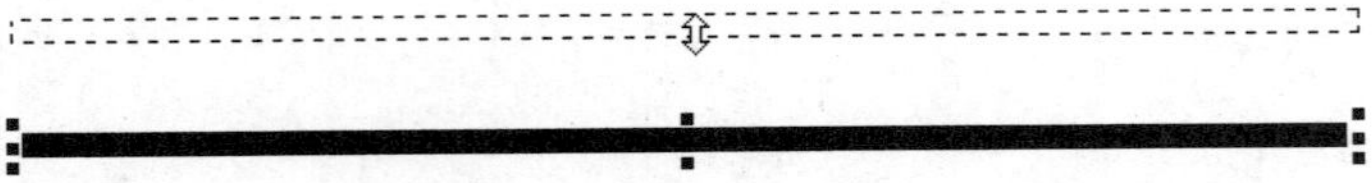

Figure 47. To resize a selected line, use the mouse to drag one of the black handles to a new location. When you release the mouse, WordPerfect redraws the line to its new thickness.

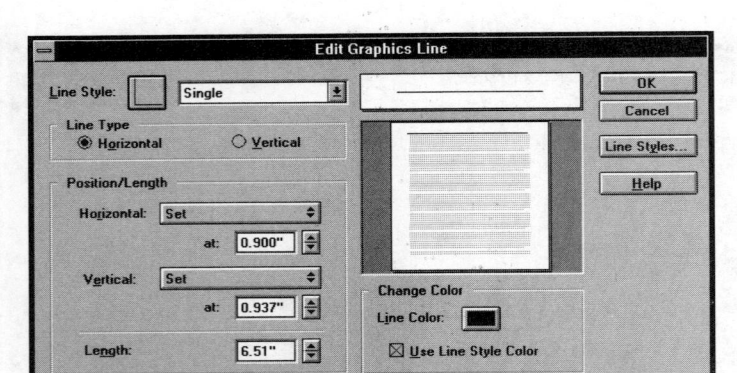

Figure 48. You can also edit any line features by double-clicking on it with the mouse. Doing this opens the *Edit Graphics Line* dialog box. Here you can change a line's style, type, position, length, color, and thickness as well as allowing you to force a distance between the line and any surrounding text.

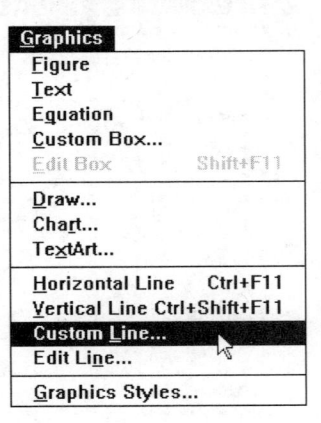

Figure 49. You can also create a custom line to insert into your document by selecting *Custom Line* from the **Graphics** menu. This activates the *Create Graphics Line* dialog box with the same choices as those in the *Edit Graphics Line* dialog box. Create a line with the available options and click on *OK* to insert it into your document.

Chapter 11: Graphics

OBJECT LINKING AND EMBEDDING (OLE) SUPPORT

The OLE support in WordPerfect 6.0 means you can run another application whose data you can include, without storing it in your document. So when you edit the source data, the data in your document is automatically updated.

Figure 50. To insert an OLE object into your WordPerfect document, choose *Object* from the **Insert** menu. In the *Insert Object* dialog box, select the name of the application from where you want to create or retrieve an object, then click on *OK*.

Figure 51. After you have created or retrieved a file, insert an object link in your document by choosing *Update* (or *Apply*) from the **File** menu in the source application.

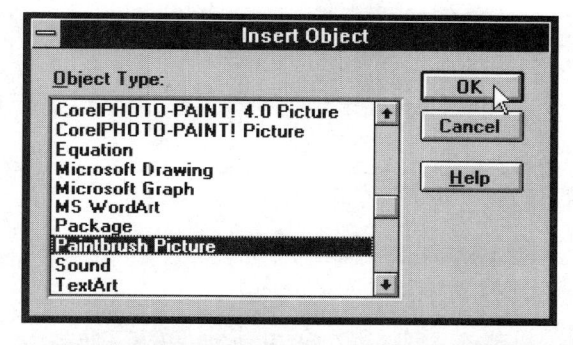

Figure 52. You can also update the embedded object when WordPerfect prompts you with a similar dialog box shown here. It is activated when you try to save the source file or exit the source application without having updated the object.

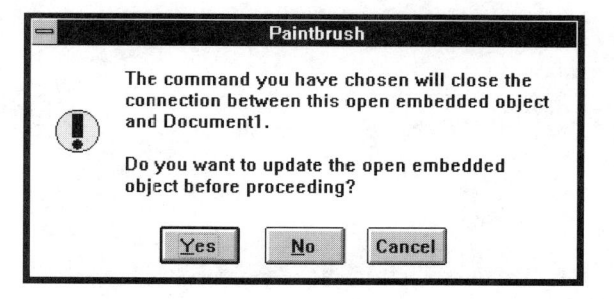

177

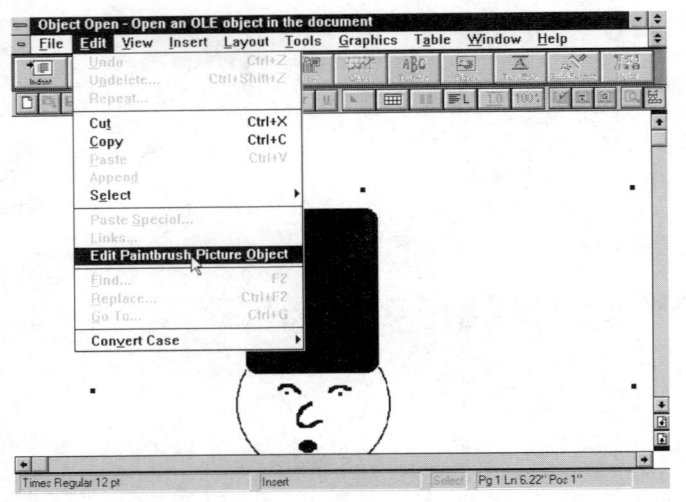

Figure 53. To open and edit an embedded object in your WordPerfect document, double-click on it, or select the object and choose *Edit Object* from the **Edit** menu. You can then make any changes you want and update the changes in your WordPerfect document.

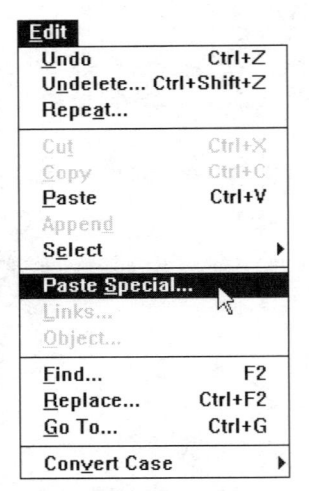

PASTE SPECIAL AND PASTE LINK

Figure 54. Use *Paste Special* from the **Edit** menu to paste the contents of the clipboard into your document in a format you choose. After copying or cutting data to the clipboard from another Windows application, put the insertion point in a new location in the document, and choose *Paste Special* from the **Edit** menu.

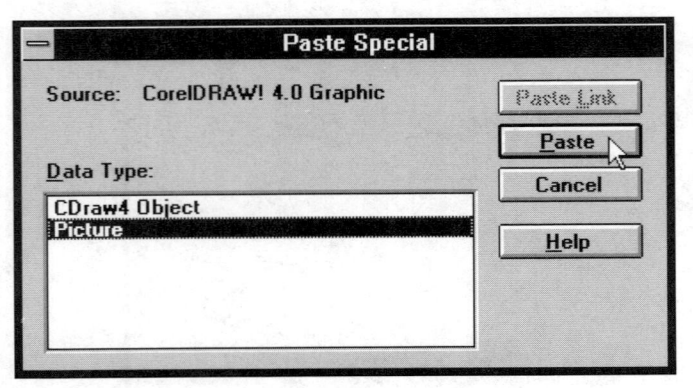

Figure 55. Then select a data type from the *Paste Special* dialog box, and click on the *Paste* button to copy the contents into your document.

Figure 56. To link a file with another document, open the application that you want to create the linked file in. Then either create and save a file, or open an existing file. Copy the image to the clipboard. Open the WordPerfect document that the file will be linked to, position the insertion point and then choose *Paste Special* from the **Edit** menu.

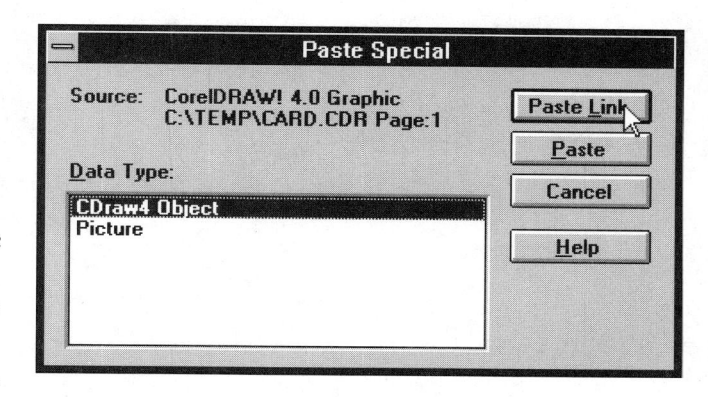

Now select the clipboard object from the *Data Type* list box and click on the *Paste Link* button. If it is not available you have not saved the file. (You can't link unsaved files.)

You can edit a linked file by double-clicking on the object. Unlike an embedded object, when you edit a linked item, the original file is updated to reflect the changes and all documents that are linked to this item are also affected.

Figure 57. Whenever the linked object is not selected you can select *Links* from the **Edit** menu. This opens the *Links* dialog box where you can view, update, edit, or cancel object links. In the *Links* dialog box, the *Update Now* button lets you update a link; *Cancel Link* lets you remove an existing link; and *Change Link* lets you edit an existing link.

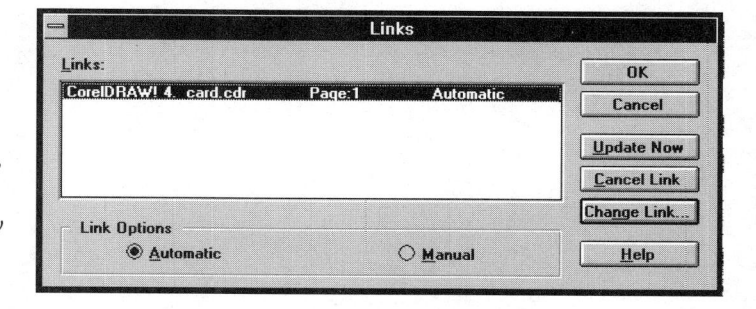

DELETING GRAPHICS

To delete any graphic, select it with the mouse and press the Delete key on your keyboard. You can also delete the graphic's code from the *Reveal Codes* screen. If you delete a graphic by mistake, you can use *Undo* or *Undelete* in the **Edit** menu to restore it.

WP Draw   12

Opening WP Draw

WordPerfect 6.0 now offers a new drawing package, WP Draw, that allows you to create and edit graphics for your document using a variety of tools and commands.

Figure 1. To start WP Draw, click the *Draw* button on the button bar or select *Draw* from the **Graphics** menu.

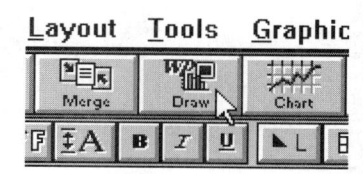

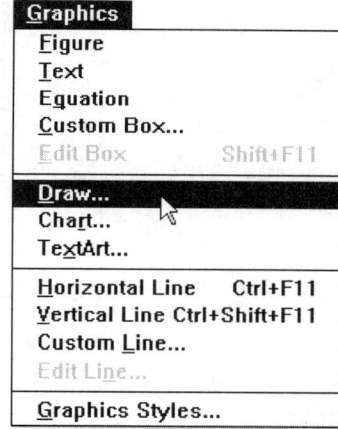

Figure 2. WordPerfect now opens the WP Draw screen with a blank drawing window ready for you to create a graphic. To the left of the drawing window is the tool bar containing a variety of drawing and graphic tools.

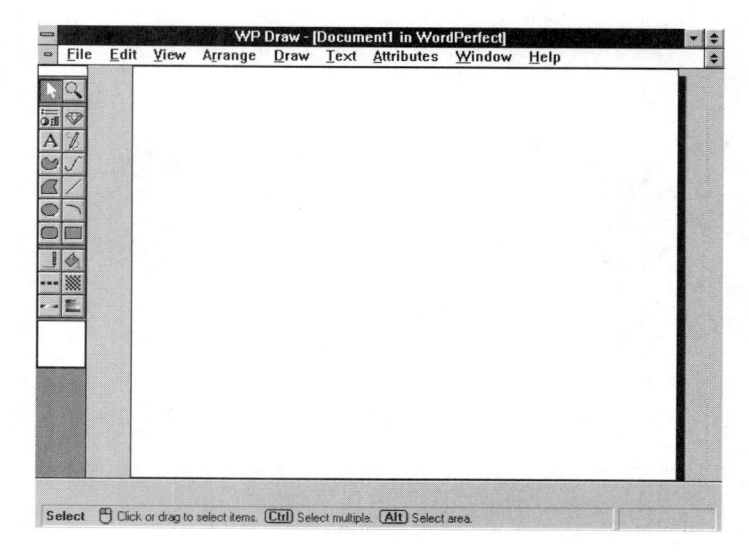

181

Chapter 12: WP Draw

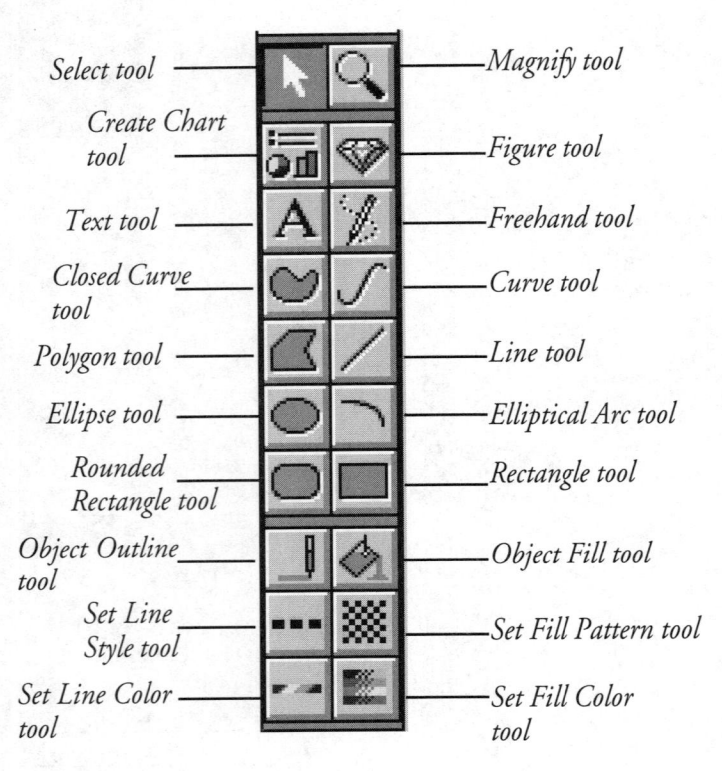

Select tool — Magnify tool
Create Chart tool — Figure tool
Text tool — Freehand tool
Closed Curve tool — Curve tool
Polygon tool — Line tool
Ellipse tool — Elliptical Arc tool
Rounded Rectangle tool — Rectangle tool
Object Outline tool — Object Fill tool
Set Line Style tool — Set Fill Pattern tool
Set Line Color tool — Set Fill Color tool

The Tool Bar

Figure 3. You can select the various tool icons within the tool bar to access a wide range of drawing and graphic functions.

Once you select a tool it remains active until you select another tool to replace it.

Function Tools

The tool bar contains two basic types of tools; function tools and drawing tools. The function tools on the tool bar allow you to manipulate images in the drawing window.

THE SELECT TOOL

You can use the *Select* tool to select, resize, move, rotate, skew, and shape objects. This is the tool that you use most often when working with your images.

Selecting Objects

Figure 4. To select a filled object with the *Select* tool, simply click anywhere in the filled area. To select an object without a fill, simply click somewhere on the perimeter of the object.

When you select an object it displays eight small black handles around its edge. To select more than one object, hold down the Shift key and click on the multiple objects.

Selecting a filled object

Selecting an object with no fill

Two objects selected

182

MARQUEE SELECTION

Figure 5. To select one or more objects in the drawing window, drag the mouse pointer over all objects that you want to select. As you do this a dotted outline defines the area that you are dragging. Any objects entirely within this outlined area become automatically selected.

MOVING OBJECTS

Figure 6. To move an object, simply click and drag it with the *Select* tool. The object moves to wherever you release the mouse. If an object has no fill, click on the border of the object and hold the mouse button down. Then drag the object to its new position.

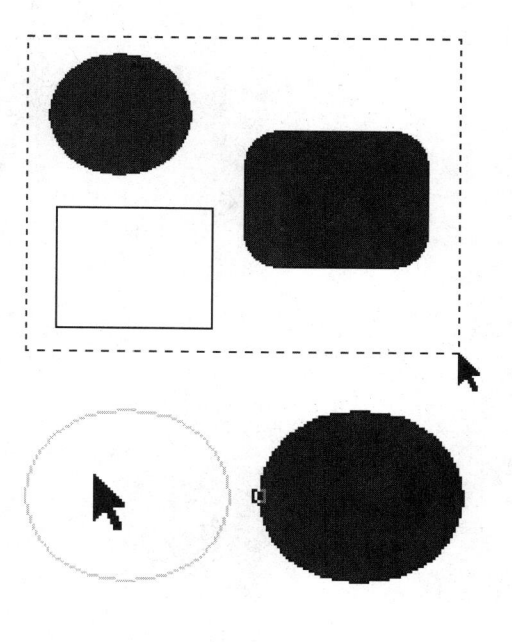

Note: When moving an object without a fill, do not click near the black handles to drag it to a new position. This avoids resizing the object by mistake (see **Resizing Objects** later in this chapter).

RESIZING OBJECTS

Figure 7. To resize an object, select it with the *Select* tool and then drag one of the eight selection handles in any direction. The object then resizes accordingly.

Resizing an object using the handles on the corners keeps the object's proportions in its new size. Dragging the handles on the sides of an object stretches it in the desired direction.

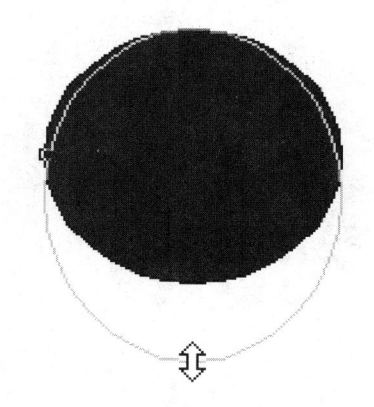

Chapter 12: WP Draw

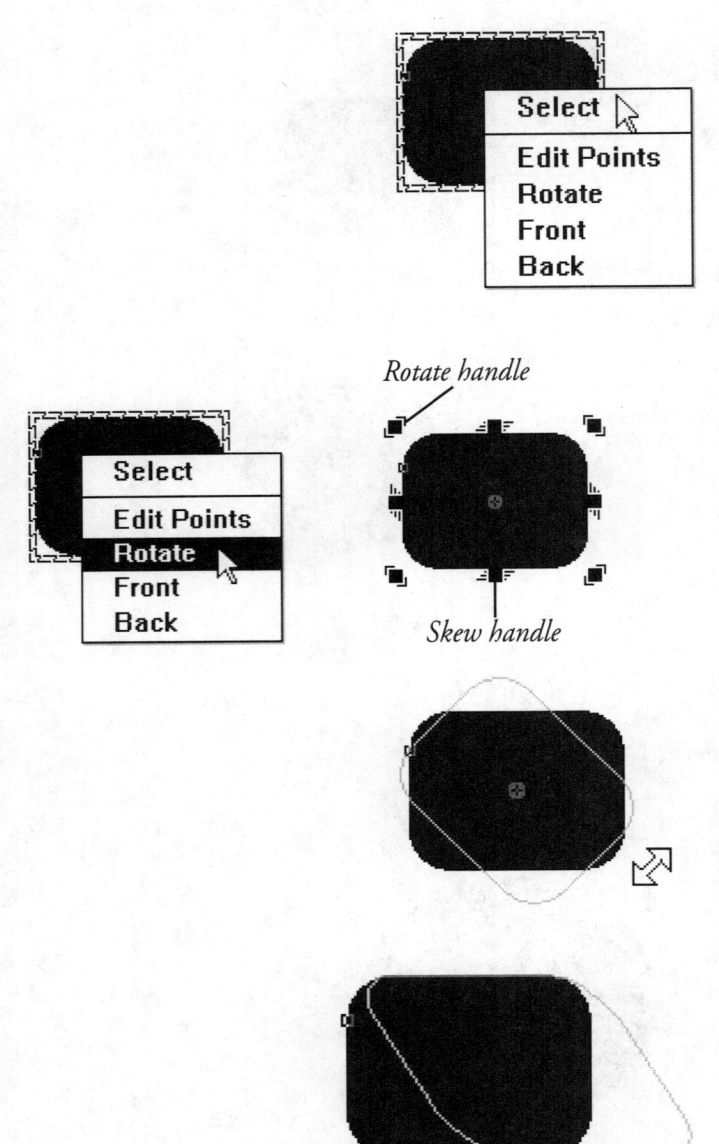

ROTATING AND SKEWING OBJECTS

Figure 8. Using the right mouse button in conjunction with the *Select* tool allows you to rotate, skew, and shape objects in the drawing window. To access these features, click on an object with the right mouse button using the *Select* tool. If the object has no fill, click on the perimeter to access this function.

Figure 9. This frames the object and activates a QuickMenu containing a variety of commands. Select *Rotate* from this QuickMenu to rotate and skew an object. This activates the rotate and skew handles.

Figure 10. To rotate an object, hold the mouse button down on any corner handle and move the object in the direction you want it to rotate. An outline of the object shows you its position as you rotate it.

Figure 11. To skew an object, hold the mouse down on a middle handle and move it in the direction you want to skew the object. Once again an outline of the object shows you its position as you skew it.

CENTER OF ROTATION

Figure 12. The small black circle containing cross-hairs in the middle of an object signifies its center of rotation. You can move this center of rotation by dragging it to a new position. Then, whenever you rotate the object, it rotates around this new center position.

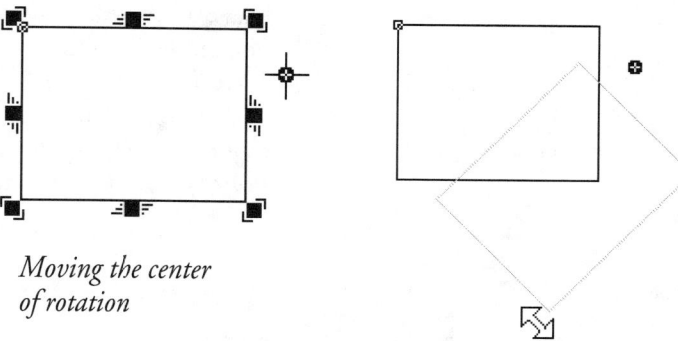

Moving the center of rotation

Rotating around the new center of rotation

RESHAPING AN OBJECT

Figure 13. To reshape an object, use the *Select* tool with the right mouse button to activate the object's QuickMenu and then select *Edit Points*. This activates an object's edit points that you can move and manipulate to reshape an object.

Figure 14. For example, to reshape a rectangle, activate its edit points and drag one to a new location.

Figure 15. You can add edit points and change their properties by activating a QuickMenu for any edit point by clicking on the right mouse button.

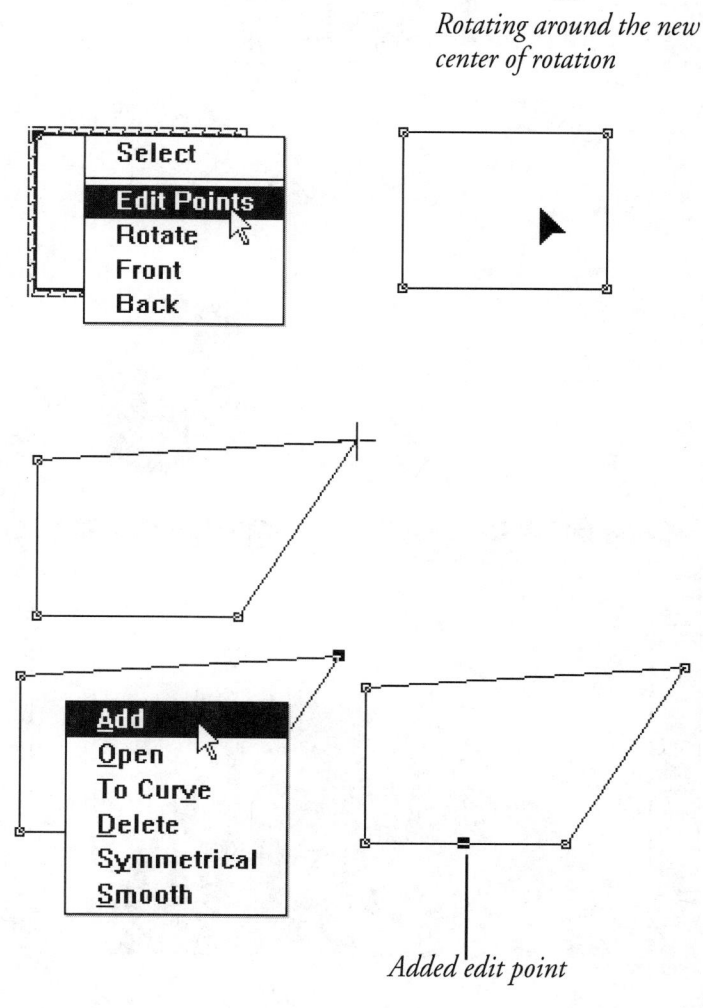

Added edit point

The *Add* and *Delete* commands add or remove edit points between two edit points. The *Open/Close* commands remove or add lines between two edit points and the *To Curve*, *To Line*, *Symmetrical*, and *Smooth* commands change the nature of a curved or straight line joining three edit points. For more information on edit point properties see your *WordPerfect Draw Guide*.

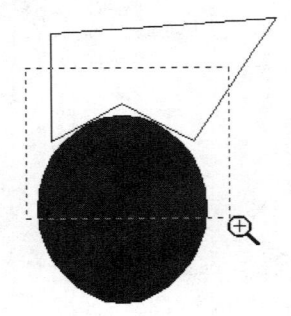

THE ZOOM TOOL

Figure 16. Selecting the *Zoom* tool activates a fly-out menu where you can change the viewing size and position of the screen. The fly-out menu contains the *Zoom In* and *Page View* options.

Figure 17. The *Zoom In* tool allows you to select an area of your graphic to view at a larger magnification. To do this, click and drag an area with the *Zoom In* tool.

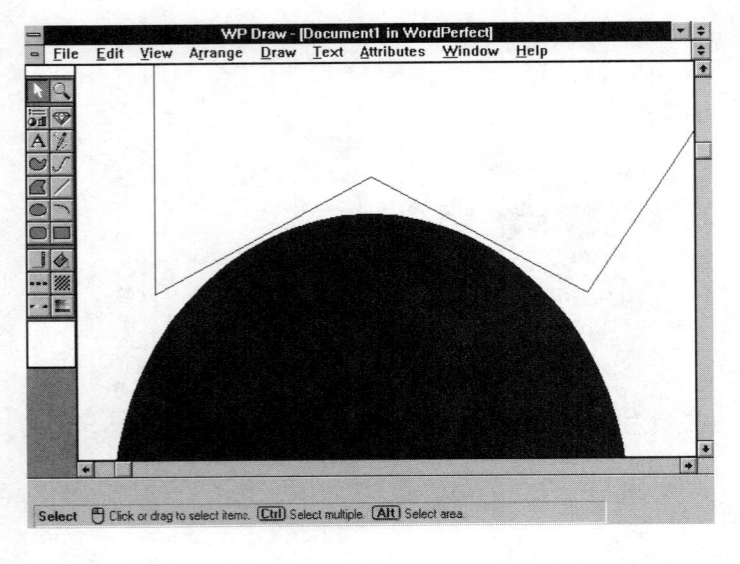

Figure 18. The area outlined by the *Zoom In* tool now fills the entire screen.

Chapter 12: WP Draw

Figure 19. To change back to a full page view, select the *Page View* tool from the *Zoom* tool's fly-out menu.

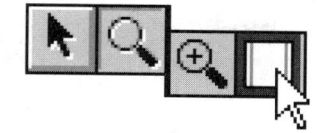

THE CHART TOOL

The *Chart* tool allows you to define an area in the drawing window where you wish to create a WordPerfect chart.

Figure 20. Select the *Chart* tool and click and drag an area in the drawing window where you want to insert a chart. The resulting outline defines the area where the chart will appear.

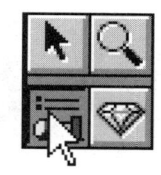

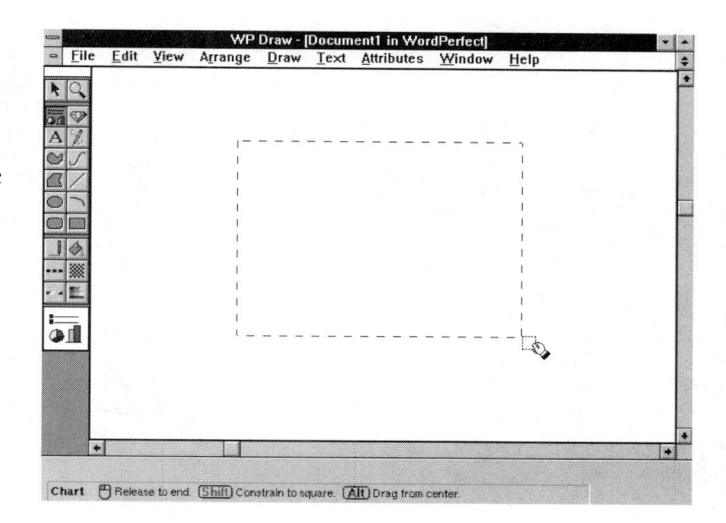

Figure 21. When you release the mouse button the *Create Chart* dialog box appears where you can specify what kind of chart you want to create. Clicking *OK* opens the Chart Editor screen where you can create your chart (see **Chapter 9** for information on creating charts).

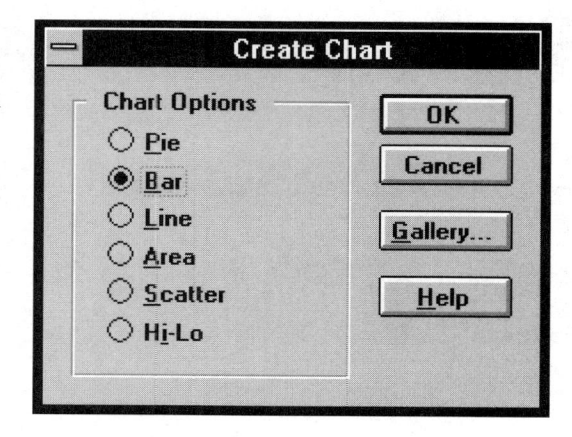

187

Chapter 12: WP Draw

THE FIGURE TOOL

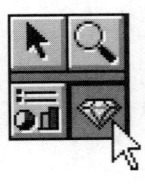

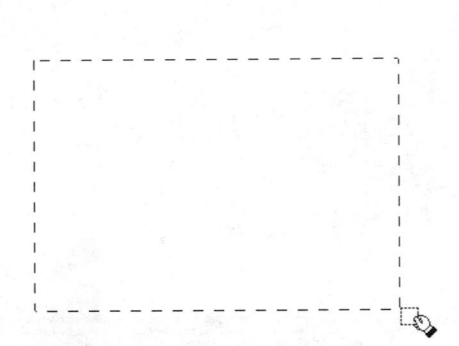

Figure 22. Use the *Figure* tool to define an area in the drawing window where you want to insert a graphic file figure. Click and drag an area in the drawing window where you want the figure to appear.

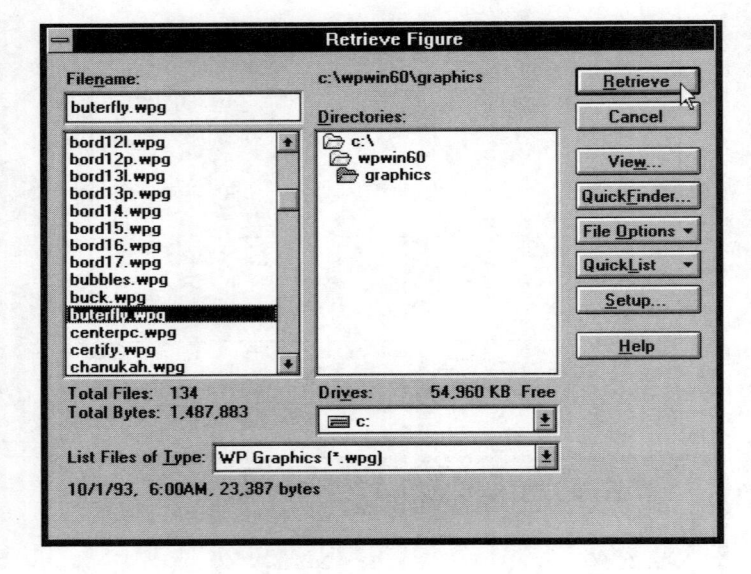

Figure 23. When you release the mouse pointer, WordPerfect opens the *Retrieve Figure* dialog box. Use this dialog box to search the available drives and directories for the figure you want and then double-click on its filename.

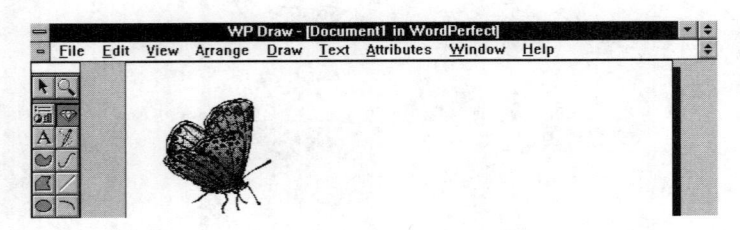

Figure 24. WordPerfect now inserts the figure into WP Draw for you to edit as you wish.

188

THE OBJECT OUTLINE/ FILL TOOLS

Select the *Object Outline* and *Object Fill* tools to turn an object's outline or fill on and off.

Figure 25. Select an object with the *Select* tool and then select the *Object Outline* or *Object Fill* tool. This activates a fly-out menu where you can specify if you want the object to have an outline or fill.

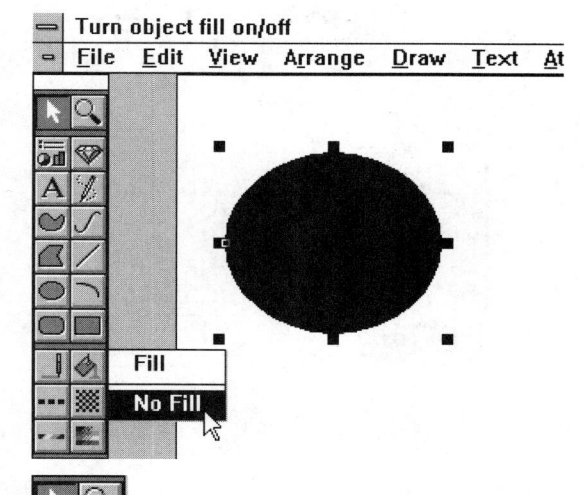

Figure 26. Alternatively, you can select the *Object Outline* or *Object Fill* tool before drawing an object to determine if the object will include an outline or a fill.

Note: You cannot specify for an object to have no outline and no fill. If you turn off one characteristic for an object, the other is activated by default.

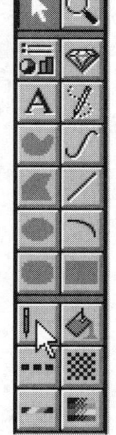

THE SET LINE STYLE/FILL PATTERN TOOLS

The *Set Line Style* and *Set Fill Pattern* tools can also be used for selected objects or objects that you want to draw. These tools let you specify line types and fill patterns for objects you draw in the drawing window.

Chapter 12: WP Draw

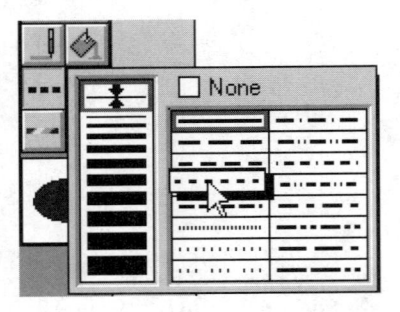

Figure 27. Click on the *Set Line Style* tool to activate a fly-out menu of line types and thicknesses. You can now select any type or thickness of line to apply to a selected object.

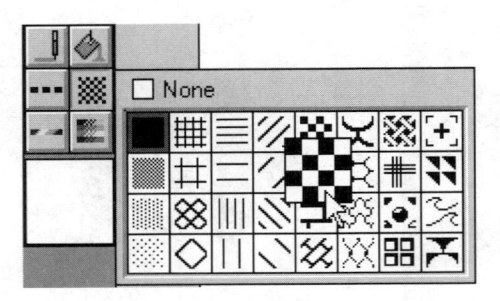

Figure 28. Click on the *Set Fill Pattern* tool to activate its fly-out menu of fill pattern types that you can apply to a selected object.

THE SET LINE/FILL COLOR TOOLS

The *Set Line Color* and *Set Fill Color* tools determine the line and fill colors for selected objects, or objects that you draw in the drawing window.

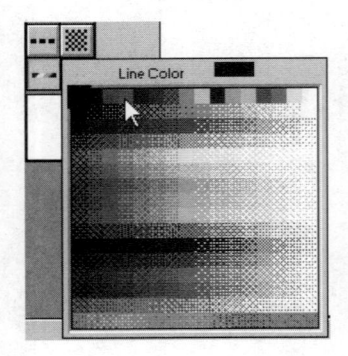

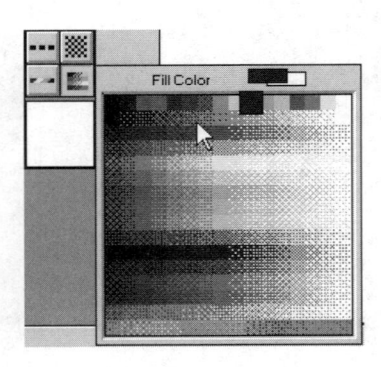

Figure 29. Click on the *Set Line Color* or *Set Fill Color* tool to activate a fly-out color palette where you can choose a color for your lines or fills.

DRAWING TOOLS

The rest of the tools on the tool bar allow you to draw various types of objects and lines in the drawing window.

THE TEXT TOOL

Select the *Text* tool to insert text in the drawing window. You can then edit and format the text as you wish, or resize and manipulate the text box to suit your needs.

Figure 30. Select the *Text* tool and then drag an outline where you want to insert text in the drawing window.

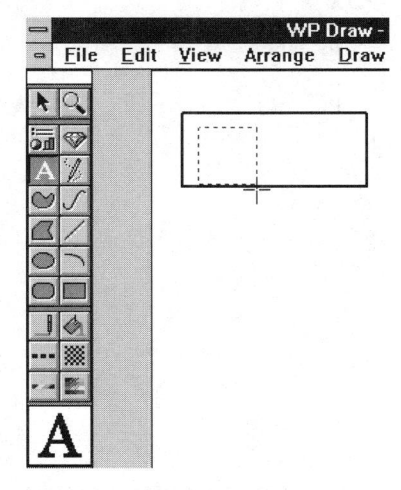

Figure 31. WordPerfect selects the outlined area as an object and the insertion point appears, ready for you to enter text. You can format the text using the **Text** menu.

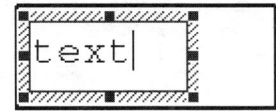

Figure 32. You can manipulate a text box at any time using the *Select* tool. You can also edit text by activating a text box QuickMenu with the *Select* tool and selecting the *Edit Text* command.

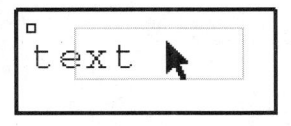

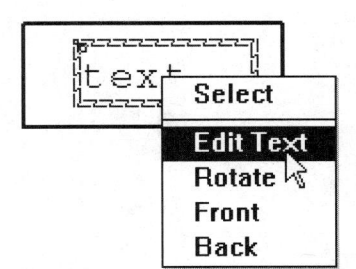

THE FREEHAND TOOL

The *Freehand* tool allows you to draw freehand lines in the drawing window.

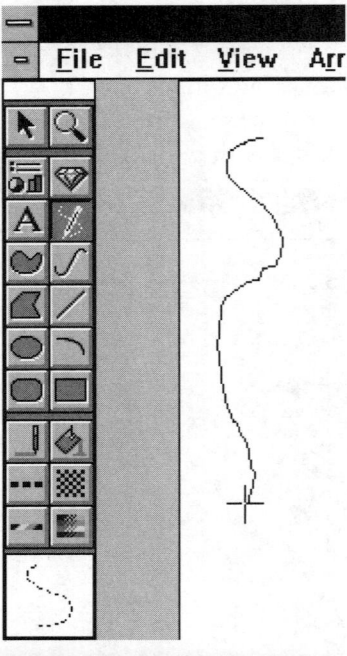

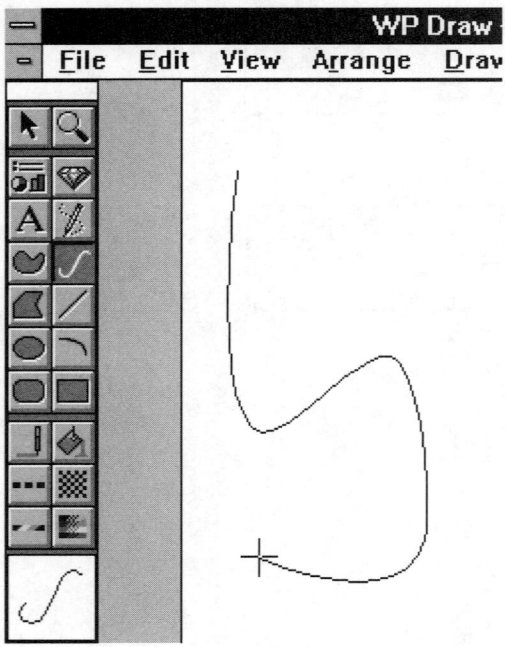

Figure 33. Select the Freehand tool and then click and drag the mouse pointer in the drawing window to draw freehand lines like you would with a pencil. When you release the mouse button, the line you are drawing ends.

Once you have drawn a line with the *Freehand* tool you can select and manipulate it using the *Select* tool.

THE CURVE TOOL

Use the *Curve* tool to draw curved lines in the drawing window.

Figure 34. After selecting the *Curve* tool, click the mouse pointer in the drawing window where you want your line to begin. Now, as you move the mouse, a line extends from the starting point to the mouse pointer position. To draw a curve, click the mouse button again to specify the curve point. The line now curves to wherever the mouse pointer is. Repeat this process as many times as you need and double-click to end your line.

Once you have drawn a line with the *Curve* tool you can select and manipulate it using the *Select* tool.

THE CLOSED CURVE TOOL

Use the *Closed Curve* tool to draw solid curved objects.

Figure 35. Select the *Closed Curve* tool and click in the drawing window to begin tracing the perimeter of your object. Click again to create a curve. You will see a shadowed outline tracing a curve from the pointer back to the starting point of the perimeter. Double-click to finish drawing your object, and the shadowed line finishes the perimeter of your image to become solid.

Once you have drawn an object with the *Curve* tool you can manipulate it with the *Select* tool.

THE LINE TOOL

Use the *Line* tool to draw straight lines in the drawing window.

Figure 36. After selecting the *Line* tool, click the mouse pointer in the drawing window to begin your line. As you move the mouse, a line extends from this starting point to the mouse pointer. Click the mouse button to specify a corner point for your line. The line now extends from this corner point to the mouse pointer and so on. To finish your line, double-click.

You can manipulate the line using the *Select* tool.

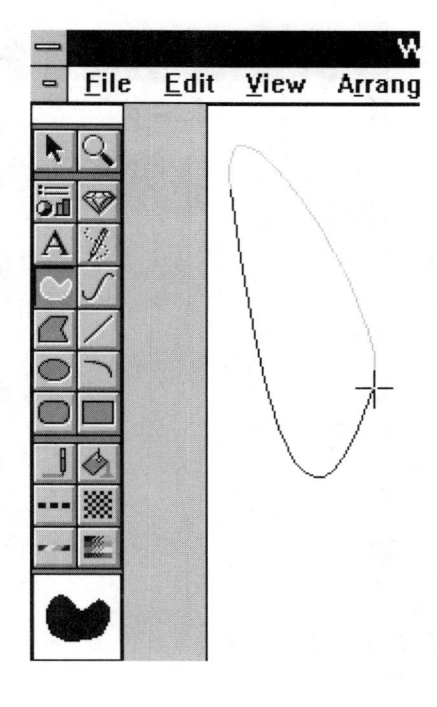

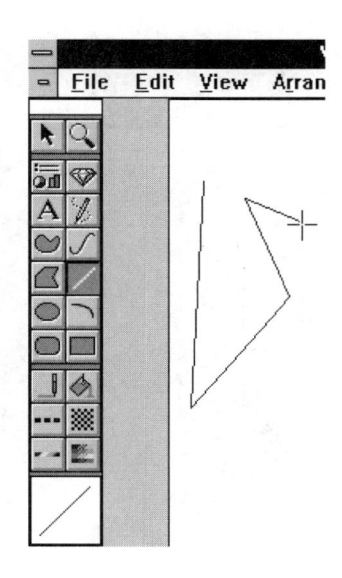

THE POLYGON TOOL

Use the *Polygon* tool to draw polygons.

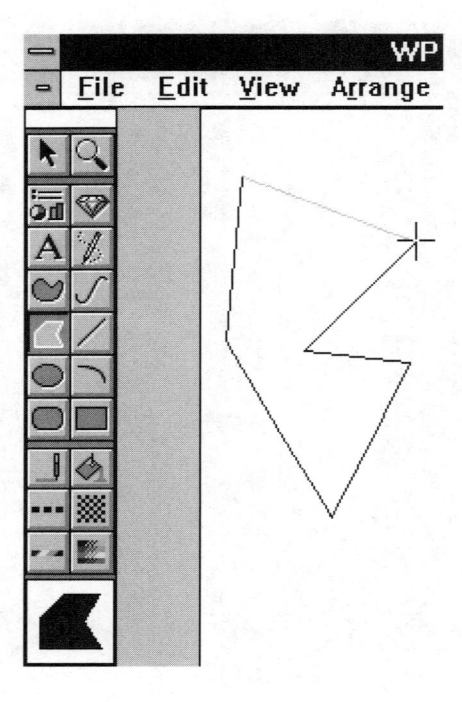

Figure 37. Select the *Polygon* tool and click in the drawing window where you want to begin tracing the perimeter of your polygon. The *Polygon* tool now operates in exactly the same way as the *Line* tool, except that a shadowed outline traces a line from the cursor back to the starting point of the perimeter. When you double-click to finish drawing your object, this shadowed outline becomes solid to finish the perimeter of your image.

You can manipulate the polygon using the *Select* tool.

THE ELLIPTICAL ARC TOOL

Use the *Elliptical Arc* tool to draw sections of an ellipse.

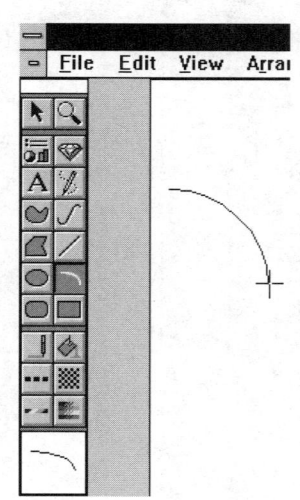

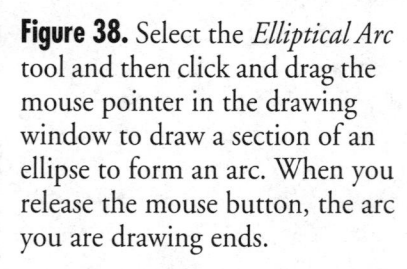

Figure 38. Select the *Elliptical Arc* tool and then click and drag the mouse pointer in the drawing window to draw a section of an ellipse to form an arc. When you release the mouse button, the arc you are drawing ends.

Once you have an arc you can manipulate it using the *Select* tool.

THE ELLIPSE TOOL

Use the *Ellipse* tool to draw an ellipse.

Figure 39. Select the *Ellipse* tool and then click and drag the mouse pointer in the drawing window to draw an ellipse. When you release the mouse button, the ellipse becomes a solid image.

You can manipulate an ellipse using the *Select* tool.

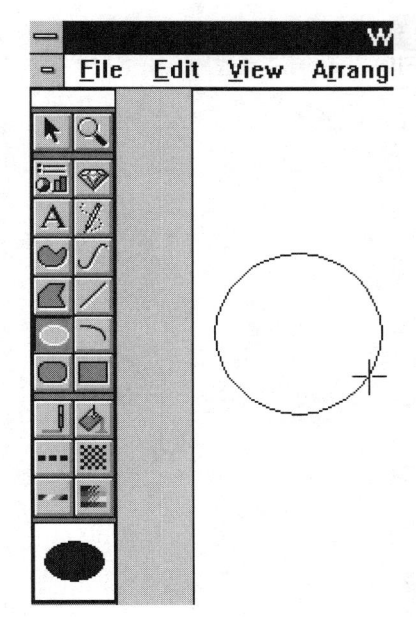

THE RECTANGLE AND THE ROUNDED RECTANGLE TOOL

You use the *Rectangle* tool and the *Rounded Rectangle* tool to draw rectangles.

Figure 40. You use these two tools in exactly the same way as the *Ellipse* tool to create these types of rectangles.

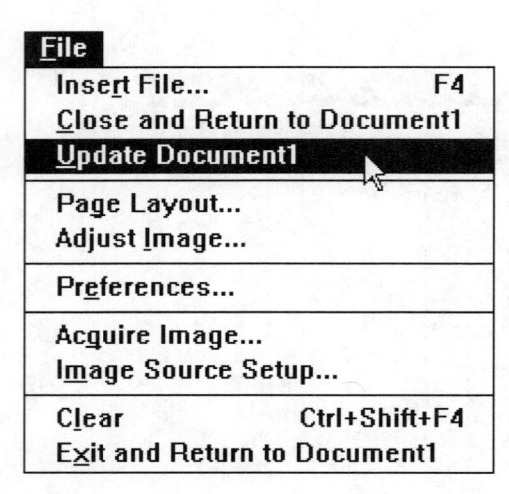

Updating Your Document

Figure 41. You can insert your figure into your document at any time by selecting *Update Document* from the WP Draw's File menu. This inserts your figure in its own graphics box at the insertion point in your document while you remain in WP Draw.

Alternatively, whenever you select *Close/Exit and Return to Document*, you are prompted to update your document with your latest WP Draw image. Click on *Yes* to update your document and exit WP Draw.

The WP Draw Menus

There are many more commands in the WP Draw menus that allow you to manipulate and work with your figures. For an explanation of the menu commands see your *WordPerfect Draw Guide*.

TextArt 13

TextArt

WordPerfect now allows you to create graphically enhanced text that you can insert into your document as a graphic through the TextArt feature. You can then edit your text graphic at any time, change its wording and attributes and update your document as you wish. You can even save your TextArt as files that you can access at any time in the future.

Starting TextArt

Figure 1. To start TextArt, click on the *TextArt* button on the button bar or select *TextArt* from the **Graphics** menu.

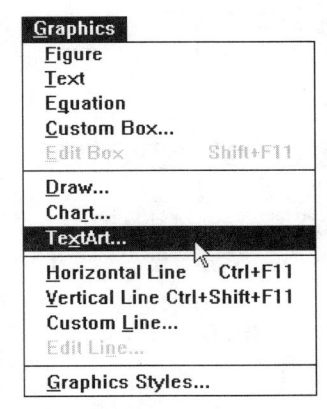

Figure 2. This opens the *TextArt* dialog box where you can create your TextArt graphics.

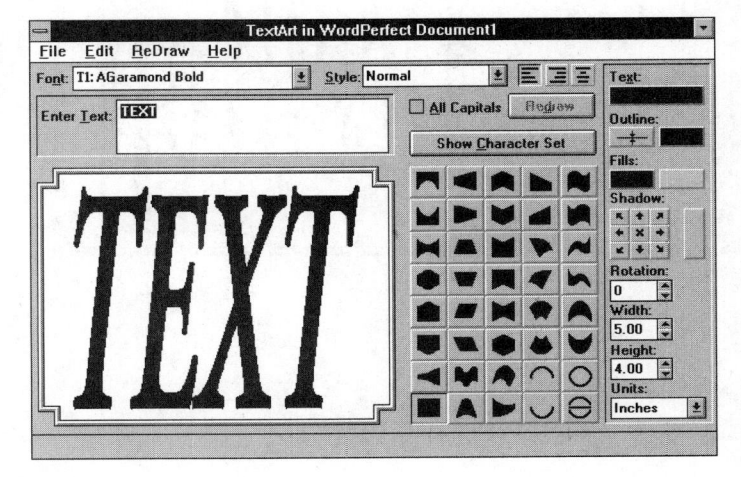

197

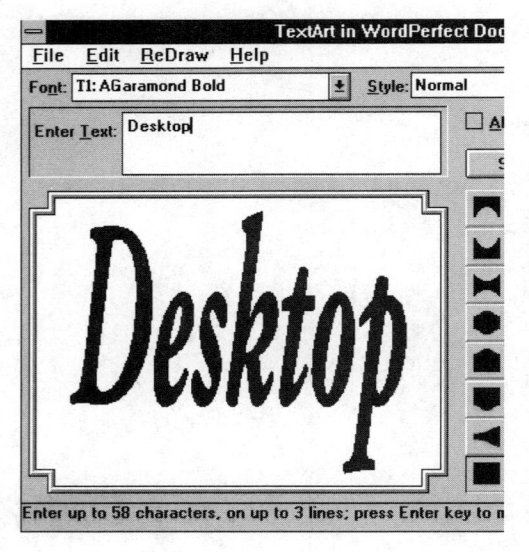

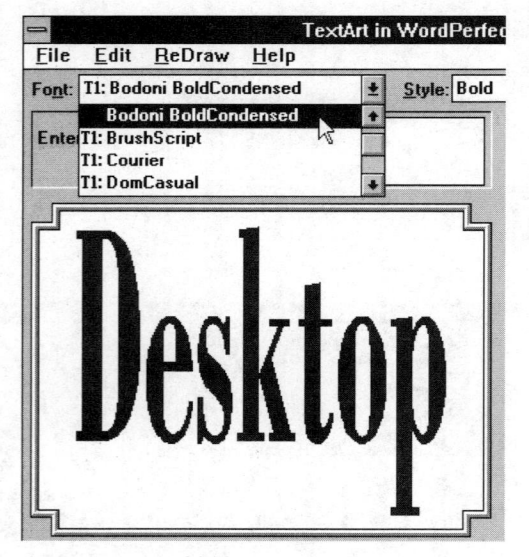

CREATING TEXT

Figure 3. The *Enter Text* text box currently contains the highlighted word "TEXT." This is where you enter the text that you want to include as your TextArt image. Simply type the text that you want into this entry box.

As you do so, the display window below the *Enter Text* text box redraws to show what your TextArt image looks like. Any changes that you make in the dialog box are shown in this display window.

CHANGING FONTS AND STYLES

Figure 4. The *Font* section of the dialog box lets you change the font of your TextArt image. Click on the down arrow to activate a drop-down list of available fonts that you can choose from.

Figure 5. The *Style* section of the dialog box allows you to change the style of the text in your TextArt image. Activate the *Style* drop-down list and choose an available style.

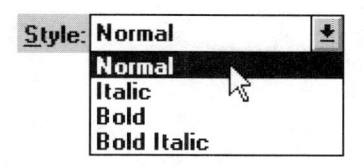

TEXT ALIGNMENT

Figure 6. The three icons to the right of the *Style* section allow you to set the justification of your TextArt text image if it is more than one line long. Click on the first of these icons to align your text to the left, click on the middle icon to align text to the right, and click on the last icon to center your text.

REDRAWING TEXT

Figure 7. The *Redraw* button below the alignment icons allows you to redraw the display window after you have made changes in the dialog box. If this button is grayed out it means that the redrawing setting is on *Auto*. To change to manual redrawing, select *Manual* from the **ReDraw** menu.

The *Redraw* button becomes active. Now, whenever you make changes in the dialog box you must click on the *Redraw* button to see your changes in the display window.

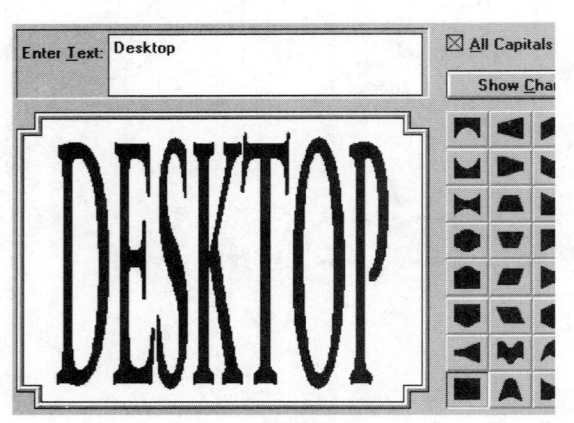

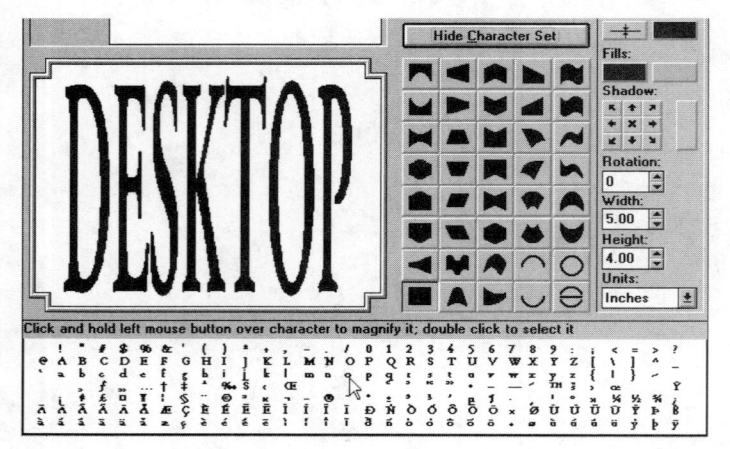

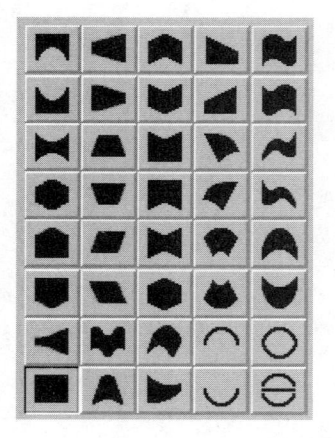

TEXT ATTRIBUTES

CAPITALIZATION

Figure 8. Select the *All Capitals* check box to change your TextArt text into all capitals. When you do this, only the display window reflects the change, the original text remains unaltered.

WP CHARACTERS

Figure 9. Select the *Show Character Set* button to display a window at the bottom of the dialog box containing a variety of text characters. You can now select any of these characters to include in your text by double-clicking on it. To remove the set, click on *Hide Character Set*.

TEXT MOULDS

Figure 10. Below the *Show/Hide Character Set* button is a variety of text moulds. Click on any of these moulds to change the shape of your TextArt image. As you click a mould, your text bends into the shape of that mould.

Figure 11. The display window shows you the effect of each mould on your text.

COLORS AND FILLS

Figure 12. The *Text* section of the *TextArt* dialog box allows you to change the color of your text. Click on the button shown to produce a drop-down palette of colors that you can choose from.

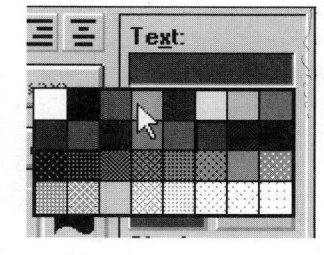

Figure 13. You can also change the color of the outline around your text using the *Outline* section of the dialog box. Click on this button to activate another drop-down color palette for you to choose from.

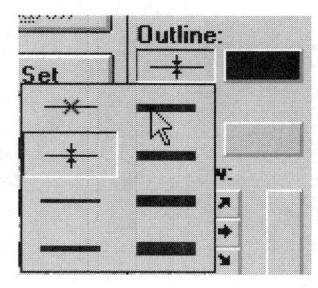

Figure 14. The two buttons in the *Fills* section of the dialog box allow you to determine the fill type and background color for your text. Click on the first button to activate a drop-down list of possible fill types to choose from. If you select a fill type that is not a solid color you can then specify a background color with the second button.

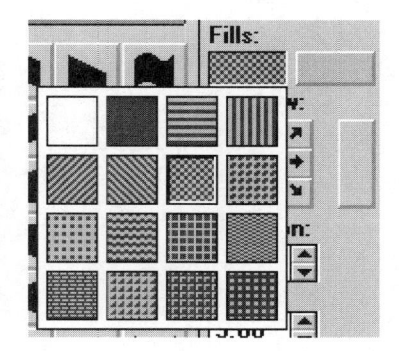

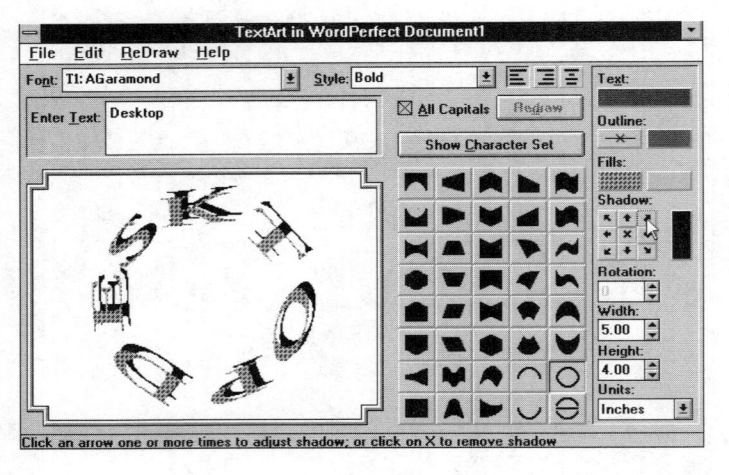

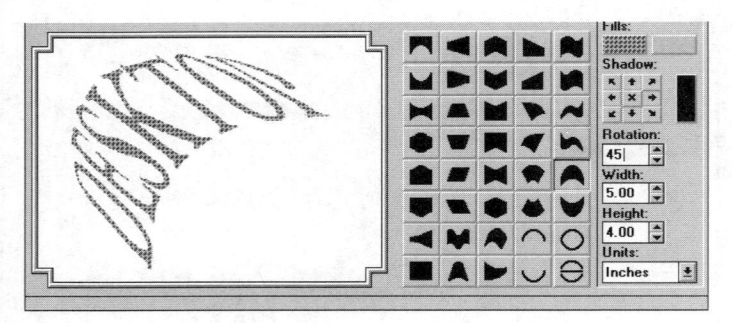

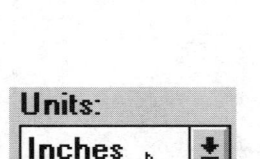

SHADOWS

Figure 15. The *Shadow* section of this dialog box allows you to add a shadow to your text, and to pick the shadow's color. Click the arrows in the *Shadow* section of the dialog box to nudge the shadow once in the direction indicated.

When the shadow is in the position that you want, you can change its color through the button in the *Shadow* section. Click on the button and select a color from the drop-down palette that appears.

ROTATING TEXT

Figure 16. You can adjust the rotation, width, and height of your text by adjusting the values in the spin boxes with the arrows.

UNITS OF MEASURE

Figure 17. Click on the down arrow in the *Units* section of the dialog box to activate a drop-down list of measurement units that you can choose from for determining the height and width of your text.

TEXTART MENUS

Figure 18. Use the **Edit** menu to undo your last command, or to copy any text in the *Enter Text* section of the dialog box to the clipboard.

Figure 19. When you have finished creating your TextArt image, use the **File** menu to save your TextArt images, or exit TextArt and return to your document. You can also select the *Update WordPerfect* command to update your document with the current settings of the *TextArt* dialog box. Alternatively you can create new TextArt images, or open existing TextArt files to include in your document.

Figure 20. This is how your TextArt is placed in your document. You can resize and move it like you would any other graphic.

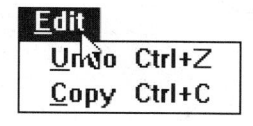

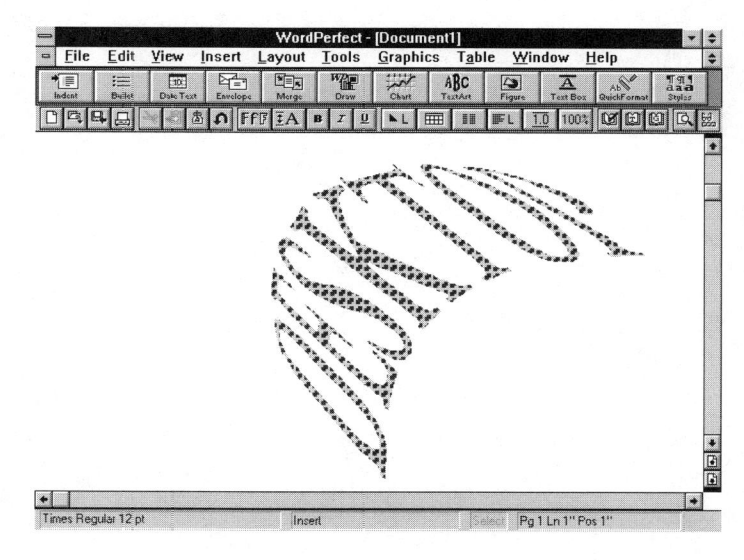

MERGING 14

THE MERGE COMMAND

When you use the *Merge* command in WordPerfect, you can combine a list of variable information (data file) with a standard document (form file) to create multiple documents. This type of merge is often called a mail-merge, because generally you combine a form letter with a data file of names and addresses that are merged into the letter. In this case, the letter is known as the *form file,* while the list of names and addresses is the *data file*.

THE DATA FILE

A data file is made up of fields and records. It may be, for instance, a list of names and addresses. All the particulars about one person are called a *record* and each separate piece of information in that record, such as a name or an address, is a *field*.

Figure 1. As an example of a data file, we will produce a file containing four records (three people's information), with three fields in each record.

```
J. AustenENDFIELD
23 Bridge Way
Northsville 45903ENDFIELD
WriterENDFIELD
ENDRECORD

B. WilesENDFIELD
23 Remuera Rd
Peaksville 490328ENDFIELD
MusicianENDFIELD
ENDRECORD

C. TwainENDFIELD
2/67 Bower Rd
Clontarf 89907ENDFIELD
ArtistENDFIELD
ENDRECORD
```

Figure 2. To do this, click on the *Merge* button on the button bar, or select *Merge* from the **Tools** menu.

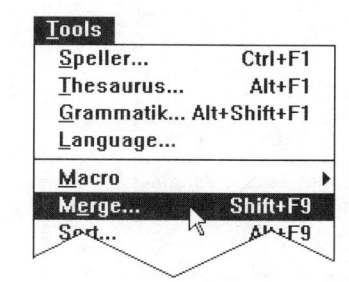

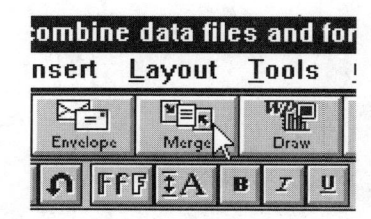

205

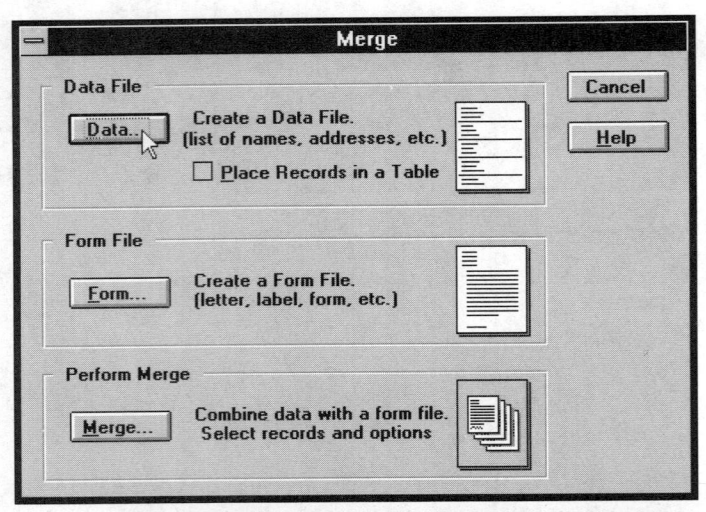

Figure 3. This opens the *Merge* dialog box, where you can specify the type of merge file that you are creating, in this case a data file. To do this, simply click on the *Data* button in the *Data File* section of the dialog box.

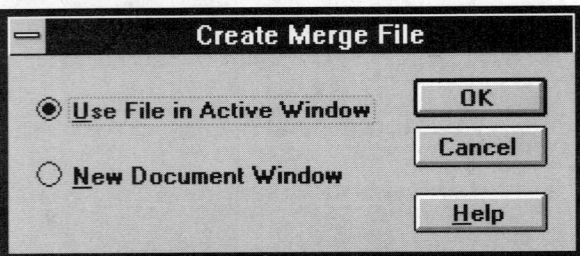

Figure 4. In the *Create Merge File* dialog box, click on *OK* to create the file in the current document.

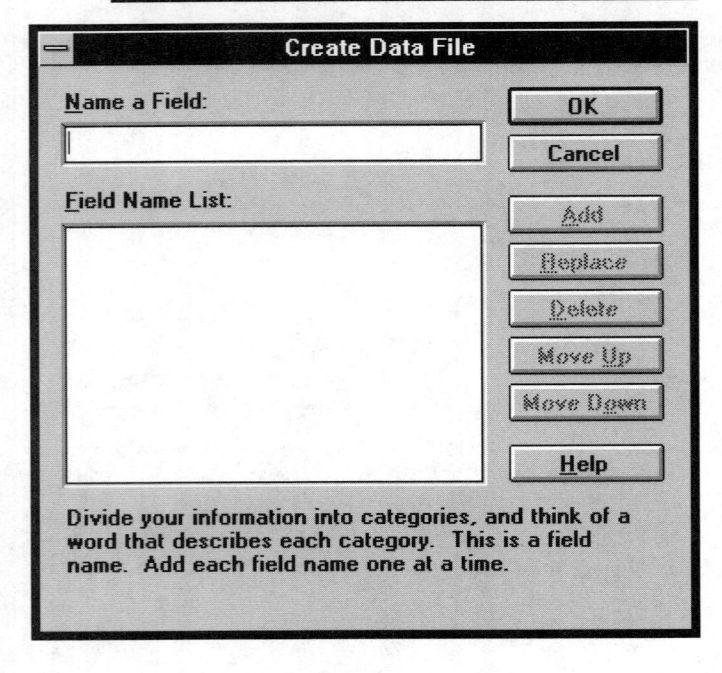

Figure 5. WordPerfect now opens the *Create Data File* dialog box. In this dialog box you specify all of the field names that you want to include in each record. For example, you might wish to have fields that record the name, address and occupation for each record/person in your data file.

Chapter 14: Merging

Figure 6. In the *Name a Field* text box of the dialog box, type the first field name that you want in each record, in this case "Name." Now click on the *Add* button or press Enter to add the field name to the *Field Name List* list box.

Figure 7. Repeat this process to add "Address" and "Occupation" to the *Field Name List* list box. When you have finished creating your field names, click on *OK*.

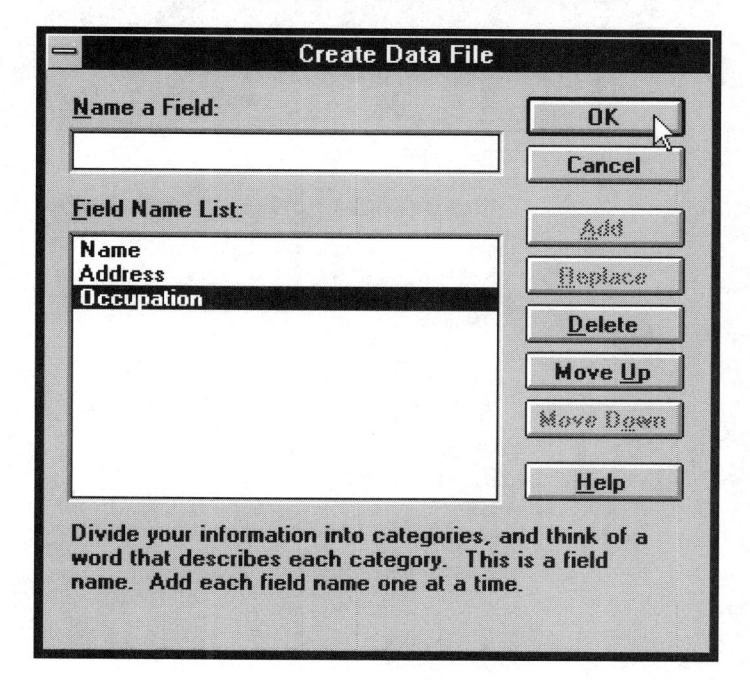

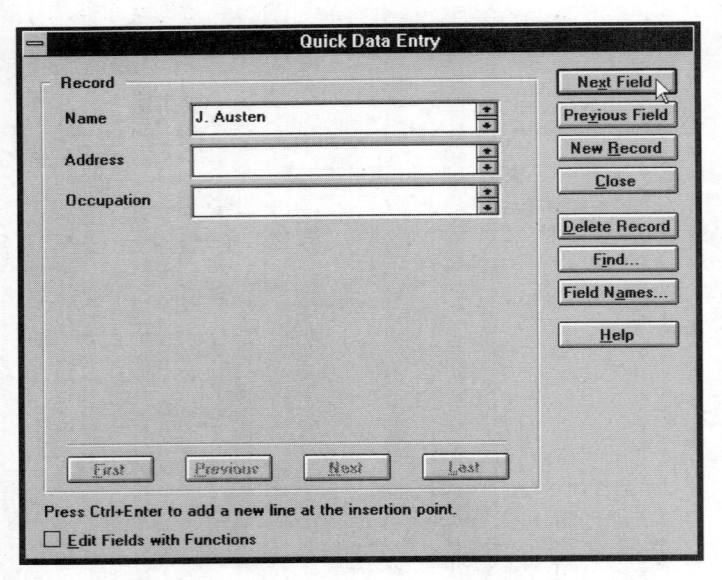

Figure 8. This activates the *Quick Data Entry* dialog box, where you can enter the information for each record of your data file. The *Record* section of the dialog box lists the field names that you created earlier, ready for you to enter your information.

Type the name of the first person in the *Name* text box in this dialog box and then click on the *Next Field* button or press Enter.

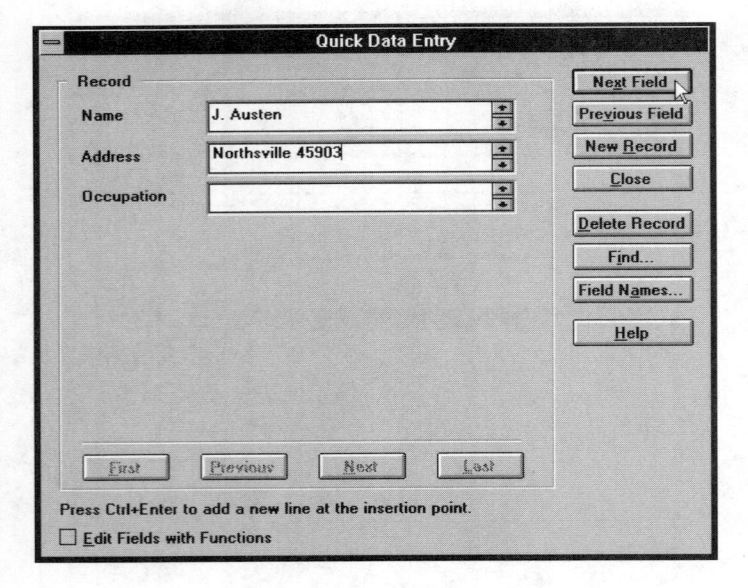

Figure 9. Now type the address of the first person in the *Address* text box.

If you want to include more than one line in a field entry you must press the Ctrl + Enter keys and not just the Enter key because pressing Enter moves you to the next field. You can use the arrows in the text entry boxes to scroll to any field entry lines that you cannot see.

Finally, enter the first person's occupation in the *Occupation* text box.

Figure 10. Because you are in the last field for this record, click on the *Next Record* button or press Enter to begin a new person's record.

Figure 11. Now continue to create records for each person in your list by entering their details in this way. When you have finished entering your information, click on the *Close* button.

WordPerfect prompts you to save this data file so that you can use it later to perform your merge. Click on *Yes* to save your data file.

Now name your file and specify a directory to save it to in the *Save Data File As* dialog box (see **Chapter** 4 for more information on saving files).

Figure 12. This returns you to the editing screen with your information displayed in document form. Each field and record is signified by an ENDFIELD and ENDRECORD code.

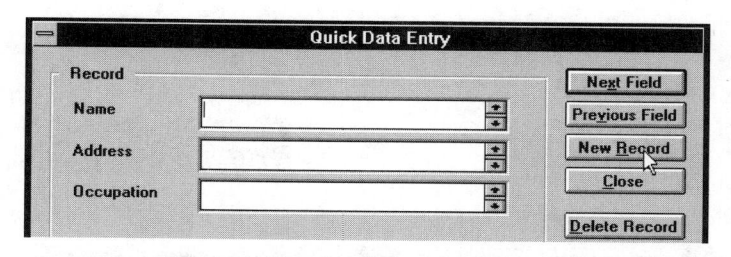

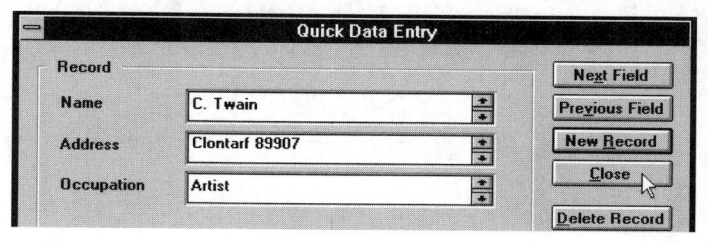

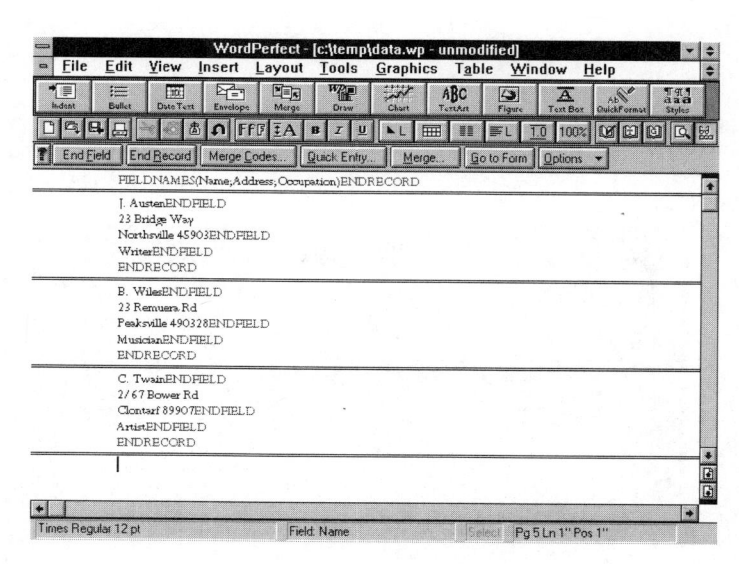

THE FORM FILE

Once you have created and saved your data file, WordPerfect returns you to your document with the *Merge* feature bar activated. You now have to create a form file that can be merged with your data file's field entries.

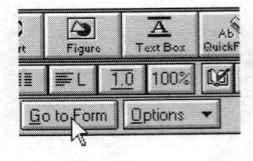

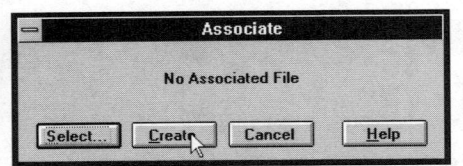

Figure 13. To create your form file, click on the *Go to Form* button on the *Merge* feature bar. This activates an *Associate* prompt box because you haven't associated any form file with the current data file. Either select an existing form file or click on the *Create* button to create a new one.

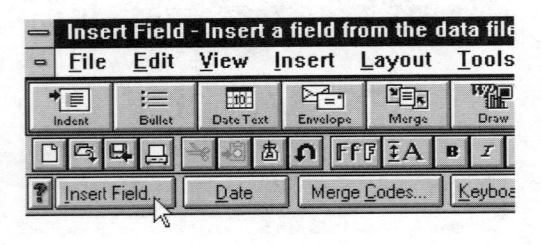

Figure 14. WordPerfect now takes you to a new document. In this example, the form file (or standard document) is a letter. Start creating your letter in the same way you would create any letter. However, when you reach a section of the letter which requires information from the data file, click on the *Insert Field* button on the *Merge* feature bar.

Note: Make sure you put a space after the text so the field code appears one space away.

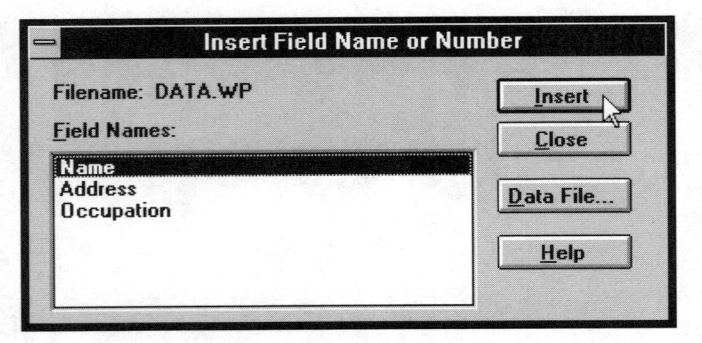

Figure 15. WordPerfect displays the *Insert Field Name or Number* dialog box, where you can specify which data field to insert into your letter. Either double-click on the field name, or highlight it and select *Insert* to insert it into your form file. Then click *Close* to return to your document.

Figure 16. Repeat this process until you have finished creating your letter with field entries for all of your data file fields. Once you have typed the letter with field codes inserted, save the document. (See **Chapter 4** for more information on saving files.)

Merging Files

Figure 17. You can now merge the form and data files to produce a series of "form" letters. To do this, click on the *Merge* button on the *Merge* feature bar.

Figure 18. Once again this opens the *Merge* dialog box. Now to merge the files, click on the *Merge* button in the *Perform Merge* section of the dialog box.

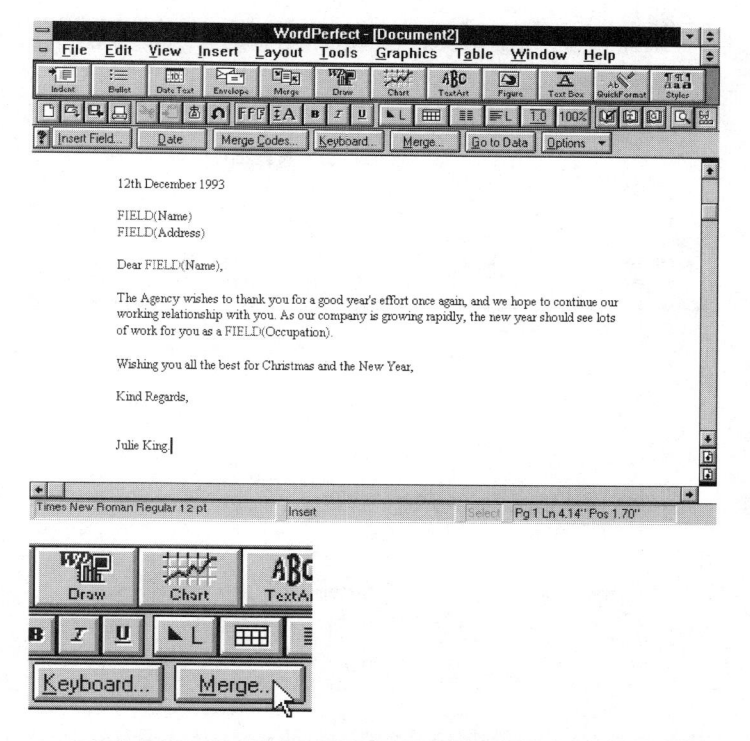

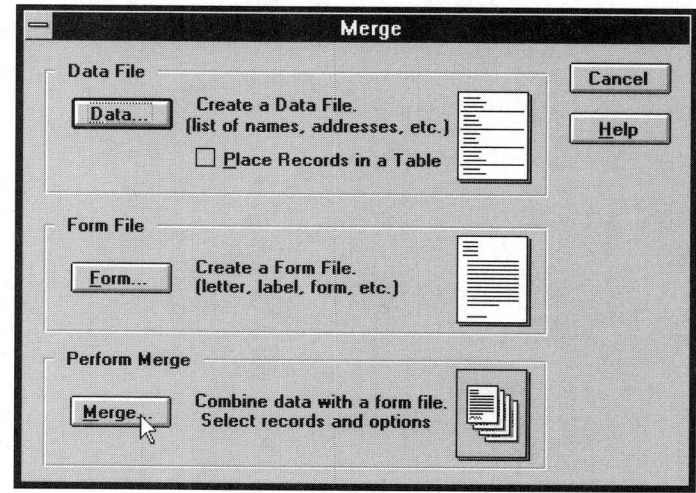

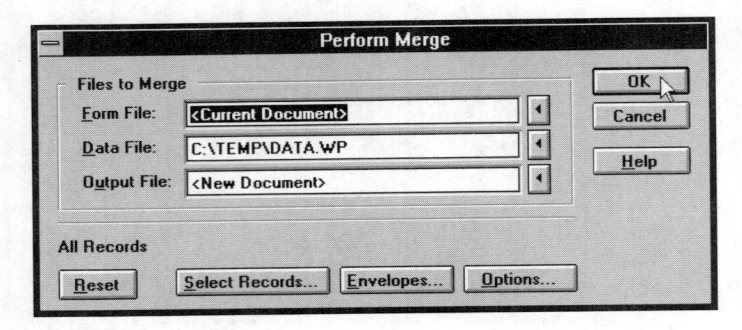

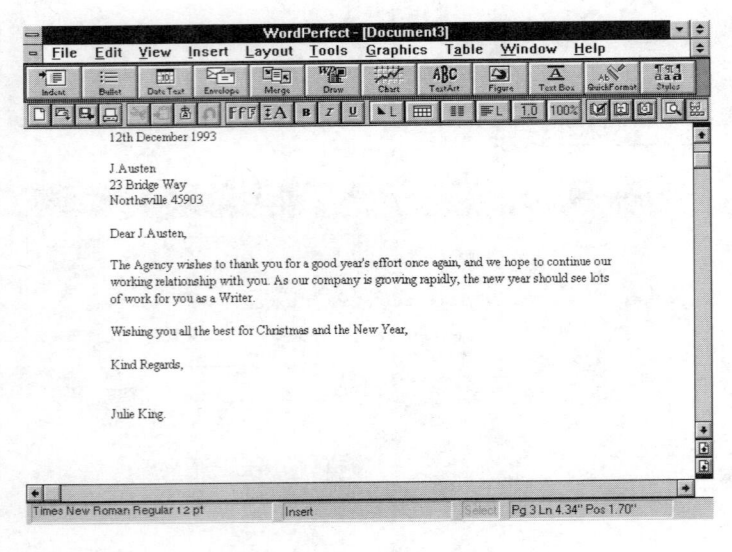

Figure 19. This opens the *Perform Merge* dialog box where you can specify the form, data, and output files. The *Form File* text box contains the words "Current Document." This means you will use the form file that you just created for the merge. Check that the *Data File* text box contains the filename of the data file that you want to use. You can also specify an output file to contain the merged letters, in this case the output file is a new document. Click *OK* to perform the merge.

Figure 20. WordPerfect now creates a new file with the merge completed. There is one form letter for each data record and each letter contains the field information at the appropriate points. WordPerfect inserts a hard page break between the documents of each record.

This newly created document is untitled, so you may wish to save it before printing. Use the vertical scroll bar to view the other letters in the merge.

CREATING MACROS   15

USING MACROS

You use macros in WordPerfect to record a series of commands to perform a task. You can then play them back quickly and easily to achieve this task. Almost anything you can do in WordPerfect for Windows can have a corresponding macro command.

WordPerfect comes with some pre-recorded macros that you can select from the *Play Macro* dialog box (see Figures 7 and 8). You can also create and play back macros through the *Macro* submenu in the **Tools** menu.

RECORDING A MACRO

Figure 1. To begin recording a macro, select *Record* from the *Macro* submenu in the **Tools** menu.

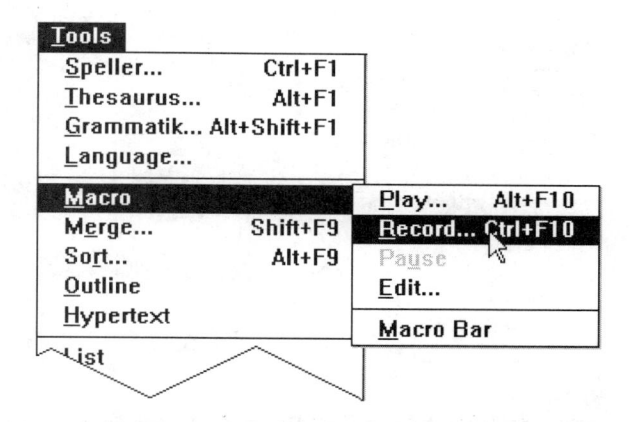

Figure 2. This opens the *Record Macro* dialog box. Type a filename for your macro in the *Name* text box. If you do not specify a directory, WordPerfect saves your macro into the *Macro* directory by default. WordPerfect also automatically appends a *.wcm* extension to your filename if you do not specify one. To begin recording your macro, click on the *Record* button.

213

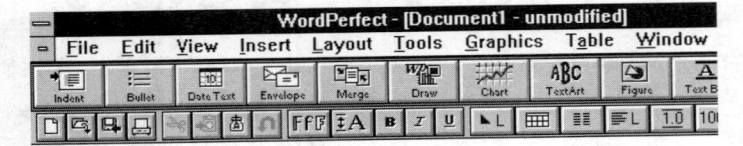

Chapter 15: Creating Macros

Figure 3. You are now returned to the document window with the status bar indicating that you are currently recording a macro. The pointer changes shape when over the editing screen, reminding you that you can't change the position of the insertion point with the mouse when recording a macro.

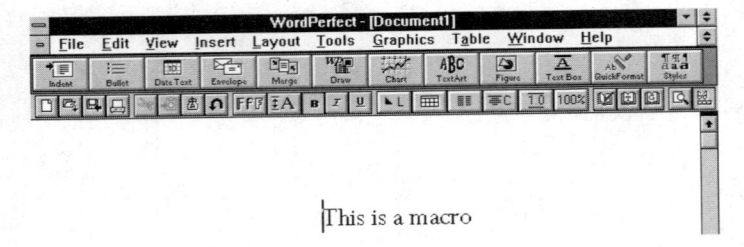

Figure 4. Now, any commands you select from the menus or steps you perform are recorded in the macro. In this example we have entered the text "This is a macro" and formatted it using menu commands.

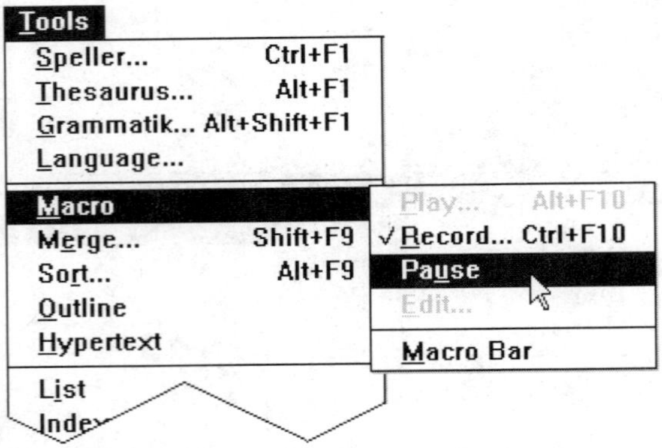

Figure 5. The *Pause* command in the *Macro* submenu lets you pause when recording a macro. Anything you do after selecting *Pause* is not part of the macro. Select *Pause* again to resume recording the macro.

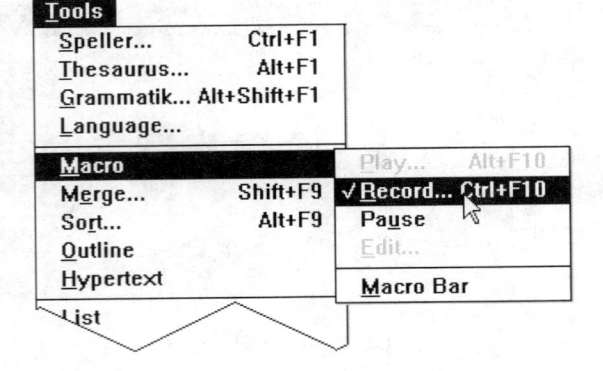

Figure 6. When you have finished performing your macro task, re-select *Record* from the *Macro* submenu to finished recording the macro. The check mark next to the command disappears.

214

PLAYING MACROS

Figure 7. To play a macro in any WordPerfect document, select *Play* from the *Macro* submenu in the **Tools** menu.

This opens the *Play Macro* dialog box. Now click on the list button to open the *Select File* dialog box where you can search for the macro that you want to play.

Figure 8. Find the macro file that you want to play and then double-click on its filename to insert it in the *Play Macro* dialog box.

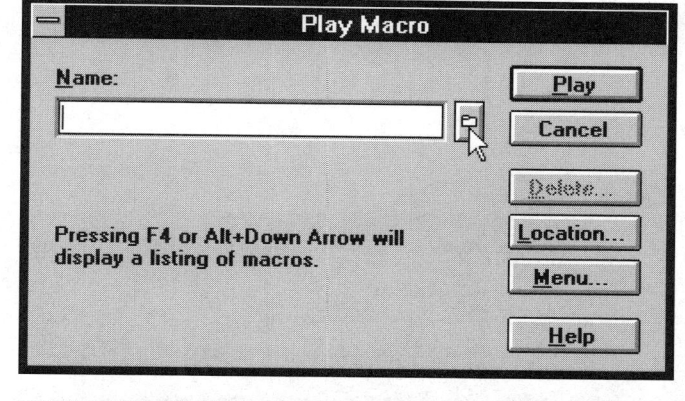

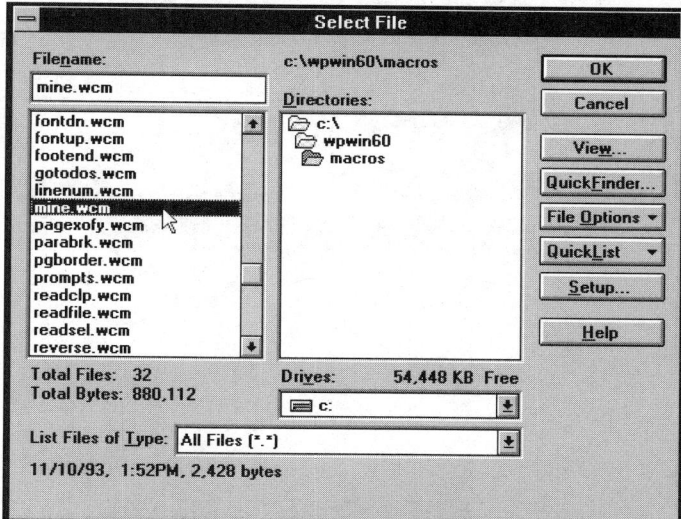

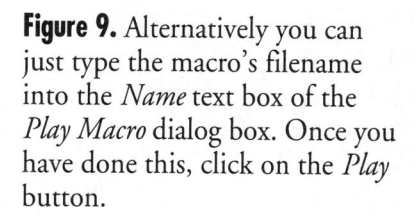

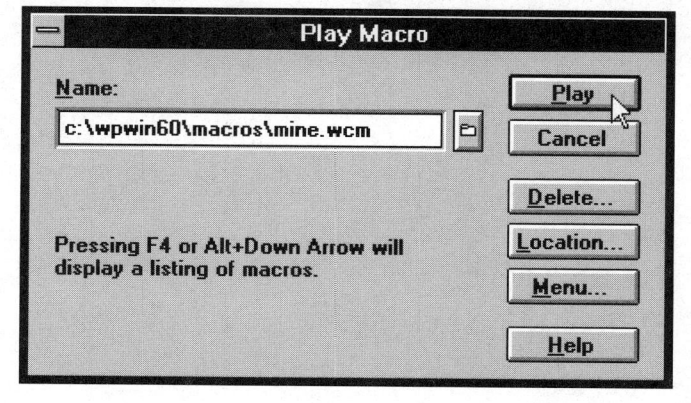

Figure 9. Alternatively you can just type the macro's filename into the *Name* text box of the *Play Macro* dialog box. Once you have done this, click on the *Play* button.

215

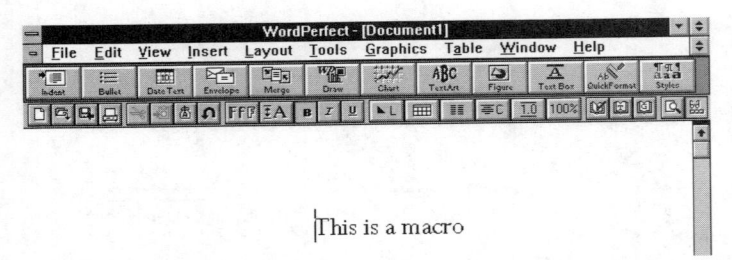

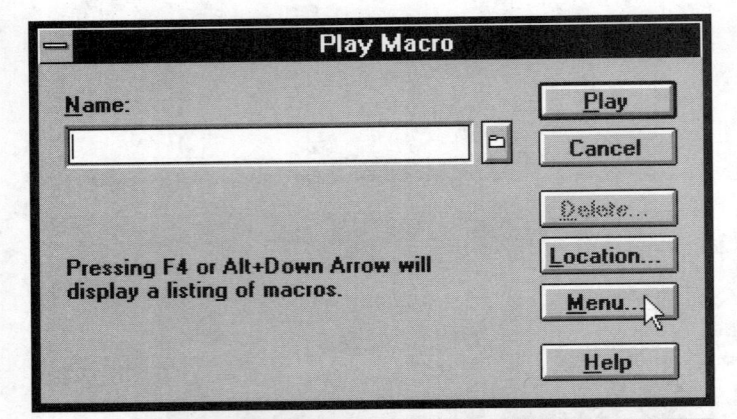

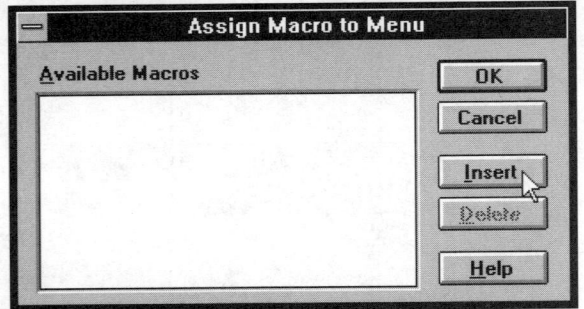

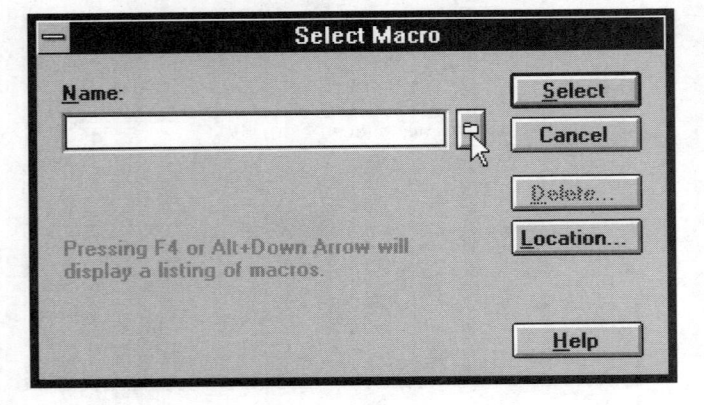

Figure 10. After a few moments, WordPerfect plays the macro you selected in the *Play Macro* dialog box.

PUTTING MACROS IN THE MENU

Figure 11. To simplify the way you use macros, you can add any macro to the *Macro* submenu. To do this, first select *Play* from the *Macro* submenu.

In the *Play Macro* dialog box, you can click on the *Menu* button to assign macros to the *Macro* submenu.

Figure 12. Now in the *Assign Macro to Menu* dialog box click on the *Insert* button to specify macro names that you want to assign to the menu.

Figure 13. This activates the *Select Macro* dialog box where you can choose which macros to include. Click on the list button to open the *Select File* dialog box where you can select the macro that you want.

Chapter 15: Creating Macros

Figure 14. Use this dialog box to find the macro that you want and then double-click on its filename. This returns you to the *Select a Macro* dialog box with the macro inserted in the *Name* text box. Click on the *Select* button to include this macro in the *Available Macros* list.

Figure 15. WordPerfect now returns you to the *Assign Macro to Menu* dialog box with the macro name listed in the *Available Macros* section. Now click on *OK* and then close the *Play Macro* dialog box.

Figure 16. The macro is now listed at the bottom of the *Macro* submenu in the **Tools** menu. You can now play this macro at any time by simply selecting it from the *Macro* submenu.

Note: The four most recently played macros are also listed at the bottom of the Macro submenu. You can play any of these by selecting them directly.

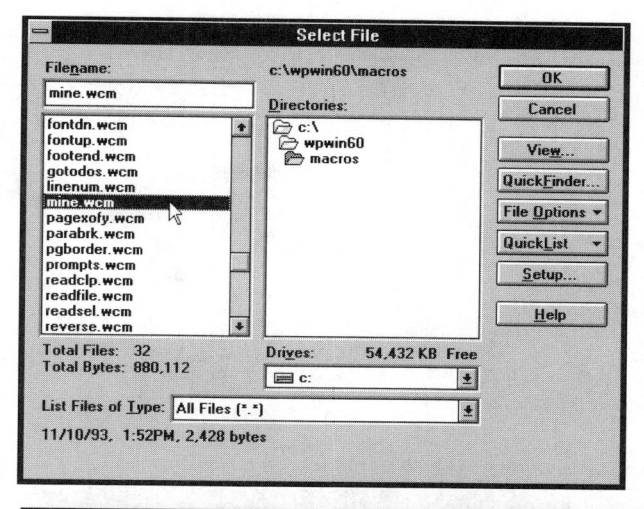

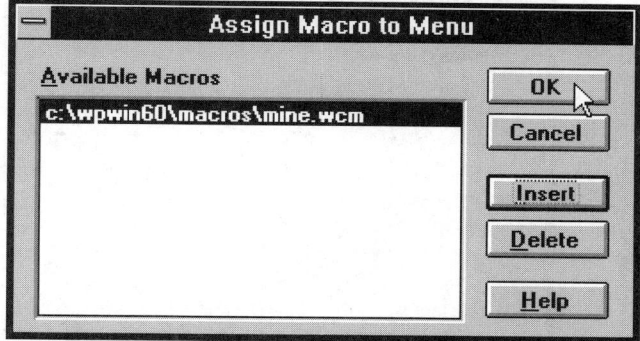

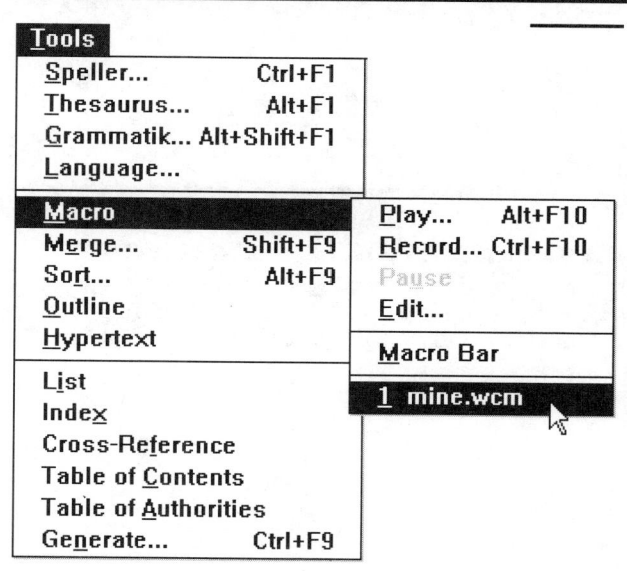

217

Chapter 15: Creating Macros

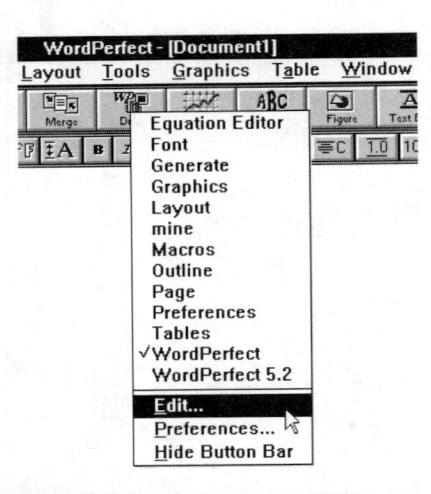

Figure 17. You can also assign macros to the button bar. To do this, select *Edit* from the button bar's QuickMenu.

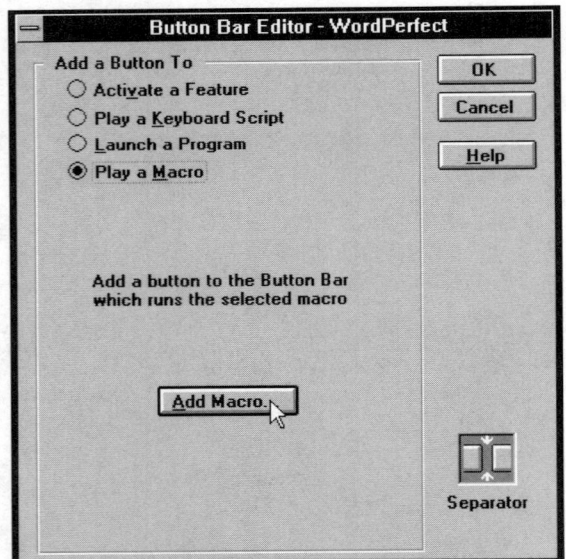

Figure 18. Now select the *Play a Macro* radio button in the *Add a Button To* section of the *Button Bar Editor* dialog box. As you select the *Play a Macro* option, WordPerfect displays the *Add Macro* button. Click on this button to open the *Select Macro* dialog box where you can select a macro to include on the button bar.

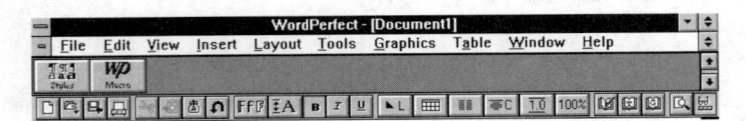

Figure 19. Once you have finished adding macro buttons, close the *Button Bar Editor* dialog box to return to your document. A macro button now appears on the button bar.

For more information on the button bar, see **Chapter 1**.

218

DOCUMENT TOOLS 16

INTRODUCTION

WordPerfect contains a wide variety of additional features to help you organize, structure and work with your documents. This chapter discusses these document tools and how to use them.

BOOKMARK

You can use the *Bookmark* command in WordPerfect to mark a location in your document so that you can return to that location quickly at a later date. Any bookmarks that you create in your documents are saved with the document.

CREATING A BOOKMARK

Figure 1. To create a bookmark, position the insertion point or select the text where you want the bookmark and select *Bookmark* from the **Insert** menu.

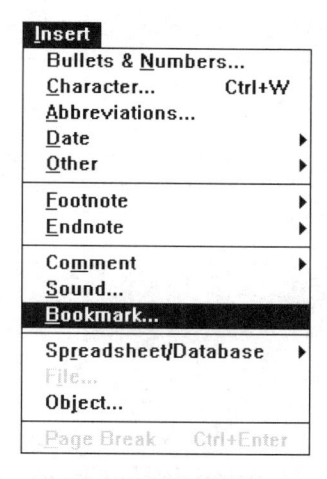

Figure 2. This opens the *Bookmark* dialog box. Now click on the *Create* button to open the *Create Bookmark* dialog box where you can name your bookmark.

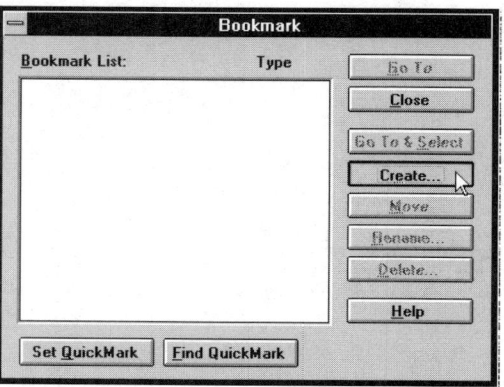

219

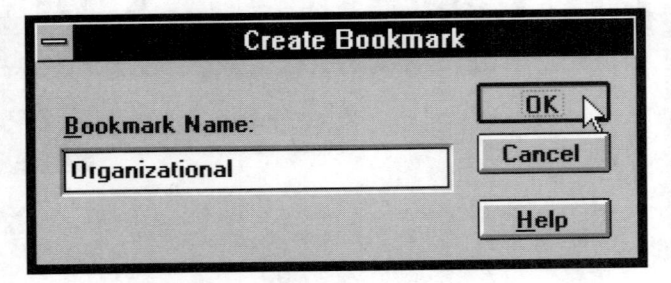

Figure 3. WordPerfect highlights text in the *Bookmark Name* section of the dialog box based on the text in your document at the bookmark position. Click *OK* to accept this name, or type in a new name for your bookmark and click on *OK*.

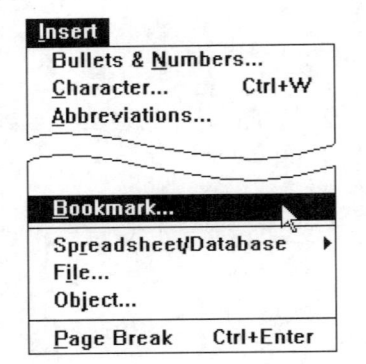

USING BOOKMARKS

Figure 4. You can move directly to your document bookmarks in any document where you have set them. To do this, select *Bookmark* from the **Insert** menu.

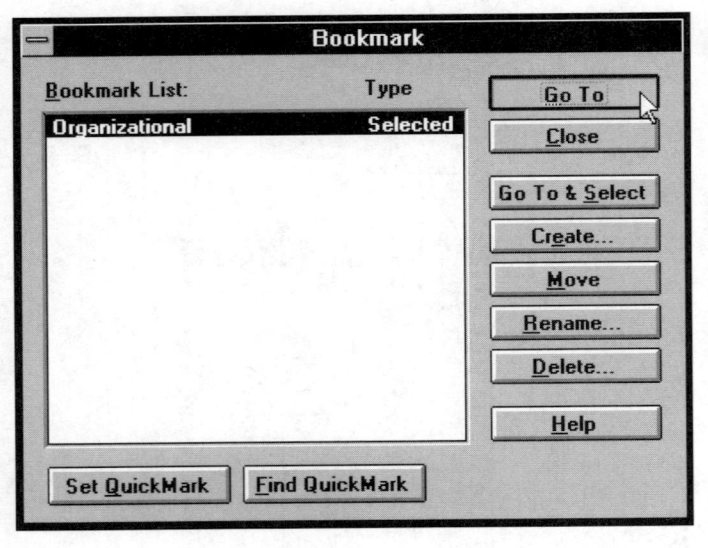

Figure 5. This opens the *Bookmark* dialog box with all of the document's bookmark names displayed in the *Bookmark List* section of the dialog box. To go to a bookmark, simply double-click on its name or highlight it and click on the *Go To* button.

Chapter 16: Document Tools

Figure 6. WordPerfect now takes you directly to the bookmark in your document.

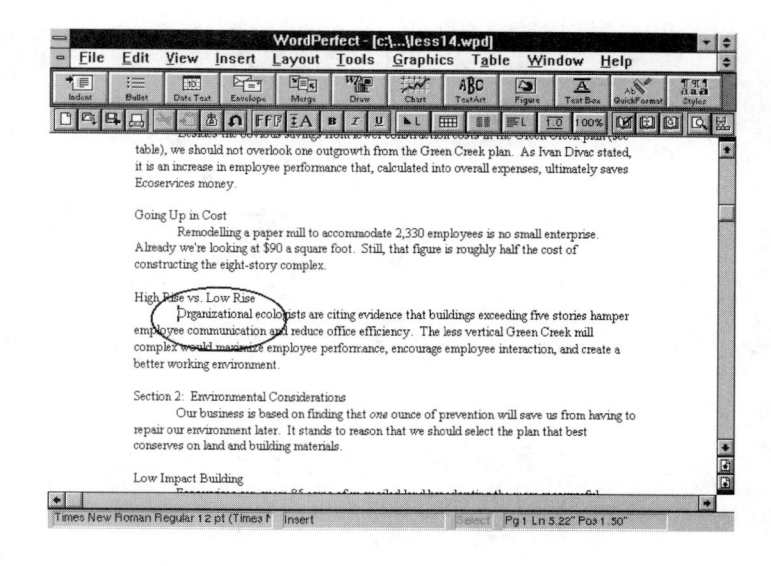

QUICKMARK

You can also place a quickmark in your document that you can set and find quickly through the *Bookmark* dialog box. To do this, position the insertion point or select the text that you want as a quickmark and then select the *Bookmark* command from the **Insert** menu to open the *Bookmark* dialog box.

Figure 7. Now click on the *Set QuickMark* button. You can only set one quickmark in your document so you do not have to name it. WordPerfect then returns you to the editing screen.

You can also set a quickmark in your document at any time by pressing Ctrl+Shift+Q. This sets the quickmark at the insertion point.

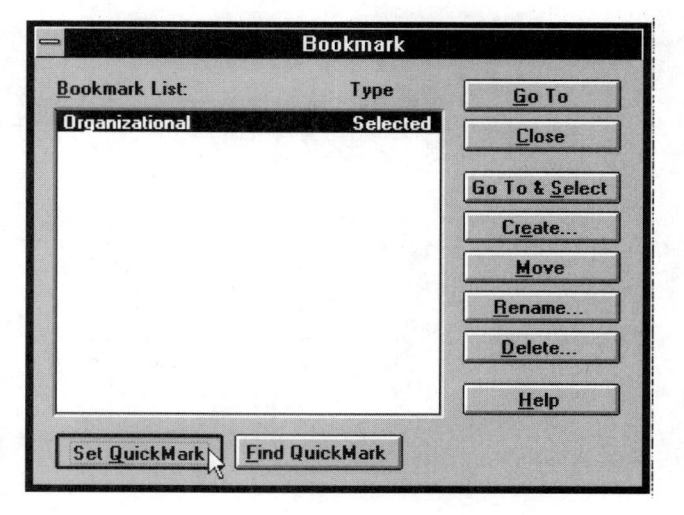

221

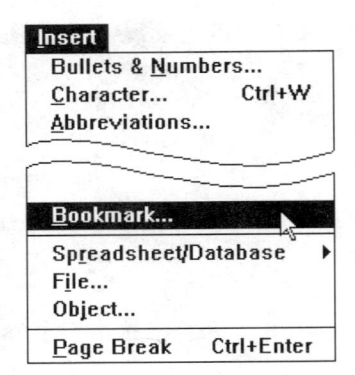

Figure 8. To go to a quickmark, simply select *Bookmark* from the **Insert** menu to open the *Bookmark* dialog box.

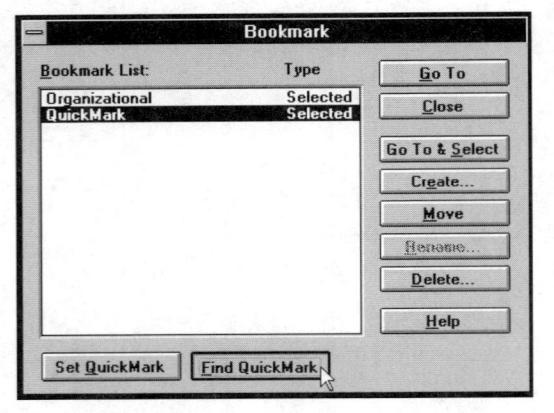

Figure 9. A "Quickmark" entry appears in the *Bookmark List* section of the dialog box. To go to your quickmark, click on the *Find QuickMark* button. This takes you directly to your quickmark in your document.

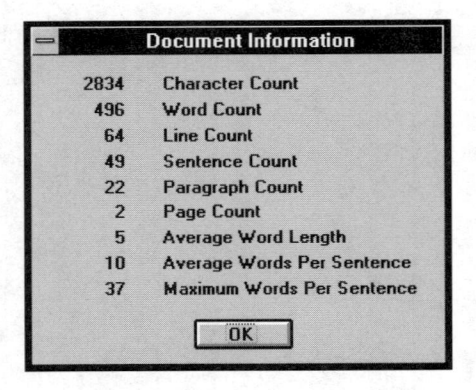

DOCUMENT INFORMATION

Figure 10. Selecting *Document Info* from the **File** menu displays information on your document from a character count to a page count, as well as information like average word length and words per sentence.

You can also use the *Document Info* command to view information on a selected range of text in your document.

DATE

Figure 11. The *Date* command in the **Insert** menu allows you to insert the date into your documents more quickly and easily.

Figure 12. Select *Date Text* from the *Date* submenu to insert the current date in the document at the insertion point. The date is inserted as normal text, just as if you had typed it yourself.

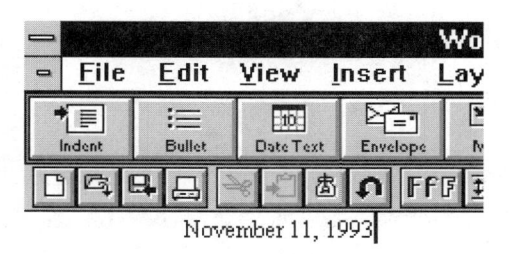

Figure 13. The *Date Code* command in the *Date* submenu inserts the date as a code so that every time you open the document in the future, the date changes to reflect the current date.

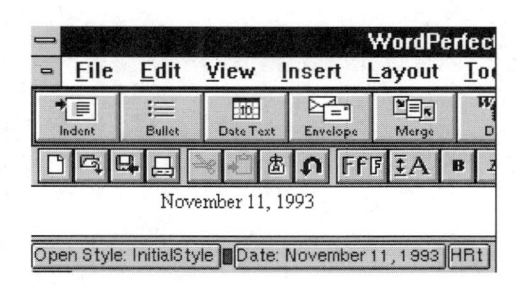

Figure 14. The *Date Format* command in the *Date* submenu activates the *Document Date/Time Format* dialog box. The options in this dialog box let you change the way the date appears in your document. You can select a standard option from the *Predefined Formats* list, or you can customize your date display through the *Custom* button.

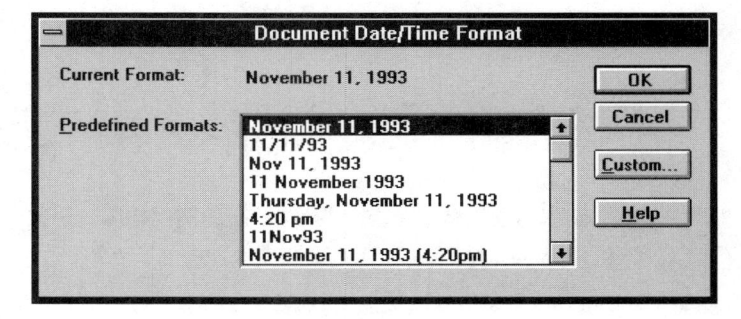

DOCUMENT COMMENTS

You can create and add comments to the text in your document that you can view in WordPerfect but are not included when you print.

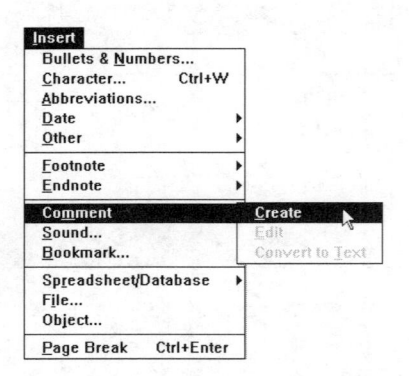

CREATING A COMMENT

Figure 15. To create a comment in your document, place the insertion point where you want the comment to appear and select *Create* from the *Comment* submenu in the **Insert** menu.

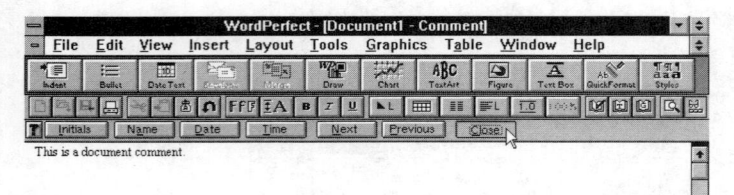

Figure 16. WordPerfect now opens a blank comment editing screen with the *Comment* feature bar at the top of the editing window. The *Initials* and *Name* buttons allow you to insert your user initials and name for creating comments. You set these, as well as your user color, through the *Environment Preferences* dialog box.

You can insert the date and time by clicking on their relevant buttons and you can move between document comments using the *Next* and *Previous* buttons.

To create your comments, simply type in the text that you want to include and then click on the *Close* button. WordPerfect then returns you to your document.

Figure 17. If you are in *Draft* view, your comment appears in the text with a gray highlight.

Figure 18. In *Page* and *Two Page* views, a document comment icon appears in the left margin of your page.

To view this comment, simply click on the comment icon to display a comment box in your document. Click anywhere in your document to hide this comment box again.

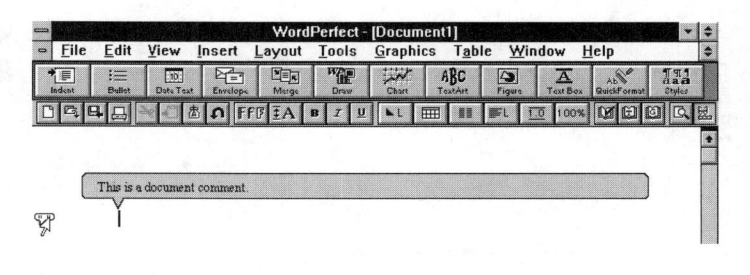

EDITING A COMMENT

Figure 19. To edit a comment, simply place the cursor near the comment you want to edit and select *Edit* from the *Comment* submenu in the **Insert** menu.

Alternatively you can simply double-click on the comment text in *Draft* view or the comment icon in *Page* and *Two Page* views.

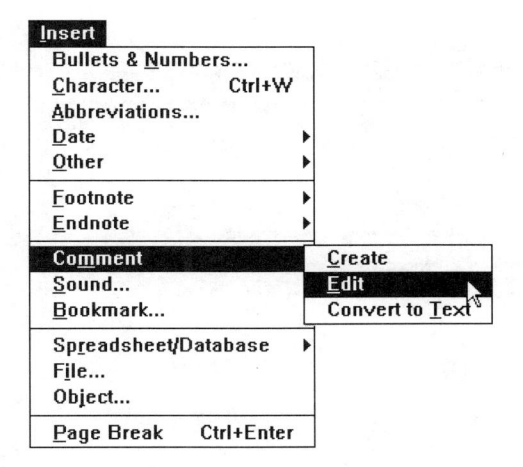

Figure 20. This takes you to the comment editing screen where you can edit your comment as you would normal text.

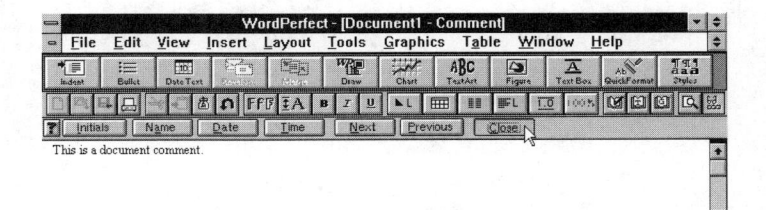

Chapter 16: Document Tools

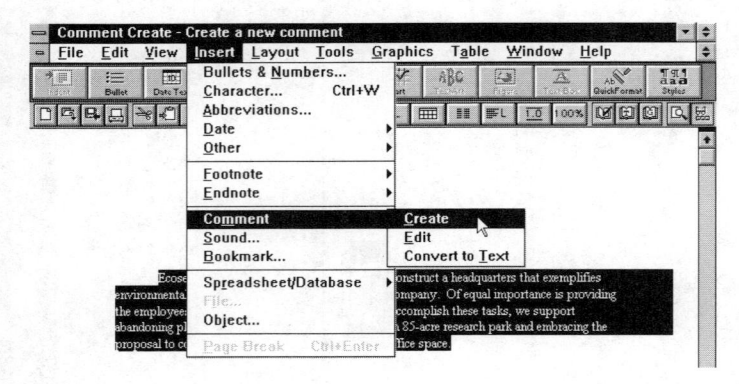

CONVERTING

Figure 21. To convert text into a comment, first highlight the text and then select *Create* from the *Comment* submenu.

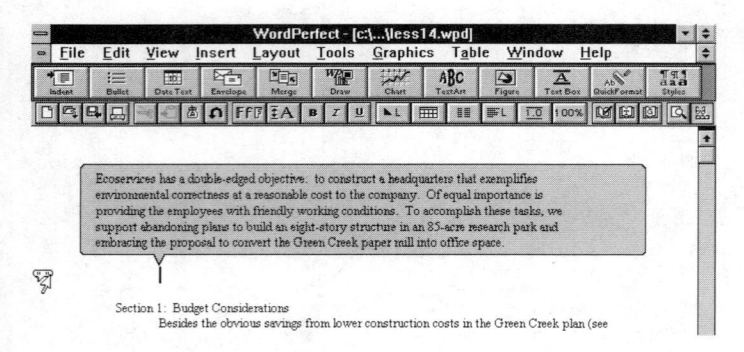

Figure 22. This automatically converts the selected text into a comment.

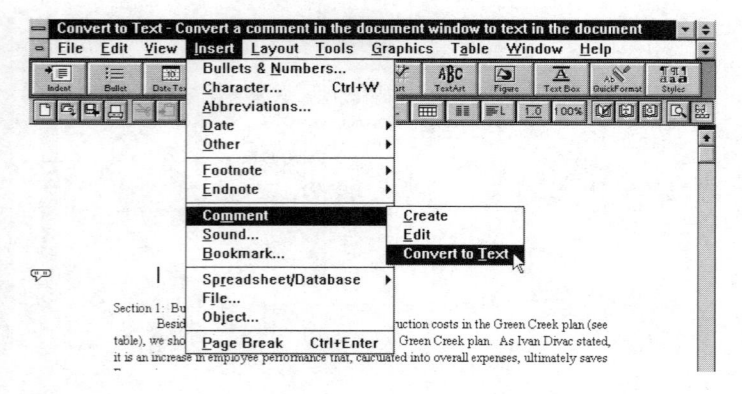

Figure 23. To convert a comment to text, place the insertion point near the comment where you want the text to appear and then select *Convert to Text* from the *Comment* submenu.

WordPerfect then inserts the comment as text at the insertion point.

FOOTNOTES AND ENDNOTES

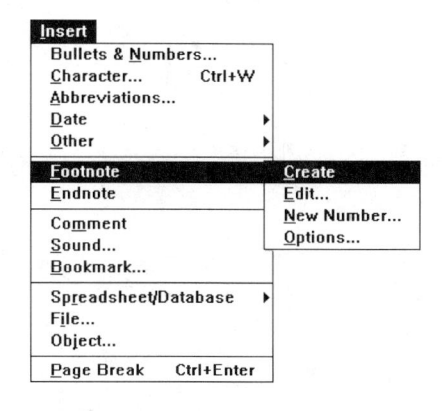

Figure 24. To add a footnote in your document at the insertion point, select *Create* from the *Footnote* submenu in the **Insert** menu.

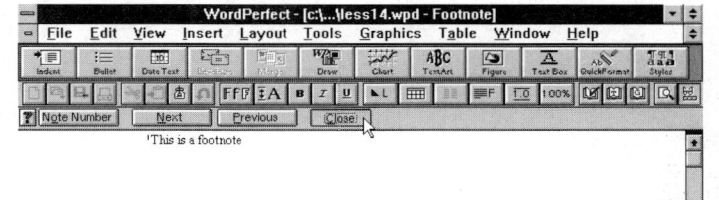

Figure 25. WordPerfect automatically activates the *Footnote/Endnote* feature bar and inserts the footnote number at the insertion point. If you are in *Draft* view, WordPerfect takes you to a footnote editing screen where you can enter the footnote text next to its number. Click on the *Close* button on the feature bar to return to your document.

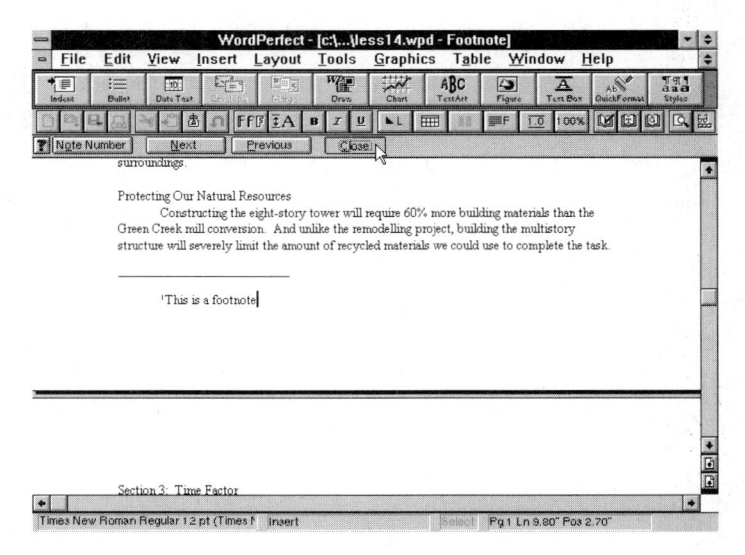

Figure 26. If you are in *Page* view, WordPerfect takes you to the bottom of the current page below the footnote separator line. Now simply enter your footnote text here next to its number and click on the *Close* button on the feature bar to return to the insertion point.

Note: You can only view the footnote text in Page or Two Page view.

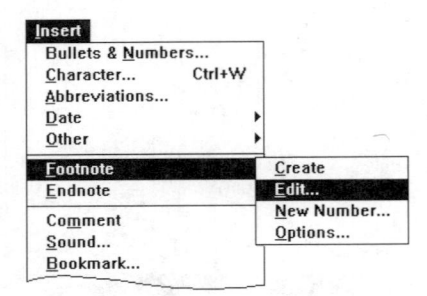

Figure 27. To edit a footnote, select *Edit* from the *Footnote* submenu in the **Insert** menu.

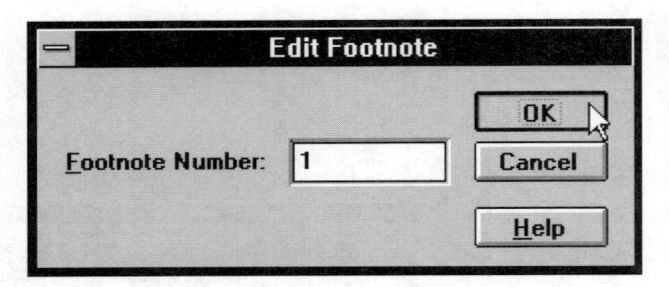

Figure 28. In the *Edit Footnote* dialog box that appears, key in the footnote number you want to edit, and click on *OK*. This takes you to the relevant footnote text for you to edit.

Figure 29. You can delete a footnote in the document by deleting its reference number. WordPerfect automatically updates the remaining footnote numbers.

Figure 30. The *Next* and *Previous* buttons in the *Footnote* feature bar take you to the next or previous footnote if you have created more than one.

Figure 31. The *New Number* option in the *Footnote* submenu lets you start a footnote with a new number of your choice or increase/decrease the existing footnote numbers.

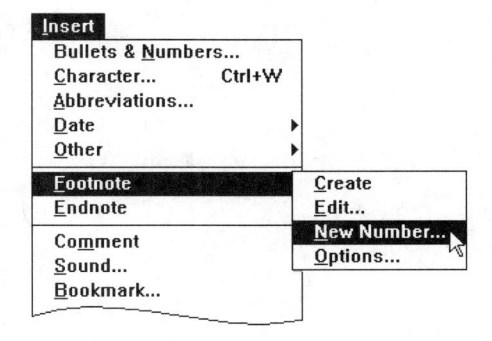

Figure 32. The *Options* command at the bottom of the *Footnote* submenu activates the *Footnote Options* dialog box. This lets you change the style, format, numbering, and spacing of your footnotes as well as the separator options for the end of each page.

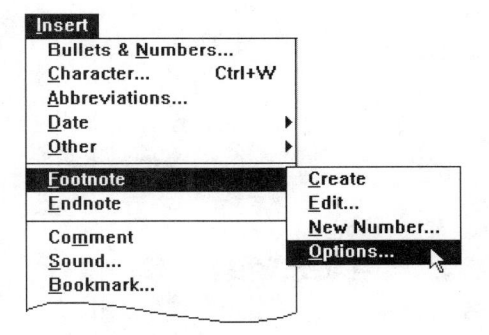

Figure 33. You create endnotes in the same way as footnotes, only endnotes appear at the end of a document. To make endnotes appear before the end of a document, select *Placement* from the *Endnote* submenu in the **Insert** menu.

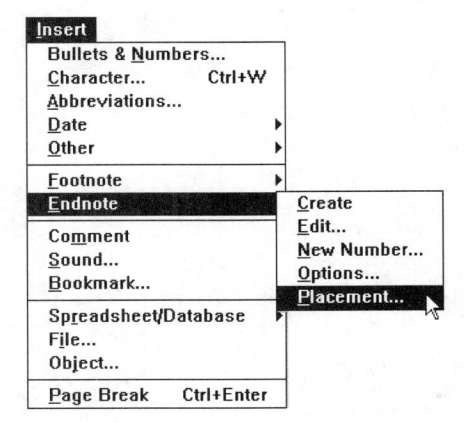

DOCUMENT SUMMARY

WordPerfect allows you to create a document summary for your documents that you can print, save, and view at any time to give you an overview of what a document contains. By default a document summary that you create is saved with your document.

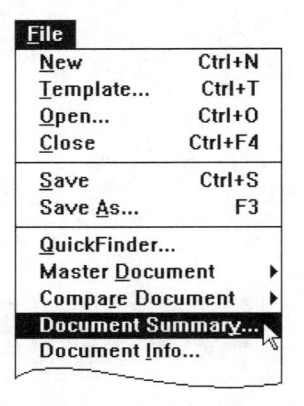

Figure 34. To create a document summary for the current document, select *Document Summary* from the **File** menu.

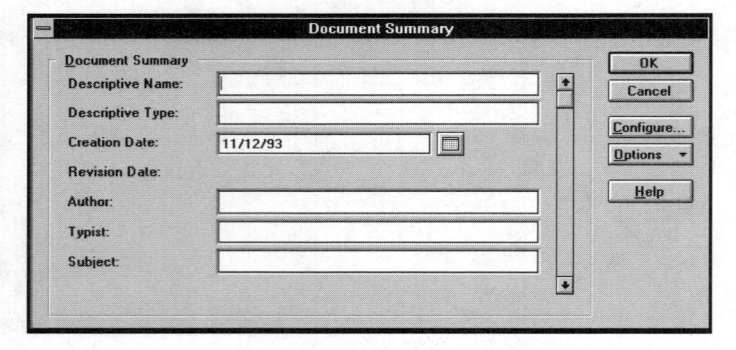

Figure 35. This opens the *Document Summary* dialog box with a range of summary fields that allow you to summarize your document's contents.

Type the relevant information into the entry fields using the scroll bars to access further field options.

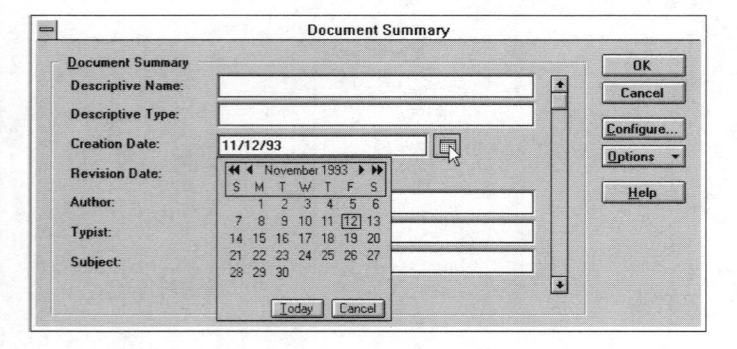

Figure 36. The button beside the *Creation Date* text box activates a calendar where you can specify the date you want.

Chapter 16: Document Tools

Figure 37. Select the *Configure* button to open the *Document Summary Configuration* dialog box where you can specify the field types and order for your document summary.

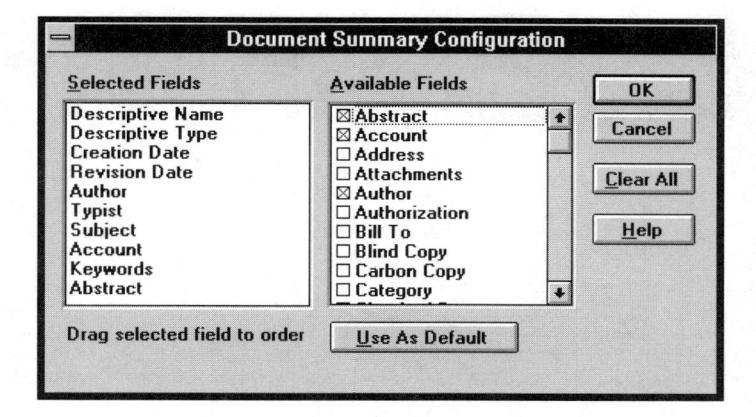

Figure 38. The *Options* drop-down list allows you to print and delete a document summary or save the document summary as a new document. You can also use the *Extract Information From Document* command to fill in some of the summary fields by extracting the information directly from the document.

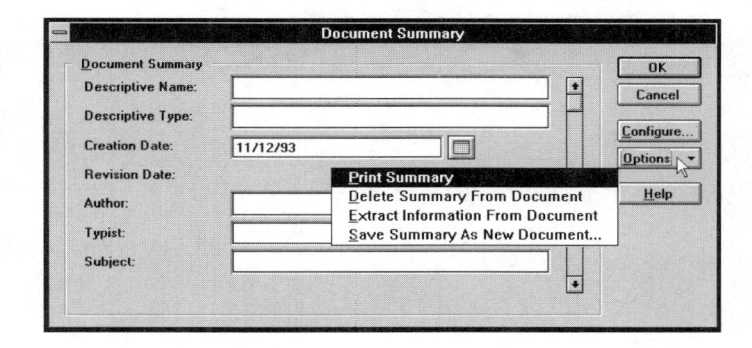

Click on *OK* to close this dialog box and return to your document. You can then view the document summary at any time in the future to give you an overview of your document's contents.

DOCUMENT COMPARE

Figure 39. *Compare Document* lets you compare two versions of a document and note the differences between them. The first option in the *Compare Document* submenu from the **File** menu is the *Add Markings* command. Use this command to compare a document with another and mark the passages that differ.

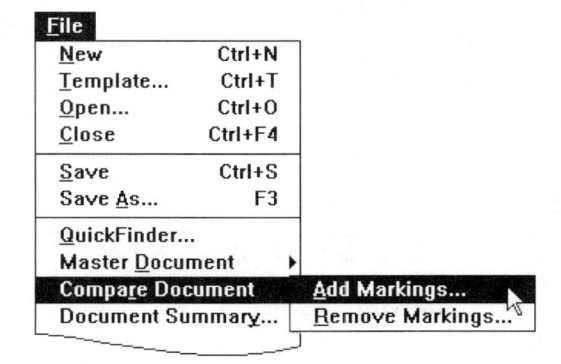

231

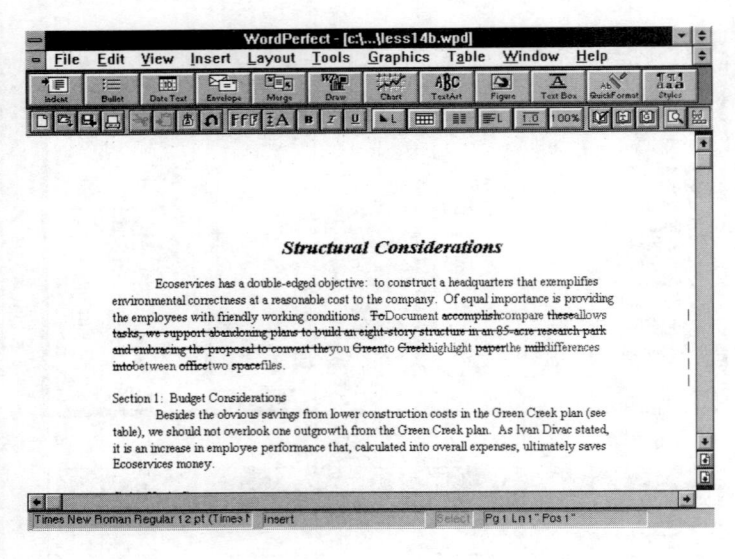

Figure 40. WordPerfect marks the changes made to the document with *Redline* codes, *Strikeout* codes, or messages indicating if any text has been moved.

The *Remove Markings* command in the *Compare Document* submenu takes out the markings and restores the document to the way it was before you made the comparison.

MASTER DOCUMENT

The *Master Document* command in the **File** menu allows you to manage very large documents. The master document contains codes linking it to subdocuments, such as chapters in a book.

The options in the *Master Document* submenu let you include any number of subdocuments in the master document. Subdocuments are just normal WordPerfect files except they are included as part of a larger document, the master document.

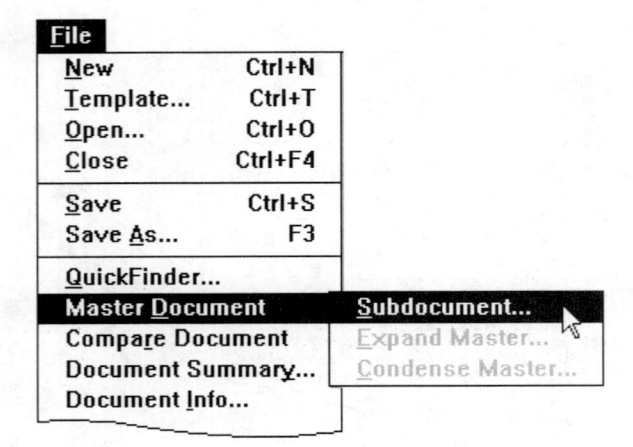

Figure 41. The first command from the *Master Document* submenu in the **File** menu is the *Subdocument* command. Select this command to activate the *Include subdocument* dialog box.

Chapter 16: Document Tools

Figure 42. Choose a filename from the *Files* list and click on the *Include* button.

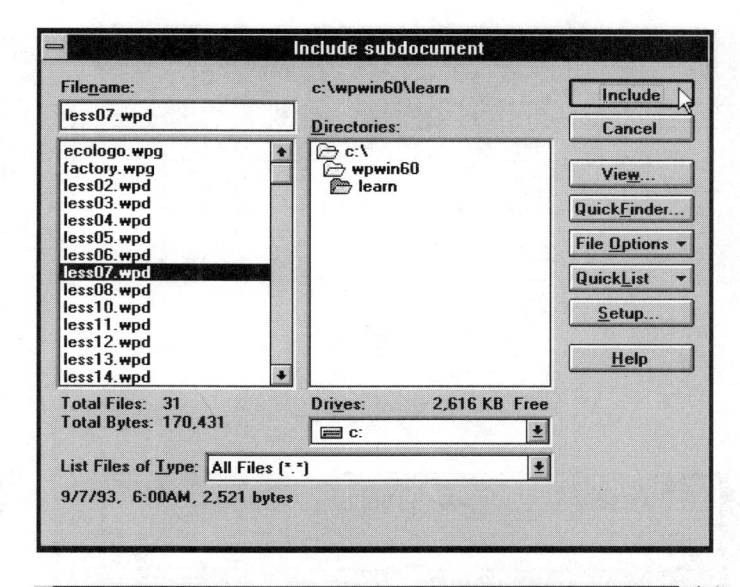

Figure 43. An icon, representing the selected file, appears in the document where the cursor is. The file represented by this icon is a subdocument linked to the master document. You can click on this icon to reveal the filename of the subdocument at any time. In Draft mode the subdocument name is displayed on a gray highlight.

Now simply continue adding subdocuments to this master document. The order that the subdocument icons appear in this file determines the order in which the files appear in the master document.

Figure 44. Select *Expand Master* from the *Master Document* submenu to open the *Expand Master Document* dialog box where you can specify which subdocuments you want to retrieve into the master document. Click on *OK* to expand the master document.

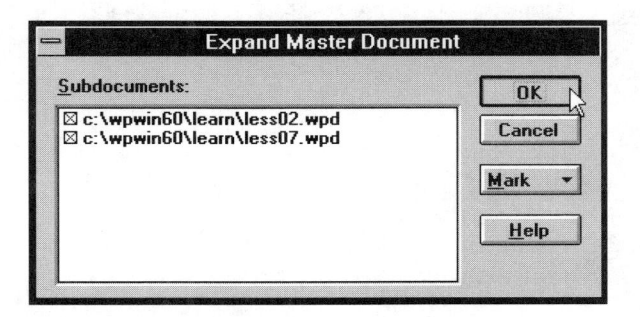

233

Chapter 16: Document Tools

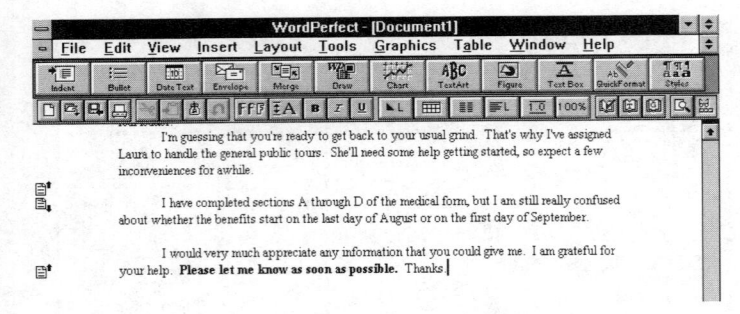

Figure 45. The subdocuments now expand into the master document. Icons appear before and after each subdocument in the master document in Page and Two Page mode. In Draft mode the filename of the document is highlighted in gray.

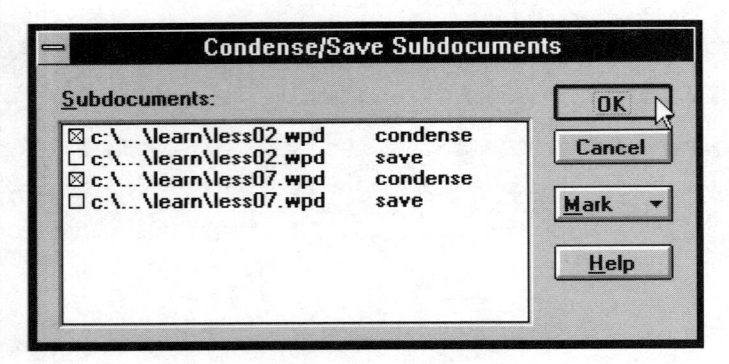

Figure 46. Choose *Condense Master* in the *Master Document* submenu to open the *Condense/Save Subdocuments* dialog box where you can specify which subdocuments you want to condense. You can also mark subdocuments that you want to save whether or not you condense the master document. Click on *OK* to condense the selected subdocuments.

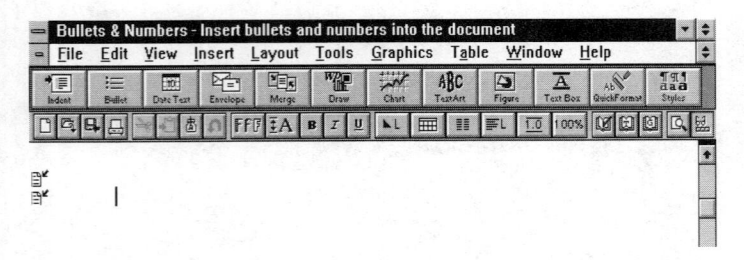

Figure 47. This removes the subdocuments from the master document. They still remain linked and the icons remain in the master document.

SORT

Figure 48. Select *Sort* in the **Tools** menu to display the *Sort* dialog box. In this box, you can sort selected text or the whole document alphabetically or numerically.

Specify what document is sorted and where the sort information will appear in the *Input File* and *Output File* section of the dialog box. In the *Sort By* section, choose the type of information you want to sort. If the information for each record only takes up one line, then you should select the *Line* option. If the information for each record takes up more than one line, then you should choose the *Paragraph* option. Select *Merge Record* if you are sorting a secondary merge file containing end field and end record codes. If your cursor is inside a WordPerfect table, the default is *Table Row,* which allows you to sort a WordPerfect table.

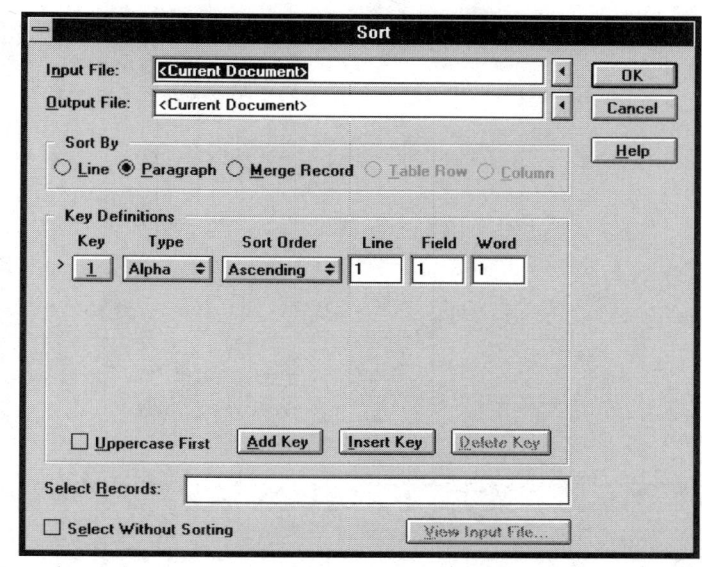

In the *Key Definitions* section, the *Type* drop-down list lets you select either *Alpha* or *Numeric,* depending on whether you are sorting words or numbers.

The *Sort Order* drop-down list lets you indicate whether you want items sorted from A–Z (*Ascending*), or from Z–A (*Descending*).

The *Field, Line,* and *Word* options let you determine how WordPerfect selects and sorts the items—these vary depending on what you choose in the *Record Type* section. (For example, if you have *Table Row* selected as the *Record Type,* then these options change to *Cell, Line,* and *Word.*) For sorting purposes, a *line* ends with a Return code; a *word* is separated by a space; and a *field* is separated by a tab.

As an example, you may have a list of names such as:

> Danny Hills
>
> Charles Brown
>
> Agatha Hills
>
> Karyl Hills
>
> Bruce Woodward

You can use the key definitions to determine the priority of how you want to sort this information. For example, you may want to sort the above list by surname, with a second priority to first names when the surnames are the same. This requires two keys.

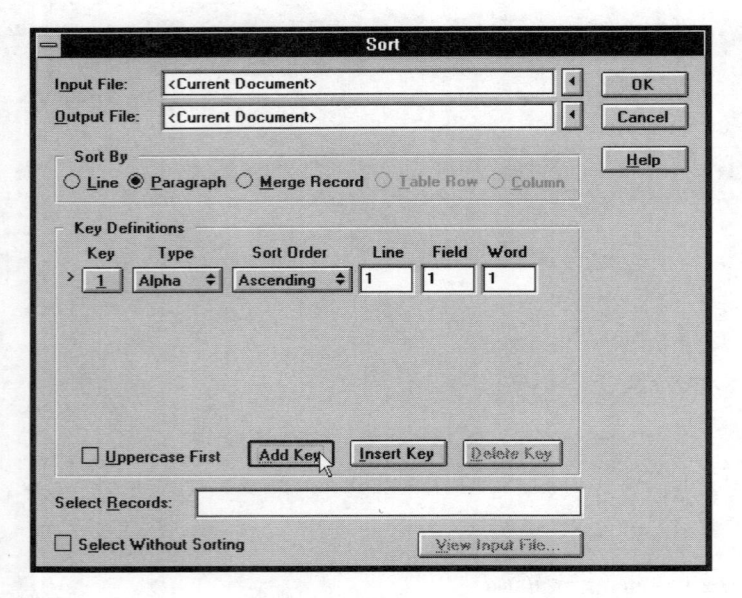

Figure 49. Click on the *Add Key* button to give you another key so that you can enter primary and secondary priority details for sorting. (You use *Insert Key* to add keys between other keys.)

Figure 50. Now, to determine your first priority, enter your sort details into *Key 1*. Under *Word* in *Key 1,* enter "2" to give sorting priority to the second word of each line.

The *Key 2* default of *Word 1* is correct as you want the sort to have a secondary priority of sorting the first word in each line.

Click on *OK* for WordPerfect to use these settings to sort the second word (the surname) in each line first with a secondary priority for the first word.

Back in your document, the result is as follows:

>Charles Brown
>
>Agatha Hills
>
>Danny Hills
>
>Karyl Hills
>
>Bruce Woodward

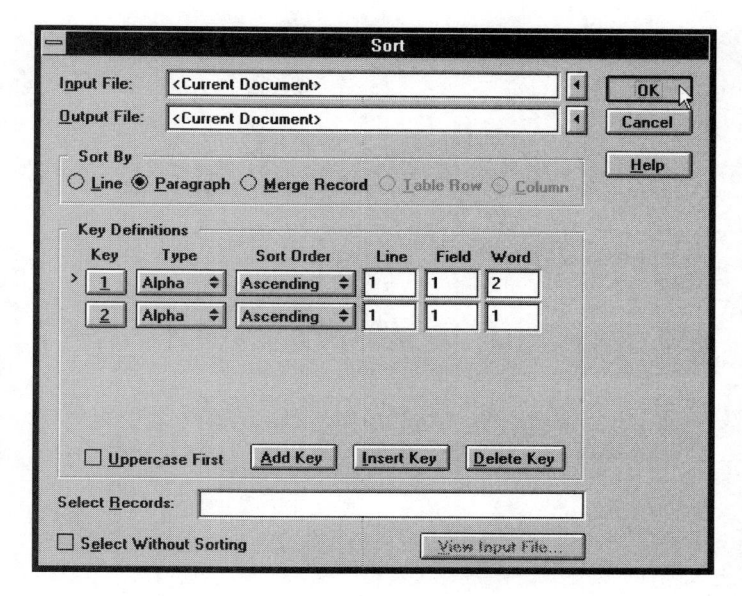

REFERENCING TOOLS   17

MARK TEXT, DEFINE, AND GENERATE

WordPerfect has a number of generating features that operate in similar ways allowing you to create document references. The *List*, *Index*, *Cross Reference*, *Table of Contents*, and *Table of Authorities* features in WordPerfect all involve the process of marking entries and generating the output.

CREATING AN INDEX

WordPerfect allows you to create an index for your documents that you can mark, define and generate as you want. WordPerfect indexes can include two heading levels and can draw on a concordance file to avoid marking each text entry manually.

Figure 1. To create an index for a document, select *Index* from the **Tools** menu. This activates the *Index* feature bar at the top of the editing window.

Figure 2. There are two ways of specifying index entries in WordPerfect; marking text and creating a concordance file.

To mark text, simply select it in your document and then click in the *Heading* or *Subheading* text box, depending on what level entry you want the text to be. The selected text then appears in the relevant text box. Now click on the *Mark* button.

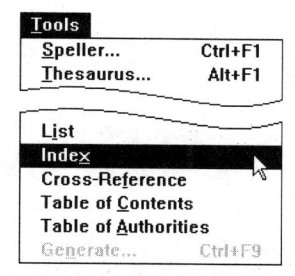

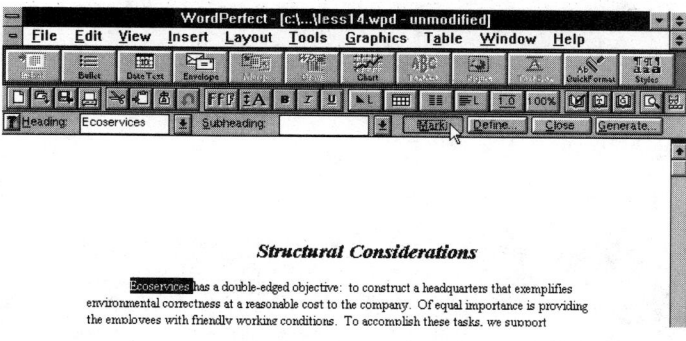

After you click on *Mark*, this text is marked to be included in the index (when you generate it). To create more index entries, select the text that you want and repeat this process.

CREATING A CONCORDANCE FILE

As an alternative to marking text manually, you can create a concordance file. A concordance file is a WordPerfect document that contains the words or phrases that you want to include in your index.

Using a concordance file, WordPerfect automatically searches a document for each occurrence of the words in your file and creates an index without you searching through the entire document to select each word that you want indexed.

You can mark index entries within a document and use a concordance file as well.

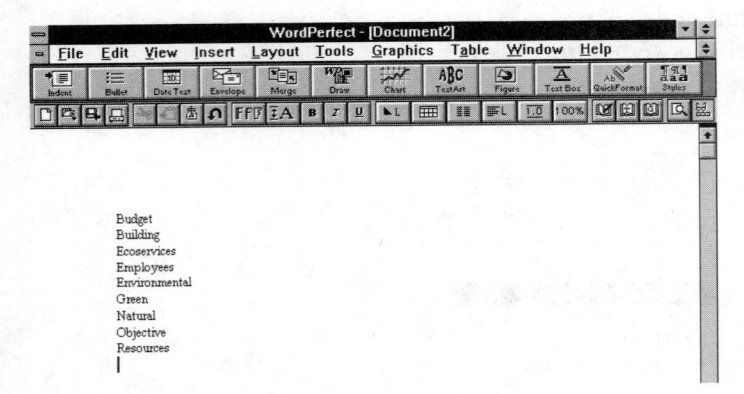

Figure 3. To create a concordance file, start a new WordPerfect document. In this new document, list all words you want to appear in the index and sort them into alphabetical order.

Once you have done this, save and name your concordance file. When you define your index, you can then specify this filename to use as your index concordance file.

DEFINING AN INDEX

Once you have marked your index entries and/or created a concordance file, you are ready to define your index in your document.

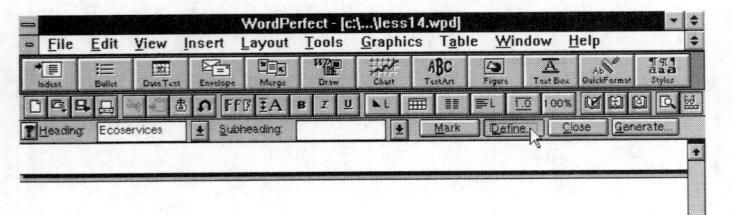

Figure 4. Open the document you want to create the index for and place the insertion point at the end of the document. Choose *Page Break* from the **Insert** menu to create a new page.

Now click on the *Define* button on the *Index* feature bar to open the *Define Index* dialog box.

Figure 5. From the *Numbering Format* section of the dialog box, choose the *Position* drop-down list to determine the style and position of numbering for your index.

There are five different *Position* options, differing only in the position and formatting of text and page numbers. The example box below the pop-up list shows you what the index looks like with a particular option.

Figure 6. If you are using a concordance file, enter its filename into the *Filename* text box of the *Concordance File* section or click on the list button and select it from the *Select File* dialog box that appears. Once you have specified the settings for your index, click on *OK*.

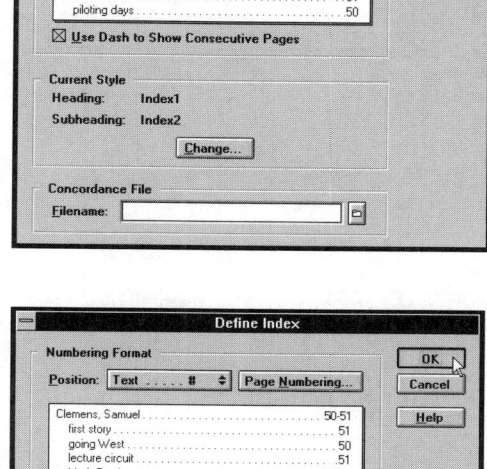

Figure 7. This returns you to your document with the text "Index will generate here" at the insertion point.

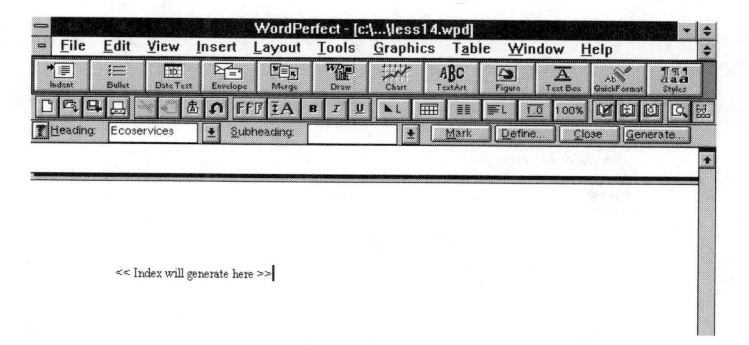

Chapter 17: Referencing Tools

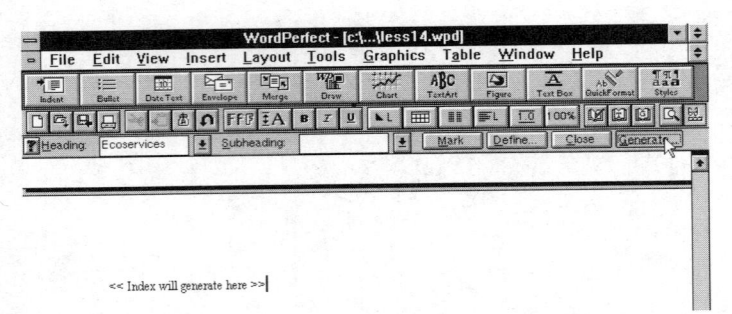

GENERATING AN INDEX

Figure 8. To compile the index, simply click on the *Generate* button on the *Index* feature bar.

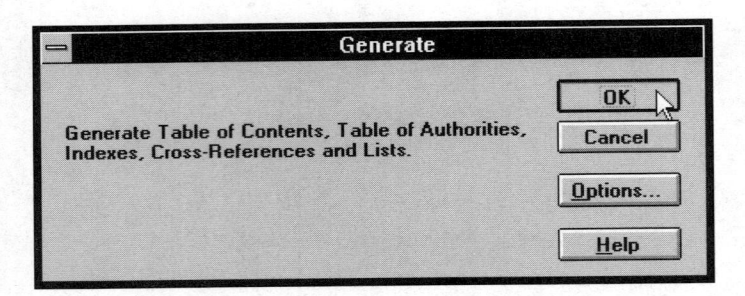

Figure 9. Selecting *Generate* activates the *Generate* prompt box. Click on *OK* to begin creating the index.

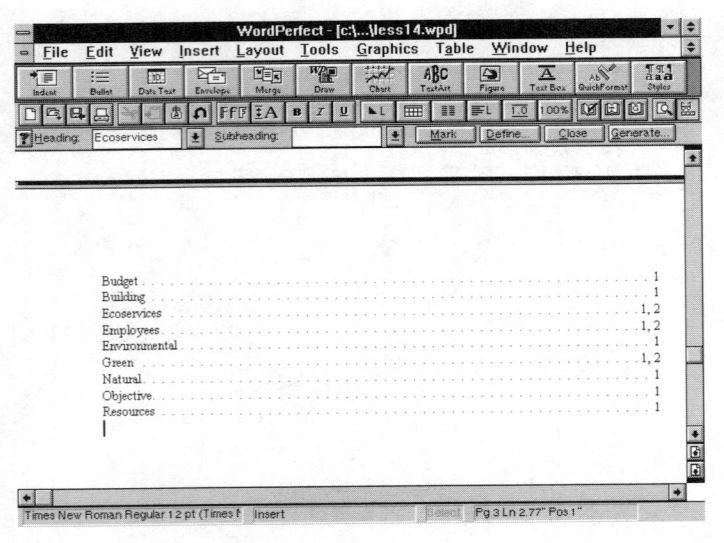

Figure 10. After a few moments, the index appears at the insertion point. You can edit this like any other text in a document.

242

CREATING LISTS

Creating a list is similar to creating an index; you need to mark, define, and generate your list entries. You can use the list feature for such things as figures or captions in a document and you can create multiple lists within the one document. When WordPerfect generates a list, the items appear in the order that they occur in the document.

Figure 11. The first step in generating a list is to select the *List* command from the **Tools** menu.

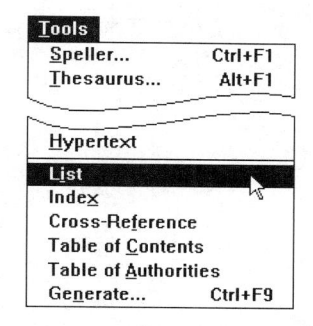

Figure 12. This activates the *List* feature bar at the top of the document window, giving you access to all of the controls necessary to create a list.

Figure 13. To mark text for your list, you first have to specify the list name that you are creating. To do this, click in the *List* text box on the *List* feature bar and type a name for your list.

Figure 14. Now, simply select the text in your document that you want to include in your list and click on the *Mark* button on the *List* feature bar.

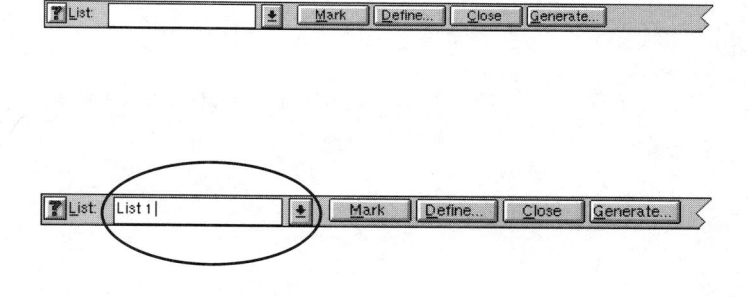

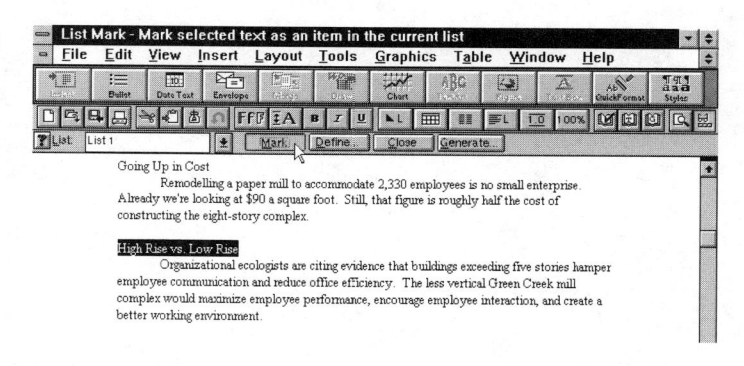

Figure 15. Once you have selected and marked all the text you want in the document, place the insertion point where you want the list to appear. Then click on the *Define* button on the *List* feature bar.

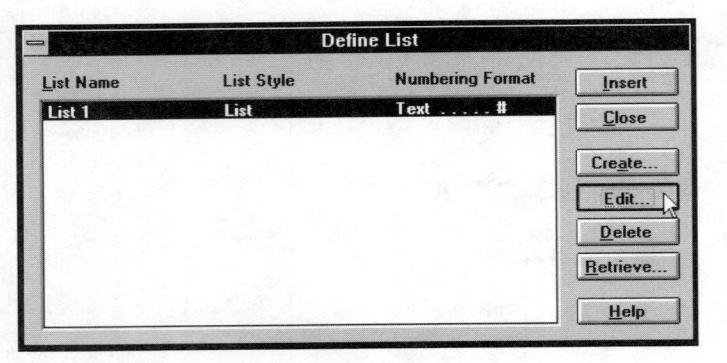

Figure 16. This activates the *Define List* dialog box. Select the list name that you assigned to the selected text and then choose *Edit*.

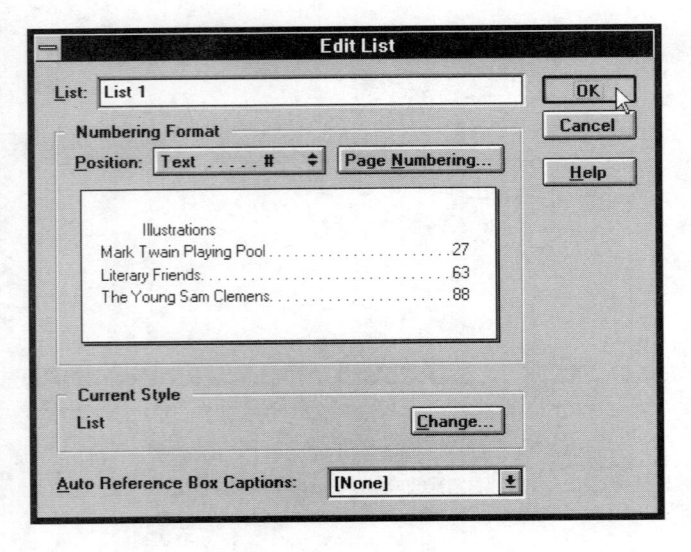

Figure 17. This opens the *Edit List* dialog box where you can edit the definition for your list numbers and position. Click on *OK* to return to the *Define List* dialog box.

244

Chapter 17: Referencing Tools

Figure 18. Click on the *Insert* button in the *Define List* dialog box (Figure 16) to insert your list definition into your document at the insertion point. The text "List will generate here" marks the position of the list in your document.

Figure 19. Now click on the *Generate* button on the *List* feature bar to generate your list.

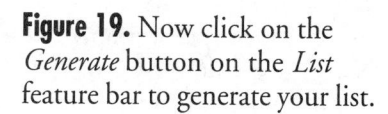

Figure 20. After clicking on *OK* in the *Generate* prompt box (Figure 9), WordPerfect generates the list in your document. As with the index, you can edit it like any text in your document.

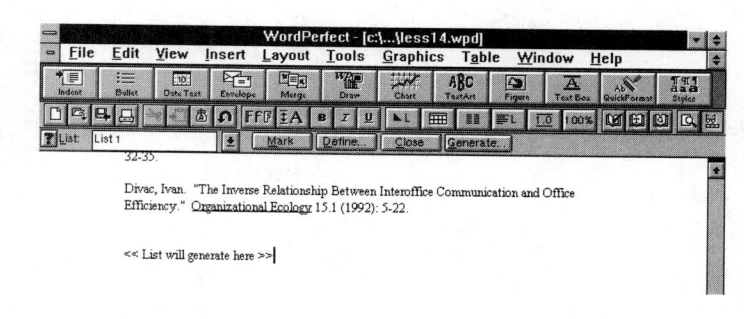

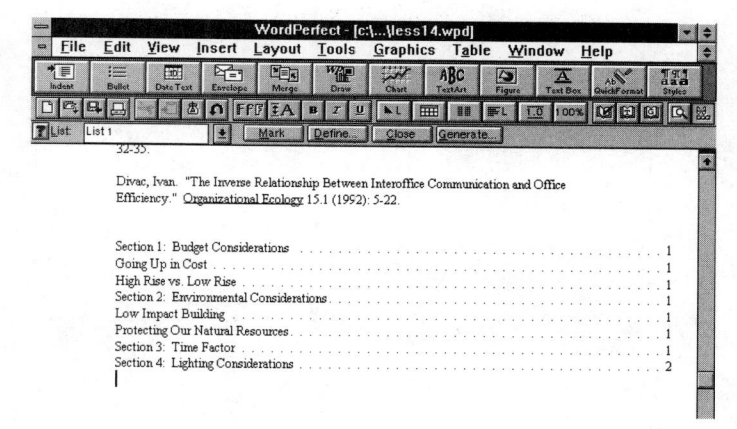

TABLE OF CONTENTS

Figure 21. WordPerfect can generate an automatic table of contents for your document. To do this you need to mark the text; define the table location and format; and generate the table.

To begin, select *Table of Contents* from the **Tools** menu.

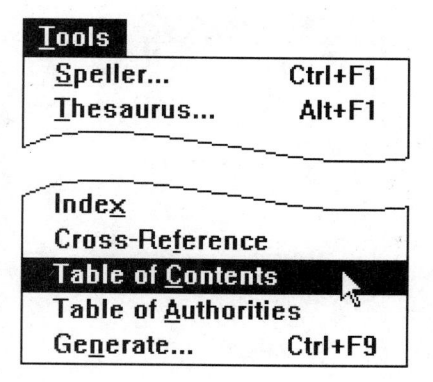

245

Chapter 17: Referencing Tools

Figure 22. This activates the *Table of Contents* feature bar at the top of your document window, giving you access to all of the tools you need to create your table of contents.

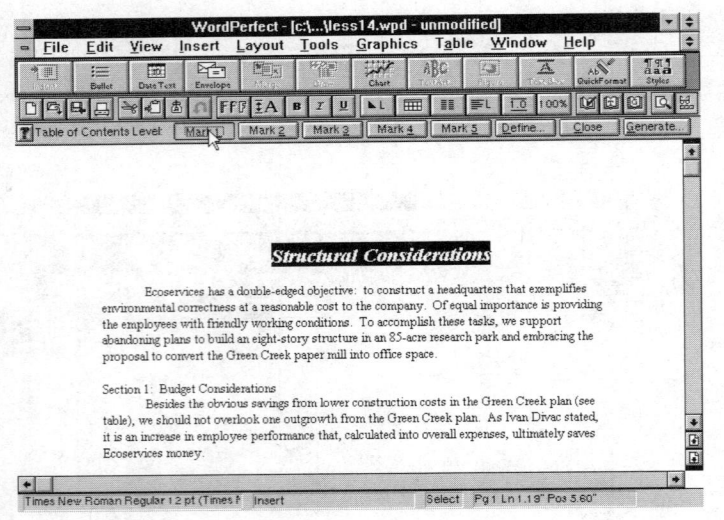

Figure 23. To mark the text for your table of contents, simply select the text you want to include and then choose one of the five *Mark* buttons on the *Table of Contents* feature bar. A major heading is considered *Level 1,* the next subheading as *Level 2* and so on.

Follow these steps for all the headings, subheadings, and text you want to include in the table of contents.

Figure 24. Once you have marked all the entries for the table of contents, move to the beginning of the document and create a new page.

Place the insertion point where you want the table of contents to appear and click on the *Define* button on the *Table of Contents* feature bar.

Chapter 17: Referencing Tools

Figure 25. This activates the *Define Table of Contents* dialog box.

Use the arrows in the *Number of Levels* section of the dialog box to specify the number of levels you have in your table of contents. Then for each level, select the numbering style you want in each of the *Position* pop-up lists that correspond to each level.

Click on *OK* once you have set up this dialog box.

Figure 26. This returns you to your document with the text "Table of Contents will generate here" at the insertion point. Now, to create the table of contents, click on the *Generate* button on the *Table of Contents* feature bar.

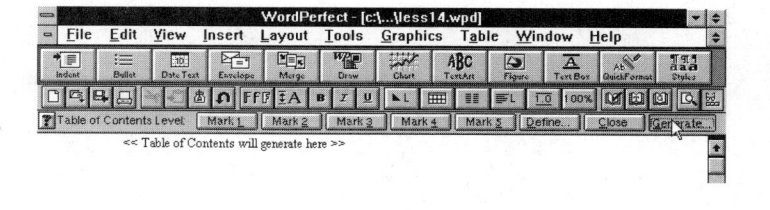

Figure 27. Click on *OK* in the *Generate* prompt box (Figure 9) and after a few moments, the table of contents appears in your document. You can edit the table of contents in the same way as other text in your document.

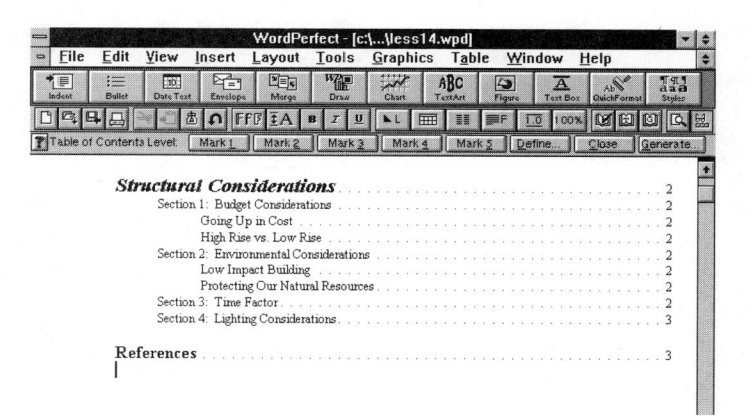

247

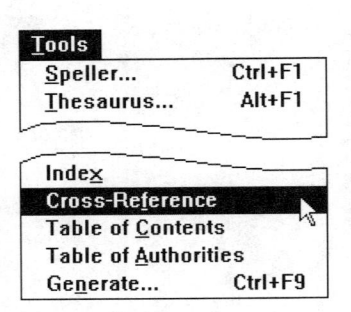

CROSS-REFERENCE

Figure 28. WordPerfect provides a cross-reference capability where you can update references to such things as page numbers and figure numbers as these target numbers change. To create cross-references, select *Cross-Reference* from the **Tools** menu.

Figure 29. This activates the *Cross-Reference* feature bar at the top of the editing window. The options on this feature bar allow you to create cross-references throughout your document.

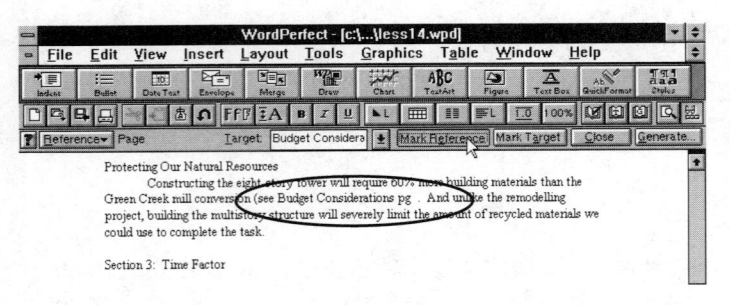

Figure 30. The *Mark Reference* button creates a reference point at the insertion point. However, when you create references and corresponding targets, you must name them in the *Target* text box so they are linked.

To mark a reference, enter the target name in the *Target* text box and then click the *Mark Reference* button. (Before selecting this button, you may like to type some cross-reference text such as "Refer to" or "See" in the document to appear before the cross-reference.)

Chapter 17: Referencing Tools

Figure 31. Use the *Mark Target* button to mark the place where you are telling the reader to look. Again, first put the insertion point where you want to create the target and then select the target name from the *Target* drop-down list.

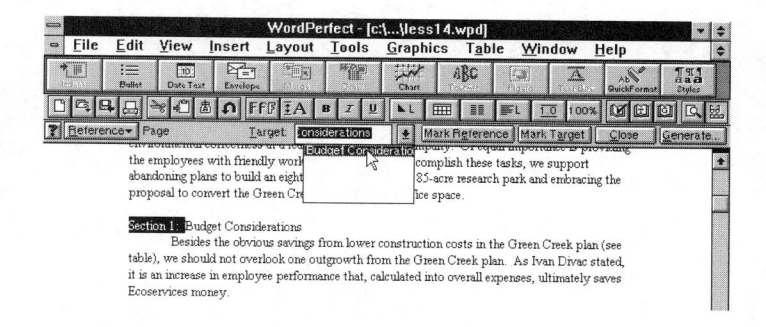

Figure 32. Now click on the *Mark Target* button.

Figure 33. Now use the *Reference* drop-down list to determine what the cross-reference is tied to. The default option is *Page*.

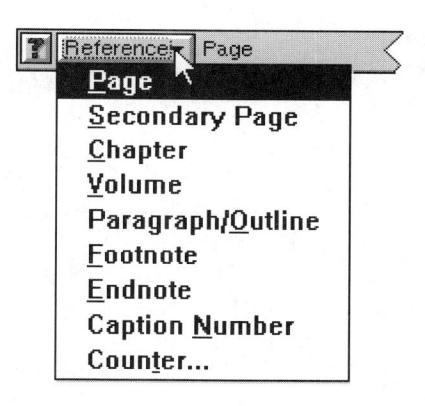

Figure 34. Once you have marked the reference and target points in the document, select the *Generate* button and click *OK* in the prompt box that appears (Figure 9) to link the cross-references together.

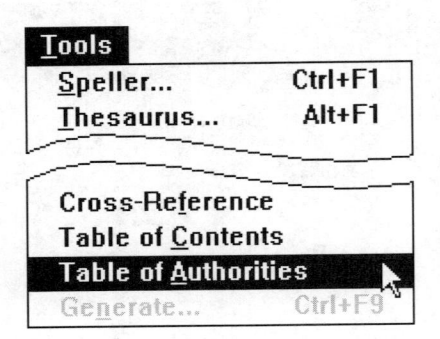

TABLE OF AUTHORITIES

Figure 35. The *Table of Authorities* feature of WordPerfect is used mainly in the legal profession to list citations. For more information on tables of authorities, see the *WordPerfect Reference Manual*.

HYPERTEXT

You can use the hypertext function within WordPerfect to jump from one part of a document to another place in that document or even another document altogether.

CREATING HYPERTEXT LINKS

A hypertext link is like a cross-reference for open WordPerfect documents except through the hypertext link you can "jump" directly to the cross-referenced information.

You can create hypertext links to bookmarks within the current document or other documents, to other files, or to macros. In order to create a hypertext link you must create these other bookmarks, files, or macros first.

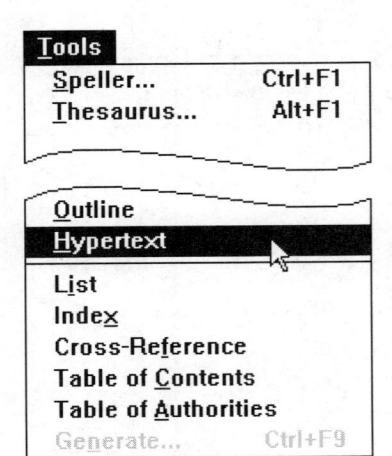

Figure 36. Once the bookmarks, files, or macros that you want to link to have been created, open the document that you want to place the hypertext links in and select *Hypertext* from the **Tools** menu.

Chapter 17: Referencing Tools

Figure 37. This activates the *Hypertext* feature bar at the top of the editing window, giving you access to all of the necessary tools to create and edit hypertext links. Now select the words that you want to use as the hypertext link and click on the *Create* button.

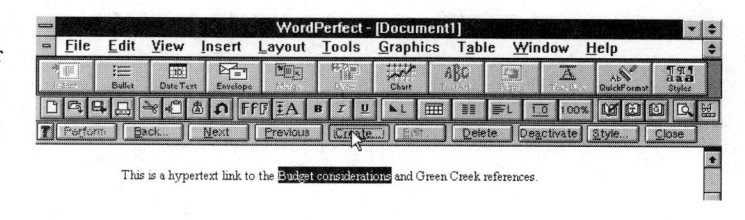

Figure 38. This opens the *Create Hypertext Link* dialog box. Select a radio button from the *Action* section of the dialog box depending on what you want to link to and then specify the relevant filename and/or bookmark name.

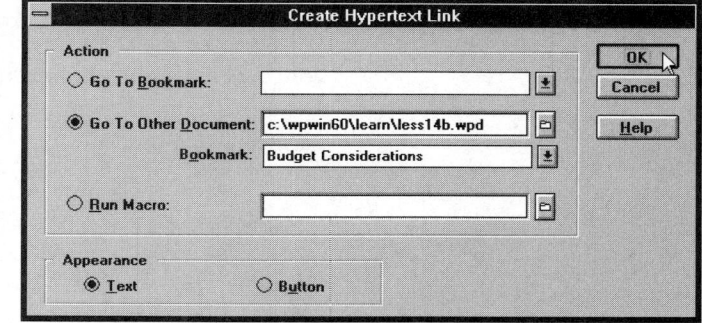

The list buttons allow you to open the *Select File* dialog box where you can search for any files you want.

Then select a radio button to specify the appearance of your hypertext link. The *Text* option highlights the hypertext link as underlined green text in your document, whereas the *Button* option creates a button around the selected word.

Click on *OK* to return to your document with the hypertext link created.

Once you have created your hypertext links, save your document to ensure that the links are maintained.

USING HYPERTEXT LINKS

Figure 39. To use your hypertext links, simply click on the highlighted text or button in your document. This automatically takes you to the bookmark, document, or macro that the link represents.

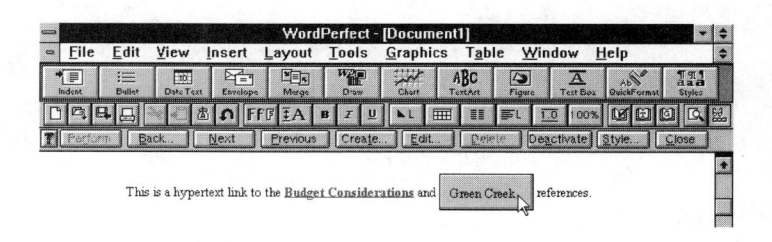

251

Chapter 17: Referencing Tools

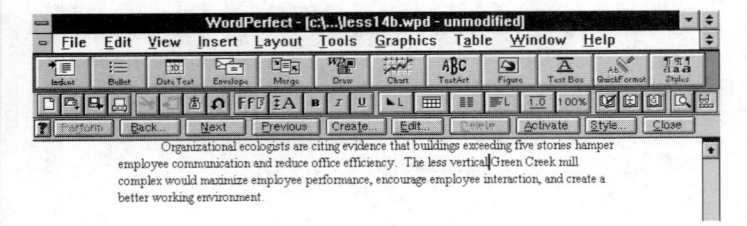

Figure 40. Click on the *Back* button on the *Hypertext* feature bar to jump back to the original document containing the links after viewing a bookmark.

Click on the *Next* or *Previous* button to find the next or previous hypertext link in your document.

The *Deactivate* button allows you to disable the hypertext links in your document. When you do this, the button changes to an *Activate* button, allowing you to activate the links when you want to.

Use the *Perform* button to make a hypertext jump when a link is inactive.

Click on the *Delete* button to delete the current or selected hypertext links.

EDITING HYPERTEXT LINKS

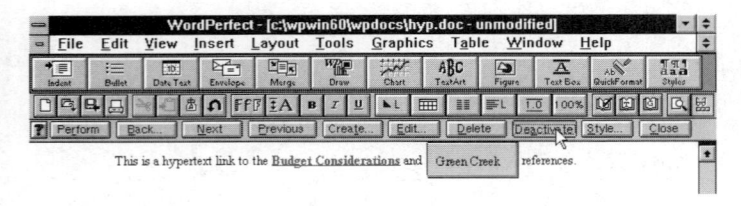

Figure 41. To edit a hypertext link, you must first disable the document's links by clicking on the *Deactivate* button.

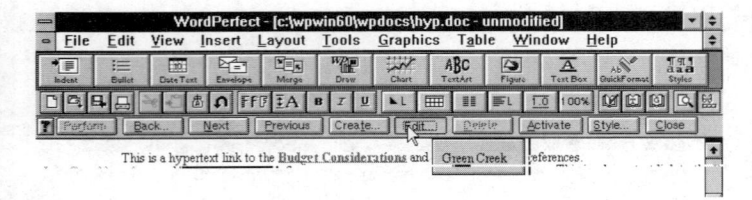

Figure 42. Once you have done this, place the insertion point near the button or within the text you want to edit and then click on the *Edit* button.

Figure 43. This opens the *Edit Hypertext Link* dialog box where you can make the changes that you want. Click on *OK* once you have finished.

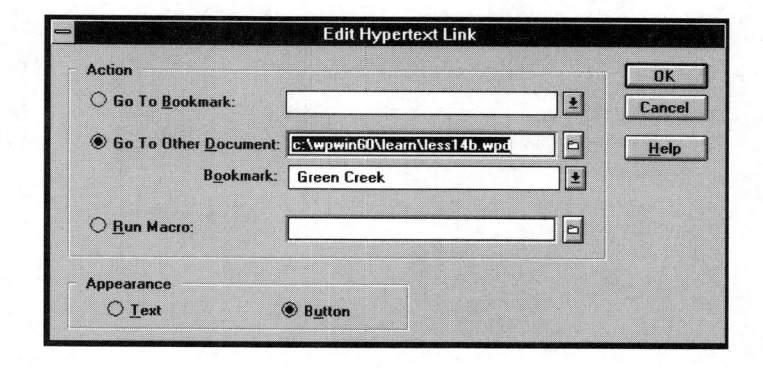

Index

A

abbreviations, 25
   creating an abbreviation, 25
   expanding an abbreviation, 27
   inserting an abbreviation, 26
Add Markings command, 231
adding macro buttons to the button bar, 218
Advance command, 60
antonyms, 98
Append command, 15, 16
applying styles, 147
assigning macros to menus, 217

B

back tab, 43
backspace key, 13
binding, 49
Block Protect, 46
Bookmarks, 219
   creating, 219
Border/fill option, 47
button bar, 1, 5
   adding macro buttons, 218
   creating, 83
   customizing, 81
   display options, 85
   editing, 82
   selecting, 81
button bar preferences, 77

C

calculating formulas, 131
Cascade command, 67
cell reference, 117
cells, 118
   alignment, 118
   attributes, 118
   Ignore Cell When Calculating option, 118
   selecting, 115
   selecting text in, 116
   vertical alignment, 118
Center command, 40
Center of Rotation, 185
Center Page command, 45
chaining styles, 146
character styles, 144, 146
characters, 31

Chart, 135
chart button, 135
Chart Editor, 136
Chart Gallery, 137
Chart menu, 137
chart titles, 139
Chart tool, 187
chart types and styles, 137
Charting
   data, 136
   display options, 140
   Options menu, 139
   placement, 142
   redraw, 136
charting tables, 135
clipboard, 15, 16, 100, 127
Close command, 69
Closed Curve tool, 193
codes, 17
   delete, 21
   open codes, 20
   paired codes, 18
   Reveal Codes screen, 17
   scroll bar, 18
columns, 43
   balanced newspaper, 43
   icon on the power bar, 44
   newspaper, 43
   parallel, 44
comments, 224
Compare Document command, 231
concordance file, 241
Condense Master Document command, 234
Conditional End of Page option, 46
Control menu box, 2, 3
Convert Case command, 17
Copy command, 15
copying formulas, 132
Creating
   graphics lines, 176
   bookmarks, 219
   captions, 169
   concordance files, 240
   new styles, 145
   indexes, 239
   button bars, 83
   endnotes, 229

Index

footnotes, 227
form files, 210
graphics, 164
hypertext links, 250
lines, 175
styles, 143
tables, 113
tables from existing text, 133
Cross Reference command
    Generate button, 249
    Mark Reference button, 248
    Mark Target button, 249
    reference, 249
    target, 248
    feature bar, 248
Current Dir, 64
cursor
    mouse, 2
Curve tool, 192
customizing the screen, 81
    button bar, 81
    power bar, 85
    status bar, 88
Cut command, 15

D

data file, 205
data fill, 131
Date, 223
    code, 223
    format, 223
    text, 223
deactivate hypertext, 252
defining an index, 240
Delay Codes option, 45
deleting
    table columns, 125
    table rows, 125
    tables, 125
    graphics, 179
    styles, 151
Delete key, 13
directories, 64
display preferences, 76
display settings, 4
displaying outlines, 155
Document Comments, 224
    converting comments, 226
    creating a comment, 224

editing a comment, 225
Document Compare, 231
    Add Markings option, 231
    Remove Markings option, 232
document formatting, 54
    Initial Codes Style, 55
    Initial Font, 54
    Redline Method, 55
Document Information, 222
document preview, 107
document styles, 146
document summary, 230
    preferences, 77
double indent, 42
Drag and Drop, 16
    copying text, 16
    moving text, 16
Draw button, 181
Drawing tools, 190
drives, 65

E

Edit menu, 179
editing
    button bars, 82
    endnotes, 229
    footnotes, 228
    graphics, 164
    hypertext links, 252
    keys, 13
    styles, 145, 148
    the power bar, 86
    the status bar, 88
    table structures, 123
editing methods
    Append, 15
    Copy, 15
    Cut, 15
    Drag and Drop, 16
    Insert mode, 12
    moving the insertion point, 11
    Paste, 15
    selecting text, 14
    Typeover mode, 12
    Undelete, 13
    Undo, 13
Ellipse tool, 195
Elliptical Arc tool, 194
End Outline, 154

Index

ENDFIELD code, 209
endnotes, 227
   creating, 229
   editing, 229
   placement, 229
ENDRECORD code, 209
environment preferences, 76
Equation Editor, 174
equations, 174
Exit command, 70
Expand Master Document command, 233

F

families, 154
Feature Bars, 10
   Cross-Reference, 248
   Footnote/Endnote, 227
   Graphics Box, 160
   Hypertext, 251
   Index, 239
   List, 243
   Merge, 210
   Outline, 153
   Table of Contents, 246
fields, 205
Figure tool, 188
File Info command, 65
file management, 70
   File Attributes, 71
   File Options, 71
   Open dialog box, 70
   QuickFinder, 74
   QuickList, 71
   QuickMenus, 70
file preferences, 77
filename, 64
Find command, 21
Find and Replace Text dialog box
   Direction menu, 24
   Match menu, 24
   Options menu, 24
   Replace menu, 24
   Type menu, 24
Find Text dialog box
   Action menu, 23
   Match menu, 23
   Options menu, 22
   Type menu, 23
Flush Right command, 40

Font dialog box, 27
   Color options, 29
   Font Appearance, 28
   Font Face, 27
   Font list, 28
   Font Position, 28
   Font Size, 28
   Redline, 28
   Relative Size, 28
   Strikeout, 28
Font Face button, 27
Footers, 56
Footnote/Endnote feature bar, 227
Footnotes
   creating, 227
   editing, 228
Force Page command, 46
form file, 210
formatting, 27
   Font, 27
   paragraphs, 41
   QuickFormat, 30
   text in tables, 117
Formula bar, 128
Formula Edit text box, 130
formulas, 129
   calculating, 131
   copying, 132
   functions, 129
   Sum button, 129
Freehand tool, 191
Function tools, 182
Functions, 129

G

generating an index, 242
Grammar Checker, 102
   Advice box, 102
   Check menu, 102
   Formality Level option, 102
   Options menu, 102
   Writing Style option, 102
graphics, 159
   B & W attributes, 168
   borders and fills, 171
   color attributes, 167
   creating, 164
   captions, 169
   lines, 175

Index

deleting, 179
editing, 164
Equation Editor, 174
equations, 174
fill attributes, 168
height, 163
Image settings, 165
Image tools, 165
Mirror Image, 167
Miscellaneous options, 168
Move Image command, 166
moving, 161
Position, 161
putting text in boxes, 173
QuickMenu, 162
resizing, 163
retrieve, 159
Rotate Image, 167
Scale Image, 166
Text Wrap, 170
width, 163
graphics box contents, 172
Graphics Box feature bar, 160
Graphics Editing
    WP Draw, 164
graphics in styles, 152
graphics in tables, 132

H

hanging indent, 42
headers, 56
headword, 98
Hide Family button, 155
horizontal line, 175
Hypertext, 250
    button, 251
    create button, 251
    deactivate, 252
    editing links, 252
    text, 251
    using, 251
Hypertext feature bar, 251
hyphenation, 39

I

I-beam, 2, 11
Ignore Cell When Calculating option, 118
Image settings
    graphics, 165

Image tools
    graphics, 165
import preferences, 80
Include Subdocument command, 232
Indent command, 42
    Double Indent option, 42
    Hanging Indent option, 42
Index
    concordance file, 240
    create, 239
    define, 240
    define button, 240
    generate button, 242
    generating, 242
    mark button, 239
Index feature bar, 239
Initial Codes style, 55
Initial Font, 54
inserting
    bookmark, 219
    date, 223
    Document Comments, 224
    formulas, 129
    QuickMark, 221
    table columns, 124
    table rows, 124
Insert Field button, 210
Insert File, 66
Insert key, 12
Insert mode, 12
Insert Object command, 177
Insert Special Codes dialog box, 40
insertion point, 2

J

join cells, 126
justification, 61

K

Keep text together, 46
    Block Protect option, 46
    Conditional End of Page option, 46
    Orphan, 46
    Widow, 46
Key Definitions, 235
Keyboard preferences, 78

L

Layout menu, 35
    Document submenu, 54

Index

Justification submenu, 61
Line submenu, 35
Page submenu, 44
Paragraph submenu, 40
Letterspacing command, 60
Line Height command, 37
Line Hyphenation command, 39
Line Numbering command, 38
Line Spacing command, 38
Line tool, 193
lines
   creating, 175
lists, 243
   Define button, 244
   edit, 244
   Generate button, 245
   Mark button, 243
List feature bar, 243
List Files of Type option, 65

M

Macros, 213
   adding macros to the button bar, 218
   directory, 213
   pause, 214
   playing, 215
   putting macros in the menu, 216
   recording, 213
   using, 213
Margin Release command, 43
margins, 7, 61
   guides, 7
   markers, 7
Margins dialog box, 7
mark text, 239
marquee selection, 183
Master Document command, 232
   condense, 234
   expand, 233
   subdocument, 232
maximize button, 2, 3
menu bar, 1
   control menu box, 3
   maximize button, 3
   minimize button, 3
menu bar preferences, 79
menus, 3
Merge, 205
   creating form file, 210

creating records, 208
data files, 205
ENDFIELD code, 209
ENDRECORD code, 209
fields, 205
form file, 210
Insert Field button, 210
naming fields, 207
perform merge, 212
Quick Data Entry, 208
records, 205
Merge button, 205, 211
Merge feature bar, 210
merging files, 211
minimize button, 2, 3
moulds
   TextArt, 200
mouse pointer
   I-beam, 2
   insertion point, 2
moving families, 154
moving graphics, 161
moving objects, 183

N

naming fields, 207
naming tables, 130
new files, 63
   New command, 63
   title bar, 63
new styles, 145
next page button, 4
numbering lines, 38
numbering pages, 47

O

object linking and embedding (OLE) support, 177
Object Outline/Fill tools, 189
OLE, 177
open codes, 20
opening files, 64
   current dir, 64
   directories, 64
   drives, 65
   file info, 65
   filename, 64
   List Files of Type option, 65
   Open button, 64
   Open command, 64

Index

Open File dialog box, 64
View button, 65
View window, 65
opening WP Draw, 181
orphan, 46
Other Codes command, 40
outline definitions, 156
outline displays, 155
Outline feature bar, 153
outline options, 156
outlines, 152
    ending, 154
    families, 154
    Hide Family button, 155
    moving families, 154
    Show Family button, 155
    using, 152
Overstrike, 60

P

page break
    soft, 53
page border/fill, 47
page break, 53
page layout, 44
page margins, 7
page numbering, 47
page numbering dialog box, 47
page views, 33
    Draft, 34
    Page, 33
    Two Page, 34
paired codes, 18
paper orientation, 51
paper size, 50
    paper orientation, 51
    text adjustments, 51
paragraph, 40
    indent, 42
paragraph border/fill, 41
paragraph styles, 144, 146
Paste, 15
Paste Link, 178
Paste Special, 178
Perform Merge, 212
placement of endnotes, 229
placing charts, 142
playing macros, 215
Polygon tool, 194

positioning graphics box, 161
power bar, 1, 6, 13, 27
    customizing, 85
    editing, 86
power bar preferences, 78
Preferences command, 75
previewing documents, 107
    Page view, 107
    Two Page view, 107
    Zoom button, 108
previous page button, 4
Print dialog box, 108
print preferences, 79
print quality, 110
printers
    selecting, 80
printing documents, 108
    selecting printers, 109
putting macros in the menu, 216
putting text in boxes, 173

Q

Quick Data Entry
    Merging, 208
QuickFinder, 74
QuickFormat, 30
QuickList, 71
QuickMark, 221
QuickMenu, 9, 70, 162

R

recording a macro, 213
records, 205
Rectangle tool, 195
Redline method, 55
reference chaining, 98
referencing cells, 117
Remove Markings command, 232
Replace, 21
    Find and Replace Text dialog box, 23
    Replace command, 23
reshaping an object, 185
resizing
    graphics, 163
    objects, 183
restore button, 3
retrieving graphics, 159
retrieving styles, 150
Reveal Codes, 152

Index

screen, 17
resizing, 18
rotating objects, 184
Rounded Rectangle tool, 195
row height, 120
ruler bar, 1, 6
   margin guides, 7
   margin markers, 7
   margins, 7
   page margins, 7
   tabs, 8

S

Save, 68
Save As, 68
   file format, 69
saving styles, 149
Screen
   button bar, 1
   menu bar, 1
   power bar, 1
   ruler bar, 1
   scroll bars, 1
   status bar, 1
scroll bar, 18
   next page button, 4
   previous page button, 4
   scroll button, 4
Select tool, 182
selecting button bars, 81
selecting cells, 115
selecting objects, 182
selecting printers, 80
selecting text, 14
   dragging, 14
   F8 key, 15
   multiple clicks, 14
   Select submenu, 15
   shift-click, 14
selecting text in cells, 116
Set Fill Color tool, 190
Set Fill Pattern tool, 189
Set Line Color tool, 190
Set Line Style tool, 189
setting preferences, 75
Show Family button, 155
skewing objects, 184
sort, 235
   key definitions, 235

Speller, 91
   Check menu, 95
   Dictionaries menu, 95
   Not Found alert, 91
   Options menu, 96
   Replace, 92
   Replace With, 92
   stand-alone mode, 97
   suggestions, 91
   supplementary dictionary, 95
split cells, 126
status bar, 1, 5
   customizing, 88
   editing, 88
status bar preferences, 78
styles, 143
   adding graphics, 152
   adding tables, 152
   applying, 147
   button, 147, 148
   chaining, 146
   character, 144
   character (paired), 146
   creating, 143
   deleting, 151
   document (open), 146
   editing, 148
   editor, 145
   new, 145
   paragraph, 144
   paragraph (paired), 146
   properties, 145
   QuickCreate, 144
   retrieving, 150
   saving, 149
   type, 145
styles editor window, 149, 152
styles based on existing text, 143
Styles button, 147, 148
Styles Editor, 145
Subdivide Page command, 49
subdocument, 232
Sum button, 129
supplementary dictionary, 95
Suppress Page command, 45
switching between documents, 67
   Cascade option, 67
   Tile option, 68
   Window menu, 67

Index

synonyms, 98

T

Tab Set, 35
   settings, 36
   Tab Set command, 35
   Tab Set dialog box, 35
   type, 36
table columns, 119
   delete, 125
   insert, 124
   margins, 119
   width, 119
Table Formula feature bar, 128
Table menu, 116, 113
Tables of Authorities, 250
Tables of Contents, 245
   Define button, 246
   Generate button, 247
   Mark buttons, 246
Table of Contents feature bar, 246
Table QuickCreate button, 114
table rows, 120
   delete, 125
   insert, 124
   margins, 120
   row height, 120
table structure
   editing, 123
tables, 113, 121
   cells, 114
   charting, 135
   columns, 114
   copying, 127
   create, 113
   cutting, 127
   editing structure, 123
   formatting text, 117
   join, 126
   lines/fills, 123
   naming, 130
   number types, 121
   pasting, 127
   position, 121
   rows, 114
   split, 126
   status bar, 115
tables in styles, 152
tabs, 8

templates, 64
text adjustments, 51
Text tool, 191
Text Wrap, 170
TextArt, 197
   alignment, 199
   All Capitals check box, 200
   attributes, 200
   button, 107
   characters, 200
   colors, 201
   creating, 198
   fills, 201
   fonts, 198
   menus, 203
   moulds, 200
   Redraw button, 199
   ReDraw menu, 199
   rotation, 202
   saving, 203
   shadows, 202
   starting, 197
   styles, 198
   units of measure, 202
TextArt button, 197
thesaurus, 97
   antonyms, 98
   Dictionary menu, 100
   Edit menu, 100
   headword, 98
   History menu, 101
   looking up words, 99
   reference chaining, 98
   replacing words, 100
   stand-alone mode, 101
   synonyms, 98
Tile option, 68
title bar, 2, 63, 66
   Control menu box, 2
   maximize button, 2
   minimize button, 2
   restore button, 3
tool bar, 182
Typeover mode, 12
Typesetting command, 59

U

Undelete, 13, 179
Undo, 13, 179

Index

power bar button, 13
updating your document
   WP Draw, 196

V

vertical line, 175
View button, 65
   viewing graphics, 160
View menu, 5, 6
View window, 65

W

watermarks, 58
widows, 46
width
   graphics, 163
Window menu, 67
Windows Program Manager, 97, 101
word count, 222
WordPerfect characters, 31
WordPerfect screen, 1
   button bar, 1
   menu bar, 1
   power bar, 1
   ruler bar, 1
   scroll bars, 1
   status bar, 1
Wordspacing option, 60
WP Draw, 164, 181
   center of rotation, 185
   Chart tool, 187
   charting, 136
   Closed Curve tool, 193
   Curve tool, 192
   drawing window, 181
   Ellipse tool, 195
   Elliptical Arc tool, 194
   Figure tool, 188
   Freehand tool, 191
   Line tool, 193
   marquee selection, 183
   moving objects, 183
   Object Outline/Fill tools, 189
   Polygon tool, 194
   Rectangle tool, 195
   reshaping an object, 185
   resizing objects, 183
   rotating objects, 184
   Rounded Rectangle tool, 195
   Select tool, 182
   selecting objects, 182
   Set Fill Color tool, 190
   Set Fill Pattern tool, 189
   Set Line Color tool, 190
   Set Line Style tool, 189
   skewing objects, 184
   Text tool, 191
   tool bar, 182
   updating your document, 196
   Zoom tool, 186
writing tools preferences, 79

Z

Zoom button, 108
Zoom tool, 186